'AN OFFER YOU CAN'T REFUSE'

Workfare in inter   .SOURCES CENTRE
                          nsley ♡75 3ET
perspective

Edited by Ivar Lødemel and Heather Trickey

The POLICY
PRESS

First published in Great Britain in January 2001 by

The Policy Press
34 Tyndall's Park Road
Bristol BS8 1PY
UK

Tel +44 (0)117 954 6800
Fax +44 (0)117 973 7308
e-mail tpp@bristol.ac.uk
www.policypress.org.uk

© The Policy Press 2000

British Library Cataloguing in Publication Data

A catalogue record for this book is available from the British Library

ISBN 1 86134 195 4 paperback

A hardcover version of this book is also available

Ivar Lødemel is Research Director at Fafo Institute for Applied Social Science, Oslo, Norway and **Heather Trickey** completed this work while working as a Research Associate at the Centre for Research in Social Policy.

Cover design by Qube Design Associates, Bristol.
Photographs on front cover supplied by kind permission of www.johnbirdsall.co.uk

Printed and bound in Great Britain by Hobbs the Printers Ltd, Southampton.

Contents

Acknowledgements   iv

Notes on contributors   vii

Preface   xi

one   A new contract for social assistance   I
           Ivar Lødemel and Heather Trickey

two   Between subsidiarity and social assistance – the French   41
           republican route to activation
           Bernard Enjolras, Jean Louis Laville, Laurent Fraisse
           and Heather Trickey

three   Uneven development – local authorities and workfare   71
           in Germany
           Wolfgang Voges, Herbert Jacobs and Heather Trickey

four   Workfare in the Netherlands – young unemployed people   105
           and the Jobseeker's Employment Act
           Henk Spies and Rik van Berkel

five   National objectives and local implementation of workfare   133
           in Norway
           Ivar Lødemel

six   When all must be active – workfare in Denmark   159
           Anders Rosdahl and Hanne Weise

seven   Steps to compulsion within British labour market policies   181
           Heather Trickey and Robert Walker

eight   Making work for welfare in the United States   215
           Michael Wiseman

nine   Comparing workfare programmes – features and   249
           implications
           Heather Trickey

ten   Discussion: workfare in the welfare state   295
           Ivar Lødemel

Index   345

Acknowledgements

The material for this book results, in large part, from the work of an international group of researchers who have contributed to a three-year European Union-funded project to look at the development of workfare policies in Northern Europe. Funding for this work has been made available through the European Union's targeted Socioeconomic Research Programme. We would like to thank the programme's scientific officer, Giulia Amaducci who has been a great source of encouragement for this aspect of the project's dissemination strategy. The Center for the Study of Youth Policy at the University of Pennsylvania provided Ivar Lødemel with excellent working conditions during the academic year 1998-99. In addition, we would like to thank the German Marshall Fund of the United States for the financial support that enabled Michael Wiseman to contribute to this book. At The Policy Press, Dawn Rushen, our editorial manager and Karen Bowler, Editor, have superbly assisted and encouraged us both.

As well as those who have contributed as authors of chapters, as editors we wish to thank those who have contributed to other aspects of the work of the project. These include Emma Cornwell, Bruce Stafford, Suella Harriman, Noel Smith and Sharon Walker at the Centre for Research in Social Policy, Loughborough; Steve Mckay of the Policy Studies Institute, London; Espen Dahl, Heidi Vannevjen and Axel West Pedersen at the Fafo Institute for Applied Social Science, Oslo; Laura Olsen and Lisbet Pedersen at the Danish National Institute of Social Research, Copenhagen; Eve Shapiro and Sarah Staveteig at the Urban Institute, Washington; and, Olaf Jüngens and Jüng Haider at the Centre for Social Policy Research, Bremen. Jon Are Lian, Fafo, provided crucial research assistance during the final stages.

External to the project, a number of people have been an invaluable source of help through their comments on both the content and drafting of chapters. In particular, we would like to thank Michael B. Katz and Mark Stern at the University of Pennsylvania, Andreas Cebulla and Barbara Dobson at the Centre for Research in Social Policy, Martin Evans at the Centre for Analysis of Social Exclusion at the London School of Economics and Political Science, Terry Kowal at the Inland Revenue, London, Tapio Salonen and Sune Sunesson at Lund University, Sweden, Peter Abrahamson at the University of Copenhagen and Einar Øverbye at NOVA, Norwegian

Social Research, Stephan Leibfried at the Centre for Social Policy Research, Bremen. We would also like to thank the four anonymous reviewers whose comments have enabled us to identify and correct mistakes and misinterpretations.

Finally, it remains for us to thank Susan Clark, Benjamin and Teadora, Simon Brindle and Rachel Atkinson, who, on a daily basis, have lived with and through the lumpy process of writing, editing and meshing the material together. Without their enduring moral and practical support the task of editing this book would not have been possible.

The findings and views represented in this book are those of the authors. Responsibility for any remaining inaccuracies rests with the authors.

Ivar Lødemel and Heather Trickey
December 2000

To Susan E. Clark and to Simon Brindle

Notes on contributors

Bernard Enjolras is senior researcher at the Institute for Social Research (Oslo) and associated researcher at CRIDA (Paris). His main areas of research are the economic analysis of social policies and social services and the role of voluntary associations in welfare provision and other services industries. He is the author of *Le marche providence* (Desclee de Brouwer, 1995) and of *Politiques sociales et performances economiques* (Desclee de Brouwer, 1999). He has been fellow at the Johns Hopkins University (Baltimore, Maryland) and the Universite Paul Valery (Montpellier, France).

Laurent Fraisse is researcher at the Research and Information Centre on Democracy and Autonomy (CRIDA), a team of the Sociology Laboratory of Institutional Changes (LSCI/IRESCO). His main areas of research are social and inclusion policies, third sector development and local initiatives against social exclusion. He is the author of *Exclusion, une loi cadre pour quoi faire?* (FPH, Paris). Recently, he has participated at several European research networks such as the TSER project 'Comparative social exclusion policies and citizenship in Europe: towards a new European social model' and at the Dublin European Foundation's comparative analysis about coordination in activation policies of minimum income recipients.

Herbert Jacobs is social researcher for the local authorities Frankfurt/ Main, Germany. Until January 2000 he worked at the Centre for Social Policy Research at the University of Bremen where he evaluated a local workfare scheme for social assistance recipients and researched welfare reforms in Germany and the USA. His main areas of research interest are social assistance, poverty and social exclusion. His next book deals with the history of legislation on social assistance and public discourse about social assistance and poverty in Germany between 1970 and 1996.

Jean Louis Laville is the President of Research and Information Centre on Democracy and Autonomy (CRIDA, Paris) and researcher at the National Centre of Scientific Research (CRIDA/LSCI, CNRS). His main areas of research are solidarity-based economy and third sector; daily life services and local development; social inclusion, employment and social policies; economic organisation and democracy. He is Director of the collection 'Economic Sociology' at Desclée de Brouwer Editions. He is representative of formation at the Institute for Political Sciences (Paris). He is the author of *L'économie solidaire: une perspective internationale, Une troisième voie pour le travail et Sociologie de l'association* (Desclée de Brouwer, Paris). He has participated at the OECD report *Reconciling economy and society. Towards a plural economy*, (1996).

Ivar Lødemel is Research Director at Fafo Institute for Applied Social Science (Oslo). His main areas of research are living conditions, social services and comparative studies of social assistance. He is the author of *The welfare paradox. Income maintenance and personal social services in Norway and Britain, 1946-1966* (Scandinavian University Press). Lødemel has been Humboldt Fellow at the Max Planck Institute for Foreign and International Social Law (Munich) and Visiting Scholar at the University of Pennsylvania. He has served as consultant for the World Bank, the Council of Europe and the OECD. Currently he is coordinator of the TSER-project 'Social integration through obligation to work: Current European "workfare" initiatives and future directions', the collaboration from which this book originates.

Anders Rosdahl has been Head of the Research Unit, the Danish National Institute of Social Research (Copenhagen), since 1987. His main areas of research are labour market, working life and social and labour market policy. He has headed a number of evaluations of Danish social and labour market reforms, and he is the author of several books and research reports on labour market issues. Rosdahl has also evaluated the European Social Fund and has worked as a consultant for the European Commission. Currently Rosdahl is coordinating a comprehensive Danish research programme on the Social Responsibility of Enterprises. He is lecturer at the Institute of Economics, University of Copenhagen.

Henk Spies is a post-doc researcher at the department of General Social Sciences at Utrecht University. His main research area is social policies for (young) unemployed people. He worked for some time at a research department of the local social services of Rotterdam and did extensive research on young unemployed people and drop outs from workfare programmes. Publications include among others *Uitsluitend voor jongeren? Arbeidsmarktbeleid en het ontstaan van een onderklasse (Exclusive policies for young unemployed people? Labour market policies and the emergence of an* *underclass*) (Utrecht, Jan van Arkel, 1998). He is also editor of the Dutch *Journal for Work and Participation* (*Tijdschrift voor Arbeid en Participatie*).

Heather Trickey is a social researcher with a background in health services and health promotion research. Her research interests are lifestyles and living standards and changing welfare institutions. Previous publications have been in the areas of unemployment and job-seeking and of primary care. The work for this book was carried out while she was working as a Research Associate at the Centre for Research in Social Policy, Loughborough University.

Rik van Berkel is researcher at the Faculty of Social Sciences of Utrecht University and the Centre for Social Policy Studies of the municipality of Rotterdam. His main research areas are social policies, labour-market policies and unemployment. He has been coordinator of the TSER research project 'Inclusion through Participation'. Among others, he has published on citizenship and social exclusion ('European citizenship and social exclusion', together with Maurice Roche, Ashgate) and on social movements of claimants ('Beyond marginality? Social movements of social security claimants in the EU', together with Harry Coenen and Ruud Vlek, Ashgate).

Wolfgang Voges is Professor at the Institute for Sociology and the Centre for Social Policy Research (CeS) at the University of Bremen (Germany). His main areas of research are analysis of social structure analysis and social policy, health and social inequality, methods and techniques of empirical social research, international comparative social studies. He is the editor of *Dynamic approaches to comparative social research. Recent developments and applications* (Aldershot: Avebury, forthcoming). Voges has been Visiting Fellow at the Institute for Research on Poverty, University of Wisconsin, Madison, Wisconsin/USA, the Survey Research Center, Institute for Social Research, University of Michigan, Ann Arbor, Michigan/USA, the Center for Urban Affairs and Policy Research, Northwestern University Evanston, Illinois/USA, the Department of Economics, University of Göteburg, Göteburg/Sweden and the Centré d'Etudes de Population, de Pauvreté et de Politique Socio-Economiques (CEPS/INSTEAD) Differdange/Luxembourg. Currently he is coordinator of the German part in several TSER-projects related to social exclusion.

Robert Walker is Professor of Social Policy at the University of Nottingham and was formerly Director of the Centre for Research in Social Policy at Loughborough University. His interests embrace poverty and welfare dynamics, labour market policy and policy evaluation and he is actively engaged in policy debates in Europe and North America. The latest of his 15 books is *The making of a welfare class: Benefit receipt in Britain* (co-authored with Marilyn Howard, The Policy Press, 2000).

Hanne Weise is Head of Section in the Ministry of Labour. Among her areas are analysis and development of integration policies for the weak unemployed. Before moving to the Ministry of Labour, she was a researcher at the Danish National Institute of Social Research. Her main research areas were in effects of policies to prevent marginalisation of the weakest groups on the labour market, and specially in activation of social clients.

Michael Wiseman is a Visiting Senior Fellow at the Washington office of the National Opinion Research Center of the University of Chicago and Visiting Scholar in Social Policy at the Congressional Research Service of the Library of Congress. He serves on policy and technical advisory committees for the California Department of Social Services and the Wisconsin Department of Workforce Development, and he is consultant to the Administration for Children and Families on evaluation of state welfare reform initiatives. He is a member of the Welfare Reform Advisory Committee and the Working Seminar on Social Program Information Systems of the US General Accounting Office. Before turning to independent consulting practice, he was Professor of Economics at the University of California at Berkeley (18 years), Professor of Public Affairs at the University of Wisconsin-Madison (10 years) and Senior Fellow at the Urban Institute in Washington (two years). He is affiliated with the Institute for Research on Poverty at the University of Wisconsin-Madison.

Preface

Workfare in international perspective

During the 1980s and 1990s important changes in social assistance provision took place in a number of welfare states. Whereas social assistance for unemployed people had generally been provided after a test of willingness to seek and accept regular work, people were increasingly required to participate in work, or in other activities, as part of their assistance contract. By the beginning of the 21st century the seven countries investigated in this volume had all extended the range of compulsory work activities applied to out-of-work groups.

The term 'workfare' is one that is more readily associated with social assistance programmes in the United States (US). A consequence of this is that the practice of 'working-for-benefit' has come to be associated with the lot of poor people in those countries that demonstrate a liberal-right ideology. In this book, the authors, who describe policies in a range of welfare state contexts, have taken the term workfare as a starting point for descriptions of policies that constitute 'work-for-benefit', or the nearest equivalent, in their respective countries. In doing so, this book attempts to identify similarities and differences between programmes in different countries and to chart the extent to which they diverge from an idealised quid pro quo, work-for-benefit form of policy. Using this approach, policy comparison becomes possible across a range of ideological and institutional settings, so that familiar US programmes can be considered alongside more overlooked examples of work-for-benefit policies that also exist in northern European countries.

Six northern European countries – France, Germany, the Netherlands, Norway, Denmark and the UK – have been selected for inclusion in this comparative book. Together they represent commonly understood 'types' of welfare state based on Esping-Andersen's widely used typology (Esping-Andersen, 1990), namely 'Conservative-Corporatist' (France and Germany), 'Social Democratic' (Denmark and Norway) and 'Liberal' (UK). The Dutch welfare state is understood by Esping-Andersen to share characteristics of both Conservative and Social Democratic regimes. Chapters Two through Seven, the core of this book, take each European country in turn, moving through the three 'typology' groupings. A selection of workfare programmes in the US, considered a 'Liberal' welfare regime under Esping-Anderson's typology, are described in Chapter Eight. Because the US is often viewed as being at the forefront of modern workfare, comparison with developments elsewhere allows us to examine the importance of policy convergence as against country-specific 'solutions' to variously perceived 'problems'.

The scale of the workfare programmes described in this book, in relation to the total social assistance populations in each of the countries described, varies enormously. However, programmes described in Chapters Two through Eight all have an important impact on the normative and legal foundations of the welfare state in their respective countries, and on understandings of, first, the balance between recipients' rights and obligations and, second, the balance of responsibilities between the state and individual citizens.

During the last two decades, the number of people receiving assistance has increased in all seven countries (Gough et al, 1997). This growth has prompted a renewed emphasis on measures to reduce spending, and countries have introduced both incentives and disincentives designed to further self-reliance through work. Incentives constitute a range of (mostly) supply-side measures to help ease the transition from benefit to work and to help make work a viable and attractive alternative to benefit, including voluntary training programmes, arrangements to support childcare and in-work benefits. Disincentives constitute tighter conditionality rules and stricter eligibility criteria within social assistance provision (Ditch and Oldfield, 1999).

The introduction and spread of workfare programmes at the end of the 20th century strengthened a trend towards conditionality within social assistance regimes. Workfare programmes may themselves contain incentives – for example in the form of increased access to resources – however, deterrants always constitute an underlying factor in the form of a threat of sanction for non-compliance. Whether the work requirements are viewed as 'giving less' as a result of the threat of benefit sanctions, or 'giving more' as an extension of opportunities, an important change in social assistance provision has taken place. To observe their implementation is to observe a further development of a trend whereby "social services are used to impose sanctions as well as to confer benefits upon their clientele" (Pinker, 1971, p 144). A key comparative question is the extent to which workfare impacts on the balance between rights and obligations – carrots and sticks – to fundamentally change the social assistance contract.

Compared to other aspects of social security, social assistance policies have only recently begun to receive high profile attention from policy makers. Traditionally, the focus has been on social insurance which, in many countries, catered for larger groups and consumed greater chunks of public expenditure. For much of the post-war period, policy makers in north-western European states shared the ambition and hope that the development of social insurance and social services would reduce social assistance to a residual programme. An almost universal sharp increase in expenditure on social assistance over the last two decades – for a range of reasons outlined in Chapter One – has contributed to the demise of this belief (Lødemel, 1997). As social insurance has come to be seen as a less secure way of providing for people, attitudes towards social assistance have changed. International organisations, including the World Bank and the European Union, have supported a renewed emphasis on social assistance as an integral and inevitable form of welfare provision.

The shift in political focus towards social assistance recipients has been accompanied by ideological shifts among politicians and policy makers, resulting in a resurrection of normative questions about the purpose of welfare. Policy developments over the last decade have been chiselled out through new and often unexpected political positions and alliances. In all seven countries, left-of-centre parties have recently become inclined to apply work requirements as a condition of receipt for able-bodied social assistance recipients. Support for workfare policies by reformed social-democratic parties is of particular relevance.

Social insurance is typically understood to facilitate income redistribution (between different insured people and for individuals over their lifetime). In contrast, the discourse surrounding social assistance provision is laden with different interpretations of the normative values underlying welfare provision. Renewed rhetorical emphasis on recipient behaviour is strongly associated with the shift of social assistance policy from the margins to the centre of debates about welfare (Lødemel, 1997). Bradshaw and Terum (1997) argue that social assistance policies address the 'behaviour' of their recipients to a greater extent than policies in any other area of social security. Social assistance is commonly understood as resulting from a unilateral exchange relationship, hence constituting a 'gift' (as opposed to social insurance, which is understood to be an earned right, based on the recipient having made contributions at some earlier stage). As a result questions about the 'deservingness' of the recipient group are more evident when the recipients claim social assistance. Leibfried (1993) has argued that through examining and comparing social assistance policies that lie at the margins of the welfare state, we are studying the impact of social policy on people at the margins of citizenship.

The development of Active Labour Market Policies (ALMPs), in general, and specifically the introduction of work requirements into social assistance has blurred traditional divisions between labour market policies and social policies. This has been matched by similar crossover between traditionally separate traditions of research. The concept of workfare has invited a range of academic perspectives, from industrial relations (for example Peck, 1999), economics (for example Jessop, 1993; Morel, 1998; Solow, 1998), philosophy (for example Schmidtz and Goodin, 1998) and sociology (for example Giddens, 1998). These contributions are discussed in Chapter One.

Since the first systematic comparisons of social assistance programmes emerged a decade ago, a large number of studies of social assistance provision have been published (Ditch and Oldfield, 1999). In spite of this, workfare itself remains largely unmapped from a comparative perspective. Comparisons that have been made are mainly based on evidence from one nation (Walker, 1991; Wiseman, 1991; Torfing, 1999; Peck, 1999) or two nations (Morel, 1998; Shragge, 1997). This book seeks to expand the comparative range.

This book consists of 10 chapters: an introduction to the subject matter (Chapter One); a description of policies in each country (Chapters Two through Eight); a systematic comparison of policies drawing implications for the future of workfare programmes (Chapter Nine); and a discussion of possible explanations for similarity and variation in the strategies pusued in workfare programmes (Chapter Ten).

By way of an introduction, Chapter One presents a definition of workfare as used by the authors contributing to this volume. Key elements of workfare programmes are identified: workfare is compulsory; is primarily about work; and relates to policies tied to the lowest tier of income support (social assistance). The policy context for workfare policies is outlined in a discussion of a move from 'passive' to 'active' labour market policies. The ideological context is provided in a discussion of two competing concepts – 'dependency' and 'social exclusion' – in relation to worklessness. The structural context for workfare is then given, including a presentation of key economic indicators in the seven countries and a description of differences in welfare state and social assistance regimes.

In Chapter Two we examine work-for-benefit policies in France, a country that, ideologically speaking, seems as unlikely a host of workfare programmes as any of the countries examined here. This chapter is primarily concerned with the way in which the strong republican ideology of French policy makers from the main political parties has accommodated the development of work-for-benefit policies – and indeed work-instead-of-benefit policies – by viewing them as part of a broader strategy to fight 'exclusion' and foster 'insertion'. Incremental policy developments embedded within a complex administrative system involving state agencies and autonomous elected bodies at the national, regional, department and local levels are described. For older people, these include the insertion contract which is a component of Revenu Minimum d'Insertion (RMI) (the relatively recently introduced national social assistance scheme). For under 25-year-olds, who are not entitled to RMI, they include a range of schemes culminating in *Emploi Jeunes*, that provides participants with up to five-year employment contracts. Findings from a number of programme evaluations, which suggest that the impact of these policies has not, so far, been substantial with regard to labour market insertion objectives, are given and expanded upon.

In Chapter Three we continue our tour of 'Corporatist-Conservative' welfare states and turn to Germany, a country with a long tradition of work creation schemes within a system of locally organised social assistance delivery. The chapter describes the uneven and uncoordinated development of Help Towards Work (*Hilfe zur Arbeit*) schemes across Germany, resulting in a patchwork of provision which varies in extent (completely universal to highly selective) and in strategy (highly integrative to predominantly preventive) between localities. Traditionally, these schemes have first and foremost represented a cost-cutting device for local authorities rather than a means of promoting long-term work integration. A loop-hole in the two-tier system of social security provision means that social assistance recipients can gain access to federally subsidised and administered insurance-based unemployment benefits as long as local authorities provide them with a one-year employment contract. Available evidence is weak, but suggests that, while the schemes are effective in cutting local authority expenditure and in raising feelings of self-confidence among participants, they have not been shown to promote employment integration. The chapter concludes with some indicators for the future. The authors suggest that the future is likely to involve these schemes becoming part of a federally coordinated strategy of employment integration for *young* social assistance recipients. This strategy looks set to develop a new emphasis on methods promoted in other parts of Europe and in some North American states, including the use of private placement agencies to construct individually tailored programmes.

Chapter Four takes us to the Netherlands, where the Jobseeker's Employment Act (JEA) represents a universal strategy of compulsory activation for young unemployed people and a (so far) less comprehensively developed programme for older unemployed people. This chapter traces ideological, political and economic developments that form the backdrop to policy implementation. The special character of the JEA, which is made up of three different 'regimes' suitable for people with different levels of work-readiness – forming an explicit hierarchy of 'phases' towards labour market integration – is described. The emphasis on 'measurement' of clients, so as to produce individualised, tailored programmes is underlined. The chapter concludes with an overview of research findings and themes that emerge from these, pointing especially to the very high levels of 'drop out' from JEA schemes (and so from social assistance provision) that may be considered counterproductive with respect to the objective of tackling social exclusion.

Chapter Five provides an example of a localised form of Norwegian workfare, applied selectively to a highly residualised social assistance population within an economic setting that has been relatively unaffected by a rise in the unemployment rate. Norwegian local authorities have been highly instrumental in interpreting national legislation at the local level, and so the case of Norwegian workfare is demonstrative of the importance of the implementation process in determining the character of a programme. This chapter focuses on the first years of the new conditionality and describes first how political and ideological factors have converged to support the introduction of workfare as a condition of social assistance. The chapter then describes how structural and political conditions have resulted in a distortion of poorly specified national objectives, the result being that a policy that was supposed to be applied as a systematic programme and in cooperation with agencies of the Ministry of Labour often came to be applied with limited reference to labour market insertion considerations. The last part of the chapter describes recent developments that suggest that workfare in Norway is moving in a more similar direction to policies in other European countries.

Moving to our second social-democratic state, Chapter Six describes 'activation' policy as it is applied to social assistance recipients in Denmark. Compulsory activation, applied to the vast majority of social assistance (and social insurance) recipients after a set period, is contextualised within Denmark's 'Active Line' – which is an expression of the principle that *everybody* in receipt of public income transfers should contribute to society through some activity. In addition to the striking (and increasing) universality of compulsory activation, the chapter draws attention to a number of other features that are important for comparison. First, activation represents the development of a condition that active measures *must* be taken up out of a pre-existing 'right' to a programme of active assistance. While conditionality has been strengthened, the rights-based origins of the programme is reflected in a relatively mild sanctioning strategy. Second, in comparison to labour market policies applied (until recently) to German social assistance recipients, Danish policy makers have sought, with some success, to make Labour and Social Affairs ministries cooperate in the delivery of programmes. Third, to a greater extent than elsewhere, activation policies are intended to take a human capital development approach to labour market integration and to provide recipients with the choice of a range of placements, which are supposed to be tailored to their wider needs. Finally, as unemployment has fallen since the mid-1990s, and the social assistance population has become more residualised, activation policy has swung towards accepting the necessity of a long-term strategy towards inclusion in the labour market for highly marginalised individuals.

Chapter Seven describes the trend towards compulsory work-for-benefit policies in the UK and focuses on the development of these policies by an ideologically social-democratic government operating within a 'liberal' welfare regime. The New Deal programmes – including the New Deal for Young People, the policy that comes closest to an idealised form of workfare in Britain – are part of a wider welfare reform package adopted by New Labour. This comprises three policy strands: 'welfare-to-work'; 'making work pay'; and providing 'work for those who can; security for those who can't [work]'. The chapter demonstrates that this package builds on former British programmes developed under successive Conservative administrations, as well as borrowing and adapting ideas from other, particularly English-speaking, nations. The chapter describes the structure of the New Deal for Young People in some detail, drawing on existing evaluation evidence and contextualising the programme within a broader array of policies directed to other out-of-work groups, including work-based policies for under 18-year-olds who are not usually entitled to any social assistance. The chapter concludes by pointing to some of the normative underpinnings of the New Labour government's strategy towards 'workless' people, including an emphasis on supply-side solutions to unemployment and a focus on paid work as a desirable goal for all and as a solution to poverty.

Chapter Eight takes us to the US and charts policy developments that have led to increasing levels of decentralisation and further distancing from the principle that relief from poverty is a citizenship right. The chapter focuses on workfare policies that were introduced as part of the acceleration of welfare reform during the 1990s. It begins with an overview of the social assistance system, drawing attention to a number of important features that make US social assistance programmes different from European programmes. In particular, the author points to the high degree of discretion that individual states have over provision arrangements and the variable and minimal levels of support available to single childless unemployed people of working age. Policy changes that accompanied the introduction of workfare, and that are crucial to any evaluation of the potential transferability of workfare measures, are described. These include the expansion of state latitude, the introduction of time-limits to benefit receipt and the ultimate 'end of entitlement' to cash benefits. Focusing on developments in three locations – New York City, Wisconsin and California – the chapter considers the different ways that welfare reform has played out in practice. The author presents findings from evaluations based on participants in these programmes but points to the lack of information regarding outcomes for people who have been diverted from assistance and the circumstances of families undergoing sanction.

Chapter Nine presents a systematic overview of the most 'workfare-like' workfare policies in each of the countries above. Specifically, the chapter compares programmes in terms of their aims and ideological underpinnings, their target groups, their administrative framework and the extent to which they diverge from an 'ideal-type' workfare model. From this it is clear that workfare, as defined in this book, is represented by a range of programmes and approaches, and applied to populations that are not consistent between national programmes and are heterogeneous within some of them. Patterns of variation are discussed, resulting in the identification of one distinct 'type' of workfare not associated with countries sharing a common history of either social security or social assistance provision – illustrated by the Dutch Jobseeker's Employment Act, Danish activation and the British New Deal policies. These 'European Centralised Policies' are characterised by a nationally led administrative structure, a trend towards universal application and an ideology and strategy that supports 'integrative' as well as 'preventive' aims. Chapter Nine concludes with a discussion of implications for the future of workfare based on the overview presented. It concludes that, despite their differences, workfare programmes face a common set of problems that emanate directly from the fact that they are compulsory, work-based and targeted at a population facing formidable barriers to work. The attractiveness of compulsory programmes to a range of ideological perspectives and a perceived congruence with a range of objectives means that compulsion, if not workfare, is likely to form part of activation programmes for the foreseeable future. Given this, the author points to a need for the state to refocus on the quality of programmes for people with multiple barriers to employment so as to avoid 'churning' individuals within a system that does not improve their employment prospects. This is likely to involve two things: first, clearly establishing tangible 'rights' for participants within compulsory programmes; second, providing empirical evidence to justify the operation of compulsory programmes for social assistance recipients and, in particular, for groups with multiple barriers to employment.

Finally, Chapter Ten discusses possible reasons for diversity and apparent convergence with regard to the development of workfare programmes within the countries considered here. First, the chapter considers the extent to which workfare policies are being used as part of a strategy to improve welfare services with a view to increasing labour market integration, or as a means of reducing individual autonomy for those who participate.

Second, the chapter discusses whether the introduction of workfare does herald a convergence of policies for uninsured out-of-work people in the seven countries. The author goes on to discuss four possible explanations of diversity among the programmes, presenting and evaluating the evidence for four hypotheses in turn: 'politics matters'; 'scale of the perceived problem matters'; 'policy inheritance matters'; and 'target group matters'.

References

Bradshaw, J. and Terum, L.I. (1997) 'How Nordic is the Nordic model? Social assistance in a comparative perspective', *Scandinavian Journal of Social Welfare*, vol 6, pp 247-56.

Ditch, J. and Oldfield, N. (1999) 'Social assistance: recent trends and theme', *Journal of European Social Policy*, vol 1, pp 65-76.

Esping-Andersen, G. (1990) *The three worlds of welfare capitalism*, Cambridge: Polity Press.

Giddens, A (1998) *The Third way: The renewal of social democracy*, Cambridge: Polity Press.

Goodin, R. (1998) 'Social welfare as a collective social responsibility', in D. Schidtz and R. Goodin *Social welfare and individual responsibility*, Cambridge: Cambridge University Press.

Gough, I., Bradshaw, J., Ditch, J., Eardley, T. and Whiteford, P. (1997) 'Social assistance in OECD countries', *Journal of European Social Policy*, vol 7, no 1, pp 17-43.

Jessop, B. (1993) 'Towards a Schumpeterian workfare state? Preliminary remarks on post-Fordist political economy', *Studies in Political Economy*, vol 40, pp 7-39.

Leibfried, S. (1993) 'Towards a European welfare state', in C. Jones (ed) *New perspectives on the welfare state in Europe*, London: Routledge.

Lødemel, I. (1997) *The welfare paradox. Income maintenance and personal social services in Norway and Britain, 1946-1966*, Oslo: Scandinavian University Press.

Morel, S. (1998) 'American workfare versus French insertion policies: an application of Common's theoretical framework', Paper presented at Annual Research Conference of the Association for Public Policy and Management, 29-31 October, New York.

Peck, J. (1998) 'Workfare, a geopolitical etymology', *Environment and planning D Society and Space*, vol 16, pp 133-60.

Peck, J. (1999) Workfare in the sun: politics, representation, method in the US welfare-to-work strategies, *Political Geography*, vol 16, pp 535-66.

Pinker, R. (1971) *Social theory and social policy*, London: Heinemann Educational Books.

Pinker, R. (1979) *Social theory and social policy*, London: Heinemann Educational Books.

Scmidtz, D. and Goodin, R. (1998) *Social welfare and individual responsibility*, Cambridge: Cambridge University Press.

Shragge, E. (ed) (1997) *Workfare: Ideology for a new underclass*, Toronto: Garamond Press.

Solow, R. (1998) *Work and welfare*, Princeton, NJ: Princeton University Press.

Torfing, J. (1999) 'Workfare with welfare: recent reforms in the Danish welfare state', *Journal of European Social Policy*, vol 1, pp 5-28.

Walker, R. (1991) *Thinking about workfare: Evidence from the US*, London: HMSO.

Wiseman, M. (1991) *What did the American work-welfare demonstrations do? Why should Germans care?*, Bremen: Zentrum für Sozialpolitik, University of Bremen.

ONE

A new contract for social assistance

Ivar Lødemel and Heather Trickey

Introduction

This book seeks to describe, compare and analyse a fundamental change in the way social assistance is provided. The requirement that people who are judged able to work and available for work must seek and accept work in the regular labour market is an inherent part of the contract within social assistance programmes. This contract is changed through introducing a requirement for recipients to work as a condition of receiving benefits. While developments of this kind in some parts of the United States (US) have received considerable attention, the introduction of work requirements within European countries has generally been less comprehensively observed outside of their respective national spheres.

This book describes the new work requirements within social assistance programmes on both sides of the Atlantic and presents a systematic comparison of policies in six European countries, two US states and New York City. This chapter defines the subject of comparison, 'workfare', and identifies the factors that are likely to determine whether the new contracts result in governments providing more or doing less to help people who are presently excluded from self-reliance through regular work.

Within the countries considered here, welfare provision underwent incremental growth over most of the third quarter of the 20th century. During this time policy debates relating to welfare were mainly over spending priorities, either with regard to the needs of different groups within the welfare population or with regard to levels of expenditure on welfare provision as opposed to other functions of the state. In line with this, the proclaimed 'crisis of the welfare state' in the 1980s sparked debate that was also primarily about spending priorities.

The last decade of the 20th century witnessed the development of a more fundamental challenge to welfare as a modern project. Attention shifted from debates about the level of welfare expenditure to questions about the desirability and usefulness of welfare payments (although the former contributed to the latter). This new orientation was applied to a range of welfare programmes, but was particularly focused on social assistance provision for able-bodied people who were judged to be available for work. While until recently the policy ambitions of most Western governments have been towards a reduction in overall levels of social assistance payments, selectivity and targeting within social assistance are now being restored as desirable features of welfare provision (Lødemel, 1997b).

Changes in the organisation of working life and the threat of rising welfare expenditure in a climate of increased global competitiveness led to a desire to make the welfare state more effective in terms of limiting spending and improving outcomes. Nowhere was the spending reduction objective clearer than in the US where welfare provision arrangements underwent a revolution in the mid-1990s. A cross-party consensus developed around the ambition of 'ending welfare as we know it', so that Republican and Democrat parties only differed in the extent to which they supported the balance of measures to achieve change. In north-western Europe support for some form of welfare provision has proved more solid, and a willingness to depart from established principles regarding rights to welfare is less evident. However, on both sides of the Atlantic a new 'wisdom' regarding the role of welfare emerged.

The new wisdom stated that traditional cash benefits fail to support a proportion of recipients in becoming self-sufficient. European and American policy makers began to turn to new policies, which seek to improve the skills and capabilities of workless people who have been unable to find work and attempt to reduce disincentives to take work (Heikkila, 1999). This book focuses on one part of the new policies: those that oblige social assistance recipients to work as part of the assistance contract.

The initial motivation for making this comparison was an observation of similarity between policy developments in different countries – compulsory work programmes were being introduced in a range of welfare states within a relatively short period of time and were associated with a variety of political positions and parties. The extent of policy *convergence* around workfare is discussed briefly in Chapter Ten. However, the main emphasis of this book is *diversity* in the application of workfare programmes. The aim is to highlight differences in the balance which compulsory work policies strike between promoting labour market integration and preventing social exclusion and dependency. In the first part of this chapter the concept of workfare is defined in order to facilitate transnational comparison and to distinguish workfare from related activating policies (see next section). Subsequently, the chapter discusses factors that might lead to diversity in the implementation of 'workfare-like' policies. The more generalised policy shift from 'passive' to 'active' policies on both sides of the Atlantic is discussed and ideological and structural factors are introduced and discussed that aid an understanding of differences in the character of workfare programmes in the seven countries. Two concepts used to justify the introduction of workfare are discussed: namely 'social exclusion' and 'dependency'. The structure of welfare provision by which workfare policies are framed is then outlined, and the final section introduces the programmes and schemes discussed in the subsequent chapters.

Defining workfare

At present no consensus exists regarding a single definition of workfare. The use of the term varies over time and between countries (Peck, 1998) and the language of workfare is at least as hazy today as it was a decade ago (Standing, 1990). There are two main reasons for this lack of clarity.

First, workfare has always been a politically charged term. Surveys of public opinion suggest that the idea of replacing unconditional benefits with requirements to work receives substantial support in different welfare states. In Norway, for example, a survey found that an overwhelming majority of those asked supported the idea of young recipients working in exchange for their benefit (Lødemel and Flaa, 1993). Similar results are reported in the US (see Chapter Eight). When it was coined during the Nixon administration in 1969, the term workfare was used to market work-based programmes as a very positive alternative to the passive provision of social assistance, which has not been embraced by policy makers. However, despite support for the idea of work-based programmes, the term workfare has not caught on internationally, and is now seldom used to describe policies other than by those who oppose work requirements, which they perceive to be eroding rights-based entitlement to assistance (Shragge, 1997). In Europe, the word workfare is often used by policy makers as a foil, to explain what the new policies are *not*. Only the political Right in the US still uses the term to describe policies that they advocate.

Second, in comparison to other social policies, workfare policies are not easily defined either in terms of their purpose (for example, as compared to rehabilitation policies) or in terms of their target group (for example, as compared to pension provision schemes). Policies variously described as workfare are often associated with different aims and target different groups of people.

This lack of clarity about what workfare really is, has not prevented it from increasingly penetrating public and academic discourse. In the three largest US newspapers *(New York Times, Washington Post, Wall Street Journal)* more references were made to workfare in the year 1995 than in the entire period 1971-80 (Peck, 1998). The academic literature also bears witness to this trend. Of a total of 90 articles describing workfare, only 11 were published before 1990 (Social Science Citation Index). The use of the term in the academic literature reflects its ambiguity as well as the blurred boundaries between workfare and related policies.

The growth in political and academic interest in workfare-like policies, and the confusion about what workfare actually is, means that it is important to begin any overview with a clear definition of the subject. A review of the literature reveals that a key distinction can be made between *aims-based* (Evans, 1995; Morel, 1998; Nathan, 1993) and *form-based* definitions (Walker, 1991; Wiseman, 1991; Jordan, 1996; Shragge, 1997; Mead, 1997a) of workfare.

Aims-based approaches to definition tend to distinguish between programmes which are intended to be more or less overtly punitive. For example, Morel (1998) compares the French 'insertion approach' within social assistance, with a US 'workfare approach' (see Chapter Two). She suggests that the key difference is that the 'workfare approach' is concerned with a fight against dependency, whereas the insertion approach is intended to counteract social exclusion. Nathan (1993) focuses on the programme aims when he distinguishes between two forms of workfare that can be identified in the US at that time (prior to the 1996 reforms described in Chapter Eight). He uses the term 'new-style workfare', now familiar to studies of US programmes, to refer to a range of "strategies which aim to ... facilitate entry into the labour force" (p 15). By contrast, plain workfare (elsewhere termed 'old-style workfare'), referred to US policies in the 1970s and 1980s, which were understood to be more "restrictive and punitive" (Nathan, 1993). According to Nathan, the different aims *were* reflected in the form of the policies; while the former offered little more than work in exchange for benefits, 'new-style workfare' encompassed a variety of work and training programmes designed to help welfare recipients gain access to regular jobs.

A particularly broad aims-based definition is found in several recent contributions from writers within the so-called 'regulation school' of institutional economics. According to this perspective, workfare encompasses wide-ranging changes in the aims and functions of both social and labour market policies. These writers start from the assumption that social policy is a central element in the State's social model of regulation and serves to facilitate the current reconstruction in the economy. Jessop (1993) coined the phrase 'Schumpeterian Workfare State' to describe the new social policy direction of the neo-liberal economic regime as part of the shift from Keynesian demand-side approaches, of providing benefits to those out of work, to the post-Fordist supply-side policy aimed at facilitating (re)integration into the workforce. In this system social policy is subordinate to the demands of labour market flexibility and structural competitiveness (Jessop, 1993). Following Jessop, several writers (including Grover and Stewart, 1999; Peck, 1998; Torfing, 1999) use the term workfare to describe new policies that embrace both social and labour market initiatives.

Perhaps the broadest use of the term is found in Grover and Stewart's discussion of 'market workfare'. This encompasses both what they term 'traditional workfare', which is directly coercive, *and* wider supply-side policies, which result in depressed wage levels with the result that the market itself creates 'workfare jobs' (Grover and Stewart, 1999, p 85) including direct and indirect methods of wage subsidy. According to these authors, a wide range of policies can be labelled workfare in the sense that they "force people to take work or training on the job which pays less than the current market rate for the same kind of work" (Costello, 1993). While this definition may be useful for studies that focus on wider changes in the labour market, it is too broad to be suitable for a study of arrangements within social assistance provision – the main focus of this volume. In addition, this definition focuses exclusively on workfare as a supply-side measure. As this volume shows, several countries have adopted work obligation policies that contain strong demand-side characteristics where unemployment is tackled through job creation (see Chapters Two and Three on France and Germany).

In this book workfare is defined as an ideal policy *form*, as opposed to a policy that results from a specific set of aims. The group of contributors to the book judged aims-based definitions to be unsuitable for comparative work, which is essentially about mapping a particular phenomenon in the context of the different ideological settings and different policy processes. In addition, aims-based approaches were considered to court the danger of over-simplification of the different and potentially contradictory aims that programmes address, as well as of the process whereby official objectives are translated from the higher policy-making echelons to the implementation level. The links between work-for-benefit policies and various ideological perspectives and associated labour market initiatives are clearly important. However, examination of a specific form of policy initiative permits comparison across different ideological and policy contexts. A form-based definition facilitates investigation of how, why, and for which out-of-work populations, work-for-benefit policies are used; and how and why policies vary in relation to different policy contexts.

The group of contributors sought a form-based definition that allowed the following questions to be addressed:

- whether workfare policies occur as a means of satisfying more or less identical aims and objectives across different countries or whether they arise despite these being different;
- to whom workfare policies are targeted and why;
- how different administrative set-ups interact with the operation of workfare policies;
- how the work element within workfare policies operates and how it is supplemented by other components;
- whether 'types' of workfare can be identified; and
- whether common challenges arise from a policy form operationalised within different contexts.

These questions are returned to in Chapters Nine and Ten.

For purposes of delineation and comparison, we have decided to define workfare as:

> Programmes or schemes that require people to work in return for social assistance benefits.

In this definition the term 'programme' is used to denote a prescribed generic strategy implemented in a range of locations. In contrast, 'scheme' is used to describe locally developed projects. The term 'policy' is reserved to denote the general plan of action adopted by national or local government.

The definition sets out an 'ideal type' programme and one that strongly diverges from the traditional social assistance contract. It can be argued that a proportion of social assistance recipients in each of the countries compared here experience programmes that could be described in this way. However, the programmes described in this book vary in the extent to which they meet this definition. Thus, it becomes possible to examine the extent and direction of divergence.

The definition has three elements – that workfare is *compulsory*, that workfare is *primarily about work*, and that workfare is essentially about policies tied to the *lowest tier of public income support*. In the next three sections each element is briefly discussed. This is followed by a discussion of their combined effect on the character of the social assistance contract.

Workfare is compulsory

Previous form-based definitions have focused on *compulsion* as workfare's key distinguishing feature (for example, Walker, 1991; Wiseman, 1991; Jordan, 1996; Shragge, 1997). Here a programme is defined as compulsory if non-compliance with work requirements carries the *risk* of lost or reduced benefits, even if such sanctions are not automatic under the rules of a particular programme. In some cases (see Chapter Six on Denmark) programmes are presented to social assistance recipients as a new *offer*, and the compulsory character is only revealed when this is not accepted. Because economic necessity often makes clients unable to reject the 'offer' of participation, it is perhaps best described as a 'throffer', combining offers and threats in one package (Steiner, 1994; Schmidtz and Goodin, 1998).

Compulsion within workfare reveals an assumption on the part of policy makers that at least some of the people to whom they are applied need to be coerced into participation, and, here, this is considered to be a key underlying feature of workfare policies. Whether because some people are choosing to be dependent on assistance ('rational dependency'), or because some have become so distanced from the labour market that they cannot or will not voluntarily re-enter ('irrational dependency') (Bane and Ellwood, 1994), compulsion is deemed necessary for at least a portion of the client group. Neither paid work in the regular labour market nor the work scheme itself are considered to proffer sufficient incentives or opportunities for all target group members to make use of them as a matter of choice. According to Mead, the main argument for compulsion is that it is effective in integrating participants in the labour market (Mead, 1997a). In his view, it is therefore an essential part of the 'new paternalism', which he justifies on grounds of furthering social citizenship through imposing the duty to work (Mead, 1986, 1997b).

Compulsion is important for two reasons. First, because it has a serious impact on the rights of those compelled, and second, because it reveals an underlying assumption among policy makers that the problem of worklessness is not merely a problem of a lack of the right jobs. As a result, compulsion is the most controversial feature of workfare. Critics who otherwise support 'activating' measures challenge the justification for compulsion. Criticism of compulsion is related to both normative considerations and to a perceived increased likelihood of undesirable outcomes.

First, it is argued that benefits must be unconditional in form in order to serve their function of residual safety net (Schmidtz and Goodin, 1998), and that entitlement to a guaranteed minimum income expresses the role of welfare as a guarantee of social citizenship (Marshall, 1985) which conditionality undermines. Second, it can be argued (for example, Grimes, 1997) that compulsion is counterproductive as it undermines consumer feedback, so other people are unable to reject poor quality programmes. Basing his argument on evidence from voluntary labour market programmes in Glasgow, Grimes claims that voluntary programmes are more motivating and yield better results in terms of integration into work than compulsory programmes. Finally, Jordan (1996) argues that, in combination, compulsion and poor quality programmes may further a 'culture of resistance' where participants use "the weapons of the weak; malingering, absenteeism, defection, shoddy workmanship and sabotage" (p 208).

Workfare is primarily about work

Here workfare is distinguished from other compulsory schemes through its primary emphasis on work rather than training or other forms of activation. Although work and other forms of activity operate together within workfare programmes, *work* is the primary component and unsubsidised work the official desired outcome. The distinction between work and other kinds of activity (particularly forms of 'on-the-job' training) is obviously problematic. However, it is considered to be important because of the different implications for the risk of displacement in the regular labour market and the use of workfare to fill 'regular' jobs or to carry out 'public work'. Unlike compulsory training programmes, clients who enter workfare schemes are compelled to supply their labour in exchange for financial assistance from the state – or, in the words of Laurence Mead, to "work off the grant" (Mead, 1997a, p viii).

Shragge (1997) uses a broader definition of workfare, which includes both work and *other required activities* linked to benefits; understanding workfare as a manifestation of a "new ideology for the underclass" (p 18). Torfing (1999) discusses workfare in relation to a broad social activation programme and Jordan (1996) groups workfare and what he terms 'trainfare' (to define compulsory training programmes) under the umbrella of the 'politics of enforcement'.

As Chapters Two to Eight demonstrate, the distinction between work and other compulsory activities in the programmes described in this book is not always clear. Many of the workfare programmes the authors describe include other forms of activity including 'training', which operate alongside work activities. A major area for comparison is the extent to which alternatives to work-for-benefit are available to programme participants.

Workfare is a part of social assistance

Here, workfare is defined as a *condition* tied to the receipt of social assistance. In general, the term 'social assistance' is used to refer to last-resort income support programmes, which in all seven countries have means-tested eligibility requirements (as a modern heir to previous poor law arrangements – Lødemel, 1997b). In some countries other benefits, including housing benefits and categorical benefits for older people, are means tested (Eardley et al, 1996) but are not considered as part of social assistance here.

The focus on social assistance is because the research group was interested in the fate of the most residualised population – where choice is most limited and for whom there is no further safety net.

Most other form-based discussions of workfare focus on programmes tied to social assistance. US writers use the term workfare more uniformly than European writers, referring to programmes tied to means-tested 'welfare' benefits, especially cash-based social assistance (Shragge, 1997). However, some European commentators have tended to take a broader view and to define programmes based both on social insurance and social assistance as workfare. This reflects the different composition of populations in Europe compared to the US (generally a greater number of people with insurance entitlement) and follows from a focus on 'compulsion' as the key factor. For instance, Standing (1990) focuses on compulsory 'work-related activities' so that his overview of workfare programmes includes those for insured and uninsured recipients.

Divergence from this third 'ideal-type' characteristic is important in the programmes considered in this book. Some workfare programmes considered (see particularly Chapter Six on Denmark) also extend to people with insurance entitlement – which is conditional on having paid in to the scheme rather than on the non-existence of other means of support. The extent to which policies for insured and uninsured groups overlap is discussed in Chapter Nine as one comparative characteristic. Some programmes that the authors in the book have chosen to describe can be better described as programmes that supply work 'instead of social assistance', rather than require work 'in return'. This applies to programmes for young people under the age of entitlement to income support (such policies in France and in the UK are described in Chapters Two and Seven), and to some of the Temporary Assistance for Needy Families (TANF) programmes operating in the US (see Chapter Eight).

A change in the contract of social assistance

Each of the three elements outlined in the definition of workfare used here conditions the way social assistance is delivered. Used in combination, the introduction of work and compulsion tied to the receipt of aid represents a fundamental change in the balance between rights and obligations in the provision of assistance. The crucial factor is the relationship between work and assistance.

Among the countries considered here, the extent to which access to cash-based social assistance constitutes an individual 'right' varies. In the UK, Germany, France and the Netherlands the 'right' to assistance (while conditional for some) is universal for needy people who meet the minimum age criteria and levels are legalised at the national level. The French case is unusual, as people as old as 24 are not normally entitled to assistance. In Norway and Denmark levels of local discretion over the award of assistance benefits are higher (Gough et al, 1997). Even prior to 1996, many US states had, effectively limited 'rights' to cash-based assistance to needy women with children; post-1996 the 'right' to cash-based assistance for this group was, for practical purposes, removed by new legislation (see Chapter Eight).

It could be argued that to maintain a balance of rights and responsibilities a 'right to work' should be introduced alongside a requirement to work in return for benefit. In fact, a right to work remains embedded in the constitutions of some of the countries discussed here (see France, Chapter Two and Norway, Kjønstad and Syse, 1997) although this 'right' is not understood to be enforceable at the individual level. In recent history, only the former communist countries actually instituted a right to work that corresponded to an obligation to work. Alternatively, one could argue that the balance of rights and responsibilities could involve participants having a right to participate in effective programmes to improve their chances of finding work. As Chapter Nine discusses, in some programmes (Danish 'Activation' and, in theory, through French Revenue Minimun d'Insertion [RMI] contracts) obligation to participate is explicitly matched with (universal) entitlement to be provided for within the programme. However, guarantees with regard to the 'quality' of the programmes are not made.

Although workfare programmes impact on the balance of individual rights and responsibilities, introducing a workfare programme need not necessarily reduce either the quantity or the quality of assistance provided. A programme can either be seen as an extension of opportunities to improve labour market integration chances – *giving more* – or as a means of curtailing existing rights – *giving less.* In the latter case the programme may potentially result in long-term losses for the client, in the form of a negligible or even negative impact on the chances of finding work, as well as short-term losses in the form of curtailed freedom. Clearly, the solution to the more/less equation will depend on the characteristics of pre-existing provision arrangements (including the extensiveness of opportunities to participate in voluntary programmes) as well as on the characteristics of the new compulsory programme.

It also depends on recipients' own interpretation of what constitutes 'more'. There is no single measure to determine whether a programme gives individual clients 'less' or 'more', but factors might include increased feelings of well-being, finding (sustainable) work, and increased income, among other outcomes. From the point of view of policy makers these outcomes are likely to only partially represent the aims of the programme. Some policy objectives, for example, a reduction in case loads or a cut in social assistance expenditure, are usually only coincidental to, and may even be in conflict with, the interests of individual participants as they themselves understand them. The European research group involved in the project from which this volume originates is currently pursuing qualitative studies of implementation and a review of the results of effect evaluations in the six European countries included here (Dahl and Pederson, 2001: forthcoming; Lødemel and Stafford, 2001: forthcoming).

From passive to active policies

The social consequences of worklessness continue to be a major focus for policy analysts and politicians. High levels of unemployment experienced by most western nations from the 1970s onwards impacted on fiscal policy and led to high levels of public expenditure on social security, requiring governments to develop strategies to relieve these problems. Periods of strong economic growth helped lower unemployment levels, but there is a common consensus that macroeconomic policies cannot alleviate the problems caused by unemployment alone. Governments understand themselves to be under a number of constraints related to labour market rigidities that affect their ability to use macroeconomic policy to stimulate demand for labour. In addition, policy makers are concerned with the notion that 'passive' benefits (see below) provided to workless people contribute to the rigidities that complicate macroeconomic policy and imply slow adjustment to changing economic realities. This is understood to result from moral hazard, whereby initiative is discouraged and 'dependence' is fostered so that benefit programmes actually contribute to the incidence and duration of the problem they are intended to alleviate (Giddens, 1998).

Accepting the notion that the western nations are undergoing a transition from industrial to post-industrial societies, the concept of the new 'risk society' suggests two explanations that can be applied to changes in the pattern of claims for social assistance in these countries (Beck, 1992). In terms of unemployment, the 'risk society' involves 'temporalisation': where unemployment, traditionally understood to be a static problem, is now *also* understood to be a dynamic (short-term or recurrent) problem for many individuals, and 'democratisation': where unemployment is no longer a problem confined only to 'working-class' people. The logical consequence of these changes was that policies targeted at unemployed people were required to realign to meet the needs of a broader range of individuals.

Governments have begun to seek ways to redesign social and labour market policies in line with changes in the recipient out-of-work population. An important aspect of the new policies is an extension of their reach beyond those closest to the labour market (unemployed people with good insurance contribution records) to other groups. Policy changes were based on a perceived need to 'build bridges back to work' for out-of-work groups who could benefit from "soft landings on the side of active society" (Larsson, 1998) and include the development of 'Active Labour Market Policies' (ALMPs).

The introduction of ALMPs, including workfare policies, can be understood as part of a wider change in the mode of production (Jessop, 1993). Jessop's contention is that as economies move from an industrial to a post-industrial state, the character of the welfare state is adapted to support new mechanisms to regulate labour. While the industrial welfare state was demand-side oriented – focusing on the use of macroeconomic tools – to regulate labour, the post-industrial 'workfare state' requires microeconomic instruments to improve the *supply* of labour through structural reforms. These reforms include improving education and training provision, increasing worker mobility and worker flexibility and improving incentives to seek and find new work opportunities.

On both sides of the Atlantic, the latter part of the 1990s has witnessed a decided shift away from 'passive' measures towards a more 'active' use of funds with the view to improving the availability of state training and experience programmes and furthering 'self-help' towards work among individual recipients. The boundary between passive and active measures is a fuzzy one, and the terms are used differently by policy makers in different countries. Broadly, benefit allocated without any condition to show evidence of seeking work or any offer of assistance in finding work would be at the far extreme of passive measures, while typically active measures would include training and subsidised work programmes targeted to out-of-work groups (OECD, 1999). In western Europe during the last decade, 'activation' is the key concept that describes this trend. In contrast, this term is seldom used in the US, although US commentators talk about a move towards an 'enabling state' (for example, Gilbert and Gilbert, 1989) to describe a similar process.

The origin of the present emphasis on ALMPs in Europe has been traced to Scandinavian countries (Wilensky, 1992), and, in particular, Sweden where active policies have long been used to stimulate both the demand and the supply of labour in times of economic restructuring. The rapid diffusion of active policies in recent years is largely a result of the support that they have garnered from key international organisations. In 1992, the OECD formulated a number of recommendations for member countries to reform social and labour market policies with the view to furthering integration into work as well as into other institutions in society (OECD, 1994). In 1995, a meeting of European ministers responsible for social welfare stressed the importance of active social policies, feeding their support for active policies into the 1995 United Nations Summit in Copenhagen. The European Union (EU) has adopted activation as the cornerstone of social policy development. In 1997 the EU Luxembourg Jobs Summit laid down three objectives. First, to guarantee training or other employability measures to unemployed individuals who had six months of unemployment. Second, to repeat intervention with such measures after twelve months of unemployment. Finally, to increase the use of ALMP measures so that they affect at least 20% of unemployed people at any one time (European Council, 1997). The Luxembourg Summit set in place 'Employment Guidelines' agreed annually by member states and called for annual 'National Employment Action Plans' whereby member states report on their progress against the guidelines (European Commission, 1998). The Amsterdam Treaty gives the European Commission powers to make recommendations to the European Council on member states' employment policies. These non-binding international policies together form the 'Luxembourg process'.

The activation approach can be linked to similar approaches applied to clients within general social and rehabilitation work (Hvinden, 1999) in the sense that the aim is to help clients to change their circumstances through participation. However, typically the use of the term in the context of labour market policy is narrower, in that an 'active' labour market measure is generally specifically intended to bring individuals into work. An important observation is that, in the context of labour market policy, the term 'active' is usually understood to mean 'economically active'. Workfare constitutes one form of 'active measure' (with distinctive characteristics as described above) (Heikkila, 1999; Torfing, 1999).

Active labour market policies, including workfare, are characterised by the use of a mixture of *incentives* and *disincentives* ('carrots' and 'sticks') to achieve desired aims. Such measures are based on the assumption that individuals respond rationally, at least in aggregate, to cues that help them to maximise their income. The use of this approach within the new policies has been described as demonstrating a 'fundamental shift in policy makers' beliefs about human nature and behaviour' and 'the victory of rational choice thinking' (Le Grand, 1997). An ideal-type workfare programme, as set out in the definition at the start of this chapter, would place greater emphasis on disincentives in the form of the threat of sanction than other active labour market measures (Hvinden, 1999; Abrahamsen, 1998).

The change from passive to active policies has been described above as a universal trend in developed welfare states, suggesting that the welfare states may be becoming more similar – as 'activating states' or, to use Jessop's terminology, 'workfare states' (Jessop, 1993). However, while impulse and trend can be seen to be common, in ten or twenty years from now it may become clear that the pattern of policy implementation currently occurring has resulted in variation in post-industrial states which is as marked as that described in industrial nations.

Ideological contexts for workfare

This section considers different justifications for workfare. A review of the debates around the introduction of activation and workfare policies in different countries demonstrates that a broad range of social problems and social ills are brought forward as problems to be met with compulsory participation in work activities (Hvinden, 1999; Standing, 1990). These include high levels of unemployment, high proportions of people marginalised from the labour market, expensive cash benefits, as well as the ambition of restoring civic virtues, duties and solidarities through increasing participation in society (Hvinden, 1999; Standing, 1990). In Nordic countries two sets of justifications for activating policies are outlined in the policy literature (Hvinden, 1999, p 30). The first set relates to 'the individual', the latter to the 'interest of society as a whole'. Individual-based justifications include improving skills necessary for finding and keeping work, preventing the negative personal effects of joblessness, encouraging active job-seeking and providing participants with a sense of meaning and worth through contributing to society. Societal-based justifications include improving the supply of labour, integrating unemployed people into society, and reducing pressure on public budgets (Hvinden, 1999).

The *cost* of worklessness always forms part of the reason that workfare-like programmes are introduced. Another organisational tool for workfare programmes is the different political and scientific interpretations of the *causes* of worklessness. The focus is on how different discourses express different *justifications* for workfare. Two key justifications are identified: preventing 'social exclusion' and preventing 'dependency'. The former emphasises structural causes of worklessness, resulting from industrial restructuring, regional imbalances in economic development and a skills mismatch between available labour supply and existing demand. In contrast, understandings of worklessness related to dependency justifications for workfare-like policies emphasise individual and cultural factors which result in people being less able and less willing to make the transition to work and the provision of passive assistance, which supports people in making a choice not to work. However, the two justifications are not mutually exclusive. It is possible to hold that social exclusion leads to dependency, and vice versa. Both justifications are present within the public policy discourse of all seven countries included in this book and are used to justify policies with a workfare element, although the emphasis on either justification varies between and within countries (see Chapter Nine). Chapter Nine discusses the links between the stated aims and objectives of programmes and the strategies that they employ to combat worklessness. The wider question of whether policies seeking to combat social exclusion differ in anything more than rhetorical packaging from dependency-driven programmes (Spicker, 1997) is explored further in Chapter Ten.

The main difference between the concepts of social exclusion and dependency is that the former tends to focus on structural causes of social assistance receipt, whereas dependency tends to focus on the choices that individual recipients make. Theoretically at least, different interpretations of the causes of worklessness should relate to different policy responses to the problem. However, concepts are highly mixed in political rhetoric, so that different justifications are often used to reinforce one another. The dependency concept itself is fractured into at least three sub-concepts (as described below). The following sections attempt to clarify these justifications and explain how ideally they would relate to policy initiatives.

Social exclusion and worklessness

The concept of social exclusion is European, more specifically French, in origin. It was first used in the 1970s to describe the large number of French people excluded from social insurance entitlement. The term then came to be associated with disadvantaged groups in general, and with the rise of new forms of poverty, which are distinguished more by precarious life events than by material want (Paugam et al, 1993). Social exclusion is linked to the concept of citizenship and to Republican principles established during the French revolution (see Chapter Two). The French influence on social policy-making within the EU is associated with the recent upsurge in popularity of the social exclusion concept (Leisering and Walker, 1998; Room, 1995). For some the concept is dynamic focusing on the processes of detachment from society (Castels, 1990). Elsewhere the term is used with regard to relational issues, including different levels of resources, integration and power (Room, 1995). Both dynamic and relational approaches separate the social exclusion approach from a previously dominant concern with 'poverty', which until recently, in Anglo-Saxon countries in particular, was dominant in the discourse around receiving social assistance.

The policy response to social exclusion is 'insertion'; society has a responsibility to re-insert excluded people. The emphasis is on the responsibilities of the state in facilitating *social cohesion*, and mending "ruptures in social bonds" (Morel, 1998). As an expression of solidarity, efforts to develop 'insertion' policies entail an extension of public investment in welfare rather than a retrenchment of public responsibilities (Morel, 1998). According to Silver (1994), the social exclusion concept is also associated with Durkheimian sociology, in particular with an emphasis on moral integration. Levitas adds that the solidarity concept which relates to discourse around social exclusion (see Chapter Two) "is focused on work – with work itself perceived to have social as well as moral and economic functions" (Levitas, 1998).

The social exclusion perspective emphasises the (positive) *responsibilities* of the state. However, the emphasis on state responsibility can also entail a greater stress on the *interests* of society than on the interests of the individual, as per Hvinden's distinction (Hvinden, 1999). Jordan (1996) expressed this view in his critique of the French use of the term. In his view, the motivation behind the concept of social exclusion is primarily paternalistic. This paternalism originates from a wider Continental mercantilist tradition, where the inclusion of excluded people primarily served the interest of the state rather than the interest of the individual; "the poor were more like sheep and cattle to be farmed (regulated and provided for as part of the creation and conservation of natural wealth)" (p 4). Social exclusion resulting in "tears in the social fabric" (see Chapter Two) can be understood to be as much a threat to the cohesiveness of society as it is a threat to the well-being of excluded people. It can be argued, therefore, that there is little major difference from the Anglo-American liberal tradition in which the poor are perceived as "wild animals to be tamed" (Jordan, 1996, p 4). While a social exclusion perspective can justify workfare as a tool which gives excluded people *more* through increasing their inclusion prospects, it can also justify the use of compulsion in order to ensure that general national economic and security interests are met.

Dependency and worklessness

Concern with the problem of 'dependency' on welfare is as old as statutory welfare itself (Malthus, 1998 [1798]). This concern underpinned the introduction of extreme conditionality measures in the 1834 British New Poor Law, and even at that time the focus was not exclusively British. After a visit to England in 1833 the French commentator de Tocqueville highlighted what he saw as a paradoxical situation, whereby Britain, the most prosperous country in Europe at that time, suffered the greatest problem of pauperism. In de Tocqueville's view, the riches that had enabled England to institute legal charity also explained the large scale of pauperism: "Any measure that establishes legal charity on a permanent basis and gives it an administrative form ... creates an idle and lazy class living at the expense of the industrial and working class" (de Tocqueville, 1997 [1833]). The solution proposed by de Tocqueville was similar to that of Malthus' (1998 [1798]) – the abolition of public relief. This recommendation was not taken up by policy makers at that time, and perhaps the strongest attempt to adopt the approach advocated by de Tocqueville was made more than 150 years later, when the US Congress introduced time-limited social assistance in 1996 (see Chapter Eight).

The concept of dependency is increasingly used in relation to social assistance provision throughout the developed western welfare states. As in the early 19th century, a central element in the policies that follow from a concern with dependency is compulsory work for those receiving assistance as a 'work test' to weed out people who could provide for themselves by other means. Through the dependency concept workfare-like policies are justified on the basis that far from being a solution to the problem of worklessness, passive provision is itself a main root of the problem. Hence, the dependency concept is more directly linked to workfare than the social exclusion concept, in that workfare itself constitutes a logical policy response, as it prevents dependency on passive cash assistance. Conversely, as discussed earlier in this chapter, and demonstrated in Chapter Nine, dependency is always a component of the justification for compulsory policies.

It is perhaps unsurprising that the early 19th-century concept of dependency should have re-emerged at the end of the 20th century. Both periods were characterised by fundamental changes in the mode of production: from an agricultural to an industrial economy at the time of the industrial revolution, and further on to a 'post-industrial' economy in the last quarter of the 20th century. During industrialisation, workers were often forced to accept industrial employment at below subsistence wages. The transition to a post-industrial economy has meant reduced job security for many, sometimes lower wages and new demands on workers who previously worked in industry, and changed opportunities for people newly entering the labour market (Jessop, 1993). Once again the 'work ethic' is emphasised by policy makers in support of these changes (Bauman, 1998) and once again the transition is accompanied by corrective measures targeted at people who are out of work.

Bane and Ellwood (1994) describe the current preoccupation with dependency in the US as a result of a profound shift in emphasis and tone in the debates about poverty during the 1980s and early 1990s. Prior to this period, policy makers focused on the adequacy of labour supply and labour opportunities; towards the end of the decade the focus shifted towards an emphasis on the *values* of the poor. In the words of Handler and Hasenfeld (1997), "Dependency, as used in the welfare context, is not simply being poor. It is not simply being out of work. Rather, welfare dependency is a problem of attitude, a moral failure to have a proper work ethic. It is a way of life" (p 9).

A number of different explanations for dependency are put forward, and Bane and Ellwood distinguish three models in the dependency discourse, which highlight different mechanisms. These models are not mutually exclusive, and typically those who employ the dependency concept refer to all three.

1. The *rational model* of dependency is based on the understanding that humans tend to try to maximise their circumstances in terms of gains in income and leisure. Dependency is therefore understood to result from the fact that the generosity of benefits compared to wages makes it irrational for individuals to reject benefits in favour of work.
2. The *psycho-social (or expectancy) model* of dependency more clearly sees people as 'victims of welfare'. Long periods of receiving welfare are therefore understood to deprive people of the confidence they require to move into work, even if they would like to do this.
3. The *cultural model* of dependency holds that people do not want to move on from claiming social assistance because they have developed values and behaviours and life-styles that are different from those of working people and which are congruent with passive benefit receipt. In the US this model is used to explain the development of ghettoes containing people who have different social values from those in other parts of society. Bane and Ellwood (1994) distinguish between a

conservative and a liberal version (in US terminology) of the cultural model. The conservative version, of which Murray is a proponent (1994), stresses the importance of a culture which condones immoral mores; "the new heroes of the ghetto are those who game the system" (Murray, 1994). In contrast, the liberal version is closer to the social exclusion concept, in that it emphasises structural factors, notably the loss of employment opportunities in the inner cities as a result of changes in industrial mix and the migration of both jobs and professionals from the minority neighbourhoods.

For a fuller exploration of the concept of dependency readers should turn to Fraser and Gordon's excellent review of this "single most crucial term" in the recent US welfare reforms (Fraser and Gordon, 1994). However, the positions of two US writers who have been particularly influential in giving the concept currency are worth outlining. Charles Murray (1994) chiefly employs the rational and cultural dependency models in his work. Moreover, he is the commentator most closely associated with two concepts related to the cultural model: the *culture of poverty* and the *underclass* (Murray, 1994). Ultimately, Murray's solution to the problem of dependency is not workfare but follows in the tradition of Malthus and de Tocqueville: to end welfare altogether (Murray, 1994). In contrast Laurence Mead (1997a) is the commentator who is most closely associated with the psycho-social or expectancy model. Basing his conclusions on research findings that suggest that "welfare disincentives to work are surprisingly unimportant", Mead concludes that the rational model receives little support from evidence (Mead, 1997a). Mead argues that the main reason why people do not work is that "people do not accept responsibility for themselves. They want to work in principle but they feel they cannot in practice" (Mead, 1997a). This lack of 'self-efficacy' is understood to be rooted in personal experiences of failure, so that the principal obstacle to entry to the labour market is defeatism rather than rational choice or a lack of moral fibre.

Ideal-type work-for-benefit workfare, as defined in this chapter, is a rational policy response to dependency understood in rational terms. Compulsory work changes the terms of the calculations that current recipients make, as well as those made by people considering taking up benefits. For both groups the leisure/income calculations are likely to mean that benefit receipt is a less attractive option. The policy response is therefore both corrective and preventive. Under a rational model of dependency, workfare is primarily intended to change the balance of choices which recipients face, so that more is expected from them in return for the assistance that they receive. Payne refers to workfare in this context as a "contract for uplift in the form of 'expectant giving'" (Payne, 1998).

Compulsory work policies also make sense as a response to an expectancy model of dependency, if work experience can be understood to change people's perceptions of their options. Such a 'paternalistic' approach combines 'directive and supervisory' measures to educate benefit recipients about their choices. Mead describes such an approach as a combination of 'help and hassle' intended to guide 'dependent' people to self-sufficiency through work (Mead, 1997b). The obligation to work under such a model is justified on grounds of *reciprocity*, so that it forms part of the *social contract* and is justified as an instrument for achieving self-respect among people who receive state benefits by furthering their integration into society (Bardach, 1997). Theoretically, there should be a key difference in policy response depending on whether policy makers are more sympathetic to a rational versus expectancy model of dependency. Under a rational model, policies which give 'less' to recipients are called for, while under an expectancy model 'more' provision may be justified in the form of guidance or opportunity (Bane and Ellwood, 1994) – even if this is under a regime of compulsory participation.

Policy responses to dependency in cultural terms depend on whether a conservative or liberal interpretation of the process, by which distinct subcultures with separate values come about, is adhered to. The idea of compulsory participation is congruent with both liberal and conservative interpretations. In conservative terms, workfare needs to be corrective (and give less) in order to end a system of values that is supported by non-expectant giving. The rationale is that changes in the structure of giving may result in a change in work orientation among recipient populations as long as people are left with no choice but to work. More liberal interpretations for the causes of the development of subcultures point to a greater focus on incentives and on wider measures to improve employment opportunity.

Schmidtz and Goodin (1998) take issue with the concept of dependency at a philosophical level, arguing that there is no logical reason why a person who depends on family support or a protected labour market is more 'self-reliant' than someone depending on state welfare. In addition, considering different state programmes, they argue that some forms of social security are singled out as problematic while others are not and that dependency is increasingly understood to mean long-term receipt of last-resort income maintenance among poor people of working age. In the US this includes a disproportionate number of people from ethnic minority backgrounds. Other groups of people reliant on social security – including elderly people without sufficient contribution records to entitle them to insurance-based benefits – are not bracketed within a dependent population. The impact of this distinction is shown in the fact that it was possible for Clinton to campaign to 'save social security' and 'end welfare' simultaneously. Schmidtz and Goodin argue that the distinction between 'dependency' and 'self-reliance' is inconsistent and disingenuous and can only be seen as resulting from a particular moralistic stance (Schmidtz and Goodin, 1998). The use of the words 'welfare' and 'dependency' together give both terms negative connotations. The result is that the meaning of 'welfare', as understood in political discourses in the US, has changed from a neutral or positive concept to a negative one.

Dean and Taylor-Gooby (1992) also argue that the current use of the dependency concept rests on moralistic assumptions about poor people, and is counterproductive. They argue that the implication that people who receive state assistance are "'culturally' separated from the rest of society" is inaccurate. Their critique of the idea of separateness is supported by empirical evidence. Findings from dynamic analyses of poverty on both sides of the Atlantic suggest that the majority of people in receipt of social assistance experience relatively short spells of receipt. On the other hand, a minority of recipients appears to be less mobile and to suffer longer spells of social assistance receipt (Leisering and Walker, 1998; Bane and Ellwood, 1994). Even among this group, the main determinant of longer periods of social assistance receipt appears to be the length of the period of the need resulting from unemployment, sickness or lone parenthood, rather than the impact of the experience of public transfer receipt itself. Leisering and Walker conclude that the evidence shows that "while the probability of escaping from poverty or benefits decreases with time, the simple assertion that this is evidence of dependency, of morally enervating effects of being on benefits, receives little support" (Leisering and Walker, 1998).

Structural context to the seven nations

The seven countries included in this volume are all wealthy OECD nations with well-developed welfare states. However, there are obvious differences in both sizes and systems of government. For example, in undertaking comparison it is important to remember that the population of the US is similar in size to that of the six European countries put together. Its federal structure of government is also distinctive; while Germany is also a federal state the degree of discretion afforded to the regions is considerably less in relation to social welfare issues. The seven nations demonstrate considerable variation with regard to key economic indicators; these are described in Table 1.1.

Over the past decade Nordic and Continental European nations have tended to be characterised by relatively low rates of income poverty and high levels of overall social security expenditure, with social assistance expenditure accounting for about one or two per cent of GDP. In addition, Norway and Denmark have experienced high rates of participation in paid work, whereas France and Germany have experienced low levels as well as higher levels of unemployment. In Germany and the Netherlands, long-term unemployment levels have been relatively high. In the UK, unemployment has decreased sharply in recent years, while long-term and youth unemployment remained relatively high in 1995. Norway and the US both have low levels of total unemployment.

In the US the proportion of the population experiencing poverty has been significantly higher than elsewhere and levels of expenditure on social security have been significantly lower. By contrast, UK governments have spent a greater proportion of their social security budget on social assistance than governments elsewhere in Europe. In the US, despite the low levels of overall spending, the proportion of the population receiving social assistance (including non-contributory unemployment-related benefits and income support programmes) is the highest among all seven countries (Gough et al, 1997).

Active labour market policies

Workfare bridges two traditionally separate elements of modern welfare states – labour market policies and social policies. In most countries this division has resulted in different agencies and government ministries being responsible for each set of policies. While labour market authorities supplement social policies for some groups, mainly insured unemployed people, there is variation in the extent to which social assistance recipients have access to labour market measures provided through labour authorities. Taking the case of Norway, it has been suggested that workfare policies that are residual and exist outside of wider national active labour market policies may tend to be preventive rather than integrative in character (Lødemel, 1997a). Conversely, Torfing has demonstrated that in Denmark,

Table 1.1: Key comparative data

	1	2	3		4	5	6
	Population (millions)	System of government	Extent of income poverty circa 1995 (%)		Gross public social expenditure as % of GDP	Social assistance expenditure as % of GDP	Labour market participation rate
	1999		Ca 1990	Ca 1995	1995	1992	1999
Denmark	5.2	Unitary	7.7	6.9	32.2	1.4	80.6
France	58.2	Unitary	12.9	8.4	28.0	1.8	67.8
Germany	81.7	Federal	18.2	11.4	27.1	1.6	71.2
The Netherlands	15.5	Unitary	6.5	6.2	26.8	2.2	73.6
Norway	4.4	Unitary	4.6	5.8	27.6	0.7	80.6
United Kingdom	58.6	Unitary	11.7	10.6	22.4	6.4	76.3
United States	263	Federal	17.5	17.9	15.8	1.3	77.2

Notes:

1 US Census Bureau (2000) www.census.gov/cgi-bin/, 7 September 2000

3 Luxembourg Income Study (2000) www.lis.ceps.lu, 7 September 2000. Poverty defined as income below 50% of median household disposable income.

4 OECD (1999). For France OECD (1996b)

5 Gough et al (1997)

6 OECD (2000)

Table 1.1: contd.../

	7	8	9	10		11	12	
	Total expenditure on labour market programmes as % of GDP	Total expendture on ALMPs as % of GDP	Expenditure on ALMPs as a % of expenditure on labour market programmes	Unemployment rates		Long-term unemployment rate as a % of total unemployment	Activism rate	
	1995	1999	1999	1995	1999	1999	1995	1999
Denmark	4.90	1.77	36.1	7.3	5.2	20.5	0.22	0.34
France	3.13	1.33	42.1	11.7	11.3	40.3	0.10	0.12
Germany	3.42	1.30	38.0	8.2	8.7	51.7	0.14	0.15
The Netherlands	4.61	1.80	39.0	6.9	3.3	43.5	0.15	0.55
Norway	1.29	0.82	63.6	5.0	3.3	6.8	0.25	0.25
United Kingdom	1.19	0.37	31.1	8.7	6.1	29.8	0.06	0.06
United States	0.42	0.17	16.6	5.6	4.2	6.8	0.04	0.04

Notes:

7 OECD (2000)

8 OECD (2000)

10 OECD (2000), the unemployment rate gives the numbers of unemployed persons as a percentage of the civilian workforce (the definition conforms with the ILO guidelines)

11 OECD (2000), long-term unemployment is defined as 12 months and over

12 OECD (2000) and OECD (1996a), expenditure on ALPM as % of GDP/standardised unemployment rate in 1995. See also Hvinden (1999) for a discussion of different ways to measure activism.

where workfare exists as an integral part of wider activation policies, there is a greater focus on integration (Torfing, 1999).

The seven nations differ in the length of their history with regard to activation measures. Table 1.1 refers to the mid-1990s and demonstrates differences in the scope of activation policies, measured as the expenditure on ALMPs divided by the unemployment rate (Column 12, Table 1.1). Norway and Denmark were leaders in the move towards more ALMPs at this time, whereas the UK and US demonstrated relatively low levels of activation. The different levels of ALMP development in the mid-1990s may have impacted on the role that compulsory work policies played towards the end of the decade, as consensus around the importance of ALMPs developed. The compulsory policies introduced by UK and US governments of the late-1990s were key components of the drive to a more activating approach in these countries that lagged behind in the development of ALMPs more generally.

Welfare state typologies

Social scientists have sought to categorise welfare states in a number of ways. Building on the work of Wilensky and Lebaux (1964), Titmuss (1974) made a distinction between "three contrasting models or functions of social policy" – institutionalist, handmaiden and residual models – which have informed most later typologies of western welfare provision arrangements. The three models sought to relate differences in welfare state provision to differences in ideas regarding the function of the state vis-à-vis social provision. Under the *residual* model of welfare provision, social services are provided to people who are unable to help themselves. They form a safety net which catches individuals temporarily when the 'natural' channels of welfare – the private market and the family – break down. Under the *handmaiden* model of welfare provision, social services are functional to other institutions, so that social needs are met on the basis of "merit, work performance and productivity" (Titmuss, 1974). Under the *institutional-redistributitive* model, services are provided on a universal basis and social welfare as an integrated institution in society, "providing universalist services outside the market on the principle of need" (Titmuss, 1974).

Esping-Andersen (1990) took these typologies a step further and based his models on findings from comparative research. He distinguished between three (again) idealised welfare state regimes, defined according to two dimensions: extent of decommodification (the extent to which social policy makes individuals independent of the market) and stratification (the extent to which the welfare state differentiates in the treatment of different groups). He labelled his three 'worlds of welfare' 'conservative-corporatist', 'liberal' and 'social-democratic' regimes. The first is characterised by strong emphasis on the role of social partners, on the principle of subsidiarity, and in consequence on an underdeveloped service sector and on the existence of labour market 'insiders' and 'outsiders', and is illustrated here by the inclusion of France and Germany. The second is characterised by minimal and targeted assistance measures, re-enforcement of job-seeking behaviour and promotion of systems of private welfare provision, and is illustrated here by the UK and the US. The third idealised type, the 'social-democratic' regime, exemplified by Scandinavian countries, is characterised by institutionalised redistribution, where the welfare state provides universal services, based on full employment. This type is represented here by the inclusion of Norway and Denmark (Esping-Andersen, 1990). The seventh country represented here, the Netherlands, is understood by Esping-Andersen to share elements of both the conservative and social-democratic regime types.

Workfare policies relate to the concepts of decommodification and stratification. Introducing workfare can be understood as part of a reversal of welfare expansion in that it 're-commodifies' some unemployed people. In doing so, workfare policies, selectively applied, also influence the degree of stratification between different groups of workless people. A key comparative question is therefore the extent to which the nature of workfare reflects the regime type to which the individual countries belong (see Chapter Ten).

Typologies of social assistance

The welfare typologies and regimes outlined above are biased towards descriptions of social insurance provision and therefore yield different results from comparisons focusing on social assistance (Lødemel and Schulte, 1992; Gough et al, 1997). Over the past 20 years, structural changes largely resulting from de-industrialisation have led to a rise in unemployment, to a complementary rise in long-term unemployment, to a feminisation of the labour market and to increased wage polarisation in many European countries (Walker, 1999). Together with changes in demographics and family forms, in particular the growth in lone parenthood (Eardley et al, 1996), these changes have led to increases in the number of people relying on means-tested social assistance benefits in all seven countries. The increase has been exacerbated as a growing number of long-term unemployed people are reaching the end of their entitlement for social insurance benefits. At the same time new entrants to the labour market, who have not had time to build up contributory benefits, find that they require assistance. In addition to these 'push' factors, Ditch and Oldfield (1999) note a number of 'pull' factors, including the extension of means-tested benefits in order to achieve better targeting of social security. One side-effect has been a greater reliance on social assistance (as a 'top up') among people who are working. An important change, for the purposes of this book, is that in most countries a greater proportion of social assistance clients are now unemployed than was the case two decades ago (Room, 1990).

These factors have contributed to an increased interest in social assistance among the research community. One expression of this is an increase in the number of comparative studies, and with it attempts to describe variation among nations and how they cluster. Table 1.2 includes two different typologies of social assistance. The first typology applies Titmuss' distinction between residual and institutional welfare. Social assistance itself can be seen as an embodiment of *residual* welfare provision, in that it is a last resort, safety net measure. Nonetheless, cross-national comparisons of the post-war development of social assistance programmes demonstrate the extent to which these programmes have departed from purely residual arrangements as they have incorporated institutional traits including legal entitlement for recipients and state responsibility for finance and implementation (Lødemel, 1989, 1997b). Lødemel and Schulte (1992) focus on the legal framework of programmes and the degree of programme centralisation and distinguish four European 'poverty regimes'; institutionalised, differentiated, residual and incomplete differentiated. All four regimes are represented among the seven nations considered in this book. A key distinguishing factor is the extent to which social assistance provision has been combined with social work provision, as in the cash-care multifunctional tradition of the early Poor Laws. At the time when this typology was made (before the New labour government), the UK was described as an institutionalised poverty regime, with centralised programmes providing benefits on the basis of legal entitlement without accompanying social work interventions. The 'incomplete' French system was centralised while sharing the cash-care multifunctional form of delivery with Germany, Denmark, Norway and the Netherlands. The US model of the early 1990s could be described as a combination of the institutionalised and the differentiated models.

Based on a study of all OECD countries, Gough et al (1997) provided a new and extended typology and arrived at eight different regimes. The authors included information about the number of recipients and levels of assistance that they received (Table 1.2). The combined index of programme structure is summarised in an 'exclusion score' which mirrors the legal framework dimension of the typology developed by Lødemel and Schulte.

Workfare programmes inevitably introduce an element of case-work into the provision of financial assistance. In France, Germany, the Netherlands, Norway and Denmark workfare strengthens an already established tradition of combined cash-care provisions (social workers are assigned to individual recipients). However, in the UK in particular and to some extent also in the US, workfare reintroduces a social work role to systems where cash and care have previously been separated.

The combination of case-work and financial assistance can serve to ensure that 'more' or 'less' is provided to recipients through the programme. On the one hand, case-workers can be instrumental in providing advice and support. On the other hand, they may help the state to assert firmer social control on clientele in the tradition of the early Poor Laws, alongside increased discretion and diminished entitlement (Lødemel, 1997b). Chapter Ten discusses the extent to which differences in the use of workfare-like measures reflect different typologies of social assistance, and addresses the extent of convergence between different national traditions.

Taxonomies of workfare

Until recently, while descriptions of policies described as workfare have been produced on a country-by-country basis, little consideration has been given to whether patterns of social assistance hold when the workfare policies embedded within them are considered. A first contribution has been made by Torfing (1999) who, in describing workfare policies in Denmark, makes a distinction between 'offensive' workfare (a term Torfing uses to describe Danish policies) and 'defensive' workfare (which Torfing associated with policy making in the US and in the UK). 'Offensive workfare' is integrative, reaches out to a wide range of recipient groups, including those who have problems other than unemployment, and emphasises 'activation', skill development and 'empowerment'. 'Defensive workfare' on the other hand is preventive and punitive and is concerned with 'benefit reduction', 'flexibility' and 'control'.

Table 1.2: Selected features of social assistance and welfare regimes

Column number	1	2	3	4	5	6	7
		Social assistance regimes				Total welfare	
Characteristic	Proportion of the population	Relative benefit levels after housing costs (%)	Exclusion group	Gough et al: Assistance regimes	Lødemel/ Schulte: Poverty regimes	Three worlds of welfare	Expenditure on ALMP
Denmark	Moderate (3-10%)	66	Moderate exclusion score	Citizenship-based residual	(Residual)	Social-democratic	Low
France	Moderate (3-10%)	43	Moderate exclusion score	Dual social assistance	Incomplete differentiated	Conservative	Medium
Germany	Moderate (3-10%)	44	Moderate exclusion score	Dual social assistance	Differentiated	Conservative	Low
The Netherlands	Moderate (3-10%)	43	Moderate exclusion score	Citizenship-based residual	Differentiated	Social Democratic/ Conservative	Low
Norway	Moderate (3-10%)	57	High exclusion score	Decentralised discretionary relief	Residual	Social-democratic	High
United Kingdom	High (>10 %)	42	Low exclusion score	Integrated safety net	Institutionalised	Liberal	Low
United States	High (>10 %)	Variable (under 30)	Moderate exclusion score	Public assistance state	(Institution-alised)	Liberal	Medium

Notes to Table 1.2

[1] Gough et al (1997).

[2] Gough et al: the authors constructed relative benefit levels, which they calculated by comparing disposable incomes of people receiving social assistance with disposable incomes of the same household type where the head was earning average male earnings.

[3] Gough et al (1997, p 30): the exclusion score is a combined index based on the following variables: legal and administrative framework, resource unit, treatment of income, treatment of assets and rights vs discretion.

[4] Gough et al (1997, p 36): Institutionalised = centralised, unified, separate from social work; Differentiated = categorical schemes alongside a general scheme, locally administered, but codified and distinct from social work; Residual = local, marginal scheme with a strong emphasis on social control and treatment; Incomplete differentiated = categorical schemes for the 'non-able bodied' with limited assistance tied to social control and treatment. [..] = Not included in original classification.

[5] Lødemel and Schulte (1992).

[6] Esping-Andersen (1990).

[7] See Table 1.1, column 9: expenditure on ALMP as a % of expenditure on labour market programmes.

The offensive/defensive distinction that Torfing describes relates to differences in ideology (which translates to a strategy designed to meet integrative aims) and regime type (social-democratic as opposed to liberal). While this provides a starting point for the differences which we consider here, it is important to remember that Torfing looked only at Denmark in any detail. The broader perspective that we offer allows us to consider what factors beyond ideology and regime type are associated with offensive policies. In Chapter Nine the aims, strategy and content of programmes are compared and the extent to which different national and cross-national types of workfare can be identified is discussed.

10687

Programmes and timing of legislation

This book considers the main workfare programmes or schemes operating in seven countries. These are discussed fully in Chapters Two to Eight and can be listed as follows:

- France – Insertion programmes and schemes operating under the Minimum Income and Insertion Act (1989), the Solidarity Job Contracts Act (1989), and the Jobs for Youth Act (1997).
- Germany – Help Towards Work policies, based on the Social Assistance Act (1961).
- The Netherlands – The programme outlined in the Jobseeker's Employment Act (1998).
- Norway – Local schemes resulting from the Social Services Act (1991).
- Denmark – Programmes and schemes operating under the Active Social Policy Act (1998).
- UK – The New Deal programmes for 18-24s, and for over 25s (introduced in 1997-98) which build on legislation from the Jobseeker's Act (1995). The dual-training system for 16- to 18-year-olds, of Modern Apprenticeships (introduced in 1995) and National Traineeships (introduced in 1997).
- US – programmes in New York City, Wisconsin and California resulting from the Personal Responsibility and Work Opportunity Reconciliation Act (1996).

On the whole, the introduction and evolution of workfare programmes in Europe is a 1990s phenomenon (Figure 1.1). However, while the US is often seen as the originator of workfare policies, having a history of programmes going back to the early 1970s, compulsory work-for-benefit measures also have a long history within post-1945 Europe. In Germany a provision for workfare was included in the 1961 social assistance legislation, although the policy was largely dormant until the onset of mass unemployment in the 1970s. Denmark has taken a pioneering role in the more systematic application of compulsory activation policies.

**Figure 1.1: Key legislative changes and policy developments: a
time line for the introduction of compulsory work–for–benefit
programmes in the last decades of the 20th century**

Denmark	98	**ACTIVE SOCIAL POLICY ACT** – Activation policy
France		**ANTI-EXCLUSION ACT** – TRACE programme
The Netherlands		**JOBSEEKER'S EMPLOYMENT ACT** – JEA programme
United Kingdom		New Deal for Young People (and New Deals for others)
France	97	**JOBS FOR YOUTH ACT** – Emploi Jeunes
United States	96	**PERSONAL RESPONSIBILITY AND WORK OPPORTUNITY RECONCILIATION ACT** – Increased state latitude in work obligation enforcement and raised caseload activation requirements
United Kingdom		*Project Work*
United Kingdom	95	**JOBSEEKERS' ACT** – Compulsory short programmes for jobseekers
	94	
Norway	93	*A-tiltak programme*
The Netherlands	92	**YOUTH EMPLOYMENT ACT** – *YEA programme*
Norway	91	**SOCIAL SERVICES ACT** – Local authority workfare schemes
	90	
France	89	**SOLIDARITY JOB CONTRACTS ACT** – CES programme **MINIMUM INCOME AND INSERTION ACT** – *Insertion contracts*
United States	88	**FAMILY SUPPORT ACT** – *State requirements for caseload activation*
	87	
	86	
	85	
France	84	**COLLECTIVE UTILITY WORKS ACT** – *TUC programme*
	83	
	82	
United States	81	**OMNIBUS BUDGET RECONCILLIATION ACT** – *Allows CWEP programmes for AFDC recipients*
	80	
	79	
Denmark	78	**LOCAL AUTHORITY EMPLOYMENT SCHEME ACT** – *Employment projects*
Federal Republic of Germany	61	**SOCIAL ASSISTANCE ACT (BSHG)** – *HZA schemes*

Key:

BOLD CAPITALS	Legislative changes permitting/extending workfare
Italics	Extinct, or subsequently superseded, workfare programmes
Normal type	Current programmes/schemes

Note: All legislative Acts and programmes in this figure are discussed in Chapters 2-9.

Summary

This chapter has provided an overview of different definitions of workfare and presented a form-based definition that is used as a starting point for the contributors to this book. Workfare bridges two traditionally separate areas of welfare, social services and labour market policies. The recent move towards more active labour market policies and the role of workfare within this trend has been outlined. It has been argued that the introduction of workfare involves a shift in the balance between rights and obligations of people provided with social assistance. The factors that may lead to diversity include ideological justifications for workfare and the structural context of welfare provision. Depending on what existed previously, and the character of the workfare programmes introduced, the shift can result in a 'less' or a 'more' situation for individuals, in terms of the quality of the assistance provided by the state.

References

Abrahamsen, P. (1998) 'Efter velfærdsstaten: ret og plikt til aktivering', *Nordisk Sosialt Arbeid*, Nr 3, pp 133-44.

Bane, M.J. and Ellwood, D. (1994) *Welfare realities. From rhetoric to reform*, Cambridge: Harvard University Press.

Bardach, E. (1997) 'Implementing a paternalist welfare-to-work program', in L. Mead (ed) *The new paternalism*, Washington, DC: Brooking Institution Press.

Bauman, Z. (1998) *Work, consumerism and the new poor*, Buckingham, PA: Open University Press.

Beck, U. (1992) *Risk society: Towards a new modernity*, London: Sage Publications.

Castels, R. (1990) *Extreme cases of marginalization: From vulnerability to deaffiliation*, Paper presented to a conference 'Poverty, marginalization and social exclusion in the Europe of the 1990s', Alghero, Sardinia, 23-25 April.

Costello, A. (1993) *Workfare in Britain? Some perspectives on UK labour market policy*, London: Unemployment Unit.

Dahl, E. and Pedersen, L. (eds) (2001: forthcoming) *Does workfare work? Systematic review of workfare evaluations in six European countries*, Oslo: Fafo Institute for Applied Social Sciences.

Dean, H. and Taylor-Gooby, P. (1992) *Dependency culture. The explosion of a myth*, New York, NY: Harvester Wheatsheaf.

de Tocqueville, A. (1997 [1833]) *Memoir on pauperism*, Chicago, IL: Ivan R. Dee.

Ditch, J. and Oldfield, N. (1999) 'Social Assistance: recent trends and themes', *Journal of European Social Policy*, vol 1, pp 65-76.

Esping-Andersen, G. (1990) *The three worlds of welfare capitalism*, Cambridge: Polity Press.

Eardley, T., Bradshaw, J., Ditch, J., Gough, I. and Whiteford, P. (1996) *Social Assistance schemes in OECD countries: Volume 1. Synthesis report*, DSS Research Report No 46, London: HMSO.

European Commission (1998) *From guidelines to action: The national action plans for employment*, Brussels: DG V.

European Counsel (1997) *The 1998 employment guidelines*, Council Resolution of 15 December, Brussels: DG V.

Evans, P. (1995) 'Linking welfare to jobs: workfare, Canadian style', in A. Sayeed (ed) *Workfare: Does it work? Is it fair?*, Montreal, Canada: Institute for Research on Public Policy.

Fraser, N. and Gordon, L. (1994) 'A genealogy of dependency: tracing a keyword for the US welfare state', *Signs: A Journal of Women in Culture and Society*, vol 19, no 2, p 310.

Giddens, A. (1998) *The third way: The renewal of social democracy*, Cambridge: Polity Press.

Gilbert, N. and Gilbert, B. (1989) *The enabling state: Modern welfare capitalism in America*, New York, NY: Oxford University Press.

Gough, I., Bradshaw, J., Ditch, J., Eardley, T. and Whiteford, P. (1997) 'Social Assistance in OECD countries', *Journal of European Social Policy*, vol 7, no 1, pp 17-43.

Grimes, A. (1997) 'Would workfare work? An alternative approach for the UK', in A. Deacon (ed) *From welfare to work. Lessons from America*, London: Institute of Economic Affairs.

Grover, C. and Stewart, J. (1999) 'Market workfare: social security, social regulation and competetiveness in the 1990s', *Journal of Social Policy*, vol 28, no 1, pp 73-96.

Handler, J. and Hasenfeld, Y. (1997) *We the poor people: Work poverty and welfare*, New Haven, CT: Yale University Press.

Heikkila, M. (ed) (1999) *Linking welfare and work*, Dublin: European Foundation for the Improvement of Living and Working Conditions.

Hvinden, B. (1999) 'Activation: a Nordic perspective', in M. Heikkila (ed) *Linking welfare and work*, Dublin: European Foundation for the Improvement of Living and Working Conditions.

Jessop, B. (1993) 'Towards a Schumpeterian workfare state? Preliminary remarks on post-Fordist political economy', *Studies in Political Economy*, vol 40, pp 7-39.

Jordan, B. (1996) *A theory of poverty and social exclusion*, Cambridge: Polity Press.

Kjønstad, A. and Syse, A. (1997) *Velferdsrett*, Oslo: Gyldendal.

Larsson, A. (1998) 'The welfare society: added value or excessive burden?', Speech to PES Conference, 'Reform of the Welfare State and Employment', Brussels, July.

Le Grand, J. (1997) 'Knights, knaves or pawns: human behaviour and social policy', *Journal of Social Policy*, vol 26.

Leisering, L. and Walker, R. (1998) *The dynamics of modern society: Poverty, policy and welfare*, Bristol: The Policy Press.

Levitas, R. (1998) *The inclusive society?*, Basingstoke: Macmillan.

Lødemel, I. (1989) 'The quest for institutional welfare and the problem of the residuum. Income maintenance and social care policies in Norway and Britain 1946-1966', Doctoral thesis, London: London School of Economics and Political Science.

Lødemel, I. (1997a) *Pisken i arbeidslinja*, Fafo report no 226, Oslo: Fafo.

Lødemel, I. (1997b) *The welfare paradox. Income maintenance and personal social services in Norway and Britain, 1946-1966*, Oslo: Scandinavian University Press.

Lødemel, I. and Flaa, J. (1993) *Sosial puls*, Fafo report no 156, Oslo: Fafo.

Lødemel, I. and Schulte, B. (1992) 'Social assistance – a part of Social Security or the Poor Law in new disguise?', *Yearbook*, Leuven: European Institute of Social Security.

Lødemel, I. and Stafford, B. (eds) (2001: forthcoming) *The implementation of workfare in six European countries*, Oslo: Fafo Institute for Applied Social Science.

Luxembourg Income Study http://www.lis.ceps.lu/, 07.09.2000.

Malthus, T. (1998 [1798]) *An essay on the principle of population*, Amherst: Prometheus Books.

Marshall, T.H. (1985) *T.H. Marshall's social policy*, London: Hutchinson and Co.

Mead, L. (1986) *Beyond entitlement: The social obligations of citizenship*, New York, NY: The Free Press.

Mead, L. (1997a) *From welfare to work: Lessons from America*, London: Institute of Economic Affairs.

Mead, L. (ed) (1997b) *The new paternalism: Supervisory approaches to welfare*, Washington, DC: The Brookings Institute.

Morel, S. (1998) 'American workfare versus French insertion policies: an application of Common's theoretical framework', Paper presented at Annual Research Conference of the Association for Public Policy and Management, 29-31 October, New York.

Murray, C. (1994) *Losing ground: American social policy 1950-1980*, New York, NY: Basic Books.

Nathan, R.P. (1993) *Turning promises into performance. The management challenge of implementing workfare*, New York, NY: Columbia University Press.

OECD (1994) *New orientations for social policy*, Social Policy Studies no 12, Paris: OECD.

OECD (1996a) *Employment outlook*, Paris: OECD.

OECD (1996b) *Caring for frail and elderly people: Policies in evolution*, Social Policy Studies no 19, Paris: OECD.

OECD (1999) *Labour market and social policy*, Occasional papers No 39, Paris: OECD.

OECD (2000) *Employment outlook*, Paris: OECD.

Paugam, S., Zoyem, J.-P. and Charbonnel, J-M. (1993) *Précarité et risque d'exclusion en France*, Paris: La documentation Francaise, coll. Documents du CERC, no 109.

Payne, J. (1998) *Overcoming welfare: Expecting more from the poor and from ourselves*, New York, NY: Basic Books.

Peck, J. (1998) 'Workfare, a geopolitical etymology', *Environment and planning D: Society and Space*, vol 16, pp 133-60.

Room, G. (1990) *New poverty in the European community*, Basingstoke: Macmillan.

Room, G. (ed) (1995) *Beyond the threshold: Measurement and analysis of social exclusion*, Bristol: The Policy Press.

Schmidtz, D. and Goodin, R. (1998) *Social welfare and individual responsibility*, Cambridge: Cambridge University Press.

Shragge, E. (ed) (1997) *Workfare: Ideology for a new underclass*, Toronto, Canada: Garamond Press.

Silver, H. (1994) 'Social exclusion and social solidarity: three paradigms', *International Labour Review*, vol 133, nos 5-6, pp 531-78.

Spicker, P. (1997) 'Exclusion', *Journal of Common Market Studies*, vol 35, no 1, pp 133-43.

Steiner, H. (1994) *Essays on right*, Oxford: Blackwell.

Standing, G. (1990) 'The road to workfare – alternative to welfare or threat to occupation', *International Labour Review*, vol 129, no 6, pp 677-91.

Titmuss, R. (1974) 'Social policy', in B. Abel-Smith and K. Titmuss (eds) London: George Allen & Unwin.

Torfing, J. (1999) 'Workfare with welfare: recent reforms in the Danish welfare state', *Journal of European Social Policy*, vol 1, pp 5-28.

US Census Bureau (2000) http://www.census.gov/cgi-bin/, 07.09.2000.

Walker, R. (1991) *Thinking about workfare: Evidence from the US*, London: HMSO.

Walker, R. (1999) 'The Americanisation of British welfare: a case study of policy transfer', *Focus*, Journal of the Institute for Research on Poverty, University of Madison-Wisconsin, vol 19, no 3, pp 32-40.

Wilensky, H. and Lebaux, C. (1964) *Industrial society and social welfare*, New York, NY: Free Press.

Wilensky, H. (1992) 'Active labour-market policy: its contents, effectiveness, and odd relation to evaluation research', in C. Crouch and A. Heath (eds) *Social research and social reform*, Oxford: Clarendon Press.

Wiseman, M. (1991) *What did the American work-welfare demonstrations do? Why should Germans care?*, Bremen: Zentrum für Sozialpolitik, University of Bremen.

TWO

Between subsidiarity and social assistance – the French republican route to activation

Bernard Enjolras, Jean Louis Laville, Laurent Fraisse
and Heather Trickey

Introduction

'Workfare' is not a positive term in the French policy debate. It is usually reserved to describe the kinds of strategies that policy makers want to avoid, since workfare policies are considered to focus on social exclusion resulting from individual behaviour. French activation policies are strongly rooted in a republican ideology and form part of a broader strategy to fight 'exclusion' and foster 'insertion'. Nonetheless, recent developments in job creation and activation policies have tended towards compulsory work, through the development of work insertion requirements for over 25-year-olds receiving means-tested cash assistance, and via a refusal to provide financial assistance to under 26-year-olds outside of a work or training context.

Insertion policies (policies with an official goal to re-integrate 'excluded people' either into the labour market or into social life) began to be introduced in France at the beginning of the 1980s. While France shares a European orientation towards activating social assistance recipients, it is exceptional in several key respects. In general, French policy makers place responsibility on society to enable individuals to be integrated, rather than on individuals to develop their own strategies. Unemployment has grown to a level that policy makers accept will not be absorbed through economic growth alone. Policy makers view this unemployment as a structural problem – with a shortage of low-skilled jobs seen to be

the primary cause of social exclusion among young and unskilled people
– rather than resulting from poor motivation on the part of the individual.
Nonetheless, dependency on 'passive' benefits is increasingly viewed as
highly undesirable, particularly for young people.

The administrative context for French activation is extremely complex.
Insertion policies involve state agencies and autonomous elected bodies
at the national, regional, departmental and local levels. Policy developments
have been incremental, and have built up within a complex administrative
system. As a result, French work-for-welfare requirements do not
constitute a clear set of programmes. For older uninsured people workfare
is one possible trajectory attached to the nationalised social assistance
programme. *Revenu Minimum d'Insertion* (RMI). For younger people
workfare does not replace social assistance but rather exists *instead of*
RMI since younger people are not eligible for RMI. There can be no
sanctioning and hence no compulsion to work. However, for many
young people State work programmes are the only means of guaranteeing
an income.

French welfare provision is traditionally corporatist and insurance-
based, with a strong reliance on both the contributory principle, and on
the principle of subsidiarity. Public social assistance is considered subsidiary
as it is provided when individuals, and their families, have failed to provide
for basic needs. Economic changes in the 1970s and 1980s exposed gaps
arising from the exclusion of women, young people, and long-term
unemployed people from contributory unemployment insurance
programmes. To some extent this situation has been ameliorated by the
introduction of RMI, which has a minimum income component. RMI
assistance is conditional on compliance with an 'insertion contract' –
which may include work. However, this scheme does not extend to
young people under the age of 25, whose main recourse to financial
assistance (outside of the family or education system) is still through a
confusing array of training and labour market insertion schemes. Work-
based insertion policies directed towards uninsured people who are very
distant from the primary labour market have tended to emphasise job
creation over subsidised employment.

While recent programmes have focused on insertion through work,
the process of insertion is clearly intended to integrate social *and* labour
market approaches. The boundaries between social policy and labour
market policy have been partially eroded through the development of
insertion policies which often require a labour input from their
beneficiaries, but which also, and equally explicitly, seek to tackle other

dimensions of social exclusion – including housing, health and education. The approach is centred on the individual, with a strong 'case-work' element.

Concern to overcome structural unemployment and consequent social exclusion has led to a number of policy initiatives to encourage moves into work among younger people on the one hand, and early retirement for people aged 55 plus on the other. Measures enacted by successive governments from the Right and Left during the 1980s and 1990s have included the implementation of public jobs programmes aimed at creating 'social utility activities', designed to create public jobs, to integrate excluded people, and, more recently, to activate passive benefits.

The focus of this chapter is programmes that are designed to reintegrate socially excluded *young* people into the labour market. Three types of labour market insertion programmes may be distinguished: training programmes, subsidised job programmes within the private sector and job creation programmes within the public and voluntary sectors. The focus here is on job creation programmes, since these are more easily accessed by socially excluded young people.

Alongside a concern to 'do something' about high unemployment levels, runs a second concern to meet society's needs. French policy makers believe that the market leaves important and undesirable 'public goods' gaps – for example, as a result of population migration from rural job-poor areas to urban job-rich areas. Created public jobs are seen as a key means of tackling this problem of unmet needs. Labour market and social policies have often been designed to satisfy unmet needs and to offer temporary job opportunities to excluded people simultaneously. However, these objectives have often been found to be incompatible, with the result that more recent insertion policies take a more incidental approach to meeting needs.

Labour insertion policies for young people have grown and developed through a series of stages since the early 1980s. As well as demonstrating conflict between the twin objectives of meeting needs and of providing insertion opportunities, evaluation of early programmes showed that they failed to improve employability, and had only limited success in perpetuating new activities. Despite this, the development of insertion through work accelerated following the passing of RMI law: because of the growing number of excluded people; because of the need to offer insertion opportunities to RMI recipients; and through attempts to build on the accumulated experience from early programmes.

In 1998 Jospin's Socialist government implemented a programme called

Emploi Jeunes, which attempted to overcome some of the difficulties encountered by previous programmes. Key features of this programme are that it pays a minimum wage, has a duration of at least five years, and is primarily concerned with insertion rather than unmet needs. This has been followed by the introduction of a broader based *Trajet d'accés à l'emploi* (TRACE) programme, which concentrates on integrating the most disadvantaged young people.

Key difficulties faced by current French insertion programmes include low impact on 'real' job creation and little impact on primary labour market selectivity. In addition, there is a danger that insertion jobs operating outside of the market economy can themselves become exclusion trajectories.

Insertion policies and republican ideology

The discourse within which the term 'exclusion' is embedded is strongly linked to the French republican solidarity tradition, which builds on the principles of the 1789 French Revolution, and particularly on the Declaration of Human Rights leading to a universalist conception of citizenship based on the equity of rights. The republican solidarity tradition recognises the state as responsible for maintaining 'social cohesion'. According to the solidarity principle the State is understood to be responsible for ensuring the 'inclusion' of all its members. Adherence to the principle of inclusion for all French citizens has traditionally been a common factor between major republican parties. Through solidarity the tension between individual and State is supposedly overcome.

The term 'exclusion' coined by Renè Lenoir (1974) was originally used to describe the process by which people who do not come under the umbrella of social insurance, particularly poor, physically disabled and mentally ill persons, were separated out from the rest of society. Exclusion in this context is understood to be a deficiency of solidarity, with society viewed as a single body within which the constituent parts (citizens) depend upon each other. As unemployment grew, traditional social bonds were seen to break down and the term exclusion came to be applied to the process by which broader and broader categories of socially disadvantaged people found themselves both outside of the insurance bracket and unable to rely on family support (Paugam, 1993). This understanding of the reciprocal roles of individual citizens and the State has been mobilised through the development of insertion policies. These ideological considerations are crucial to understanding the development of social policies since the mid-1980s.

While a number of programmes have been in existence for some decades, the most dramatic step in the development of insertion policy was the introduction of *Revenu Minimum d'Insertion*, a minimum income insertion scheme, in 1988. The new 'right to insertion' (*'le droit à l'insertion'*), which RMI law embodies, can itself be seen as an attempt to reconcile the French tradition of solidarity with the rise of individualism (de Foucauld, 1992). In the same way that society as a whole is held responsible for tears in the social fabric which result in social exclusion, so it is the duty of society as a whole and the State in particular to promote reintegration. The first article of the RMI law, which asserts both collective responsibility towards those who are in need and the right to insertion, is a direct translation of the solidarity principle into the law:

> All persons who, due to their age, their physical or mental state, their economic and employment situation, are not able to work, have a right to a decent means of existence from society. The social and professional integration of people encountering difficulties constitutes a national imperative. (Loi du 1 Decembre 1988, art 1)

Nonetheless, the solidarity principle has always itself been a contested concept, with different interpretations of the relationship between the individual and the State and different consequences for the type of insertion policies that have been developed.

On the one hand, Leroux and others understood solidarity to result from a democratic social bond (Le Bras and Chopard, 1992) between the individual and the State. In order to be (to feel) bonded to one another, individuals need some meeting place where they can act together, and operate through intermediaries and organisations (workers associations and voluntary associations) which mediate between the individual and the State. Solidarity is a matter of participation and of belonging and takes place within the institutions of civil society. Insertion policies that promote job creation within the third sector (voluntary and community work) can be interpreted as being based on this understanding of the solidarity concept.

On the other hand, for 'Solidarists' (including Bourgeois and Duguit) the principle of solidarity constitutes both the foundation for State intervention in the social sphere, and a means of describing its *limits*. As a result, 'subjective rights' of individuals can be identified, which should not be overridden or interfered with by the State (Donzelot, 1984). Bourgeois thought that it is necessary to point not only to the *rights*, but also to the *duties*, of each member of society (Bourgeois, 1902). Because each individual benefits from the experience of a civilised society, so each individual is obligated to repay this debt. Hence, *debt* is inherent, and precedes the rights of individuals. This legitimises State intervention to avert threats to the social fabric – for example through imposing taxes to redistribute income. Insertion policies that define the rights and duties of both the individual and society (the State) can be interpreted as being based on this 'Solidaristic' understanding of the solidarity concept.

Institutional context for insertion policies

The institutional context for insertion policies is bewilderingly complex. There are four levels of administration in France: national, regional, departmental and communal. Each ministry has its own agency at the regional and departmental levels. Each region and department has a *Prefet* who represents the national government and coordinates State agencies. The State system co-exists with locally elected bodies including regional councils (regional level), general councils (departmental level) and municipal councils (communal level). These bodies have their own administrative agencies, and reserved fields of intervention, as well as areas of jurisdiction which overlap with the State. In 1982 some domains of intervention (particularly social policies) were transferred from the State departmental administration to elected departmental councils. This took place as part of a process of decentralisation, which aimed to give more power and autonomy to local authorities.

Insertion policies are coordinated at the departmental level by the *Prefet* (the State's representative and head of State administration at the departmental level) and by the President of the General Council, who, together, share overall responsibility for implementation. Since decentralisation the General Council has had charge of social assistance, medical social assistance, and social services. At the street level, social workers employed by the General Council are responsible for receiving people with social difficulties and for assessing individual cases.

To complicate matters, the State is in charge of many work and non-work aspects of 'insertion', including employment and vocational training programmes, social housing, and public health policies. Several employment programmes implemented by the State are targeted toward RMI recipients. At the departmental level, a council for insertion (consultative body co-chaired by the *Préfet* and the President of the General Council) is in charge of planning insertion programmes.

Since the beginning of the 1980s attempts to bring greater coherence have been instigated through a network of reception, counselling and orientation agencies. These operate within infra-departmental employment policy zones (*zones emploi formation*). All actors operating within these zones are supposed to work together to produce coherent labour market and employment policy. Having identified themselves, clients are assessed by the counselling and orientation agencies. Subsequently, zone coordinators, in charge of funding, are supposed to access relevant available resources and to mediate between all the social and placement agencies. However, a selection problem emerges, as people with greater social difficulties do not tend to make use of the *Mission locale* or reception agencies.

Economic context for insertion policies

In France the rate of annual GDP of growth has reduced by one half since 1974 (INSEE, 1998). Unemployment has grown rapidly over this period, from one million in 1978 to over three million in 1993 (ILO definition). The effects have been selective, with greater rates of unemployment among young people (who have become more vulnerable to unemployment, and who are finding it harder to break into the labour market) and among low-skilled unemployed people (whose employability has declined) (Marchand, 1993).

The term 'exclusion unemployment' (*chômage d'exclusion*) was coined, during the period of unemployment expansion between 1988 and 1990, to refer to those people who were failing to break back into the labour market. Initially coined by academics (Wuhl, 1991), it has subsequently been picked up and used by policy makers. In spite of the creation of some 700,000 jobs between 1988 and 1990, unemployment scarcely fell (by about 60,000 in total) and long-term unemployment continued to grow. The inability of a segment of the population to benefit from economic recovery was considered to be a sign of structural exclusion from the labour market.

Long-term unemployment – 12 months or more – has increased, affecting 12% of unemployed people in 1982, 30% in 1990, and 37% in 1996 (INSEE, 1996). Unemployment among unqualified workers is generally understood to be structural, and due to a lack of unskilled jobs and a selective labour market. Unskilled workers account for a decreasing proportion of the active population. Transfer from industrial work to service jobs has been problematic (as service jobs need new types of relational and interpersonal skills). Meanwhile, competition in the labour market has led to 'creaming' by employers and a tendency towards over-qualification; and there is evidence that skilled workers take unskilled jobs because of the scarcity of work (Rose, 1998).

Unemployment benefits

The French welfare state has been categorised as 'corporatist', based on a statutory social insurance regime (Esping-Andersen, 1990). Despite the traditional emphasis on insurance, welfare has gradually been extended to cover people without insurance entitlement, to the extent that it is now quasi-universal. The contributory unemployment insurance system has itself been eroded, so that taxes now play a growing role in stabilising the insurance system, and in financing a secondary means-tested solidarity system for those whose insurance cover has run out.

The traditional system of unemployment benefit delivery is composed of two parts, based on loss of, rather than absence of, employment:

• an Unemployment Insurance scheme (*Allocation Unique Digressive* – AUD) managed by the social partners (trade unions and employers); and
• a 'Solidarity' regime (*Allocation de Solidarite Specifique* – ASS) managed by the State and funded through taxation.

Unemployment Insurance is a categorical benefit available to former private sector employees, but does not cover self-employed people or permanent civil servants. Self-employed people make their own social security and unemployment insurance arrangements; civil servants have no need of Unemployment Insurance since their jobs are 'for life'. In 1997 there were 19.5 million private sector employees for an active population of about 22.4 million people (87%) – with each private sector employee paying into the system.

In order to claim Unemployment Insurance a claimant must have worked at least 122 days in the previous eight months. Benefits are reduced over time, from 75% of previous earnings. The length of payment period depends on the duration of the affiliation to the insurance system and lasts somewhere between four and 60 months. Recipients must actively seek work, must enrol at the State employment exchange office, and must accept jobs where the wage is above 30% of the wage they earned in their most recent job (before becoming unemployed). In order to be designated as unemployed one has to be (1) registered at the unemployment agency, (2) not in work, education or an insertion programme and (3) immediately available for work.

When the right to the Unemployment Insurance is exhausted, government social welfare assistance steps in and pays a 'Solidarity Benefit'. The scheme has existed since 1984. This is a means-tested benefit, which is worth about half the minimum wage, paid to long-term unemployed people who have lost their right to AUD. Remuneration is not related to previous earnings, although eligibility requirements are that the claimant must have worked at least five years in the previous ten. The number of unemployed people receiving the solidarity-based ASS trebled between 1985 and 1994, from 157,000 to 449,000 (Amira, 1996).

Between 1985 and 1994 the number of Unemployment Insurance (AUD) recipients increased by 46% (from 1,287,000 people in 1985 to 1,875,000 people in 1994 (Amira, 1996). In 1995, 1.8 million unemployed people received AUD; 467,000 received ASS, and a further 700,000 were officially classed as unemployed but not receiving either form of unemployment assistance. Concern about the growth in the number of people failing to meet the eligibility criteria for ASS was one of the key factors behind the introduction of RMI.

Revenu Minimum d'Insertion (RMI)

Until 1988 there was no central government transfer system for people who fell outside of the insurance pool. Social assistance was provided on a discretionary basis with great disparities over the country and was administered and funded at departmental level through regionally elected bodies. The system was governed according to the principle of subsidiarity – as a last resort measure for people who are unable to take care of themselves, and whose family support failed them. Eligibility was based solely on an inability to work (Beck, 1994).

With unemployment growth during the 1980s the lack of a universal safety net became more apparent. Charitable organisations were experiencing a rapid increase in the number of people asking for emergency help. The introduction of RMI by Rocard's Socialist government transformed the institutional landscape, making the right to cash assistance quasi-universal by encompassing all involuntarily unemployed people over the age of 25.

Revenu Minimum d'Insertion is described in law as a 'double right': a right to a minimum income and a right to insertion. The architecture of RMI law reflects the compromise between Right-wing parties who wanted to make the minimum income conditional on participation in collective activity and Left-wing parties who wanted to make the minimum income unconditional.

Because insertion plans relate to labour market programmes and housing programmes that are both funded and administered nationally, a significant degree of coordination between different levels of government is assumed. The cash benefit is funded at the national level by the State, whereas the insertion part of the RMI is largely funded at the regional level by the departments. Local authorities themselves have to match 20% of the money spent by the State on minimum income allowance on insertion programmes funded from their own local taxation budget.

In 1998, 1,089,648 people were RMI recipients (*Ministère de l'Emploi et de la Solidarité*, 1999). Overall expenditure on RMI had risen from six billion francs in 1989 to 24.2 billion francs in 1997 (Loi de Finance, 1998). In 1997, departmental expenditure on insertion programmes had grown to 4.4 billion francs; from 3.4 billion francs in 1995, and from 2.6 billion francs in 1989 (*Ministère de l'Emploi et de la Solidarité*, 1999).

Right to a minimum income

RMI is worth around half the minimum wage. The amount was agreed on the basis of being high enough to guarantee a minimum income but not so high as to incur a work disincentive. The RMI includes a supplement of 50% for a couple and of 30% per child.

Right to insertion

Individual insertion objectives, and strategies for achieving these, are laid down in a *contract* held between the individual and (departmental level) 'commissions for insertion'. The commissions are made up of representatives of agencies likely to be in a position to help recipients – including representatives of municipalities, of the different state agencies, of voluntary organisations, and of social workers. The insertion contract is meant to prevent individuals from becoming trapped in social assistance schemes. RMI recipients are supposed to be able to be reintegrated through programmes of insertion. This includes a specification of the help to be provided by public institutions, an agenda of action to be taken both by the recipient and by the different institutions involved, and criteria for assessing results.

In theory, insertion is available 'by right'. It may cover social and family life, health, housing, vocational training, and, of course, employment. However, work-based insertion placements are in limited supply, with the result that keen and employable clients are more likely to be inserted in this way than others. In 1994, only seven in every ten RMI recipients (69%) had signed an insertion contract (*Ministère de l'Emploi et de la Soliodarité*, 1999). A third had a contract oriented toward 'social autonomy' (in other words health action, help with daily organisation/administrative problems). A further third were involved in labour market insertion programmes within the public and voluntary sectors and a final third were looking for work (Raymond, 1997).

Conditionality within RMI

RMI law is extremely ambiguous about the degree of obligation that goes along with the right to insertion, highlighting a point of conflict between different interpretations of the republican ideal (Donzelot and Jaillet, 1997). For the Rightist parties (including the RPR (*Rassemblement pour la République*) and UDF (*Union pour la Démocratie Francaise*)), insertion is seen as a means of avoiding 'passive' assistance, and the assistance is, therefore, conditional. For parties on the Left (including the Labour Party and Communist Party), the spirit of the law obliges society to provide unconditional insertion opportunities for excluded people. The latter is the view of Belorgey, considered by many to be the 'father of the RMI', a former Socialist Party MP who was president of the parliamentary social commission at the time of implementation (Belorgey, 1996). This latter interpretation is also official government policy under the Jospin administration. Attempts to clarify the issue have been made through a ministerial circular which defined the insertion contract as:

> ... the instrument allowing for each RMI recipient to assert the right to insertion recognised by the law. (Circulaire du 9 Mars, 1989, Journal Officiel du 11 Mars, 1989)

While this circular had the effect of subduing debate at the national level (at least for a period), differences in interpretation remain at the point of local implementation. Social workers, when they deal with individuals, and commissions for insertion, when they outline local insertion strategies, may *and do* interpret the contract as the basis for making financial assistance conditional on compliance. While there is no available evaluation evidence demonstrating variation in local practice, casual observations show different levels of involvement by departments in the insertion part of the RMI (Raymond, 1997). It is likely that departments that have fewer signed insertion contracts have a greater tendency to consider RMI to be a right to minimum income, whereas departments with a higher proportion of recipients with signed contracts interpret the right to the minimum income as a counterpart of insertion.

More recently, national political divisions have reappeared, but this time *within* the parties on the Left. These divisions are utterly different from the discussions about reinforcing individual responsibility that have taken place in other northern European countries over the last decade, particularly the Netherlands, Denmark and the UK (see Chapters Four, Six and Seven). The debates within the French parties of the Left concern the question of whether to keep RMI in its present form or to transform it into an unconditional income allowance based on citizenship – so that all citizens receive a non-means-tested basic income allowance. Those who advocate this proposal consider that a first step in this direction would be to suppress the RMI insertion requirement (van Parijs, 1992; MAUSS, 1996).

Sanctions occur either because of fraud (false declaration of income) or because of non-compliance. The most common cause of non-compliance is job refusal – both of 'regular' and insertion jobs. It is estimated that 30,000 people experience sanctioning every year, 0.03% of all RMI recipients (*Ministère de l'Emploi et de la Solidarité*, 1999).

Young people and RMI

Youth unemployment trebled between 1975 and 1995, to affect one in ten of all young people aged 15-29 (*Commissariat Général au Plan* (CGP), 1997) and transitions to adulthood among French young people have altered dramatically as a result of worsening labour market prospects. Traditionally youth unemployment, along with other forms of unemployment, has been considered to be primarily a labour market problem; progressively, as the problem has deepened, it has come to be seen as a broader social (and societal) problem, associated with criminality and drug addiction. Nonetheless, this is still broadly understood as a problem shared by society as a whole, rather than one which individuals have sole responsibility to overcome.

Growth in unemployment has affected young people of all levels of educational attainment. However, young people with qualifications do much better than those without (Meron and Minni, 1996). Between 1975 and 1995, unemployment rates have soared (from 8% to 35% for young people who did not complete secondary school, from 5% to 19% for secondary school graduates, and from 4% to 12% for university graduates). Young men have tended to do better than young women. In 1996 the unemployment rate for men between 15 and 24 was just over a fifth (22%) whereas it was nearly a third (31%) for women between 15 and 24 (INSEE, 1996).

For the young people who do find work, this is more likely to be temporary and insecure than the work found by older adults. A growing proportion of available vacancies are temporary or insertion jobs and these are easier than permanent jobs for newcomers to access. The proportion of employed under 30-year-olds who held precarious and publicly funded jobs in insertion labour market programmes and in subsidised work rose from 8% to 18% between 1980 and 1990.

A further effect of poor employment prospects has been that the average period of transition from school to work has lengthened. The amount of time which young people spend in education has increased dramatically, with the effect of delaying entry into the labour market. Three in every ten of 15-29 year olds were in full-time education in 1975, compared to just under half (45%) in 1995. Youth participation in the labour market has dropped, from three-fifths of 20-year-olds in 1975 to one fifth in 1995 (Meron and Minni, 1996).

The policy decision not to extend the RMI scheme to young people was and is ideologically led, reflecting a fear of generating a 'culture of dependency' among people who have not experienced working life. Associations representing unemployed people have called for the extension of the minimum income to people aged under 26 years. These organisations estimate that around 600,000 young people live in poverty without any public assistance – although there are no official statistics available to test this estimate (UNIOPSS, 1996). However, the dominant policy response, as articulated by Jospin, is that the direction away from passive assistance should be particularly adhered to for young people. Instead, absence of entitlement, plus the presence of work programmes, constitutes a kind of workfare policy for young people in need of financial help.

Because RMI is so marginal to young people, it does not itself address the problem of youth unemployment. However, the architecture of RMI, and of RMI insertion programmes, shapes the insertion strategies that currently exist for young people on a low income. The more recent preferred policy response to high youth unemployment has been to expand insertion programmes originally designed for RMI recipients to non-RMI recipients. The result is that insertion programmes target groups have become steadily younger as young people in need of financial assistance make use of them.

Expenditure context for insertion policies

Social security expenditure (Sickness Insurance, pensions, Unemployment Insurance, maternity benefits, invalidity benefits; and social assistance benefits, including RMI and disability pensions) has risen steeply as unemployment has grown, rising from 14% of GDP in 1975 to 28% in 1984 and to 30% in 1995. Total expenditure on employment policies (unemployment-related benefits such as AUD and ASS), on early retirement incentives, on vocational training (in and out of employment), and on activation expenditures (insertion programmes in the private, public and voluntary sectors) has grown rapidly. Expenditure has shifted from Unemployment Insurance and unemployment assistance towards active labour market and insertion policies. Passive expenditure (on Unemployment Insurance and on incentives to leave the labour market) has decreased. In recent years, Unemployment Insurance has accounted for only 40% of the total expenditure on unemployment. Meanwhile, active expenditure (via measures to provide job or training opportunities to unemployed people) has increased (Table 2.1).

Attempts to curb expenditure growth, through job creation and measures to facilitate greater labour market participation have been supported through key policy changes to reduce benefit eligibility. The value of unemployment assistance has reduced as the eligibility criteria for the most expensive benefits have been tightened. Eligibility for Unemployment Insurance has been cut so that, by the end of 1994, the number of AUD recipients was decreasing, despite rises in unemployment (Amira, 1996). The purchasing power of the least expensive, means-tested, benefits has been reduced; between 1991 and 1997 the purchasing power of ASS fell by 0.9%, and RMI by 0.1%. At the same time the purchasing power of the minimum wage increased by 0.2% per year (CSERC, 1997).

Table 2.1: Public expenditure on policies to assist unemployed people

	1985	1986	1987	1988	1989	1990	1991	1992	1993	1994	1995
Total expenditure (billion francs)	170	183	192	201	202	219	242	265	295	294	291
Unemployment Insurance (proportion of total)	33	35	37	38	39	40	42	43	42	40	39
Early retirement incentives (proportion of total)	34	30	26	22	20	17	13	11	10	10	10
Vocational training for unemployed people (proportion of total)	9	11	11	13	13	14	14	14	15	14	13
Vocational training for employed people (proportion of total)	13	13	14	15	17	17	17	16	15	16	16
Other activation expenditures (proportion of total)	11	12	12	11	11	13	14	15	18	20	23
Total expenditure as a proportion of GDP	3.62	3.62	3.6	3.51	3.28	3.37	3.57	3.79	4.16	3.98	3.8

Source: Direction de l'Animation de la Recherche, des Etudes et des Statistiques (DARES) (1997)

Labour market participation policies and 'unmet needs'

The aim of French labour market policy is to make economic growth 'richer in jobs' (Bruhnes, 1993). French economists tend to consider that French economic growth has been 'poorer in jobs' than growth in other OECD countries. Between 1979 and 1989 the number of jobs in France increased by 0.5%, compared to 2.8% in Germany, 3.5% in Italy, 5.4% in the UK and 18% in the US over the same period (Brunhes, 1993). During the same period the yearly-rate French GDP growth was about 2.1%, about the level of the European Community average. The main reason given for the low level of job creation in France is that the level of productivity in services activity has traditionally been higher in France than in other industrialised countries.

In order to make economic growth 'richer in jobs', three avenues were felt to be available to policy makers:

1 Through provision of incentives for labour intensive technology (for example, through taxing capital). This avenue has been broadly rejected by policy makers because of the associated risks of slowing down technological progress and productivity.
2 Through policies to influence the relationship between the number of people engaged in the production process and the level of production, through reduced hours or part-time jobs. The 1998 working hours policy (which reduced the standard working week from 39 to 35 hours) is one illustration of policies developed along this avenue. Early retirement policies to decrease the participation of older people, and measures to encourage young people to stay on longer at school also fall into this category.
3 Through creating jobs in activities (services) not directly linked to the market economy – with the intention that productivity gains realised in the market economy should be used to satisfy unmet needs in public goods activities. Job creation insertion programmes for unemployed people illustrate this strategy. Job creation policies and insertion policies are part of a broader labour market policy objective outlined in a key report to the government at the beginning of the 1990s (Bruhnes, 1993). There is however much debate about how jobs should be funded. The main idea developed within the report was that the money used to pay benefits to unemployed people (Unemployment Insurance) and to excluded (RMI) people should be activated to finance job creation programmes. Such programmes would give RMI recipients temporary

work at a wage of about the same level as RMI. However, this strategy cannot assist people who are not eligible for cash benefits.

Alongside the concern about unemployment, key reports to the government in the early 1990s began to raise concerns about *unmet needs* in French society (Greffe, 1990; Brunhes, 1993). Two types of unmet need were identified: first, unmet needs generated as a result of wider socioeconomic changes, such as the need for home care for older people (as a result of an ageing population) or childcare (as a result of women's greater participation in the labour market): second, unmet needs that occur due to the existence of economic externalities (for example, in the areas of collective transport, environment, housing, leisure, tourism and education).

Programmes to address unmet needs are often characterised as a cheap means of expanding the service sector within the welfare state. Insertion programmes have been used to provide labour in hospitals, in residential homes for elderly people, and in education. Insertion activity is also seen as a means by which state activity has been expanded beyond the formal borders of the welfare state – into environmental protection, housing, and security services – for instance, through funding minor reparation tasks, servicing of collective housing and maintaining gardens.

Policy makers have been attracted to two sets of ideas that seek to unify the aims of creating jobs and satisfying unmet needs:

• The first attempts to offer insertion opportunities to excluded people through creating new jobs to satisfy unmet needs;
• The second aims to develop new services and jobs in the service sector – and hence satisfy unmet needs without reference to insertion.

The first approach, which tries to unify an insertion objective with the objective of countering a needs gap, has been criticised on three counts (Enjolras, 1996; Laville, 1994). First, because it tends to generate a separate sector, reserved only for those who cannot work in the 'normal' labour market, and hence it is seen as stigmatising. This has negative consequences both for the individuals and for the value attached to the work being undertaken, which comes to be seen as second rate welfare work. Second, because the development of such a sector presupposes entrepreneurial activity, which is difficult to generate outside of State-led public policy development. Finally, because such a sector runs into sustainability problems, as service activities often need long-term public funding.

Politicians seem unable to choose between these two strategies for meeting unmet needs, and there is much ambiguity regarding specific policy objectives. Although rational analysis suggests the latter strategy, budgetary constraints and pressure from local politicians, keen to give 'something' to their electorate, favour insertion programmes which are less costly and offer opportunities to a larger set of excluded people.

In fact what has often happened has been that policies originally intended to follow the former approach (mixing insertion and job creation) have evolved towards the latter (job creation schemes without any reference to insertion). For example, *Emplois Familiaux* (family jobs) initiated in 1987 created home care jobs to support older people and young families and is an example of a programme to meet unmet needs associated with socioeconomic changes. It began as an insertion programme, but was reformed in 1991 to focus on job creation, since a conflict had developed between offering services of good quality, and developing insertion opportunities. Skilled workers in the field of personal services were scarce within the target population of long-term unemployed people, and training was not compatible with these jobs.

Programmes that aim to satisfy unmet needs in public goods services have a lower requirement for skilled workers. For these programmes, while the direction of change is again away from the insertion objective, the transformation is less complete, and a sedimentation of programmes which mix insertion and job creation objectives continues to exist.

In 1995, there were about 750,000 insertion participants (including long-term unemployed people, young people aged under 25 and RMI recipients) in the non-market sector. Contracts had an average duration of between eight and nine months. Just under a quarter of participants were RMI recipients, nearly two thirds were women, and 7% were aged over 50. One third of participants were aged under 26. Employment programmes set out to meet a range of objectives. The balance between these objectives has altered as this policy area has developed. Since the first policies were first implemented in 1982, three categories of labour market insertion programme have emerged (Bouquillard and Catala, 1990). Programmes which seek to:

1. adapt skills;
2. offer job opportunities within the primary labour market; and
3. provide employment meeting unmet needs outside the primary labour market.

Programmes that fall into the final category, providing employment opportunities outside the primary labour market, can most readily be described as 'workfare'. Skills programmes and primary labour market job opportunity schemes are more selective (Rose, 1998). Young people, who would be most likely to receive social assistance if the benefit existed for them, are more likely than others to be found in the last category, in work programmes outside of the regular labour market.

Collective utility work – TUC

The first work-based insertion programme in recent years was implemented in 1984 under the Fabius-led Socialist government and was discontinued in 1989. Faced with a rise in youth unemployment – attributed to a lack of skills and professional experience – the government introduced Collective Utility Work (*Travaux d'Utilité Collective*). The programme offered public and voluntary sector jobs to young people to meet unmet needs. Initially available for 16- to 21-year-olds, this programme was extended in 1986 to people aged under 25.

Participants worked under a *stagiaire* contract. This meant that they were considered as being in a training post, without the rights associated with an ordinary job contract under labour market law. Remuneration varied in relation to the age of the client. The higher rate of remuneration was only about 40% of the minimum wage.

Training opportunities were available for 10% of young people involved in the programme and could be organised externally or 'on-the-job'. Training was accessed via an employer's request to the departmental labour market agency for additional training money. The decisions about who received training were fairly arbitrary and were mainly guided by budgetary considerations.

Early work insertion programmes, including *Travaux d'Utilité Collective* (TUC) and *Contrat Emploi Solidarité* (CES), which is discussed below, were intended to be transitory rather than permanent. Participants were supposed to improve their employability and to come back to the labour market, after one, or at most two, years.

Employment Solidarity Contract – CES

The non-contract (*stagiaire*) character of TUC employment was widely criticised on the grounds of producing 'sub-jobs' in the eyes of young people and of potential employers. Instead of developing employability,

TUC stigmatised participants. Ex-TUC recipients had no subsequent advantage in securing jobs, and may even have experienced increased difficulties (Eyssartier and Gautie, 1996). CES both reformed TUC and extended the programme to long-term unemployed people and RMI recipients, opening it up to older adults. Contracts were no longer a *stagiaire*. Nonetheless, costs were kept down by only providing each participant with 20 hours employment per week (remembering that participants aged under 25 had no other automatic right to income). The result was that, on average (for 20 hours per week), wages equalled about half the full-time minimum wage.

Like TUC, CES was intended to be transitional, lasting 1–2 years, after which participants were supposed to be able to find ordinary work (*Décrets n 90-105 du 30 Janvier,* 1990; *Journal Officiel du 31 Janvier,* 1990). Also, like TUC, CES operated solely in the public and the voluntary sectors, creating employment in community services (*service de proximité*). Typical areas included caretaking and upkeep of community areas. In 1997 around 425,000 people were involved in the CES programme over all, of whom 148,000 were under 25 (DARES, 1997).

Findings from evaluations of TUC and CES programmes

TUC and CES had a number of limitations that led policy makers to question their ability to meet their stated aims. Their two major objectives of meeting unmet needs in the public sector and of providing routes to the primary labour market appeared to be incompatible. In addition, the type of work that could be undertaken through CES was found to be insufficiently well defined, with the result that employers used placements to subsidise their existing labour costs, rather than to undertake new work.

• Programmes were intended to be transitory, and to help participants improve their employability and to find unsubsidised jobs. In fact the programmes had little impact on the selectivity of the labour market, and transitional jobs did not lead to jobs outside the sphere of public programmes and voluntary work. Instead of increasing the employability of participants, the programmes generated a self-contained 'sphere of insertion' – as individuals moved from programme to programme, without ever breaking out of the subsidised sector.

Panel research, which followed individuals participating in CES in spring 1994, found that young recipients who left CES jobs in 1989 were more likely to be unemployed than those who did not participate. This was regardless of their prior qualifications. In addition, three out of ten participants who found jobs after CES found these within other labour market insertion schemes (Aucouturier, 1993). There was strong evidence of a 'creaming' effect: participants who came into the programme with higher skills were, first, more likely to be selected into the programme, and subsequently more likely to break into the primary sector labour market (Rose, 1998).

- Programmes suffered from a basic internal contradiction in terms of their two main objectives. On the one hand they were intended to meet society's unmet needs. On the other they aimed to assist people in breaking into the primary labour market. However, jobs to meet unsatisfied needs were located in the non-market economy and were intended to be temporary and transitory; indeed, public support was considered to depend on their being so. The result was that the programmes sought to meet permanent needs with temporary support. As people began to be qualified for the job (after one or two years) they left and the work was taken over by an inexperienced newcomer. In addition, there was uncertainty among employers regarding the funding of new activities. Employers were expected to take risks, to invest, yet the activity could be cut without warning if new policy orientations were decided upon.

- Surveys of employers found that they tended to use the CES as a substitute for normal forms of employment. While the majority of employers who provided CES placements reported that the programme helped them improve the *volume* and the *quality* of their services, the objective of fulfilling society's unsatisfied needs tended to be sidelined (Bernard and Lefresne, 1992). Only about one third of employers felt that the CES had allowed them to introduce new types of community service.

Youth Employment Programme – Emploi Jeunes

In 1996 an influential report by the National Council for Anti-Poverty Policies proposed creating real-wage 'social utility activity' jobs as a solution to unemployment (Conseil National de Lutte contre la Pauvrete, 1996). The report calculated that the cost of financing an RMI recipient to be inserted through contract employment would be around 45,000 francs a year, while the cost of a part-time job (30 hours a week) paid at the minimum wage is about 62,000 francs a year. By activating passive expenditure and spending as little as 17,000 francs more it would be possible to create a 'real' job. The marginal cost to the public purse for the creation of 100,000 jobs was estimated to be around 1.7 billion francs.

Partly in response to this idea, *Emploi Jeunes* was introduced by Jospin's Socialist government in October 1997, for the 'development of activities for youth employment'. Over eight billion francs were allocated in the budget to fund 50,000 jobs in 1997 and 100,000 in 1998. In total, the programme aimed to create 350,000 jobs in the public and voluntary sector over three years.

Emploi Jeunes was supposed to build on the lessons learned from earlier schemes, and is intended to operate on a more durable basis. The emphasis is on job creation rather than meeting needs, although the latter is still considered an important component. The key difference is that job creation occurs through subsidising existing employers to create 'real' jobs, rather than creating activities through subsidising new projects. In contrast to the TUC programme, young people employed within *Emploi Jeunes* have the status of wage earners and are employed according to a private employment contract that follows general employment legislation and any specific collective agreements that exist – participants are paid a minimum wage. Through the *Emploi Jeunes*, participants are able to build up Unemployment Insurance entitlement. In contrast to the CES programme, contracts are usually full time. While they may be temporary or permanent, they have a minimum duration of five years.

In order to avoid degradation of employability associated with long spells of unemployment, *Emploi Jeunes* is not merely focused on the most disadvantaged young people. *Anyone* out of work, between the ages of 18 and 26 is eligible, regardless of qualifications or whether they are actually registered as unemployed. Similarly, people aged 26 to 30 who have not registered for Unemployment Insurance can participate.

Emploi Jeunes – employers

For five years the State provides employers with a subsidy of about 80% of the minimum wage for each job (92,000 francs; 14025.5 Euros per year in 1998). In addition, employers do not have to pay social or fiscal contributions on the subsidised portion of the wage. Clear rules exist to determine the sectors where *Emploi Jeunes* jobs may be undertaken, in an attempt to prevent publicly funded and lightly regulated jobs crowding out existing (and heavily regulated) jobs in for-profit firms and in the public sector. The State support cannot be combined with any other subsidy from the State. Possible employers fall within three categories:

- public sector employers, excluding the national state administration, local governmental bodies (municipalities, departments, regions) and public establishments (public schools, public housing, and so on);
- private sector employers who are in charge of a public service, such as the Social Security institutions; and
- non-profit organisations, associations, foundations, mutual organisations and trade unions (Archambault, 1997).

Emploi Jeunes – activities

To be eligible for the programme, employers must fulfil the following three conditions:

- they must generate jobs;
- they must provide 'social utility' in the fields of sport, culture, education, environment, or community services; and
- they must seek to satisfy emergent and unmet needs.

The law explicitly excludes two types of activity: home-based services and jobs linked to the traditional work of local authorities. This is in order to avoid 'double funding' of home-based services which are publicly funded through other programmes without an insertion objective, and in order to avoid a crowd out of standard employment (*Loi du 16 Octobre*, 1997; *Journal Officiel du 17 Octobre*, 1997).

Emploi Jeunes – implementation

The *Prefet* is supposed to play a key role in the implementation of the programme. The *Prefet* has responsibility for identifying needs, fostering the emergence of projects and promoting their development and long-term sustainability by mobilising local actors from the voluntary sector, the public sector and the social partners (trade unions and employers). Calls for projects are launched at the level of local employment areas.

Employers who wish to create jobs through the programme must apply to the *Prefet* and sign a convention with the state. Applicants are required to describe the project, the nature of the work, of the contract and of the target group. The *Prefet* takes account of the likelihood of substitution in assessing applications. As a general rule, activities funded by the programme should not compete with activities in the private sector, with existing social utility activities, or with activities implemented by the local bodies. Potential employers must indicate:

- the target group: in terms of skills, duration of unemployment and degree of social difficulty;
- how activities match identified needs;
- prospects for job development and long-term sustainability;
- coherence with the general aim of integration; and
- a strategy to professionalise activities undertaken.

Young people can receive an *Emploi Jeunes* placement through the labour exchange but may also be directly employed through approaching the employer as long as they fulfil the eligibility criteria. In terms of training, participants receive vocational training by the same mechanisms as ordinary employees – employers with more than 10 employees are obliged to spend 1.5% of salary costs per year on vocational training. Employers with fewer employees may access vocational training through regional funding.

The road to employment – TRACE

Like its predecessors, *Emploi Jeunes* favours more employable people. In March 1998, the socialist government presented a three-year plan aimed towards preventing social exclusion. This plan includes a programme specifically for young people with social difficulties called 'The Road to Employment' (*Trajet d'accés à l'emploi:* TRACE). The programme supplies individual case management for the least employable young people. This programme, designed for 60,000 youths, is not itself supposed to be an employment programme, but rather a means by which the different youth employment programmes, including *Emploi Jeunes* and CES, and subsidised jobs in the private sector are coordinated and integrated with other social programmes. In this sense it mirrors the role of the RMI contract provided for older people.

Each individual follows an 'insertion itinerary', which aims to give time and training to clients to help them become sufficiently qualified to enter the labour market. The itinerary allows several insertion programmes to be utilised in succession. The insertion plans can be up to 18 months in duration – after which the client may be enrolled within CES or *Emploi Jeunes*. During this period, participants receive a payment according to the status of the programme they are enrolled in.

Evaluation evidence for French labour market programmes

Currently, there is no available evidence as to whether the TRACE programme actually assists those young people who are most distant from the labour market to break into work, as opposed to maintaining a cycle within a system of labour market programmes. However, a number of key findings emerge from wider evaluations of labour market insertion programmes.

A summary of research into schemes targeted at young people, which considered early programmes alongside *Emploi Jeunes*, provides a number of lessons (Rose, 1998):

- None of these programmes have significant impact on employment creation. This is due to (i) opportunistic behaviour by employers who use the programmes to allow them to lower their employment costs but could have created jobs in the absence of these programmes, and (ii) to 'crowding out' effects.
- Efficiency in terms of integrating participants into the labour market is variable. Programmes that offer job opportunities within the primary labour market are more efficient than other programmes.
- Programmes have little impact on labour market selectivity and fail to modify employability, or to reduce differences between skilled and unskilled young people. In fact, they tend to *reproduce* the selectivity of the labour market. Young people with the highest levels of skill have access to programmes displaying the highest levels of integration into the labour market.
- Programmes rarely contribute to modifying firms' employment policies. On the contrary, they allow firms to be *more* selective by offering them the possibility of testing the newcomers at a lower cost.
- Programmes contribute to the increasingly insecure character of the labour market since they offer only fixed-term employment contracts and often simply part-time jobs.

One could reasonably ask why, in spite of the evidence above, labour market and activation policies have continued to develop over the last decade. The explanation is probably that some labour market policies, and particularly activation policies, act as a *substitute* for missing social policies. This is particularly true for younger people, since social assistance is not made available for young people and social activation policies prevent them from falling into poverty and facilitate the extended transition phase between family dependency and personal autonomy.

Summary

Ideological factors are not merely rhetorical. They determine the domain of the thinkable, and therefore of the possible. The republican ideology, with its focus on solidarity, and its conception of the nation as a unified entity, explains why unemployment, poverty and social exclusion are generally perceived in France not as an issue of individual responsibility (or fault) but as a collective matter. This cross-party republican ideology explains the consensus surrounding the political policy agenda. Even if political divisions reappear when it comes to designing specific policies, there are no major divisions around the goal (fighting social exclusion conceived as a collective duty).

But if ideological factors help to account for the French focus on social exclusion as a collective responsibility rather than as a result of welfare dependency, they are not sufficient to explain the actual design of the activation programmes. In order to do so one must take into account policy context of these programmes. The French welfare state has undergone a number of changes, specifically through the introduction of RMI and a set of targeted insertion policies for those who are outside of the safety net. At the same time a consensus has grown up around a loose concept of 'obligation'.

Through insertion, social protection has become, in theory at least, conditional on some reciprocal activity on the part of the individual. However, in practice the RMI exercises a very loose form of constraint. Several factors mean that it is difficult to describe French insertion policies as 'workfare' (Barbier, 1998). Labour market policies and social policies (insertion) are mixed in terms of objectives and mode of implementation. For young people the schemes are, in theory, 'voluntary', are not considered by any party as 'welfare benefits' and are not targeted to benefit recipients. For RMI recipients a contract is negotiated between the recipient and the administration, whereas an 'ideal' workfare scheme might suppose that work is imposed. Failure to respect conditions rarely leads to sanctioning, although this is a possibility. This contractual dimension is even more accentuated when it comes to programmes directed towards young people since they now take the form of a labour contract.

Implementing insertion throughout labour market policies entails an important inherent contradiction. On the one hand, the State creates public jobs in order to employ those excluded from employment. This brings certain difficulties, as large scale creation of public employment is thought to interfere with the workings of the market economy, and risks over-socialising. An alternative route is for the state to generate activities clearly outside the normal regulatory frame of the labour market, allowing lower wages, or work without wages (as a requirement of the benefit). However, the existence of such work divides the population and hence increases exclusion. Normal workers, with full-fledged rights, are clearly separated from workers in insertion activities who have only partial rights. Whereas the French republican ideology and conception of citizenship supposes equality of rights, the right to insertion paradoxically generates an inequality, and undermines the citizenship principle.

Where the government has attempted to incorporate insertion activities within the regulatory frame of the labour market (for instance, by transforming TUC jobs which paid less than the minimum wage into CES jobs) the right to insertion has become more difficult to implement due to a shortage of placements. The right to insertion demonstrates the contradictions of a Solidaristic conception of the nation and a liberal conception of rights and citizenship within a market economy. On the one hand, solidarity principles suppose the State will offer a job to 'excluded' citizens and guarantee equality of rights, on the other hand the market economy requires the state not to over-socialise the economy. French insertion lies at the intersection of two not entirely satisfactory policy trajectories: (a) offering a job to everybody through the production of 'sub-jobs' without equality of rights, and (b) offering a job to everybody with guaranteed rights, but at the risk of over-socialising the economy.

References

Amira, S. (1996) *L'indemnisation du chômage en France de 1985 à 1994*, Paris: Données sociales, INSEE.

Archambault, E. (1997) *The nonprofit sector in France*, Manchester: Manchester University Press.

Aucouturier, A.L. (1993) 'Contribution à la mesure de l'efficacité de la politique de l'emploi', *Travail et Emploi,* DARES, n 55, 1/1993.

Barbier, J.C. (1998) 'La logique du workfare dans les politiques sociales en Europe et aux Etats Unis, limites des analyses universalistes', *Document de travail CEE.*

Beck, C. (1994) *Assistance et République,* Paris: Les Editions de l'Atelier.

Belorgey, J.M. (1996) 'Pour renouer avec l'esprit initial du RMI', *Revue Mauss,* vol 7, no 1, pp 297-9.

Bernard, P.Y. and Lefresne, F. (1992) 'Contrats emploi solidarité, diversité des formes d'utilisation', *Travail et Emploi,* DARES, n 52, 2/1992.

BIPE-INSEE (1992) *Nouveaux emplois des services: Les dix services de la solidarité,* Paris: Rapport BIPE-INSEE, Ministère du Travail et de l'Emploi.

Bouquillard, O. and Catala, S. (1990) *La formation en alternance et l'accés des jeunes à l'emploi,* Paris : La Documentation Francaise.

Bourgeois, L. (1902) *Solidarité,* Paris: Colin.

Bruhnes, B. (1993) *Choisir l'emploi,* Rapport au CGP, XI plan, Paris: La Documentation Francaise.

Circulaire du 9 Mars (1989) Journal officiel du 11 Mars 1989.

CSCERC (Conseil Superieur de l'Emploi des Revenues et des Couts) (1997) *Minima sociaux entre protection et insertion,* Paris: La Documentation Francaise.

Commissariat Général au Plan (1997) *Chômage, le cas français,* Paris: La Documentation Francaise.

Conseil National de Lutte Centre la Pauvrete (1996) *Les activitiés d'utilité sociales,* Paris: Rapport du Conseil National de Lutte contre La Pauvreté.

DARES (Direction de l'Animation de la Recherche, des Etudes et des Statistiques) (1997) *La politique de l'emploi,* Paris: Repères, la Découverte.

DARES (1996) *La politique de l'Emploi,* Paris: La Decouverte.

de Foucauld, J.B. (1992) 'Exclusions, inégalités et justice sociale', *Esprit,* vol 182, no 6, pp 47-57.

Donzelot, J. (1984) *L'invention du social,* Paris: Fayard.

Donzelot, J. and Jaillet, M.C. (1997) 'Europe Etats Unis: convergences et divergences des politiques d'insertion', *Esprit*, Juin.

Enjolras, B. (1995) *Le marché providence*, Paris: Désclée de Brower.

Enjolras, B. (1996) 'Activités d'utilité sociale: ateliers nationaux ou dévelopement local?', *Union Sociale*, n 89, Janvier.

Esping-Andersen, G. (1990) *The three worlds of welfare capitalism*, Cambridge: Polity Press.

Ewald, F. (1986) *L'Etat Providence*, Paris: Seuil.

Eyssartier, D. and Gautie, J. (1996) 'Dix ans de politique de l'emploi en faveur des jeunes (1985-1994)', in *Les jeunes et l'emploi*, Cahier Travail Emploi, Paris: La Documentation Francaise, pp 17-45.

Greffe, X. (1990) *Nouvelles demandes, nouveaux services*, Rapport au CGP, Paris: La Documentation Francaise.

INSEE (1996) *Enquête emploi*, Paris: INSEE.

INSEE (1998). *Comptes de la Nation*, Paris: INSEE.

Jeger-Madiot, F. (1996) 'L'emploi et le chômage des familles professionnelles', *Données Sociales*, Paris: INSEE.

Laville, J.L. (ed) (1994) *L'Economie solidaire, une perspective internationale*, Paris: Désclée de Brower.

Le Bras Chopard, A. (1992) 'Métamorphoses d'une notion: la solidarité chez Pierre Leroux', in *La solidarité: un sentiment républicain?*, Paris: PUF, pp 50-118.

Lenoir, R. (1974) *Les exclus: Un français sur dix*, Paris: Seuil.

Loi de Finance (1988) Journal officiel du 2 janvier 1998.

Marchand, O. (1993) 'Les groupes sociaux face au chômage: des atouts inégaux', *Données Sociales*, Paris: INSEE.

MAUSS (Mouvement Anti Utilitariste dans les Sciences Sociales) (1996) *Vers un revenu minimum inconditionnel?*, La Revue du MAUSS semestrielle, n 7, 1 semestre.

Meron, M. and Minni, Cl. (1996) 'L'emploi des jeunes: plus tardif et plus instable qu'il y a vingt ans', *Données Sociales*, Paris: INSEE.

Ministère de l'Emploi et de la Solidarité (1999) *Les 10 ans du RMI*, Dossier de Presse, Nov.

Paugam, S. (ed) (1993) *La societé Française et ses pauvres, L'experience du RMI*, Paris: PUF.

Raymond, M. (1997) 'Pauvreté, précarité, RMI', in *La protection sociale en France*, Paris: La Documentation Française, pp 37-47.

Rose, J. (1998) *Jeunes et débutants face à l'emploi*, Paris: Désclée de Brouwer.

UNIOPSS (Union Nationale des Oeuvres et Organismes Sanitaires et Sociaux) (1996) 'Pour la participation de tous, lutter contre la pauvreté et l'exclusion: une priorité nationale', mars.

van Parisjs, P. (ed) (1992) *Arguing for basic income. Ethical foundations for a radical reform*, London: Verso.

Wuhl, S. (1991) *Du chômage à l'exclusion*, Paris: Syros.

THREE

Uneven development – local authorities and workfare in Germany

Wolfgang Voges, Herbert Jacobs and Heather Trickey

Introduction

Work creation schemes have a long tradition in Germany, and are an essential element of the German welfare system. The Bismarckian welfare state included a discretionary workfare component, which functioned primarily as a test of recipients' willingness to work. Discretionary workfare became part of the legal basis for social assistance in 1961 – when the Federal Social Assistance Act (SAA) was passed in the West German Federal Republic (Schulte, 1988) – so that the Federal social assistance law has always required recipients to work for their social assistance where an offer of work is made. Since implementation of the SAA, local administrations, who themselves fund social assistance, have been able to create new jobs for recipients. However, because the recipient population had, until recently, consisted largely of people who were considered unable to work, the workfare condition remained dormant. As unemployment has risen and the proportion of social assistance recipients who are unemployed has grown, local authorities have sought ways to reduce expenditure and to test recipients' willingness to work. As a result, local authorities have 'remembered' this area of law and use of the workfare measure has been rekindled.

The German designation for these job creation schemes is *Hilfe zur Arbeit*, which can be translated as 'Help Towards Work' (HTW). Two forms of HTW are used by local authorities: first, work which comes with an employment contract subject to social insurance and standard wages; and second, a more casual kind of work without these conditions. In addition, HTW may constitute vocational training. Over time, contract-type work has come to make up an increasing proportion of HTW places, and training has become more important. However, a patchwork of policies prevails. Help Towards Work schemes are implemented differently from location to location and important differences in practice exist between the new and old *Länder* (former East and West Germany).

Some local authorities monitor the results of their HTW projects, but most do not. Data about the extent of HTW, let alone effect, are minimal. The studies that have been carried out indicate that HTW is effective at reducing local authority social assistance expenditure, but that, currently, this is achieved by 'creaming off' the most work-able recipients and inserting them into the federally funded insurance-based system. Nationally, concern about the level of unemployment remains, and the process of reintegrating social assistance recipients is considered a high priority by policy makers. Under Chancellor Schroeder, policies (including local level HTW policies) which seek to reintegrate unemployed social assistance recipients, particularly young recipients, into the primary labour market, have received greater *Federal* attention and funding.

The German welfare state as a frame for job creation and Help Towards Work (workfare) policies

German welfare acts according to the principle of subsidiary (see Chapter One) with different institutions and actors on three levels: at the national level, at the level of the Federal states (*Bundesländer*) and at the level of local municipalities. This multiplicity of actors means that there is a great heterogeneity in how, and to what extent, employment provision programmes are implemented. To understand this, familiarity with four main characteristics of the German welfare regime is necessary (Alber, 1988).

1. *Fragmentation of programmes* – There are a large number of uncoordinated and decentralised employment programmes. Many autonomous institutions and organisations are responsible for the administration and provision of social services, with different organisations responsible for different benefits and/or different target groups.
2. *Emphasis on cash benefits* – The majority of benefits provided Federally are income maintenance cash payments. These payments are supposed to protect people from temporary loss of other major income sources.

3. *Reliance on social insurance* – Individuals are not normally entitled to income maintenance benefits on the basis of citizenship, but rather as members of contributory social insurance programmes. Contributory benefits are usually earnings-related, and aim to maintain the standard of living attained by the recipient during his or her working life (Alber, 1988).

4. *Importance of labour legislation* – All social policies are embedded in an elaborate system of labour market regulations; for example, concerning working conditions, dismissal arrangements and systems of codetermination at plant level[1].

These traits result from a welfare regime based on three principles. These are:

1) the social security principle (*Versicherungsprinzip*);
2) the maintenance principle (*Versorgungsprinzip*); and
3) the public welfare principle (*Fürsorgeprinzip*) (Table 3.1).

The principle of social security

Social insurance dominates the welfare system, with implications for economic well-being, employment promotion and risks of social exclusion within Germany. There are several branches of social insurance which cover typical or foreseeable risks incurred over the life course; among them, unemployment, invalidity, illness, needing care, old age and occupational injuries. Insurance-based benefits are granted where specific events have been covered by insurance contributions. For example, people who have paid insurance contributions for at least one year in the last three are entitled to draw Unemployment Benefit. Insured people may draw Unemployment Benefits for, at most, half the time they worked before having become unemployed, though people under 45 years of age are able to draw for only 12 months at most. Unemployment Benefit is worth about two thirds of previous income. Once entitlement to Unemployment Benefit is exhausted, previously insured unemployed people may claim Unemployment Assistance (a second tier insured benefit), worth about half of their previous income, for an unlimited period. Furthermore, people can claim Unemployment Assistance if they have been in contributory employment for at least five of the last twelve months.

Table 3.1: Basic principles of the German welfare state

Dimension	Principles of construction		
	The social security principle *Versicherungsprinzip*	The maintenance principle *Versorgungsprinzip*	The public welfare principle *Fürsorgeprinzip*
Support requirements	For insured loss	For specific inalienable rights	For individual needs
Covered persons	Members of the social insurance programme	Specific target groups (for example, ethnic Germans[b])	All resident citizens (including EU citizens)[a]
Scale of support	Standardised according to insured events	Standardised according to the maintenance trait	Individualised according to type and degree of need
Eligibility requirements	Payment to the social insurance fund	Sacrifice or other performance for the community	Means-tested need
Financing	Social insurance contributions with supplements from the Federal government	Federal taxation administered through Federal agencies	Federal taxation, but distributed to local authorities on a per capita basis
Institutions	Social insurance (for example, unemployment insurance)	Maintenance system (for example, pensions for war victims, public staff)	Minimum income support (for example, social assistance)
Job creation scheme	Employment office programme – *ABM*[c]	None	'Help Towards Work' *HzA*[d]. Social assistance workfare program

[a] Asylum-seekers and non-resident foreigners without a residence permit are not entitled to the social assistance programme. Since 1994 they are entitled to benefits from a similar (but not identical) programme in accordance with a specific law.
[b] German resettlers (*Aussiedler*) from the former Eastern bloc countries.
[c] *Arbeitsbeschaffungsmaßnahme* according Articles 91-93 of the Employment Promotion Act (*Arbeitsförderungsgesetz*).
[d] *Hilfe zur Arbeit* according Articles 18-20 of the Federal Social Assistance Act.

Benefits are usually earnings-related (except where nursing care is needed, and flat-rate benefits are granted) and are usually independent of personal income or assets. Contributions are paid mutually by employees and employers (each paying half) with supplements from the Federal government. In contrast to private insurance, the amount of contribution does not vary with estimates of individual risk, but, rather, with income from employment. A second feature distinguishing *social* insurance from private insurance arrangements is that contributions are compulsory. Employees have to pay unemployment insurance contributions if they work more than half the working hours that full-time employees work, according to wage agreements for the relevant trade.

The social components of social insurance, compulsion and income-related contribution, result in a form of *social equalisation* among insured people. Some groups, however, do not contribute to social security and are therefore excluded from the system. The social insurance system is focused on the traditionally male full-time employed population. Workers who have been more or less continuously employed at a relatively high wage are better protected than others are. People who have worked at home (more commonly women) and those who have worked in marginal employment situations are excluded from insurance-based social protection.

Unemployment Benefit and Unemployment Assistance Benefit are administered through locally-based Federal employment offices. These offices are also responsible for job and traineeship placement and assisting claimants with searching for jobs. Labour market programmes organised through these offices are federally funded and insured claimants are relatively well placed to access support in the form of job creation opportunities.

The principle of maintenance

Non-contributory forms of support, financed through general taxation, exist to provide a standard income for people in specific groups. Programmes operating under the principle of maintenance include compensatory payments – for war victims[2], people injured during military service, people suffering the complications resulting from publicly recommended vaccinations, and victims of crime. Most benefits of this type are granted irrespective of individual need. The main difference between these social compensations and the insurance-based social benefits described above is that payment is not justified on the basis of protecting individuals' standard of living, but rather to compensate for a loss borne by society as a whole (Schulin, 1994).

Other non-contributory social benefits include social promotion schemes or benefits designed to equalise family burdens. Social promotion schemes are designed to improve equality of opportunity; and include grants for education, vocational training and housing. These forms of support *are* dependent on the economic situation of the person concerned and are therefore means-tested. Benefits concerned with the function of balancing out financial burdens resulting from bringing up children include the children's allowance.

The principle of public welfare

A final set of benefits (of most interest here) operate according to the welfare principle, with *social assistance* being the primary example. Social assistance is financed through local taxation and relies on a universal (non-categorical) and unlimited right to basic financial support at a minimum standard of living[3]. Social assistance is financed and administered by local authorities and has two branches: 'Assistance in Special Situations' (*Hilfe Besonderen Lebenslagen*) and 'Cost-of-Living Assistance' (*Hilfe zum Lebensunterhalt*). Assistance in Special Situations is targeted towards ill or disabled people and towards people in need of costly care. This mainly takes the form of benefits in kind, including personal social services. Cost-of-Living Assistance is targeted towards people living in private households with insufficient income.

By way of comparison, the US social assistance system is categorically fragmented with eligibility rules and benefit levels varying widely between states and localities, and with a special bias against the 'working poor' or the 'able bodied'. Policy uniformity is present only in few Federal programmes, such as Supplemental Security Income (SSI) and food stamps. Seen from the US perspective, the German welfare system looks like a universal/national system for all who fall below a certain income level, but administered locally (immediately paid out of the local funds – but within the framework of a *national general* revenue sharing system). In contrast, the UK system represents a rare case of a fully national system – introduced in 1948 after centuries of a more or less local administration of poor relief – in which, unlike the Germany, the able-bodied poor are separately from the non-able-bodied poor.

In the following we only refer to Cost-of-Living Assistance. This form of social assistance is underpinned by two main objectives: to promote independence and to guarantee a level of income sufficient for 'human dignity' (Article 1, Federal SSA).

Minimum income support is provided in the form of benefits based on social assistance standard rates, with extra allowances for additional needs and assumed housing costs. Standard rates are intended to cover 'standard need'. The ordinance (Standard Rate Ordinance) issued by the Federal government defines what this standard need includes. Agencies of the Federal states determine these rates on the first of July of each year. There is some variation in the standard benefit level between East and West German Federal states (usually lower in the East).

The amount of money provided under Cost-of-Living Assistance is intended to cover basic needs, including food, housing, clothing, hygiene, household effects, heating and personal needs. It is also intended to enable the recipient to take part in social and cultural life. The amount of social assistance granted to any individual depends on specific circumstances and particularly on cost of housing. In West Germany in 1998 a single adult recipient of social assistance received on average 1,157 DM (593 Euros) per month, a married couple without children 1,844 DM (946 Euros) and a married couple with two children 2,881 DM (1,477 Euros) (Breuer and Engels, 1998).

As there are no general minimal social protection benefits apart from social assistance within the contributive social security system, the aim of social assistance is to support the existing system of benefit programmes. It is subsidiary to other forms of aid, and therefore is a last resort safety net. Other possible income sources – be they private (family) or public (insurance benefits and maintenance benefits) – have to be exhausted first. The local authority's social assistance administration checks the entitlement of new social assistance applicants, and assesses whether these people can otherwise support themselves through Unemployment Benefit, Unemployment Assistance or private means. If other means are available, social assistance may still be claimed in order to top up income to a social assistance threshold.

The Federal SSA of 1961, which forms the legal basis for social assistance, contains sufficiently clear entitlement rules to regard social assistance as a *national* programme. Local variation in granting social assistance does exist, but differences in *entitlement* should not be overemphasised. The 16 Federal states may clarify national regulations; and these may be further refined at the county and municipal level, where the programme is administered. Such clarifications and refinements are usually only to the extent of defining 'adequate' housing costs, or determining the amount of benefit which should be provided for clothing.

Bavaria is the one Federal state where a minimum standard of need is established and *local authorities* are allowed to increase the benefit level according to particular local conditions. As a result of this practice, there is greater variation in benefit levels among counties and municipalities in Bavaria than in other Federal states.

The German government considers social assistance adequate to avoid or remove poverty. However, welfare rights organisations and poverty researchers contest this assumption, as did members of the Social Democratic party during their time in opposition. Critics contend that the level of support is too low to sufficiently alleviate poverty and that there is the problem of non-take-up. Research suggests that the take-up rate is between 50% and 66%, meaning that between a third and a half of entitled persons do not claim. Older people in particular are reluctant to claim social assistance.

Social assistance claims are *processed* through local authority assistance offices, though these offices are supposed to send able-bodied claimants to the Federal employment office for support in jobseeking. Under SAA legislation, able-bodied recipients of Cost-Of-Living Assistance must take any job offered to them either through employment offices or through local authority social assistance offices. However, exceptions exist. Recipients do not have to accept:

1) overtaxing work;
2) work which endangers the future pursuit of a previous occupation; or
3) work which endangers the rearing of children in a family.

Trends in social assistance recipiency

Social assistance recipiency has grown as a result of changes in the level of unemployment as well as changes in entitlement legislation. Following unification, the unemployment rate for East and West Germany together rose from 7.6% in 1992 to 12.1% in 1997. Social assistance expenditure for unemployed recipients rose to 7.3 billion DM in 1996 (Fuchs, 1997, p 27) from 6 billion DM in 1993 (Fuchs, 1995) and from 3.4 billion in former West Germany in 1989 (Brinkmann et al, 1991).

Since 1984 the wage replacement rate of Unemployment Benefit and Unemployment Assistance has been cut several times. Because of these reductions, increasing numbers of people who claim insurance-based unemployment related benefits are also dependent on social assistance (Brinkmann et al, 1991). By the end of 1996, 43% of unemployed social assistance recipients in West Germany and a third of unemployed social assistance recipients in East Germany were also receiving Unemployment Benefit or Unemployment Assistance (Breuer and Engels, 1998).

There are important differences in the profile of social assistance clientele in the new and old *Länder*. The unemployment rate in the east (16%) is much higher than in the west (9.2%). More than half of social assistance recipients in the new *Länder* (including East Berlin) are unemployed compared to only one third in the old *Länder* (Breuer and Engels, 1998; Hauser and Voges, 1999).

Despite the fact that a rise in social assistance claims has occurred alongside a rise in the rate of unemployment, statistically the relationship is not uniform (Table 3.2). In East German cities, including Dresden and Leipzig, very high unemployment rates coincide with very low levels of social assistance recipiency. The low overall social assistance rates in eastern Germany (Seewald, 1999) may be, in part, due to the fact that the social assistance risk for older people is lower than in the west, as older people tend to have pensions above the social assistance benefit level. Another reason may be that the economic activity rate of women is higher in the east than in the west, so that many families have incomes over the social assistance minimum rate despite the fact that many male adult members are unemployed.

Unemployment was predicted to start to level off in the year 2000, but only to stabilise, at around 8%, in about 2010. The importance of the agricultural and industrial sectors, which have traditionally employed less skilled individuals, is predicted to continue to decline until 2010. Meanwhile, employment in the service industry, in both public and private sectors, is likely to continue to command a growing share of the employed labour force. As a result, the demand for skilled and qualified labour will continue to increase (Tessaring, 1994). It is predicted that by 2010, 90% of the labour force will require a qualification in order to work, with one fifth needing a university or higher education qualification. In contrast, the rate of unqualified employees is predicted to decrease to 10% (from 20% in 1991).

Within the unemployed population, social assistance recipients have worse placement prospects than other unemployed people do. As might be expected, they are more poorly qualified and are also more likely to have been long-term unemployed (Brinkmann et al, 1991). Unemployed social assistance clients with no qualifications have a significantly higher risk of remaining long-term recipients in the social assistance programme (Voges and Klein, 1994)[4]. More than three quarters (77%) of unemployed social assistance recipients have been unemployed for more than nine

Table 3.2: Indicators for labour market participation and poverty alleviation for selected regions and cities in Germany (1997)

Region/ cities	Unemployment rate (%)[a]	Unemployment social assistance rate (%)[b]	Rate of social assistance recipients (%)	Workfare rate (%)[c]
City states				
Hamburg	13.0	7.7	32.5	5.5
Bremen	16.5	9.5	37.2	3.4
Berlin	17.5	6.7*	45.8*	1.2*
North Rhine Westphalia and Lower Saxony				
Hanover	12.2	7.6	49.0	3.9
Dortmund	17.3	7.8	na	4.2
Duisburg	17.4	6.8	27.7	2.0
Düsseldorf	13.7	6.3	35.0	3.4
Essen	14.0	6.4	40.8	4.5
Cologne	14.3	7.3	40.8	2.7
East Germany				
Dresden	15.9	1.9	47.1	na
Leipzig	17.3	3.0	44.3	19.9
Rostock	19.4	4.4	66.9	2.4
South Germany				
Frankfurt/Main	11.4	6.1	42.8	6.1
Munich	7.9	3.7	27.7	4.2*
Stuttgart	8.4	4.4	38.5	4.9

Note: [a] ratio of the number unemployed to the total number of all employed and unemployed persons; [b] ratio of the number of recipient of income maintenance recipients to the number of inhabitants; [c] ratio of the number of workfare participants with a first labour market contract to the number of all working-aged social assistance recipients; data for 1997 except * 1996.
na = not available
Source: Bundesanstalt für Arbeit (1997, p 1742ff); Lungfiel and Gelhaar (1998)

months, compared to just under one third of other unemployed people. Women returning to the labour market after caring for children have a higher risk of remaining on assistance (Hauser and Voges, 1999). Unemployed social assistance recipients are younger than the registered unemployed population as a whole. Half are under 35 and one fifth under 25, compared to two fifths and just over one tenth respectively in the wider unemployed population (Krug and Meckes, 1997; Statistisches Bundesamt, 1995). In addition, a higher proportion of social assistance recipients than Unemployment Benefit recipients are believed to have severe personal barriers to working, including drug addiction and alcoholism.

Unemployment is not the only reason for the increase in the number of social assistance claimants. Other factors include increases in the number of low income single person households, as well as increased numbers of single mothers with dependent children (Seewald, 1999). Of all age groups, children under the age of seven have the greatest risk of being dependent on social assistance benefits. Until 1993, refugees and asylum-seekers, who were not permitted to work, also contributed to increases in the number of recipients (Voges and Weber, 1997).

Forms of work within Help Towards Work

The Federal government has introduced a plethora of initiatives to facilitate occupational mobility among *Unemployment Benefit* recipients through a variety of programmes, under the third section of the Social Code (*Sozialgesetzbuch*), the former Employment Promotion Act (*Arbeitsförderungsgesetz*). These include job placement, vocational and occupational guidance, vocational training or retraining, employment rehabilitation, settling-in allowance, wage subsidies, short-time working allowance and job creation schemes with wage subsidies for the employers. In contrast to the HTW programme for social assistance recipients, these job creation schemes are administered and funded by the employment offices and only target recipients of Unemployment Benefit or Unemployment Assistance. In 1997, more than 300,000 Unemployment Benefit recipients participated in such job creation schemes and nearly 450,000 participated in vocational training or retraining (*Bundesministerium für Arbeit und Sozialordnung*, 1998, Table 8.14A).

Help Towards Work, the workfare-like component of social assistance, consists of a graduated series of measures whose policy goal is the (re)integration of social assistance recipients into the primary labour market. Depending on the job placement difficulties, HTW may involve a temporary position in the secondary labour market (Figure 3.1). Each step up the gradient affords a greater approximation to a 'real work' situation. Local authorities may apply none or all of the stages of the gradient to able-bodied recipients.

Figure 3.1: Possible measures for reintegrating social assistance recipients into the labour market through Help Towards Work (strategy)

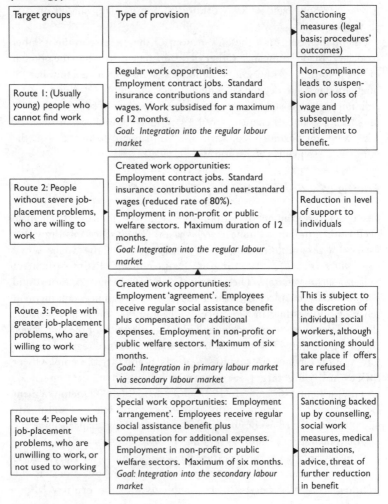

Target groups	Type of provision	Sanctioning measures (legal basis; procedures' outcomes)
Route 1: (Usually young) people who cannot find work	Regular work opportunities: Employment contract jobs. Standard insurance contributions and standard wages. Work subsidised for a maximum of 12 months. *Goal: Integration into the regular labour market*	Non-compliance leads to suspension or loss of wage and subsequently entitlement to benefit.
Route 2: People without severe job-placement problems, who are willing to work	Created work opportunities: Employment contract jobs. Standard insurance contributions and near-standard wages (reduced rate of 80%). Employment in non-profit or public welfare sectors. Maximum duration of 12 months. *Goal: Integration into the regular labour market*	Reduction in level of support to individuals
Route 3: People with greater job-placement problems, who are willing to work	Created work opportunities: Employment 'agreement'. Employees receive regular social assistance benefit plus compensation for additional expenses. Employment in non-profit or public welfare sectors. Maximum of six months. *Goal: Integration in primary labour market via secondary labour market*	This is subject to the discretion of individual social workers, although sanctioning should take place if offers are refused
Route 4: People with job-placement problems, who are unwilling to work, or not used to working	Special work opportunities: Employment 'arrangement'. Employees receive regular social assistance benefit plus compensation for additional expenses. Employment in non-profit or public welfare sectors. Maximum of six months. *Goal: Integration into the secondary labour market*	Sanctioning backed up by counselling, social work measures, medical examinations, advice, threat of further reduction in benefit

Subsidised regular job opportunities (top tier, Figure 3.1): at the highest point of the gradient, for the most employable clients/recipients, local authorities may provide subsidised work. These are 'real' jobs. Contracts are drawn up and wages paid according to the conditions in the for-profit sector, but on a time-limited basis. An employment contract is signed according to the wage agreement in the appropriate sector (public or private) with full employee rights and duties for the former social assistance recipient, while the employer receives a wage subsidy. In general, the employment contract lasts for one year. If the former recipient is not hired permanently when the contract expires, s/he becomes eligible for unemployment insurance benefits and can participate in Federal job creation programmes through the employment office.

Community and additional work (middle tier, Figure 3.1): local authorities may finance public work for clients who have greater job placement difficulties. Such work must satisfy the conditions of being both for the community good and work that would not otherwise be carried out through the private market – the so-called 'additional' requirement. These jobs may be 'real' jobs based on a regular employment contract, as above, or on a non-contract 'employment agreement' between the authority and recipient. Jobs with time-limited normal employment contracts may be financed at a reduced wage level. Participants on employment agreements continue to receive social assistance (plus an additional small supplement for work-related expenses), and are exempt from normal employment rights.

Specific work opportunities (bottom tier, Figure 3.1): at the lowest level are jobs which constitute special individually tailored work opportunities, which have the character of a 'social activation'. Such placements are used for recipients who have severe barriers to employment, mental health or addiction problems. Local authorities use such measures both to acclimatise recipients to the demands of occupational activity, and to test readiness to work. In recent years such measures have come to play a less important role. The activation programmes are cost intensive and do not bring down the payrolls of local authorities.

In addition, local authorities use HTW to supply *Education and training placements:* explicit education or training phases do not form part of the legal basis of integration. However, with a rise in the number of long-term unemployed claimants with low skills, the importance of training phases within HTW programmes is increasing. However, due to the high cost, the use of education and training is variable from locality to locality.

Social assistance offices are supposed to send all unemployed social assistance recipients to the local employment offices, where they are registered as unemployed. The employment office is then supposed to maintain contact with unemployed assistance clients throughout their periods of receipt. The employment office is the agency usually responsible for helping unemployed social assistance clients with good placement prospects to find regular unsubsidised work. However, some local social assistance administrations will themselves occasionally organise placements through temporary private or public employment agencies. In addition, most local authorities have special departments which provide training resources, and help clients to develop 'individualised life plans' to move towards self-sufficiency (Schaak, 1997; Wilk, 1997). Individuals who are *not* considered to have good immediate placement prospects may be referred to a HTW scheme.

In some locations innovative practices are being introduced, which change the relationship between social assistance offices and their clients. Some cities have adapted the Dutch use of private placement agencies to provide *Maatwerk*, or made-to-measure work, which test recipients' aptitude for different Help Towards Work placements and seek appropriate placements. Other offices have instituted performance-based contracts with outside agencies that seek to place recipients in the primary labour market *without* wage subsidies to the employer. In other words, the only difference from traditional placement procedures is that the task of job placement assistance is contracted out, so that there is a profit incentive on contractors to achieve a high number of placements. This is much cheaper than subsidising contract-type work, but may be less efficient in placing recipients who have a great number of barriers to work, because there is no special incentive (subsidy) to employers to take difficult cases. The system of contracting out and providing 'rewards' to the placing agency, rather than employers, was first introduced in Hamburg. At the end of 1995, the local social assistance office contracted an agency to place 300 recipients in the primary labour market within 12 months (Brockmöller, 1997). The agency received 4,000 DM (2,051 Euros) per placement, as long as former recipients remained employed for at least six months. Other local administrations have gradually followed suit.

Non-contract Help Towards Work (workfare-additional community work)

When local authorities require recipients to take up jobs without an employment contract (bottom and bottom middle tiers, Table 3.1) clients retain their status as 'benefit recipients' but may receive a small extra payment for additional expenses. Such jobs are fixed-term, and generally only last a few months. They are restricted according to the number of permissible working hours and are usually not full time. Remuneration rates tend to be low, with participants generally receiving between 2-4 DM (1-2 Euros) per working hour on the top of their benefit.

Contract-type Help Towards Work (subsidised and created work)

Social assistance is funded from Federal taxation, but on a per capita basis. Hence, as unemployment has risen it is *local authorities* that have borne the costs of the rise in the number of recipients. Naturally, local authorities have sought ways to diminish their financial burdens. Short of removing social assistance entitlement entirely, expenditure can be best reduced by creating insured employment opportunities (Lüsebrink, 1993, 1994; Trube, 1994). Through financially supporting recipients into insured employment on a temporary basis, local authorities are able to shift responsibility for their future well-being to the unemployment insurance system. Hence, local level policy makers have sought to create contract-type Help Towards Work (top tier, and top middle tier, Table 3.1) as a means of re-inserting clients into the insured pool of labour.

Contract-type HTW may include vocational training. Local authorities can make use of European Social Fund money (administered by the Federal states) to provide such training. No representative data are available regarding the portion of contract-type jobs that include a vocational training component. However, in one small study of 16 local administrations surveyed in 1998, half of 2,194 HTW jobs with employment contracts had a vocational training element (Deutscher Bundestag, 1998). Such training usually made up 20% of worked hours at most; very few HTW programmes consisted of full-time training components.

Until 1993 contract-type HTW took place exclusively in the public, charitable and non-profit sectors. This restriction was meant to ensure that the jobs were for the community/public interest (*Öffentliches Interesse*) and additional work (*Zusätzlichkeit*). The SAA stipulates these two conditions in order to avoid competition with private sector enterprises. However, since 1993 the social assistance administration has been permitted to disregard these restrictions especially (but not only) for younger recipients who are not eligible for the Federal job creation programme. Local social assistance administrations can now provide subsidised work by paying part of the wage of former recipients for some months after they have gained employment, and participants now usually work in the private sector.

Funding the whole salary of an insured employee directly through HTW is expensive. In the 1980s, local authorities, who wanted to find out what the return on their investment was, commissioned studies to evaluate the cost-benefit of such a strategy. These studies concluded that returns on investment usually occurred in the second or third year after participants leave contract-type HTW (Dieckmann et al, 1986; Reissert, 1988). The level of return depended on the type of household (the pay-off for larger households being quicker) and the wage paid to the participant during the Help Towards Work job. Even if former participants become unemployed immediately after having left subsidised contract jobs there is some pay-off for local authorities as these people can claim unemployment benefits and do not immediately return to the social assistance population. Families with children are more likely to return to needing social assistance to fund at least part of their income.

Sanctioning

Recipients who refuse to participate in either contract or non-contract HTW are supposed to be sanctioned. In this sense the job offer acts as a second means test to eliminate people who can sustain themselves without accepting job offers. Under the SAA legislation, local administrations have always been able to cut the benefits of recipients who refuse to take up such offers but have traditionally used their discretion not to sanction recipients. However, since 1993 local authorities have been *required* by federal law to sanction recipients who do not alter their behaviour after a threat of sanctions has been issued by a social worker.

In principle, recipients who refuse to actively seek employment or to accept a HTW job offer are subject to an initial benefit reduction of up to a quarter of their benefit. People who continue to remain non-compliant may be denied their individual part of their household benefit. The benefits of dependent family members are protected, with the intention being to punish the non-compliant recipient. Nonetheless, the reduction in support presents a problem where families are concerned because each member of the community of persons in need, as defined by the social assistance administration[5] (*Bedarfsgemeinschaft*), suffers as a result. Consequently, social workers sometimes hesitate to issue a threat of benefit cuts so as to avoid having to carry out sanctioning.

There is no clear representative evidence regarding the proportion of recipients who refuse to participate in HTW activities. Survey evidence suggests that the proportion of refusals for initial offers may be very high (as much as a quarter) in some cities (*Deutscher Städtetag*, 1997) and it is clear that in the majority of locations refusal does not usually result in sanctioning

Workfare and its rise since the 1980s

The rise in workfare, and a recent 'remembering' of the workfare component in the SAA, is in part pragmatic and in part ideological (Voges, 1998). Key factors behind the re-introduction of HTW are the desire of local governments to curtail social assistance spending and to support for greater 'work-testing' of unemployed people. Secondary objectives of HTW programmes are: to provide help to social assistance recipients seeking work in the primary labour market; to increase employment in the local area; to increase the self-confidence of participants; to reduce poverty; to help charitable associations to do things which they otherwise could not do; and to carry out work that local authorities themselves think to be important (for example, environmental protection or redevelopment of run-down town quarters).

The first and major step to reactivating the workfare clause was taken in Berlin (*Senatsverwaltung*, 1992). Here, between 1983 and 1989, social assistance offices offered about 100,000 jobs *without* any employment contract to of social assistance recipients – more than in all other western Federal states together. The main objective of this programme was to test willingness to work. Refusing the offer was subject to sanction. The impact on social assistance receipt was surprisingly limited. Only 2,000 recipients (2%) refused to participate, and the social assistance office reduced benefits paid to these recipients. A further 4,000 people (4%) abandoned social assistance completely (Albert, 1989). Analysts concluded that 'additional' work jobs and conditions of strong sanctioning do not act as a deterrent to the vast majority of social assistance recipients. The decrease in social assistance expenditure was negligible.

In contrast, studies demonstrated cost-benefit savings from contract-type HTW jobs, discussed above (Diekmann, 1986; Lüsebrink, 1993, 1994; Reissert, 1988; Trube, 1994) have led to the increased use of created insured work placements. The number of participants in contract Help Towards Work schemes rose from 14,000 in 1988 (Pilgrim, 1990) to 50,000 in 1993, and to about 100,000 in 1996 (Fuchs, 1995, 1997). This trend has been reflected in the types of activities undertaken. In 1993, 80% of all participants in HTW did things which otherwise would not have been done (*Zusätzlichkeit*, additional work) and which were for the community/public interest (*Öffentliches Interesse*). Three years later the proportion was only 56%, and [of these] more than 50% of all jobs were of employment contract type (Fuchs, 1997). The increased utilisation of insured employment is occurring even in the smaller cities and rural districts, where it is estimated that more than one third of HTW participants are involved in contract-type employment activities.

Variation in the delivery of workfare

Help Towards Work schemes are not part of a single nationwide political programme. While nearly all local authorities now create HTW jobs for unemployed social assistance recipients, this has occurred as a result of their facing similar problems and through learning, bilaterally, from one another, rather than through any coordinated programme. As a result, many different local HTW measures exist, with a range of objectives. Some schemes are targeted to the general pool of unemployed recipients while others are provided for specific groups of recipients, including single mothers, younger unemployed people and poorly qualified people.

Local authorities vary in their implementation of HTW, according to:

1) the composition of their target groups;
2) the extent to which they use contract-type as opposed to non-contract-type employment; and
3) the way in which delivery is organised.

The description of variation below focuses on differences between cities, as data is more readily available than for rural areas.

Variation in targeting

Table 3.2 illustrates the extent of variation in the use of HTW by region. In many municipalities, particularly in rural areas, only some dozen jobs are offered (*Deutscher Bundestag Drucksache*, 13/10759). In Hamburg, while all unemployed able-bodied social assistance clients, have to declare a willingness to work, job placements exist for fewer than 10%. In contrast, in the city of Leipzig, HTW is an almost comprehensive job-creation scheme, and every unemployed recipient is offered work with an employment contract. Leipzig has a higher rate of recipients in HTW schemes than cities with similar general unemployment rates among recipients of employable age.

While the SAA itself does not favour targeting some age groups above others, local authorities can do so. In Hamburg, for example, the local job centre of the social assistance administration only provides contract-type employment to recipients who have at least two of the following attributes: unemployed for longer than one year; on social assistance for longer than one year; no formal qualifications; holds foreign citizenship; has Eastern Europe ethnic German status and is over 40 years of age; in debt; has previous convictions; is re-entering the labour force after caring for children.

Most local administrations only provide HTW jobs to recipients who rely exclusively on social assistance. Since about 40% of all unemployed recipients also draw Unemployment Benefit or Unemployment Assistance, this practice represents a significant inclusion requirement. The reasoning behind this targeting measure is that partially insured recipients are entitled to participate in employment schemes funded by employment offices.

Variation in type

Differences in the ratio of contract to non-contract jobs that local authorities offer explain differences in the average duration of schemes from municipality to municipality. Larger cities tend to provide more contract jobs, and hence activities are of longer duration. In cities of up to 50,000 inhabitants, just under half (46%) of the HTW schemes have a duration under seven months, whereas in cities with over 200,000 inhabitants only one fifth (20%) of schemes are of such a short duration (Fuchs, 1997). Only a very few recipients are placed with employers via a wage subsidy (top tier, Figure 3.1). This compares with more than 73,000 participants who were funded directly through the local authority with or without employment contracts (top middle and bottom middle tiers, Figure 3.1) (Fuchs, 1997).

Variation in administration and delivery

Two main ways of administering HTW can be identified (Schaak, 1997; Wilk, 1997): schemes organised through the local offices and those organised through contracted companies.

Help Towards Work organised by the local administration

Many cities and some rural districts use special HTW units based within local social assistance administration offices. Help Towards work employment takes place within a variety of organisations and enterprises of the private and the charitable sector and within departments of the administration of the city with whom the local administration makes contact. The cities of Bremen, Berlin, and Cologne use this approach. The result is great variation in the type of activity undertaken by HTW participants, including work for poorly qualified people as well as jobs for people with higher educational qualifications. In some cases, participants are employees of the organisations and enterprises in which they work and are paid by them. Alternatively, participants are employees of HTW units (as in Berlin) and are paid by these units while employers maintain a supervisory role.

Help Towards Work organised by contracted companies

Some local authorities separate the organisation of HTW from the business of social assistance administration and make use of a specific job creation company (*Beschäftigungsgesellschaft*) which is, itself, owned by the local administration. This happens, for example, in Hamburg, Leipzig and Saarbrücken. These organisations tend to employ most HTW participants within their own enterprises. The enterprises may have hundreds and in some cases more than a thousand employees. In the cities of Leipzig and Hamburg these contracted companies employ more than 1,500 former recipients of social assistance. Leipzig (which was the second largest city in the former East Germany), after East Berlin, is now a premiere site for this kind of HTW implementation, providing a HTW model for other East German cities. In no other East or West German city has a job creation company (*Beschäftigungsgesellschaft*) been as successful as in Leipzig, where the HTW programme is generally considered to be effective in rapidly removing people from the social assistance programme *and* in producing valuable community work (including, the re-naturalisation of former canalised rivers). The activities organised by such companies tend to be less varied than in cities where HTW is organised through the social assistance office.

Differences between the new and old Länder

In general, the aim of the HTW programmes in the eastern and western German cities are the same. However, the east's restricted labour market, higher unemployment rate, but proportionately lower social assistance rate, have resulted in very different target populations.

In most western German cities HTW is not intended to provide employment opportunities for all social assistance recipients. Some cities offer HTW to recipients who *volunteer* to participate, so that the offer cannot be said to constitute 'workfare' at all. Others require participation after set periods of receipt. In some cities HTW operates in conjunction with a broad array of circumstances under which it is acceptable for recipients to reject the HTW offer. Even ability to work is not questioned in all cities, mainly due to cost factors.

Most eastern German cities do not have the necessary administrative infrastructure to implement HTW on any great scale, though many policy makers regard Leipzig as a model. The city of Leipzig attempts to offer HTW assignments to *all* social assistance recipients, including those with a disability or with severe social problems caused by alcohol or drug abuse. More typically eastern German cities, like western German cities, focus on claimants with few job placement difficulties.

There are gender differences in the characteristics of the HTW clients in the new and old *Länder*. A 'right to work' in pre-unification East Germany means that employment has a significant role in the lives of eastern German women. Under Communism, female labour force participation was high in East Germany, compared to West Germany, and the disparity has remained following unification. Correspondingly, a greater proportion of women participate in HTW programmes in the eastern cities. In the east HTW programmes tend to have much broader work opportunities for women. While in the west, women tend to be assigned to activities in the service sector, women living in the east are more often assigned to construction or carpentry work.

The age profile of the HTW clients in the east is beginning to approach that of cities in the west as the proportion of young east German clients rises. In HTW, work offers are also changing. Until recently, providing education or training as a legitimate form of HTW was a west German practice. In the East, education has been used mainly as an introduction to employment and made available to very few clients. This difference stems from differences in the educational level of the client populations; the proportion of skilled workers with professional qualifications within the social assistance population has been much higher in the former GDR. However, following the downturn in the east German labour market, young people have had fewer opportunities to enter the dual system of vocational training and to so achieve a qualification in their preferred profession[6]. As a result HTW schemes in parts of eastern Germany are beginning to change to meet the needs of this new population.

As one example of a HTW initiative designed to buck this trend, the Leipzig HTW company has introduced a training programme for 'organic butchering'. In general, while work is available, the occupation of 'butcher' is stigmatised in Germany. The training programme is intended to remove this stigma so that trainees became 'professional' butchers. The programme has a long list of applicants and limited dropout during training.

Other east/west differences concern how extensively non-contract 'Additional and Community Work' (bottom middle tier, Figure 3.1) is utilised. In some western German cities, this extra work has been used extensively where it has been seen to meet a local need for community services, including the maintenance of public areas. In the east the 'additional and community work' measure has tended to be used for short periods of 2-3 months in order to establish the capabilities of recipients before offering them an employment contract.

There are also east/west differences in sanctioning policy. Administrators in the west vary greatly in their willingness to reduce benefits where clients refuse to participate. Some cities (including Bremen and Dortmund) regard sanctions as counterproductive because of possible resultant increases in delinquency. The thinking is that in the long run it is cheaper not to sanction, as sanctioned clients become costly to the State as a result of increased poverty or increased crime. Eastern German sanctioning practices are more uniform, and in general reflect a greater readiness to reduce benefits. For example, in Berlin and Leipzig sanctioning is seen as a necessary condition for programme effectiveness and as the most effective way of establishing a willingness to work among recipients.

Political differences

At the level of national politics, both of the main political parties, Social Democrats and the Christian Democrats, support HTW, and believe that occupational activity is the best means of fulfilling one of the major aims of social assistance – helping recipients to leave it. Both parties support compulsory measures backed by sanctions. However, clear political differences underlie policy justifications, and beliefs about the kinds of HTW jobs that should be undertaken and the way in which HTW should be delivered (Gebhardt et al, 1998). Social-democratic rhetoric has tended to emphasise the need to support rather than to punish. Developing a secondary labour market through created insured work is a favoured route. Christian Democrats, on the other hand, have tended to emphasise the 'work-testing' and the obligatory nature of HTW job offers. They also tend to oppose insured employment, as this constitutes a 'wage subsidy' incompatible with the free play of market forces.

Social Democrats favour policies to transfer jurisdiction over Cost-of Living Assistance recipients to employment offices, and oppose moves by local authorities to establish administrative HTW units with similar responsibilities as employment offices (Hartmann, 1998). They maintain that unemployment should be addressed by a single agency. This view is justified in part by current funding arrangements in which both social assistance and Unemployment Assistance are branches of public welfare, funded by tax revenues.

Locally, however, the way in which HTW schemes are organised (the number of jobs, type of work and establishment of a *Beschäftigungsgesellschaft*) does not seem to be associated with specific political parties; Bremen, Cologne and Leipzig, which have different systems of administration, all have social-democratic mayors. In fact, economic circumstances, differences in unemployment rates and the proportion of unemployed people in the social assistance population better explain the differences. Perhaps unsurprisingly, it appears that the higher the unemployment rate and the greater the proportion of unemployed people in the social assistance population, the greater the number of HTW jobs.

Evaluation and outcomes

Local authorities are not obliged to evaluate their HTW measures under the SAA. Together with the heterogeneity of the local HTW schemes, this creates a significant challenge to efforts to determine 'what works' –

namely, how to obtain comparable information in order to evaluate current practice and inform effective policy reform. What is more, because there is so much variation in practice, as well as in aims and objectives, it would be extremely difficult to decide on a useful suite of measures for comparative outcomes analysis, even if it were possible to collect such information. Currently available data in most cities is very poor, due to limited monitoring. Even those cities that do have data collection practices produce incomparable data. Some cities monitor the financing of HTW programmes while others monitor the number of clients. Follow-up information about HTW clients after their period of participation is not usually collected. Even the quality of the sociodemographic and employment history data collected about clients varies considerably. Most authorities do not produce an annual statistical report. Some cities do not know how many HTW clients they have, who they are, or what kind of problems they have. Though they have a general overview of their HTW programme this is gathered from information passed by social workers on a case by case basis.

At the Federal level, problems occur because, within the same Federal state cities, may have different policies and produce different outcome data, or none at all. High numbers of HTW clients with a regular employment contract can be an indicator of high numbers of socially deprived long-term social assistance recipients, or of a generous municipality which readily moves recipients into employment activities. Similarly, low numbers of HTW clients can indicate a problem-free situation, or restricted access to the programme. The situation is often better in small cities where a programme overview is more readily obtained.

The three city-states, Berlin, Bremen and Hamburg provide exceptions to this general picture. Here local and Federal governments converge under one administration, and the cash and motivation for evaluation are available due to an interest beyond moving participants out of social assistance and into the Federal social insurance system (as this would not relieve the states of their funding dilemma). The ministries responsible for social assistance in the city-states have commissioned studies of HTW schemes that provide participants with regular employment contracts. More recently ministries of other Federal states and even local administrations have begun to commission their own evaluations. In general, evaluations have tended to focus on three objectives:

1) assisting social assistance recipients in finding unsubsidised work;
2) achieving local authority social assistance expenditures; and
3) improvements in well-being.

Finding unsubsidised work

A number of city-state surveys have investigated the destinations of participants of *contract-type* HTW schemes. In Bremen (Jacobs, 1996), in Hamburg (Häntsch and Mirbach, 1994a, 1994b), and in Berlin (Tiemann and Markert, 1995) questionnaires were sent to all former participants who had completed a period of participation lasting for one or more years. Questionnaires were sent several months after they finished their programme. Although the response rate was never greater than 30%, the respondent profiles resembled the general participant populations sufficiently such that levels of bias were deemed to be insignificant.

Participants were asked whether they had obtained employment after leaving the programme. As Table 3.3 demonstrates, approximately two thirds of former contract-welfare participants in all three city-states were, once more, out of work at the time of the survey. Only one fifth of former participants from Bremen and Berlin were in work, compared to

Table 3.3: Employment status and income resources or former contract-type workfare clients in three cities (%)

| | City-states (*Bundesländer/Stadtstaaten*) | | |
	Berlin	Bremen	Hamburg
Employment status:			
Employed in the primary labour market	21	21	31
In a job creation scheme funded by the employment office	12	6	2
Unemployed or not employed	58	57	58
In education or job training	6	3	9
Left the labour force for some time or permanently	3	10	1
Income resources:			
Social assistance only	10	32	20
Drawing Unemployment Benefit or Unemployment Assistance	40	28	39
Earnings from employment	38	33	33
Other income resources	12	7	8

just under a third of former participants from Hamburg, a difference which may be due to the better labour market situation in Hamburg. More than one in ten former participants from Berlin were re-entering the job creation scheme system – but this time through the insurance offices. Unsurprisingly, people with formal qualifications and with stronger employment histories were more likely to have found work.

Reducing social assistance expenditure

As already stated, studies carried out during the 1980s demonstrated a savings effect for local authorities who provided HTW jobs with an insurance-based employment contract. Savings occurred even when participants returned to unemployment at the end of the contract, because of renewed entitlement to unemployment benefits, to Unemployment Assistance, or to participate in employment promotion measures funded by the employment office (Dieckmann et al, 1986; Reissert, 1988).

Improvements in well-being

Contact-type HTW schemes appear to improve the well-being of participants. A comparison of HTW participants, with a similar control group of unemployed social assistance recipients, carried out in Dusseldorf, demonstrated significant differences. Most former clients said they would participate in contract-type HTW employment again, even if they were to become unemployed after its completion (Jacobs, 1996; Trube, 1997). Only one fifth of HTW participants expressed serious concern about financial difficulties compared to four fifths of the control group, unsurprising as the economic situation of contract-type HTW participants was significantly better than for the benefit claimants. In addition, participants were able to be relatively optimistic due to renewed eligibility for the Federal job creation scheme. Only 10% of participants said that they felt 'superfluous' compared to two fifths of the control group (Trube, 1994). Other studies have found similar differences in well-being and self-confidence between participants and non-participants, in addition to stronger contacts with friends and relatives (Häntsch and Mirbach, 1994b; Jacobs, 1996; Kempken and Trube, 1997; Meendermann, 1992; Tiemann and Markert, 1995).

The future

While HTW assists local authorities in relieving the strains on social assistance budgets, not all participants benefit to the extent of finding work. This is, in part, due to the fact that social assistance administrations tend to select recipients with good formal skills and few or no barriers to participate in contract-type HTW (Priester and Klein, 1992). Some municipalities, including Hamburg, aim to avoid such 'creaming' by requiring *all* to be available for work. However, the limited number of job placements means that these go to the most 'work ready'.

The ambition of moving as many recipients as possible into employment is inconsistent with the aim of reducing expenditure on social assistance. Social assistance clients who are poorly qualified and who have been unemployed for a long time need more support to find work than others do. Increasing support, for instance by extending training components, increases the cost of the HTW schemes and diminishes and defers any pay-off to the local authority. Passing the task of supporting and placing clients onto external placement agencies is likely to increase this creaming effect; as such (private sector) agencies have an even greater incentive to invest in easy wins.

The very limited range of findings described above raise a number of issues for further evaluation:

- First, as discussed there is a dearth of information of sufficient quality or consistency to support evaluation.
- Second, while the findings demonstrate that contract-based HTW has been successful in removing people from social assistance, and in improving their well-being, it is completely unclear whether the fact that, at best, one third of participants go on to employment represents 'success' or 'failure'. Effect and cost-benefit evaluations are lacking.
- Third, there are no common standards against which to evaluate HTW schemes. The stated aim of programmes is more usually to help people to take up employment, rather than to move a specific proportion of participants into work.

Despite the lack of evidence for their effectiveness in moving clients into employment, the use contract-type job creation schemes is likely to increase. The general public is broadly supportive of HTW measures and of the idea that social assistance recipients should work in return for the help that they receive (Gebhardt et al, 1998). Questions about whether compulsory work is desirable are much lower down the agenda than the broader concern with *doing something* about unemployment. The success of the schemes in cutting social assistance expenditure means that creating insured employment, as opposed to non-contract work, is likely to continue to be considered a more sensible course of action than paying benefits.

Nationally, Chancellor Schroeder's Social Democratic-Green government has emphasised the need to reintegrate unemployed people into the primary labour market and has committed itself to providing jobs and training places for *younger* unemployed people who are not eligible for participation in the Federal job creation programme. The government is likely to increase the material incentives for assistance clients to take up employment through wage subsidies or subsidised insurance contributions for low wage earners. Both instruments have the potential to raise the net incomes of unemployed people if they take up low wage employment.

In October 1998 more than 400,000 young people under the age of 25 were registered unemployed. In November 1998 the (then) new government adopted a 'Cornerstones of Action' programme to reduce youth unemployment, consisting of a combination of work and training, to achieve qualifications and employment of young people. The programme was intended to provide support for 100,000 young people (Martens, 1999). This programme offers tailored forms of support, including training, education and job placements for unemployed young people. Employers receive wage subsidies for employing unemployed young people. Young unemployed people who are not ready to be placed into regular jobs may participate in job creation schemes to gain practical work experience and additional skills. In 1999, the programme budget was two billion DM, made possible by a Federal government subsidy to the budget of the Federal Employment Office, as well as money from the European Social Fund. This fund gives local authorities greater opportunity to expand and tailor their programmes to the needs of the local community. New policies at the Federal and state level support local administrations in accessing this money.

Notes

[1] There is no (official) minimum wage in Germany. Collective agreements between labour unions and employers' organisations cover most jobs.

[2] The greater generosity of the German welfare state towards ethnic Germans is an effect of this principle. (Voges et al, 1998).

[3] This law guarantees social assistance (*Sozialhilfe*) as the basis for minimum incomes for legal residents in Germany. However, asylum seekers (since 1993) and adult higher education students are excluded from receiving social assistance and are entitled to draw other benefits (Voges and Weber, 1997).

[4] The increasing number of social assistance recipients without formal skills has raised the importance of a qualification component in to Help Towards Work measures. As a result many cities now implement vocational training within the Help Towards Work programmes.

[5] This does not cover members of a household or a family. The rules for defining 'a community of persons in need' in the Social Assistance Act are very vague. As a result there are several inconsistencies (Klein, 1999).

[6] The dual system of vocational training differs from the purely academic vocational education customary in many other countries. Most learning does not take place in schools, but rather in private business and industry. Trainees are released for set periods of time to attend a part-time vocational education (*Berufsschule*). Young people receive training three to four days per week in their company, and one to two days per week at the vocational school. Vocational training is provided by more than 500,000 firms in all branches of business and industry as well as by the independent professions and the public services. Vocational training possibilities are highly related to firms' willingness to collaborate in the dual system. This becomes specifically a problem in regions experiencing an economic downswing.

References

Alber, J. (1988) 'Germany', in P. Flora (ed) *Growth to limits. The western European welfare states since world war II*, Vol 2, Berlin: de Gruyter, pp 1-154.

Albert, F. (1989) 'Arbeit für erwerbslose Hilfeempfänger – Grundlagen und Ergebnisse des Berliner Modells', *Nachrichtendienst des Deutschen Vereins für öffentliche und private Fürsorge*, vol 69, pp 228-33.

Breuer, W. and Engels, D. (1998) *Basic information and data on social assistance in Germany*, Bonn: Federal Ministry of Health.

Brockmöller, B. (1997) 'Maatwerk – Arbeit nach Maß. Zwischenbilanz zum Modellprojekt im Sozialamt Harburg', Freie und Hansestadt Hamburg, Behörde für Arbeit, Gesundheit und Soziales (ed): *Sozialhilfereport*, no 8, pp 14-19.

Brinkmann, C., Friedrich, D., Fuchs, L. and Lindlahr, K.-O. (1991) 'Arbeitslosigkeit und Sozialhilfebezug Sonderuntersuchung der Bundesvereinigung der kommunalen Spitzenverbände in Zusammenarbeit mit der Bundesanstalt für Arbeit im September 1989', *Mitteilungen aus der Arbeitsmarkt- und Berufsforschung*, vol 24, pp 157-77.

Bundesanstalt für Arbeit (1997) *Amtliche Nachrichten der Bundesanstalt für Arbeit*, vol 45.

Deutscher Bundestag (1998) *Drucksache 13/10759: Antwort der Bundesregierung auf die Große Anfrage der Abgeordneten Ulf Fink, Eva-Maria Kors, Wolfgang Lohmann (Lüdenscheid), weitere Abgeordneter und der Fraktion der CDU/CSU sowie der Abgeordneten Dr. Gisela Babel, Sabine Leutheusser-Scharrenberger, Uwe Lühr, Dr. Dieter Thomae und der Fraktion der FDP – Drucksache 13/8687 – Hilfe zur Arbeit – vom 22.5.1998*.

Dieckmann, H., Münder, J. and Popp, W. (1986) 'Dauerarbeitslosigkeit und Arbeitshilfen. Aspekte des gesellschaftlichen Umgangs mit der Dauerarbeitslosigkeit am Beispiel der 'Hilfen zur Arbeit' nach dem BSHG – Ergebnisse eines Forschungsvorhabens', *Nachrichtendienst des Deutschen Vereins für öffentliche und private Fürsorge*, vol 66, pp 468-73.

Fuchs, L. (1995) 'Kommunale Beschäftigungsförderung – Ergebnisse einer Umfrage über Hilfe zur Arbeit nach dem BSHG und Arbeitsbeschaffungsmaßnahmen nach dem AFG', in Bundesministerium für Gesundheit (ed) *Hilfe zur Arbeit, Dokumentation der Fachtagung des Bundesministeriums für Familie und Senioren am 23 Juli 1994 in Bonn*, Baden-Baden: Nomos, pp 133-66.

Fuchs, L. (1997) *Kommunale Beschäftigungsförderung – Ergebnisse einer Umfrage von 1997 über Hilfen zur Arbeit nach dem BSHG und Arbeitsbeschaffungsmaßnahmen nach AFG*, Köln: Deutscher Städtetag.

Gebhardt, T., Jacobs, H., Leibfried, S. and Seeleib-Kaiser, M. (1998) *Globalisierung und Sozialpolitik. Der Fall der Sozialhilfe in der Bundesrepublik Deutschland und den USA, DFG-Abschlußbericht, Projekt 'Sozialhilfe und Arbeit: Zwischen 'Standortdiskussion' und Regionalisierung. Nationale politische Thematisierung von Sozial(hilfe)politik in Deutschland und den USA*, Bremen: Centre for Social Policy Research, unpublished manuscript.

Häntsch, U. and Mirbach, T. (1994a) 'Kommunale Beschäftigungsgesellschaften als Instrument zur Bekämpfung von Arbeitslosigkeit und Ausgrenzung', *Zeitschrift für Sozialreform*, vol 40, pp 577-94.

Häntsch, U. and Mirbach, T. (1994b) *Von der Sozialhilfe zum Tariflohn. Eine empirische Begleituntersuchung zur arbeitsmarkt – und sozialpolitischen Wirkung des Arbeitsangebots der Hamburger-Arbeit-Beschäftigungsgesellschaft*, Hamburg: 2a-Verlag.

Hartmann, H. (1998) 'Arbeitslosenhilfe und Sozialhilfe – zwei Systeme für das gleiche soziale Problem?', *Nachrichtendienst des Deutschen Vereins für öffentlich und private Fürsorge*, vol 78, pp 9-12.

Hauser, R. and Voges, W. (1999) *Poverty and poverty policy in Germany*, Bremen: Centre for Social Policy Research, working paper.

Jacobs, H. (1996) *Evaluierung von Maßnahmen der 'Hilfe zur Arbeit' in Bremen*, Frankfurt/M: Deutscher Verein für öffentliche und private Fürsorge.

Kempken, J. and Trube, A. (1997) *Effektivität und Effizienz sozialorientierter Hilfen zur Arbeit. Lokale Analysen aktivierender Sozialhilfe*, Münster: Lit.

Klein, P. (1999) 'Die Auswahl der 'Zieleinheit' Haushalts- oder Bedarfsgemeinschaft', in W. Voges (ed) *Kommunale Sozialberichterstattung*, Opladen: Leske + Budrich.

Krug, W. and Meckes, R. (1997) *Hilfe zur Arbeit – Arbeitspotentialschätzung 1994*, Schriftenreiche des Bundesministeriums für Gesundheit Bd 90, Baden-Baden: Nomos.

Lungfiel, H. and Gelhaar, R. (1998) 'Sozialhilfe in Hamburg 1996/97. Ergebnisse des Benchmarking zur Hilfe zum Lebensunterhalt der 15 größten Städte Deutschlands', Freie und Hansestadt Hamburg. Behörde für Arbeit, Gesundheit und Soziales (ed) *Sozialhilfereport no 13*.

Lüsebrink, K. (1993) 'Arbeit plus Qualifizierung. Kosten-Refinanzierungsrechnung eines anspruchsvollen Instruments aktiver Arbeitsmarktpolitik', *Mitteilungen aus der Arbeitsmarkt – und Berufsforschung*, vol 26, pp 53-62.

Lüsebrink, K. (1994) 'Bewertung fiskalischer Effekte kommunaler Arbeitsmarktpolitik – das Instrument der Kosten-Refinanzierungsrechnung', in M. Schulze-Böing and N. Johrendt (eds) *Wirkungen kommunaler Beschäftigungsprogramme. Methoden, Instrumente und Ergebnisse kommunaler Arbeitsmarktpolitik*, Basel: Birkhäuser, pp 155-65.

Martens, E. (1999) '100,000 Hoffnungen – mehr nicht', *Die Zeit*, no 15/ 1999.

Meendermann, K. (1992) *Die 'Hilfe zur Arbeit'. Zugangschance oder Ausgrenzungsmechanismus*, Münster: Waxmann.

Pilgrim, A. (1990) 'Die Praxis der Sozialhilfeträger bei der 'Hilfe zur Arbeit'. Ergebnisse einer bundesweiten empirischen Untersuchung', *BBJ Consult INFO*, Ausgabe II 1990, pp 2-38.

Priester, T. and Klein, P. (1992) *'Hilfe zur Arbeit', Ein Instrument für die kommunale Arbeitsmarktpolitik?*, Ausburg: Maro.

Reissert, B. (1988) 'Wie Münchhausen aus dem Sumpf? Finanzieren sich kommunale Beschäftigungsinitiativen für arbeitslose Sozialhilfeempfänger selbst', in C. Reis (ed) *Die 'Hilfe zur Arbeit' im Spannungsfeld von Sozialhilfe und lokalen Beschäftigungsinitiativen*, Frankfurt/M Deutscher Verein für öffentliche und private Fürsorge, pp 205-18.

Schaak, T. (1997) 'Die 'Hilfe zur Arbeit' nach dem Bundessozialhilfegesetz', in Behörde für Arbeit, Gesundheit und Soziales der Freien und Hansestadt Hamburg (ed) *Armut in Hamburg II, Beiträge zur Sozialberichterstattung*, pp 78-148.

Schulin, B. (1994) 'Models and instruments for social security', in B. von Maydell, E. M. Hohnerlein (eds) *The transformation of social security systems in central and eastern Europe*, Leuven: Peeters Press, pp 135-76.

Schulte, B. (1988) 'Zur Tradition der Arbeitshilfe in Fürsorge und Sozialhilfe', in C. Reis (ed) *Die 'Hilfe zur Arbeit' im Spannungsfeld von Sozialhilfe und lokalen Beschäftigungsinitiativen*, Frankfurt/M Deutscher Verein für öffentliche und private Fürsorge, pp 57-71.

Seewald, H. (1999) 'Ergebnisse der Sozialhilfe – und Asylbewerberstatistik 1997', *Wirtschaft und Statistik*, No 2/1999, pp 96-110.

Senatsverwaltung für Soziales Berlin (ed) (1992*) Hilfe zur Arbeit. Ein Weg ins Berufsleben für Sozialhilfeempfänger*, Berlin: Senatsverwaltung.

Statistisches Bundesamt (1995) *Statistisches jahrbuch für die Bundesrepublik*, Stuttgart: Metzler-Poeschel.

Tessaring, M. (1994) 'Langristige Tendenzen des Arbeitskräftebedarf nach Tätigkeiten und Qualifikation in den alten Bundesländern bis zum Jahre 2010. Eineerste Aktualisierung der IAB Prognos-Projektionen 1989/ 91', *Mitteilungen aus der Arbeitsmarket und Geufsforschung*, vol 1, pp 5-19.

Tiemann, F. and Markert, S. (1995) 'Wege aus der Sozialhilfe? Eine Evaluationsstudie', in F. Tiemann (ed) *Soziales Europa. Von der Sozialhilfe ins Erwerbsleben*, Bonn: Dümmler, pp 51-92.

Trube, A. (1994) 'Fiskalische und soziale Aspekte kommunaler Arbeitsmarktpolitik. Eine vergleichende Analyse sozioökonomischer Effekte von Arbeitslosigkeit und Beschäftigungsförderung vor Ort', *Arbeit und Sozialpolitik*, vol 48, no 7-8, pp 20-31.

Trube, A. (1997) *Zur Theorie und Empirie des Zweiten Arbeitsmarktes. Exemplarische Erörterungen und praktische Versuche zur sozioökonomischen Bewertung lokaler Beschäftigungsförderung*, Münster: Lit Verlag.

Voges, W. (1998) 'Hilfe zur Arbeit: Vom Instrument sozialer Kontrolle zur Rehabilitationsmaßnahme?', Working paper for the conference 'Hilfe zur Arbeit als Instrument der Sozialpolitik' of the Centre for Social Policy Research, Bremen/Germany and the Government of the Province South Tyrol/Italy on 3.10.1998 in Bozen/Italy.

Voges, W. and Klein, P. (1994) '"Creaming the poor" in Beschäftigungsprogrammen als Ergebnis unsystematischer Ansprache von Adressaten', in M. Schulze-Böing, N. Johrendt (eds) *Wirkungen kommunaler Beschäftigungsprogramme. Methoden, Instrumente und Ergebnisse der Evaluation kommunaler Arbeitsmarktpolitik*, Basel: Birkhäuser, pp 135-53.

Voges, W. and Weber, A. (1997) 'Sozialhilfe im Strukturwandel Auswirkungen von Zuwanderung, Arbeitsmarkt und gewandelten Haushaltsstrukturen', in I. Becker and R. Hauser (eds), *Einkommensverteilung und Armut*, Frankfurt/M Campus, pp 131-59.

Wilk, C. (1997) *Erfolgskriterien von Maßnahmen der Hilfe zur Arbeit. Expertise im Auftrag des Bundesministeriums für Gesundheit*, Baden-Baden: Nomos.

FOUR

Workfare in the Netherlands – young unemployed people and the Jobseeker's Employment Act

Henk Spies and Rik van Berkel

Introduction

Over the last decade the provision of social security in the Netherlands has undergone a paradigmatic shift. The emphasis has moved from protection, through the provision of income and/or services to those who find themselves out of the labour market, to promoting participation through incentives to encourage people to provide for themselves by means of paid work (WRR, 1996; Teulings et al, 1997; van Berkel et al, 1999). The introduction of the Youth Employment Act (YEA), a workfare policy that became operative in 1992, can be seen as a key consequence of this shift. From the time of its introduction, people aged 18-22 who had been unemployed for six months were no longer entitled to a minimum income (a benefit), but rather to minimum job rights. In 1998 the YEA was merged with previously non-compulsory training and employment programmes for older long-term unemployed people through the Jobseeker's Employment Act (JEA). The results of this development are twofold. On the one hand, a workfare policy has been broadened out to include a wider range of recipients. On the other hand, the form of the policy has changed from 'workfare' to a broader form of 'activity fare'. That is, elements that fall under the umbrella of the JEA include subsidised work and training, but also unpaid work activities (notably voluntary work). While the JEA has two main target groups: unemployed people aged under 23, and long-term unemployed people aged over 23, young people remain the major focus. The JEA does not apply to physically and/or mentally disabled people, for whom a separate employment programme exists. Mothers with children under five are not required to be available for work or to participate in the JEA. However, mothers are increasingly being stimulated to enter JEA, with part-time work and nursery placements being made available.

The policy's stated aims are:

> ... to stimulate long-term unemployed people, and especially the young, to participate in activities that promote entry into the labour market and prevent social exclusion. (Jobseeker's Employment Act, Preliminary Considerations)

For young unemployed people the JEA is a generic policy measure. Participation is compulsory for all. The government has committed itself to supplying sufficient subsidised employment and training opportunities. As applied to long-term unemployed people, however, workfare is discretionary and, currently, participation is enforced less rigorously. For older people inclusion depends, on the one hand, on the availability of state-subsidised employment and training opportunities, and, on the other, on an assessment of the situation of each individual. In terms of future direction, the selective nature of the JEA, as applied to older age groups, is set to disappear. Within the next five years the national government has stated its intention to generate enough employment and training opportunities for *all* (younger and older) newly-unemployed people. Whether economic and budgetary conditions will allow this ambition to be realised, remains to be seen. Nonetheless, some of the distinction between old and young will be retained. Young people will continue to be activated through the JEA after six months, whereas older people will wait for 12 months (*Sociale Nota*, 1999). Another distinction may be the length of activation periods. For young unemployed people participation only ends when they reach the age of 23, whereas for older unemployed people it is not yet clear what happens after they finish a scheme.

Workfare emerged in the Netherlands in the context of growing unemployment, as a result of economic crises in the 1970s and the early 1980s, and as a result of a process of economic restructuring. The structure of the unemployed population changed as it became increasingly made up of young and long-term unemployed people. In this context the government pursued a macroeconomic policy which increasingly focused on decreasing the public sector deficit. In the field of social security this led to cutbacks in benefit levels and to measures aimed at limiting the number of recipients. Workfare, however, was developed somewhat independently of the general policy of cutting back social security expenditure. Although it can be viewed as economically motivated, as an attempt to make social security more efficient in the sense of stimulating outflow into employment, ideological developments are as important as economic circumstances in understanding this specific strand of welfare reform.

This chapter begins by providing an overview of social security provision in the Netherlands. The focus then shifts to economic developments and their impact on unemployment and macroeconomic policy. Ideological developments are traced as a backdrop to developments in workfare policy. As workfare is a form of labour market policy as well as part of social security, the context of labour market policies that surround the JEA are outlined. With the contextual sketch in place, the JEA is presented in some detail. The options and schemes available are discussed in terms of their 'workfareness'. Administrative arrangements and funding issues are outlined, along with recent administrative developments and management tools intended to assist policy implementation. The chapter concludes with an overview of research findings and themes that emerge from these, including the persistent problem of 'drop-out'.

Social security provision in the Netherlands

Social assistance provides a complement to unemployment insurance. Unemployment insurance is partly funded through contributions, and confers to an entitlement of a maximum of 70% of a previous wage in case of involuntary unemployment. The system of unemployment insurance was developed at the beginning of the twentieth century by trade unions. In 1907 the city of Amsterdam started subsidising the unemployment funds of the trade unions, which provided an important impetus for the growth of unemployment insurance. In 1916, when unemployment reached new heights as a consequence of the First World War, this became national policy (de Rooij, 1979).

There are two important entry requirements for unemployment insurance. First, claimants must have worked for 26 of the previous 39 weeks. Second, they should have worked in four of the last five years. The maximum duration for receipt of this wage-related benefit is five years, with the period of receipt being dependent on the number of years worked. The right to unemployment insurance is conditional on not becoming unemployed through one's own fault or volition, on looking actively for work, and on accepting 'suitable' employment offers (Unemployment Act – WW, Article 24).

Social assistance, on the other hand, constitutes a citizenship-based, state-guaranteed subsistence level. The first Poor Law in the Netherlands dates from 1854. It stated that the government would provide relief in case charity failed to do so. In the 1880s traditional charity and poor relief were reformed. Support was only given after a thorough investigation and the poor were compelled to be self-supporting as much as possible (de Rooij, 1979). The 1920s saw the introduction of the *steun* (support) system, which reformed poor relief further in the direction of unemployment insurance. In its emphasis on control it nevertheless resembled old-fashioned poor relief.

Modern social assistance came into being in 1965, when the General Social Assistance Law (*Algemene Bijstandswet* – ABW) was passed through parliament and was revised again in 1996. The ABW states that local government has the obligation to provide for its inhabitants where they cannot provide for themselves. The purpose of social assistance is 'to enable recipients to provide for themselves' (ABW, Article 111). It is conditional on being available for work. More specifically, Article 112 of the ABW states that recipients must:

- actively look for work;
- register as unemployed with the Employment Office;
- accept a suitable job;
- refrain from anything that prevents insertion into the work process;
- respond to calls concerning work;
- cooperate with investigations into means of insertion into the work process, or suitability for schooling or education; and
- attend schooling or education considered necessary to promote capacity to be self-providing.

The level of social assistance for single people is half of the minimum wage; for single parents it is 70%. A bonus for housing costs (normally worth about 20% of the minimum wage) is additionally available to both groups. Families receive benefit to the value of the whole minimum wage.

Insurance benefits have also always been conditional in the sense that recipients have to be available for work (except when this is not possible for medical or social reasons, as judged by delivering agencies). Conditionality has increased over the last decade, but markedly so for social assistance recipients. This has happened largely within the boundaries of existing legislation, through stricter application of rules. However, it is also reflected in changes in legislation; for example, in the way the requirement 'to accept a suitable job' is operationalised.

In the 1980s, only a job that matched the qualifications of the unemployed person was considered suitable, but this is no longer the case. For school leavers, including those who have completed professional or academic education, *any* job that pays the minimum wage is now considered to be suitable. In addition, qualifications are now considered to lose their value over time, so that someone who previously worked as a professional or an academic, now has to take unskilled work after two years of unemployment. Finally, *created employment* has come to be considered suitable employment, opening the way for workfare through enforced participation.

Economic developments and unemployment

Between 1970 and 1985 employment growth stagnation was triggered by economic strain arising from the two oil crises of 1973 and 1979. At the same time women were entering the labour market in increased numbers and the working population grew (WRR, 1996). The result was extensive unemployment in the early 1980s. Between 1980 and 1984 unemployment figures more than doubled, from 260,000 to 550,000 registered unemployed people (SCP, 1992). Youth unemployment, especially, reached unprecedented levels. Two fifths of all registered unemployed people were between the ages of 16 and 24. This exceptional growth in youth unemployment was probably because those who most recently entered employment were most likely to be the first to be dismissed when redundancies were necessary. As a result, economic fluctuations affected the employment chances for young people more than for others.

Since the mid-1980s, economic conditions have improved. The explanations most commonly given for economic recovery and falling unemployment are that there have been very moderate rises in wages and a pronounced increase in the amount of part-time working. Approximately 38% of all jobs in the Netherlands are part-time jobs, compared to 16% in Germany and France (Ministry of Social Affairs and Employment, 1998). GDP and employment are growing faster than average in the European Union (EU) and inflation is under control. Per capita GDP has grown from 7700 Euros in 1980, to 14,800 Euros in 1990, to 19,500 Euros in 1996 (*Sociale Nota*, 1998). In 1997, GDP increased by a further 3.3%. Between 1985 and 1994, GDP in the Netherlands increased, on average, by 2.4% annually as against 2.3% in the EU as a whole.

Employment has also grown strongly – at a rate of one and a half percentage points per year between 1985 and 1994 – putting Dutch employment growth on a par with growth in the US (SCP, 1996). Correspondingly, unemployment has decreased. In 1994 the unemployment rate was 7.5% (7.1% according to OECD assessments), subsequently falling to 5.75% in 1997 (5.2% by OECD measurements). Youth unemployment levels also decreased (gradually approaching unemployment levels for other groups), falling from 11.1% of the population between 15 and 24 years of age in 1994 to 6.2% in 1997. By comparison, over the same period average levels of unemployment in the EU decreased only slightly, from 11.1% to 10.6% (data; cited in *Sociale Nota*, OECD, 1999). The government's own unemployment figures put the number of unemployed at 270,000 between May and June 1998. This represents a fall of some 9,000 unemployed people a month between mid-1997 and mid-1998. Unemployment figures on the last quarter of 1998, however, suggest that the decrease of unemployment is starting to slow down (CBS, http://www.cbs.nl).

Despite the fall in unemployment generally, long-term unemployment has remained at a persistently high level. In contrast to youth unemployment, long-term unemployment appears to show little response to economic fluctuations and has remained more or less stable since 1983 (de Beer, 1997). Approximately half of all unemployed people have been unemployed for more than one year. This persistence is commonly explained as a result of a growing structural mismatch between available job opportunities and the ambitions and qualifications of a large proportion of people in this group. In part, it may also be the result of demoralising effects of unemployment on individuals. People with low levels of education, and particularly migrants, are over-represented among the long-term unemployed.

There is no doubt that the structure of employment in the Netherlands has changed, characterised by a shift towards a 'post-industrial' labour market (SCP, 1996). The share of total employment accounted for by 'traditional' employment sectors – such as agriculture, industry and transport – has diminished from three fifths (60%) in 1960 to one third (35%) in 1994. Correspondingly, commercial services including trade, hotel and catering, banking and insurance have expanded up to 30% of total employment in 1994 as compared to 21% in 1960. The share of non-commercial services increased from 19% in 1960 to 34% in 1994. Highly skilled work (scientific and other professional work, executive and managerial functions) now makes up a quarter of all employment (SCP, 1996). As the trend continues, the demand for technically skilled workers continues to decrease, and the demand for people with administrative, commercial or health care qualifications grows.

The lower, unskilled end of the labour market can be defined as consisting of traditional manual labour, low paid flexible employment and part-time work in the service sector. The size of this labour market has been fairly stable since 1980. However, even this labour market has seen a shift in emphasis, with an increase in the importance of 'flexiwork' and part-time work (mostly in the trade and catering industries) and a decrease in traditional manual labour jobs. Flexible working conditions are not usually associated with high quality working conditions. Earnings are uncertain and often insufficient to feed a family, and the existence of poverty traps in the social security system means that they offer little financial gain. The result is that these jobs lack appeal for unemployed people (de Beer, 1997; Beukema and Valkenburg, 1999). Part-time jobs in the service sector generally offer somewhat better prospects for improvement in earnings or qualifications in the long term. However, the evidence is that employers prefer to hire newcomers and people re-entering the labour market, for example, after a period of looking after children, rather than to hire long-term unemployed people (van Beek, 1993; de Beer, 1997).

Developments in macroeconomic policy

Since the end of the 1970s, successive governments have concerned themselves with the aim of decreasing the size of the public sector deficit, and interest payments have long been the most important item on the national budget. In this they have been relatively successful. Between 1993 and 1998 public expenditure decreased from 52.2% to 48.7% as a percentage of GDP (OECD 1998). The Netherlands was one of the first countries to meet requirements for entry into the European Monetary Union.

In order to achieve this, cuts have been made in expenditure on social security and health services. Measures that were taken included raising the entry requirements for social insurance. For example, claimants become eligible for unemployment insurance only after having worked in four out of five years, instead of three out of five, and having worked in 26 out of 39 weeks preceding unemployment, instead of 26 out of 52. Benefit levels have been cut back. For example, unemployment insurance confers to 70% of the last wage instead of 80%, and the level of social assistance benefits has been fixed, rather than index-linked to increases in average wages. Moreover, agencies that deliver the policy and the development of 'activation' policies have been privatised to stimulate outflow from social assistance and social insurance into work.

Expenditure on social security as a percentage of GDP decreased from 26.9% in 1993 to 23.5% in 1997 (*Sociale Nota*, 1999, p 157). Only one seventh of this expenditure (3.5% of total GDP) is spent on unemployment related benefits (Table 4.1). In contrast to most other European countries, expenditure on disablement pensions is relatively high (SCP, 1996, p 166). One possible reason for this is that the Disablement Act has been used as an 'opting-out' scheme for older workers who became redundant during the economic recession of the 1970s and 1980s (WRR, 1990; SCP, 1998). In contrast to insurance-based unemployment benefits, insurance-based disability pensions used to be allocated for an indeterminate period of time. In many cases this prevented older workers from falling into poverty or into reliance on means-tested social assistance at the end of their working lives.

Ideological shifts

The policy reaction to the growth of unemployment in the 1970s and 1980s can be characterised as an attempt to decrease labour force participation and to redistribute unemployment. Young people were stimulated to stay in the educational system for a longer period of time, thereby increasing their qualifications. Unemployed people aged 57.5 and over were no longer required to be available for work. Older workers were stimulated to retire early through the introduction of early retirement schemes, in order to make way for younger workers (SCP, 1998). The beginning of the 1990s, however, produced a paradigmatic shift in unemployment policies (Teulings et al, 1997; van Berkel et al, 1999). Increasingly social security provision aims at stimulating people to provide for themselves by means of paid work. Instead of focusing on protection, policy now focuses on promoting participation in paid work for all groups.

This shift is to be explained by ideological rather than economic developments.

Back to full employment

An increase of the proportion of the population participating in paid work came to be seen as necessary for maintaining the social security arrangements of the welfare state. In an influential report, the Dutch Scientific Council for Government Policy argued for a reappraisal of work (WRR, 1990). Drawing on Durkheim's classic analysis of the division of labour in society (Durkheim, 1965 [1893]), the Council considered work to be the only institution that could still create solidarity and prevent societal disintegration. Also, drawing on Jahoda's classical study of unemployed people in Marienthal (Jahoda et al, 1933), the Council emphasised the meaningful nature of work for individuals. Increasing the proportion of the population participating in paid work came to be seen as a desirable and *feasible* target. '*Work, Work, Work*' has become a dominant policy slogan and has gained widespread political support. In their campaign for the 1998 elections, all major political parties emphasised the importance of job creation.

Discovery of 'the calculating unemployed'

Over the past 10 years, the concept of the 'calculating unemployed' has begun to manifest itself in influential Dutch research reports investigating the world of long-term unemployed people (Engbersen, 1990; Engbersen et al, 1993). With reference to the work of the US commentator Charles Murray, and on the basis of research on unemployed people, Engbersen developed a typology of Dutch unemployed people, which features the 'calculating unemployed' as a distinct category. These are defined as citizens who are considered to have made a rational decision to remain or become dependent on benefit. Although these calculating unemployed people made up only one fifth of a research population (whole population= 221 long-term unemployed people), the problem of the calculating unemployed subsequently came to dominate public and political debates. The image of *homo economicus* is convenient and encouraging to policy makers, as it suggests that people's behaviour can be easily influenced through financial incentives and disincentives.

The result has been an increased perception of unemployed people as 'undeserving' (Oude Engberink, 1993). Control and surveillance of unemployed people has intensified, and preventing and combating fraud has become a priority in the delivery of welfare. This is exemplified by the introduction of a law regulating fines and penalties (*wet boeten en maatregelen*) in 1997, making it easier for local social services to sanction clients who do not (fully) cooperate, as well as for national government to force agencies to sanction such clients.

An activating labour market policy

In 1987 the Dutch Scientific Council for Government Policy argued for an activating labour market policy (WRR, 1987). The underlying contention behind this policy recommendation was that social policy in the Netherlands had focused too much on 'care' when it should have been offering opportunities for self-sufficiency. Thus, dependency has been stimulated. Through activation, the Council believes that unemployed men and women can be assisted to re-enter the labour market. An extension of opportunities should be complemented with firmer surveillance and tougher benefit sanctions, with individuals being held explicitly co-responsible for their underprivileged status.

Dutch activating labour market policies can be viewed as a mix of Scandinavian and Anglo-Saxon ideas. Therborn (1986) propagates a Scandinavian model, based on an institutional commitment to full employment and an active use of government money (on education, training and employment projects) instead of a passive use (on unemployment benefits). Mead's (1986) emphasis on the obligations of unemployed citizens and the implicit assumption that unemployed people are at least partly to blame for their status have been influential in Anglo-Saxon debates. The mix of these ideas in the Netherlands resulted not in an *active* labour market policy, that focuses on institutions, but in an *activating* labour market policy that focuses on unemployed individuals. Social policy of the last 10 years can to a large extent be interpreted as the process of bringing about activating labour market policies.

The re-emergence of 'poverty'

After having been absent from political and public debate for some 10 years, 'poverty' has re-emerged as an important policy topic (Engbersen et al, 1996, 1997). Under Christian Democrat–Social Democrat administrations, cut backs in social security expenditure have, to a large extent, been achieved through a lowering of the real level of social assistance benefits by not raising them in line with average wage rises (SCP, 1998). In addition, for many people the insurance system no longer provides a benefit with an income above subsistence level (Vlek, 1999). The result has been that more people have become dependent on a minimum benefit, and that the level of this minimum has been relatively lowered (Oude Engberink and Post, 1994).

Two years after the new 'purple' coalition government[1] of Social Democrats, Liberals and Social Liberals, came into office in 1994, the Ministry of Social Affairs and Employment started funding research into poverty. The results of this poverty monitor indicate that 11% of all households have an income under or only slightly over (up to 105%) the level of a social assistance benefit, which is taken to be the poverty line (SCP and CBS, 1998). The policy response has tended to occur in the form of marginal, indirect and one-off measures; for example, a cold weather bonus to compensate for extra heating expenses, and extension of possibilities to remit local taxes. While such anti-poverty policy measures have certainly been meaningful to those affected, they have not had any significant impact on the amounts which welfare claimants in general receive.

Developments in labour market policy

With the goal of increasing work participation, a general policy of deregulation of the labour market has been pursued and the national government has stimulated trade unions and employers to create more entry level jobs. While this is intended to open up opportunities for unemployed people, it has also reduced the security of those in employment. Another measure that had consequences for employment in the retail industry was the extension of the legal length of opening hours in 1997. The extension of opening hours called for more flexibility in working hours.

The Flexibility and Security Act was passed in January 1999 to limit insecurity resulting from deregulation. This act aims both to increase flexibility in labour relations *and* to strengthen legal coverage of 'flexiworkers'. The most important points of this act are: the introduction of a labour contract where necessary to clarify labour relations; stand-by workers to be paid for at least three hours work; shorter probation periods for short contracts; automatic fixed term contracts where short contracts are repeated three times; and a full labour contract after 26 weeks of employment. In return for this general strengthening of legal coverage of flexiworkers, the employer's period of notice is shortened to between one and four months, depending on the duration of the contract.

In addition to stimulating flexibility in regular employment, there have been a number of subsidised and created employment initiatives which specifically aim to stimulate the participation of unemployed groups. In 1997, approximately 180,000 people worked in subsidised jobs, making up 3% of the working population (SCP, 1998). These included people working in a programme of sheltered employment for disabled people.

Prior to the introduction of the JEA, the most important employment and training initiatives for unemployed people included:

• *Reducing income tax payments and social insurance contributions for employers hiring long-term unemployed people* (unemployed for more than 12 months). This has resulted in lowered wage costs for the provision of low-paid work. This policy was introduced in 1996, but was preceded by similar policy measures in existence since 1986.
• *Creating regular jobs in the public sector for long-term unemployed people.* This has been especially important in public security, health care, childcare, education and social services. Between 1994 (the start of the programme) and the end of 1998 some 40,000 extra jobs had been created in this way.
• *Creating temporarily subsidised jobs for long-term unemployed people.* This has been especially important in providing subsidised work in the private sector. Jobs are created using money that would otherwise have been spent on benefits. The maximum time limit for subsidised employment is two years. Some 22,000 such jobs have been created between 1994 (the start of the programme) and 1998.
• *Creating subsidised 'Jobpool' employment in the public sector for very long-term unemployed people* (more than three years) since 1990. These people are considered to have no chances of finding regular employment, and are not considered eligible to participate in the employment programmes listed above. In 1997, some 23,500 jobs of this type were created.
• *A Youth Employment Scheme,* initiated in 1991. This involved the creation of supplementary, subsidised employment for young unemployed people. In 1992 this scheme came to replace traditional social assistance for young unemployed people. In 1997, some 21,000 young unemployed people participated in this scheme.
• *Social Activation.* Since 1996, municipalities have been permitted to set up programmes of unpaid activities. In most cases participation in these programmes is voluntary, but some municipalities experiment

with obligatory participation. The intention is to prevent and combat isolation and 'social exclusion' and, in doing so, to simultaneously promote individuals' emotional and social well-being and provide a first step towards future labour market participation.

The government accepts that subsidised employment will, to a limited extent, replace regular work. Because the insertion into the labour market of unemployed people – especially young people – is considered essential, such substitution is tolerated. However, five safeguards exist to minimise this substitution (article 6 of the JEA):

1. Secondments are open to employers in all sectors (so as not to favour one economic sector over another).
2. The number of secondments per company or agency is limited to a maximum of 10% of all employees.
3. Secondment is not permitted where a regular employee doing the same work has recently been fired.
4. Employers need approval from the Works Council to take people on secondment.
5. Local government has to stipulate a compensation for work on secondment that is high enough not to influence competition to an unacceptable degree.

The Jobseeker's Employment Act (JEA)

The schemes listed above now make up the principal schemes which exist within the overall JEA programme. It is useful to distinguish between them as they vary in two respects with regard to what might be called their 'workfareness': first, the type of activity required (the 'work'-ness) and, second, the degree of obligation (the 'fare'-ness).

Each new JEA entrant is supposed to receive an assessment. This assessment is a joint responsibility of local government (which often delegates this responsibility to social services and employment organisations) and employment offices (which operate more or less autonomously in relation to local government). In practice, several agencies are involved in assessing (potential) participants, and it is often not clear how responsibilities are divided between these agencies. This can result in clients being assessed several times, by different agencies and with different results. Also, differences exist between municipalities, as decentralisation of responsibilities to local governments is an important feature of the JEA.

The assessment interview is carried out to determine whether it is likely that a client will find regular employment or education by him or herself, with a little help, or whether it is unlikely that he/she will find employment within a reasonable amount of time. The objective of the interview is to determine an appropriate route to work. If that is unrealistic then a route to social activation is sought. Where it is considered unlikely that employment will be found within a reasonable amount of time, a more extensive assessment interview takes place at short notice. The period between entering the JEA Programme and the actual start of a scheme is flexible, but ultimately one year after becoming unemployed a route has to be determined, regardless of whether the individual had initially been considered capable of finding work by themselves. Individuals are consulted in the process of determining a route. Agreements are documented in a written plan.

In principle, a scheme consisting of subsidised work and/or training and social activation is available to every young unemployed person. Presently, the participation of older, long-term unemployed people is selective, as the number of schemes available is limited. Selection criteria are unspecified, but it is likely that clients who are keen to participate are more likely to be included (Lipsky, 1980).

Participation is compulsory. For young people, the right to social assistance beyond six months is limited to the time it takes to find a subsidised employment opportunity. After this, participants receive a wage. The only exception to this is for people offered a 'training and social activation' placement. In this case the right to a benefit remains on condition that the individual complies with the scheme. For long-term unemployed people aged 23 or over the scheme becomes obligatory once it has been offered.

Sanctions underpin obligation. A person who refuses to participate, or who drops out of a JEA scheme for illegitimate reasons (for example, through dismissal for regularly showing up late or not at all, or not fulfilling assigned tasks) may be sanctioned by withdrawal of the right to a benefit for a period of one month. After this period a person may have their entitlement to benefit renewed if they are considered to be cooperating. In practice, this 'ultimate' sanction of withdrawing the right to a benefit is often preceded by several warnings and minor sanctions. For example, a person who shows up late may be sanctioned by deducting a corresponding part of the wage or benefit.

Figure 4.1: Trajectories within the Jobseeker's Employment Act

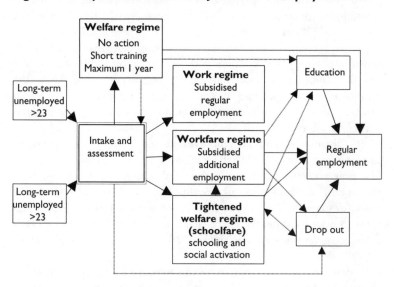

Three principal schemes are available: subsidised employment with a regular employer in the profit or non-profit sectors; subsidised employment with a municipal employment organisation; and/or training and social activation. The schemes are designed as single pathways, but may be combined. So, for instance, it is possible to work in a subsidised job for two days a week and attend training for another two days. Alternatively, placements may follow on from one another. For instance, a person may start a social activation scheme in order to overcome functioning problems (such as being on time, keeping appointments, dealing with authorities) and follow on with a subsidised employment placement (Figure 4.1).

Subsidised employment with a regular employer

Local governments are able to create work experience opportunities with regular employers. The national government provides such employers with a budget of 17,000 guilders (7,600 Euros) per participant per year as an incentive to offer work experience placements. The budget can be used to compensate for the potentially low productivity of the employee, as a contribution towards labour costs, or to finance coaching and support or education. Funding is limited to a period of two years.

The (formerly) unemployed people who participate in this form of subsidised work have a contract with the employer which lasts for at least six months. Their conditions of employment are regulated through collective agreements in the sector. Generally, participants work part-time for 32 hours a week, although there is variation, for example in the case of a single parent with children. Pay is generally a little above the minimum wage (depending on the collective agreement). Going from welfare to this form of subsidised work in most cases considerably improves participants' incomes.

This form of subsidised employment was not available to young unemployed people under the earlier Youth Employment Scheme. However, with the expansion of the Youth Employment Act into JEA, this option was opened to all. Evaluations which consider subsidised work for older people indicate that this option can provide a successful route to work for those who participate. On a yearly basis the chances of finding regular employment are 50-70% (Gravesteijn-Lighthelm et al, 1998).

Due to the relatively high cost of this subsidised work (in comparison to training) this scheme has been less used in recent years. A comparable employment project, specifically aimed at creating subsidised employment in the private sector, has come into existence more recently and has now been incorporated into the JEA scheme. National government provides funding for 20,000 subsidised jobs in the private sector.

Subsidised employment with municipal employment organisations

The official purpose of created municipal work is to provide employment experience and to help people find regular employment. However, while such outflow into regular employment is considered desirable, it is accepted that, for some, this form of subsidised employment is an 'end station'. For young unemployed people this kind of employment ends when they reach the age of 23 at which stage they return to a traditional welfare regime; for older people there is no limit to the duration of municipal work.

The participant has a labour contract with the municipal employment organisation and is placed on secondment with a regular employer in the public or private sector. Typical jobs include: school caretaker; sorting files for government agencies; clearing stables at the zoos; maintenance work at marine barracks, schools and community centres; maintenance of green areas; and assisting in workshops, garages or construction sites.

Going from welfare to subsidised employment with a municipal employment organisation is, generally, more beneficial to younger participants than to older unemployed people. A 20-year-old living alone might expect an increase in income by a factor of three. In contrast, the income of a family breadwinner might be expected not to improve at all. Contracts are, in principle, for 32 hours a week, and pay is at the level of the minimum wage. This adds up to 1,435 guilders (650 Euros) a month for those aged over 23 and who live alone, and 772 guilders (350 Euros) for 18-year-olds who live alone. For older unemployed people, who are unlikely to move into the regular labour market, pay can be increased to up to 120% of the minimum wage. It is possible to vary the number of working hours; for example, when an individual needs to work more than 32 hours a week to be lifted out of the welfare system, or when the care for a young child or a disabled person prevents individuals from working the standard 32 hours.

Young unemployed people are able to attend training courses within contract hours as long as their actual working time is at least 19 hours a week. Training is permitted where it contributes to the individual's functioning at work, and/or improves their chances of finding regular employment. Decisions regarding whether a particular training programme meets these criteria are taken by the municipal employment organisation. Attending regular secondary education is not permitted, as this is accessed through a separate system of scholarships.

Nationally, some 50,000 unemployed people participate in this kind of employment scheme. About 21,000 of these are young unemployed people. As in the option of subsidised employment with regular employers outlined above, local governments, again, have a budget of 17,000 guilders (7,600 Euros) per participant per year at their disposal to realise this form of subsidised employment.

Training and social activation

Individuals who take up training or social activation placements remain on welfare. Their income is generally somewhat below the income level of individuals in subsidised employment. For young unemployed people it is well below this level, in line with the very low level of social assistance benefits for this age group. Again, the purpose of training is to help the individual find regular employment or, if that is not realistic, to enable the individual to enter subsidised employment. Again, regular education (leading to a certificate) is not possible within this option as regular education scholarships are available.

Training and social activation is mainly intended for people who are not ready for employment because of personal factors or for whom training is the best way of improving their chances in the labour market. An example of this would be the provision of Dutch language training to new immigrants. Care programmes are also available for people with, for instance, drug-abuse-related or other personal problems. The only prerequisite for a care programme is that an exact plan is clearly recorded.

Approximately 3,000 young unemployed people participated in these kind of schemes at the end of 1996. It is anticipated that in the near future some 6,000 will participate in care programmes. For long-term unemployed people, experiments with social activation were introduced in 1996. Approximately 4,000, mostly very long-term unemployed people, participate in these experiments.

The JEA as workfare?

From the point of view of an unemployed client, the different schemes within the JEA constitute different regimes, as each scheme constitutes a different set of rights and obligations. Three regimes can be said to exist within the JEA, on a continuum from welfare to work (see Figure 4.1). The first – subsidised employment with a regular employer – can be considered to comprise a work regime. The second – subsidised employment with a municipal agency – comprises a workfare regime. The third – training and social activation – comprises a (tightened) welfare regime.

Young unemployed people who participate in subsidised employment with a municipal agency and who are sent on secondment can be regarded as making up the workfare core of the JEA. It is for this group that welfare, in the sense of an entitlement to a minimum income, has been most rigorously replaced by workfare, in the sense of a (government-created) job.

For participants working in subsidised employment with regular employers, the rights and obligations they experience do not differ from those of any other worker in the sector. They are regulated in a contract of employment that is based on a collective agreement between employers and trade unions. Those who work with a regular employer can therefore be considered to be part of the working population, to whom a 'normal' work regime applies. They have the same security of employment (protection against dismissal) as other workers. If they were to lose their job they have the same right to social security provisions as other employees or, in case of voluntary unemployment, they would be excluded from this right like anybody else.

The rights and obligations of those who have a contract of employment with a municipal agency and are sent on secondment differ significantly from those of regular workers. In many respects (conditions of employment, earnings, content of work) their jobs can be considered to be 'second rate'. Moreover, their work consists inherently of partly superfluous activities (at least in an economic sense) because their activities are permitted to replace regular work only to a very limited degree. This form of subsidised employment constitutes a form of social security. It is radically different from traditional welfare because of the requirement that one has to work rather than merely be willing to work. It can clearly be labelled 'workfare'.

People who participate in training or social activation continue to receive a benefit. With regard to this option, it seems to be necessary to distinguish between the two target groups of the JEA. For young unemployed people, participation in training and social activation schemes is strictly compulsory whereas for long-term unemployed people, to date, participation in social activation experiments has been largely voluntary. (While possibilities for more obligatory social activation activities exist for older people, as yet these have rarely been put into practice.) For young people, participation in training and social activation schemes can be said to imply a tightened welfare regime. It could be argued that the requirement to participate in training or social activation activities distinguishes this regime from workfare as much as from traditional welfare, so that 'schoolfare' could be a more appropriate term. For long-term unemployed people, a more traditional welfare regime continues to exist.

Funding and implementation

Nationally, some 900 million Euros (approximately 1.98 billion guilders) are spent on JEA schemes, which amounts to 6.8% of total expenditure on social assistance and 1.2% of total expenditure on social security. In 1997 some 230 million Euros (approximately 0.5 billion guilders) were spent on the YEA (the workfare scheme for young unemployed people that has since been incorporated into the JEA). This is equal to some 2% of total expenditure on social assistance, and only 0.3% of total expenditure on social security (including the social insurances). Total expenditure on young unemployed people is actually two to three times higher than the total expenditure on JEA schemes for young people because a large proportion of potential clients still do not actually participate in the programme and receive unemployment benefit (Spies, 1994; Angenent and den Hesten, 1998).

The responsibility for employment policies within the JEA has been partly transferred from national to local government, allowing more flexibility and policies to be tailored to the local context. The national government checks only whether the local delivery of the JEA is in accordance with the law, and whether the use of discretionary responsibilities stays within legal boundaries. Municipalities have a 'work fund', subsidised by the national government, which provides them with the financial means to coordinate the various agencies involved in the delivery of the JEA. These include employment offices, social services, municipal employment organisations and training facilities.

Cooperation between social services and employment offices has not been optimal, especially with regard to the 'hard core' of unemployed people. Employment offices generally concentrate on the better qualified unemployed people because they hope that, by referring the most qualified unemployed people to employers, every now and then these employers may be inclined to also take on someone less qualified (the hard core unemployed). Social services, on the other hand, cannot give up on the hard core unemployed as easily (if only for legal reasons). Nonetheless, they cannot offer subsidised placements by themselves, and so need the cooperation of other agencies, most notably the employment offices.

Cooperation is likely to be further stimulated by the projected development of Centres for Work and Income in the year 2000. Income provision and (re)integration into employment have traditionally existed as separate tasks for separate institutions. In these Centres for Work and Income, clients will receive a single counter service for all matters concerning benefits and activities to improve their chances of finding employment. By legally determining that social services and employment offices have to cooperate behind the same counters within the same centres, it is hoped that cooperation will improve with regard to the harder to employ population. As yet it is unclear whether this policy will succeed. In many regions there is still only limited commitment to cooperation, so that for some time to come cooperation between employment offices and social services will probably improve only slowly.

Since responsibilities are decentralised to local governments, differences in delivery exist between municipalities. Two policy instruments are being developed to limit these local differences. First, a 'measuring rod' is used to categorise unemployed people with regard to their 'distance to the labour market'. Second, a computerised information system containing information regarding the historical backgrounds of clients is being developed. These instruments are to be used by all organisations in the field of work and income provision (employment offices, social services, social insurances agencies, municipal employment organisations).

The 'measuring rod' is used with newly unemployed people and is intended to help determine what provisions are necessary to insert the client into the labour process. Criteria include education, work experience, age, unemployment history, social skills, motivation/flexibility, mobility, preferred occupation, hindrances for taking up employment and the condition of the labour market. Clients are distinguished as belonging to four categories or, to use the official term, 'phases':

1   people who are likely to find work without any help;
2   people who, with a short spell of training, will have good chances of finding employment;
3   people who, with intensive coaching and training, will have a chance to find employment;
4   people who are not likely to find employment.

Persons in categories three and four are considered to make up the core JEA target group. Clients in category two might be referred to the employment office for short training courses.

By describing these categories as 'phases' policy makers imply a process of (upward) movement between categories. This conceptualisation is underpinned by a technocratic understanding of the problems of unemployed people and the means by which they might be overcome. The implicit idea is that people who are in category four may be moved up through the categories, by means of, for example, social skills training, then intervention to improve knowledge, then further intervention to help with jobseeking, then guidance about how to secure a job, and finally through finding primary employment. Little research is available about the existence, or lack of existence, of such a process of movement through the categories.

Monitoring and research

Policy monitoring is important in order both to measure the output of the policy and to provide lessons from experience. The JEA can be seen as an attempt to address several important problems: persistent long-term unemployment; the inadequacy of traditional welfare provision in combating societal segmentation; the disconnected nature of specific employment schemes for different target groups; the tension between national regulations and differing local contexts; the defective cooperation of delivering agencies; and last, but not least, the supposed incompetence and supposed lack of social morality of unemployed people. In order to learn how far the JEA succeeds in addressing these problems, monitoring and research are necessary.

The primary source of information for monitoring the delivery and effects of the JEA is the information gathered for monitoring the legitimacy and efficacy of the delivery. Such material includes the annual reports of the delivering agencies. In addition to this administrative information, data on individual participants collected by delivering agencies is made available at the national level. The aim is to develop a systematic, periodical procedure for collating information which allows statistical tracking of individuals over time.

A comparison of the research evidence demonstrates that workfare is not an adequate route to employment for everyone, and that there is a serious drop-out problem. In 1996, 54% of all YEA scheme leavers left because they found regular employment. An additional 8% went back to school or regular education. A quarter dropped out and consequently lost their right to a benefit. The rest (13%) left for other reasons, including moving home and no longer belonging to the target group (Verkaik et al, 1998).

Drop-outs from YEA (and now JEA) schemes face a serious risk of severe marginalisation, being left totally to their own resources for survival. This risk can be considered to be even more serious given that those who drop out generally have more problematic social backgrounds than other participants (Spies, 1996). Research (Spies, 1996) suggests that about half of those who drop out come from single-parent families, and from families which are headed by parents who are, themselves, unemployed or disabled. In addition, a large proportion of young people who drop out from such schemes describe very problematic relations with their parents. This leaves them in a vulnerable position, which explains why so many of them (approximately 40%) have been in contact with institutions for welfare assistance and so many (again, approximately 40%) have run into trouble with the police. As the social support networks of these young unemployed are in themselves very vulnerable, it is highly questionable whether, and for how long, they can be counted on to provide subsistence. Interviews with some drop-outs revealed that they had intensified their criminal activities in order to provide for themselves after being excluded from the right to an income. It seems that too rigorous application of a workfare regime can have a counterproductive effect, in terms of reducing social exclusion. For some groups, policy may have to settle on the less ambitious aim of preventing further exclusion and marginalisation.

Research on young unemployed people suggests that selection for schemes reflects the prior social backgrounds of young unemployed people, probably as a result of a process of 'creaming' (Spies, 1996, 1998). Research on employment programmes that preceded the JEA suggests that institutional interests play a significant role in determining what scheme is offered to whom (Engbersen, 1990; see also Lipsky, 1980; Harmon, 1995). In general, all public institutions, to a greater or lesser extent, select their clients on the basis of how cooperative they are and tend to be more dismissive to those who are not cooperative. Dismissal and the subsequent sanctioning of clients has the unintended effects of marginalisation. Hence, careful intake, assessment, and subsequent guidance and coaching are important. One challenge for research is to find, describe and further develop good practices, that can serve as a model for other municipalities and perhaps also for other countries.

Another area of potential interest is the use of national government 'management instruments', such as: the 'measuring rod' used to categorise unemployed people with regard to their distance to the labour market; a computerised central information system used by all agencies involved in the delivery of the JEA; and the Centres for Work and Income that serve as single counter services for clients. As yet, it is not known how far these instruments will reduce institutional interests in favour of the individual interests of unemployed people, how far they will actually contribute to the coordination of all agencies involved, or the extent to which they will lead to a reduction in 'creaming' of the target population.

Summary

The introduction of workfare in the form of the YEA, and subsequently the JEA, can be seen as the culmination of an activating labour market policy, following a shift in the aims of social security provision from protection to participation. In general, activating labour market policies in the Netherlands constitute a mix of Scandinavian and Anglo-Saxon models. On the one hand, they incorporate an institutional commitment to full employment, with emphasis on active social policies (education, training and employment projects) rather than passive measures (unemployment benefits). On the other hand, they emphasise a set of obligations for individual clients that have to be fulfilled in order to access welfare. The resultant mix is not so much an *active*, but an *activating* labour market policy, reflecting the Anglo-Saxon emphasis on individuals (unemployed people) rather than on institutions (delivering agencies) in an otherwise Scandinavian active policy design.

With the introduction of the JEA in 1998, a workfare programme for young unemployed people (the YEA) was brought under one umbrella with other employment, training and social activation programmes for other groups of unemployed people. As a consequence of this, participation in these other programmes became more obligatory, although differences continue to exist. At the same time, more options became available for participants, and schemes can now consist of subsidised work, schooling, training and unpaid (voluntary) work, and combinations of these. Consequently, the JEA as a whole is probably better characterised by the term 'activityfare' rather than 'workfare'. However, different regimes continue to co-exist within the JEA. These differ with regard to the degree that they are obligatory and to the degree in which they focus on work or on training and social activation. Secondments to subsidised employment for young unemployed people can be considered to be workfare in a more or less 'pure' form in that it is focused on work, and participation is compulsory. However, other schemes in the JEA are less 'workfare-like'. As there are several schemes and regimes to choose from, the question of how individuals and schemes are matched becomes more important. In other words, how intake and assessment take place, how suitable schemes are determined, and the form of further guidance and coaching become the crucial questions.

Notes

[1] This is a historically important event reflecting the end of the conflicting 'grand narratives' of Socialism and Liberalism, as for the first time in Dutch history a coalition was formed without the Christian Democrats, thus uniting the political

Left (associated with red) and Right (associated with blue) in a pragmatically oriented coalition.

References

Angenent, F.J.A. and den Heeten, J. (1998) *Jongeren op afstand. Een onderzoek naar jongeren die langer dan een jaar in de bijstand zitten en de inzet van het werkgelegenheidsinstrumentarium*, The Hague: Ministry of Social Affairs and Employment.

Beukema, L. and Valkenburg, B. (1999) 'Atypical employment in the Netherlands', in J. Lind and I.H. Møller (eds) *Inclusion and exclusion: Unemployment and non-standard employment in Europe*, Aldershot: Ashgate, pp 111-30.

de Beer, P. (1997) 'Langdurig zonder werk', in K. Schuyt (ed) *Het sociaal tekort. Veertien sociale problemen in Nederland*, Amsterdam: De Balie, pp 23-44.

de Schamheleire, J., Garcia S. and Gomez, A. (1998) *A comparative review of research on work and social inclusion*, Report to the European Commission in the context of the TSER project 'Inclusion through participation', Utrecht: Utrecht University.

Durkheim, E. (1965, originally 1893) *The division of labor in society*, New York, NY: The Free Press.

Engbersen, G. (1990) *Publieke bijstandsgeheimen. Het ontstaan van een onderklasse in Nederland*, Leiden/Antwerpen: Stenfert Kroese.

Engbersen, G., Schuyt, K., Timmer, J. and van Waarden, F. (1993) *Cultures of unemployment: A comparative look at long-term unemployment and urban poverty*, Boulder/San Fransisco, CA/Oxford: Westview Press.

Engbersen, G., Vrooman, J.C. and Snel, E. (eds) (1996) *Arm Nederland. Het eerste jaarrapport armoede en sociale utsluiting*, The Hague: VUGA.

Engbersen, G., Vrooman, J.C. and Snel, E. (eds) (1997) *De Kwetsbaren. Tweede jaarrapport armoede en sociale uitsluiting*, Amsterdam: Amsterdam University Press.

Giddens, A. (1994) *Beyond Left and Right: The future of radical politics*, Cambridge: Polity Press.

Gravesteijn-Lighthelm, Arents, M., Jonker, K.C., Olieman, R., de Koning, J. and van Nes, P.J. (1998) *Wordt succes bepaald door de vorm? Onderzoek naar de doorstroom van gesubsidieerde naar reguliere arbeid*, The Hague: Ministry of Social Affairs and Employment/Elsevier bedrijfsinformatie.

Harmon, M.M. (1995) *Responsibility as paradox: A critique of rational discourse on government*, Thousand Oaks, CA/London: Sage Publications.

Jahoda, M., Lazarsfeld, P.F. and Zeisel, H. (1933) *Marienthal: The sociography of an unemployed community* (English translation 1972), London: Tavistock Publications.

Lipsky, M. (1980) *Street-level bureaucracy: Dilemmas of the individual in public services*, New York, NY: Russel Sage Foundation.

Mead, L.M. (1986) *Beyond entitlement: The social obligations of citizenship*, New York, NY: The Free Press.

Ministry of Social Affairs and Employment (1998) *Sociale Nota*, The Hague: SDU.

Murray, C. (1984) *Losing ground: American social policy, 1950-1980*, New York, NY: Basic Books.

OECD (Organisation for Economic Cooperation and Development) (1998) *Economic outlook*, preliminary edition, Paris.

Olieman, R., Gravesteijn-Ligthelm, J.H., van der Weijde, I., Verkaik, A., Nijhuis, P.F.H. and de Koning, J. (1996) *Evaluatie Jeugd Werk Garantiewet*, The Hague: VUGA.

Oude Engberink, G. (1993) 'Over de culturele en morele factor in het onderzoek van sociale problemen', in *Tijdschrift voor Arbeid en Bewustzijn*, no 17/2, pp 85-90.

Oude Engberink, G. and Post, B. (1994) *Grenzen van de armoede. Risico's en risicogroepen op het sociaal minimum*, Rotterdam: dienst SoZaWe.

Rooj, P. de (1979) *Werklozenzorg en Werkloosheidsbestrijding 1917-1940*, Landelijk en Amsterdams beleid, Amsterdam: Van Gennep.

SCP (Social and Cultural Planning Bureau) (1992) *Sociaal en Cultureel Rapport 1992*, The Hague: VUGA.

SCP (1996) *Sociaal en Cultureel Rapport 1996*, The Hague: VUGA.

SCP (1998) *Sociaal en Cultureel Rapport 1998*, The Hague: VUGA.

Social and Central Planning Bureau of Statistics (1998) *Armoedemonitor 1998*, The Hague: SCP.

Sociale Nota (1998) The Hague: Ministry of Social Affairs and Employment/ VUGA.

Sociale Nota (1999) The Hague: Ministry of Social Affairs and Employment/ VUGA.

Spies, H. (1994) *Geen ervaring rijker. Over jongeren die niet in de JWG komen*, Rotterdam: Dienst Sociale Zaken en Werkgelegenheid.

Spies, H. (1996) 'Workfare: emancipation or marginalisation?', in M.P.M. de Goede, P.M. de Klaver, J.A.C. van Ophem, C.H.A. Verhaar, A. De Vries (eds) *Youth: Unemployment, identity and policy*, Aldershot: Avebury, pp 191-212.

Spies, H. (1998) *Uitsluitend voor jongeren? Arbeidsmarktbeleid en het ontstaan van een onderklasse*, Utrecht: Jan van Arkel.

Teulings, C., van der Veen, R. and Trommel, W. (1997) *Dilemma's van sociale zekerheid. Een analyse van 10 jaar herziening van het stelsel van sociale zekerheid*, Den Haag: Vuga.

Therborn, G. (1986) *Why some peoples are more unemployed than others. The strange paradox of growth and unemployment*, London: Verso.

van Beek, K. (1993) 'To be hired or not to be hired, the employer decides. Relative chances of unemployed job-seekers on the Dutch labor market', Thesis, Amsterdam.

van Berkel, R., Coenen, H. and Dekker A. (1999) 'Regulating the unemployed: from protection to participation', in I. Møller and J. Lind (eds) *Inclusion and exclusion: Unemployment and non-standard employment in Europe*, Aldershot: Ashgate, pp 89-110.

Verkaik, A., van der Ende, M., van Tiggelen, M., de Vries, E., de Koning, J. (1998) *JWG-signalement Jaaroverzicht 1996*, The Hague: VUGA.

Vlek (1999) 'Paars tussen armoedebevordering en armoedebestrijding', in *Tijdschrift voor Arbeid en Participatie*, no 20/3, Utrecht: Jan van Arkel, pp165-84.

WRR (1987) *Activerend Arbeidsmarktbeleid*, The Hague: SDU.

WRR (1990) *Werkend Perspectief. Arbeidsparticipatie in de jaren '90*, The Hague: SDU.

WRR (1996) *Tweedeling in perspectief*, The Hague: SDU.

FIVE

National objectives and local implementation of workfare in Norway

Ivar Lødemel

Introduction

This chapter focuses on the implementation of a work requirement introduced by the 1991 Social Services Act in Norway. The analysis rests on an understanding that workfare can be used to further objectives ranging from supporting the integration of unemployed people into the labour market, to a cost-cutting device designed to discourage claims from recipients and thereby reduce spending on social assistance (see Chapter One). In order to determine which is the outcome of programmes we need robust effect evaluations, which have yet to be carried out in Norway. Whereas this book focuses mainly on the analysis of programmes, as laid down in law and regulations, the theme of this chapter is that the way policies are altered in implementation may provide a clearer understanding of the balance between different objectives of a programme.

The inherent potential for pursuing different objectives makes studies at the implementation level particularly important in order to to understand how workfare functions. In addition to this, workfare is always implemented at the local level (Nathan, 1993). Workfare in Norway differs from the programmes in the other six countries reviewed in this book in two important ways. With a tradition of strong local autonomy in the implementation of social assistance, and now workfare, Norway represents an interesting, if not necessarily representative, case. Workfare in Norway is, moreover, highly selective and used as a condition tied to social assistance for a minority of recipients. Its selective nature is in part explained by the existence of well-developed Active Labour Market Policies (ALMPs). While the main target groups of the latter schemes are insured unemployed people, many of these programmes are open to recipients of assistance on a voluntary or compulsory basis. This chapter therefore focuses on a form of workfare targeted at those most distant from the labour market. It is likely that workfare is more open to an implementation which is in conflict with official objectives in the Norwegian system, in comparison with systems where the central government introduces a programme with clear rules for implementation and where resources are allocated to the implementing agencies. Based on a study of implementation (Lødemel, 1997a) this chapter focuses on workfare as it was introduced and implemented in the early and mid-1990s. The introduction of workfare was part of a wider change in the Norwegian welfare state. The sections which follow consider these recent re-orientations, the official objectives and criteria for workfare, the policy context and political background to the particular nature of the Norwegian approach to workfare, findings from a study which addressed the nature of local implementation, its degree of divergence from official objectives and possible effects on spending, and the objectives pursued by local authorities are discussed in view of the results from the implementation study. The final section gives an overview of changes in workfare in the five years since our survey was carried out.

A change of orientation in the Norwegian welfare state

The introduction of workfare in 1991 must be understood in light of wider changes in the Norwegian welfare state during the 1980s. This period witnessed both extensions of entitlement and services and at the same time curtailment of welfare for some groups. Examples of the first include services for mentally disabled people, improved welfare for families with children and extensions in the education system. Of the second, the entitlement to disability benefits was restricted and services in psychiatry remained poor compared to other parts of the Norwegian welfare system. However, there is no reason to talk about a crisis in the Norwegian welfare state. Beneficial economic developments, in particular over the last five years, have shielded Norway from many of the shocks experienced by other western countries. This suggests that the shared international emphasis on the need to curtail entitlement for some groups, is as much a result of *ideological changes* as *financial constraints*. While economic constraints have figured in the Norwegian debate, the fear regarding them is more for the long-term consequences of increased welfare expenditure than for present-day problems in financing the welfare state.

Attitudes and positions formerly associated by Right-wing parties are today subject to support across most of the political spectre. In political programmes and in government papers we today find new signals with the following features:

- Macroeconomic concerns are more prevalent in the sociopolitical debate;
- Individual responsibility and obligations receive greater emphasis than individual rights;
- Means-testing is no longer viewed as an unfortunate remnant from the past and has been restored in the more positive term 'targeting' (Dahl et al, 1995).

It is emphasised that while welfare may further a dignified life for some, extensive rights to generous benefits may undermine the individual's ability to become self-sufficient.

In Norway, Labour has been the dominant party in the latter half of the 20th century. Often seen as the creators of the Norwegian model of welfare, the Labour Party is also central to the current reorientation of this model. The term 'work approach' expresses the party's adherence to this new thinking. An 'approach' is here defined by its counterpart: in the rhetoric 'social security approach' is the expression of the party's view that Norway has gone too far in facilitating *exit* from the labour force (Dahl et al, 1995). The change of orientation was therefore not the result of a welfare backlash initiated by a Right-wing opponent to the rights-oriented social-democratic welfare model. Instead, the change came from within: it was the Labour government headed by Gro Harlem Brundtland, which initiated the change, coined the terms and introduced the first legislative reforms. In this way the Norwegian Labour Party appears to be part of a political change whereby modern Social Democrats lead the way in transforming the welfare state. A non-Socialist centre coalition, which took office in 1997, continued the work orientation introduced by Labour. In the spring of 2000 a new Labour government took office, and early signs indicate that the Stoltenberg administration aims for wide-ranging reforms in the direction described above. An overhaul of the welfare programmes, and in particular of the large public sector, is at the top of his political agenda.

The work approach appears to rest on both a positive and a negative view of work. The positive understanding lies in the emphasis to enable everybody who wants to work to get a job. This finds expression in both extensions of the welfare state in terms of jobs, and in advancing active labour market policies. The negative understanding rests on the view that some do not share the ideal that gainful employment is attractive enough to make it their first choice (White Paper, no 35, 1994-95).

Both views see people as rational actors who either seek security and a good life through gainful employment or seek the good life in idleness and reliance on public transfers. It follows from this understanding of human nature that people's choices can be influenced by incentives and disincentives. It also follows that while this may take the form of positive sanctions ('carrots') and support, others may need 'sticks' in order to act.

In the implementation of the new work approach we find elements of both. While, for example, tax relief enables pensioners to work part time, harsher measures are needed for able-bodied people who choose not to work. In this perspective, the workfare arrangement is an example where the 'sticks' in the work approach is emphasised over 'carrots'.

Workfare in Norway

With the enactment of the Social Services Act in 1991, a new principle was introduced into modern Norwegian social assistance. For the first time in 60 years, local authorities were allowed to require that recipients of minimum protection carried out work in exchange for benefits. (A separate provision to cash 'residence in workhouse' was carried on from the Poor Law in the 1969 Social Care Act. This was removed in 1991.) Even if the reform was in breach of practices established in the post-war period, the reintroduction of work requirements is best understood as a culmination of curtailments in access to social assistance which started in the mid-1980s. As such, the reform is a part of a wider process of a change of direction of the Norwegian welfare state, with a renewed emphasis on work and activity as opposed to the passive provision of aid.

The dual objective in the Norwegian social assistance legislation, as introduced with the first modern scheme, the 1964 Social Care Act, provides a background to the 1991 reform. On the one hand, the legislation aims to further security and care, while on the other hand, the key objective is to provide help in a way that enables the recipient to be self-sufficient. While the dual aims can be combined, for example when services are provided to disabled people in order to enable them to continue living at home, in other cases the principles may be at odds. In the current sociopolitical climate in Norway it is increasingly accepted that too much care and security may undermine the individual's ability to be self-sufficient. This ability is to be both furthered and tested. In the latter we find the subsidiary nature of all social assistance schemes. Only when all other legitimate sources of aid are exhausted should benefits be provided. In order to secure this objective, a number of conditions are tied to the entitlement to aid. In western societies, gainful employment is the most important source of income. The requirement to seek and to take work that is offered has therefore been a key element in social assistance. With the introduction of the 1991 Act, an important step was taken to strengthen this principle of subsidiarity. The subheading of the paragraph regulating conditions for aid states: "It can be made a condition that the recipient carries out suitable work in the town of residence for as long as the person receives benefits" (Social Services Act 1991, Article 5-3.2.2).

The regulation of workfare in Norway is therefore limited to a condition to the receipt of benefits. The local authorities decide whether to use this condition or not. As such, it is not a programme in the strict sense. This assessment is based on an understanding that a programme in public policy is a set of rules regulating a policy, with corresponding financial means available to pay for the implementation of this policy.

It is important to note that the Norwegian system of workfare serves a residual function while at the same time the boundaries between workfare and other programmes are blurred. It is residual because it focuses exclusively on clients of social assistance and because it targets those within this group who have failed to make use of other services which are available to them. The boundaries are blurred for two reasons. First, because other programmes are available to unemployed recipients of social assistance. Second, because some local authorities use Article 5-3 to make the participation in ALMPs and other training programmes a condition for continued receipt of aid (Vik-Mo and Nervik, 1999). From a comparative perspective it is therefore important to stress that while workfare in Norway has no defined options or trajectories, alternative programmes outside of workfare therefore represents options and trajectories for participants and for the social workers in the social services.

The objectives behind the work requirement

Theoretically, the use of workfare may serve different objectives, ranging from the integration of the individual in the labour market to curtailing benefit expenditure by discouraging claims and avoiding work in the shadow economy. The majority of the *Storting* (Parliament) limited the aim of the work condition to the interest of the individual claimant. The purpose of setting people to work in exchange for benefits was to further the overarching objective of 'self help' through rehabilitation in the social assistance legislation. By the statement:

> The desired connection between the responsibility of the individual and entitlements is particularly important to convey to young people with no work experience. (Innst. O. nr 9, 1991/92)

the Social Committee also introduced an educative and corrective justification. In the circular to the Act, the Ministry goes further and stresses that the objectives of security, care and the rehabilitation of the individual must be safeguarded (Ministry of Health and Social Affairs, 1993a). In a letter to LO (the Trade Union Congress) the Ministry moreover answered to their fear of displacement of ordinary work by stating that:

> ... the purpose of Article 5-3 is not to carry out municipal work but to help young people improve their chances in the labour market. (Ministry of Health and Social Affairs, 1993b)

A further specification of the way in which the condition could be used can be found in a decision by the Industrial Tribunal in 1993. The Tribunal tried a case where a local social service department required a social assistance recipient to work as a caretaker's assistant at a school. The question that was tried was whether the use of the work condition was in breach of tariff regulations for the public sector, thereby displacing regular employees. The Tribunal found, however, that the work condition as applied in this case was not in breach of the tariff regulations. The Tribunal stated as the reason for their decision that average working hours were limited to 15 hours per week over a limited time period. The Tribunal also emphasised that the assistant, unlike a regular worker, had no regular work tasks (Industrial Tribunal, 1993).

Specifications aimed at ensuring compliance with objectives in implementation

There are at least three ways in which the legislator and the responsible ministry can further compliance. First, Parliament can play an active role by providing detailed rules as part of the Act. Second, the Ministry can channel (tied) resources to the agencies responsible for implementation. Third, the Ministry can attach regulation to the law in the form of circulars. Among the programmes in the seven nations studied in this book, the Norwegian work condition is unique in that neither detailed regulations nor resources made available to municipalities where the condition is applied are used as instruments to further compliance. The following section therefore considers the Act, ministerial circulars and statements made by the Social Committee in the *Storting*. The analysis focuses on target group, scope, nature of work, training as part of the work, duration of work, remuneration, sanctions and inter-agency cooperation.

Target group

Workfare in Norway is a part of the social assistance programme. Therefore, the groups from which participants can be drawn is in the outset limited to those who are in receipt of assistance benefits. There are other work and training programmes designed as a condition for the receipt of insurance-based unemployment benefits, but while non-attendance may lead to the suspension of these benefits, the recipients could, at least theoretically, fall back on social assistance.

Active labour market measures are organised by the Directorate of Labour, and the local employment offices are responsible for the implementation of the programmes. Together with various local schemes coordinated by the local social services the ALMP programmes organised by the labour market authorities are also open to social assistance recipients provided that they meet the target group criteria of these programmes.

The Social Services Act gives no further indication as to the target group. The wording "condition that the recipient carries out suitable work" allows an open interpretation for the use of the condition with regard to anyone who is in receipt of aid. A first specification of the target group can be found in circulars specifying the particular Act. The Ministry of Health and Social Affairs specifies the target group by stating that this rule should in particular be used with regard to 'young recipients' (Ministry of Health and Social Affairs, 1993a).

While both the law and the circular are instruments to bind legally, this is not the status of the statements made by the Parliamentary committee preparing the law. Still, by studying these we find the intentions of the lawmakers expressed. The committee went further than the above by stating that the target group is young people who have failed to make use of the services provided by the labour market administration (Innst. O. nr 9, 1991-92). During the first years of implementation fewer programmes within ALMP were available to recipients of social assistance. In other words, the intention of the lawmakers was to create a subsidiary programme for those who were either excluded from or failed to make use of traditional training programmes organised under the umbrella of the active labour market policy.

The striking impression is one of a very weak specification of the target group. As a result, the local authorities are legally free to implement the scheme in a way that includes other social assistance recipients for whom they find workfare to be a useful instrument. As a last-resort benefit programme, social assistance targets needs rather than particular groups. It therefore comprises a wide number of need categories, with varying social needs beyond that of a necessity for financial aid. The use of workfare across the scale of need categories will therefore have widely differing consequences for the different groups. As an example, in Norway there is no particular scheme to cater for the financial needs of refugees and asylum seekers. As a result they all become social assistance recipients for at least a transitional period after arriving in the country. The local authority receives funding from central government intended to cover their expenses in meeting the financial and other needs of these groups. Another group, which is over-represented in social assistance, is single parents. During the last years their entitlement to social insurance transitional benefits has been curtailed. There is no mention of this group in the official documents outlining the work requirement. Given the weak legal restriction in the Act, local authorities may, however, choose to require that asylum seekers, refugees and single parents work in exchange for benefits.

Scope

The operation of the condition is left to the municipalities. It is therefore for the discretion of local political authorities and social workers in the social services whether to use the condition or not, as well as in determining which particular clients to include.

Two years after the Act was introduced, approximately one third of the local authorities had used the condition at least once (Lødemel, 1997a). Later evidence suggests that this number remained stable towards the end of the 1990s (Vik-Mo and Nervik, 1999). In 1995 it was estimated that less than 5% of all social assistance recipients participated in compulsory work in the local authority.

Work specifications

There is no specification in the guidelines concerning the sectors in which work should take place. With the phrase 'work in the local authority' the legislator indicates that the municipality should act as employer, and that work therefore is restricted to services provided by the local authority. The Ministry circular also use expressions such as 'work under municipal direction' and 'work for the local authority' (Ministry of Health and Social Affairs, 1993a).

Local authorities are today responsible for a large number of services. These include all the work tasks that are listed as suitable for work for social assistance clients. According to the Ministry circular this includes "cleaning up public parks, painting of buildings or helping the elderly/ disabled" (Ministry Health and of Social Affairs, 1993a). This can be organised as created work (see Chapter Nine) or participants may work alongside regular employees in, for example, the social services.

Training as part of work

Neither the Act itself nor the accompanying circular from the Ministry mentions a training component. The closest we can find is a statement in a letter from the then Minister of Social Affairs, Grete Knudsen, to the Norwegian Trade Union Confederation. The Minister states that the work should be part of "a systematic programme, individually tailored to ensure help to promote the self-sufficiency of the recipient" (Ministry of Health and Social of Affairs, 1993b). If we are to understand this systematic programme aimed at preparing people for working life, it can therefore be expected that workfare, like other active labour market programmes with a similar aim, should contain an element of training. Without further guidelines the choice of how to ensure a 'systematic programme' is, however, again left to the local authorities. In other parts of the deliberations preceding the enactment it becomes evident that the participation in work activities in itself seen as the main contribution to the training of the individual.

Duration

Neither the Act nor the Ministry provides any specification of the duration of the work requirement. With the wording "for as long as the person receives benefits" (Social Services Act, 1991, Article 5-3.2) it is theoretically possible to require that clients work for an indefinite period providing they are still in receipt of social assistance benefit. Also, the length of the working week remains unsettled. In both cases, however, the Industrial Tribunal ruled that a particular case was acceptable on the ground that duration was limited to three months and the working week seldom exceeded 15 hours (Industrial Tribunal, 1993).

Remuneration and financing

Recipients work in exchange for benefits, and no separate pay scheme is in operation for those working. In Norway the level of social assistance benefit is set locally and is subject to considerable geographical variation. There is no requirement that local authorities set aside funds for the running of the scheme, neither has central government a duty to provide funds earmarked for the operation of workfare.

Compliance and sanctions

The work requirement is included under the paragraph listing conditions for the receipt of social assistance. If a client fails to comply with a condition, benefits may be terminated. The majority of the Social Committee in the *Storting* stated that:

> ...the main rule is that the payment of benefits is stopped if the recipient fails to meet the conditions set for the receipt of benefits, unless particular circumstances are present, for example spouse or children. (Innst O. nr. 9/1991-92)

The circular to the Act states, however, that also when the client has no valid reasons not to participate a lower level of 'crisis aid' can be provided (Ministry of Health and Social Affairs, 1993a).

Inter-agency cooperation

Cooperation across departmental borders has long been an Achilles' heel in the Norwegian welfare state. Established agencies such as social insurance and the social assistance administrations, have tried and often failed in their attempts to achieve centrally established aims of increased cooperation and coordination (Hvinden, 1994). In the case of workfare, the situation is that for the first time the local assistance administration was given permission to implement an activity similar to programmes which so far have been the domain of the labour market administration.

The introduction of workfare is, however, not the first instance where the two agencies have tried to cooperate. In order to experiment with ways to further the integration of unemployed social assistance recipients, a number of pilot projects were implemented in the period 1988 to 1993 (White Paper, no 35, 1994-95). The expectation of cooperation was strengthened with the enactment of the 1991 Social Services Act. In a joint circular to their respective local agencies, the Ministry of Health and Social Affairs and the Ministry of Labour urged the services to cooperate and to coordinate efforts with the view to improving the integration of unemployed recipients with multiple problems (Ministry of Health and Social Affairs, 1991). In order to obligate the agencies to cooperate, formal agreements on leadership had to be in place.

To sum up: the work requirement is intended to be targeted at young people, offering an individually tailored programme with the aim to further labour market integration. Work is supposed to be limited in time and duration, and the social services are obliged to cooperate with the labour market authorities in implementation. There are, however, very few binding specifications designed to ensure that these principles are followed in implementation. The next section attempts to explain how this situation was made possible.

How can we understand the particular nature of workfare condition in Norway?

The programme outlined above may appear to contradict the nature of the Norwegian welfare state as a highly developed system, with clear rules providing universal benefits and services. This part highlights two aspects that may offer at least a partial explanation for why Norway introduced a workfare programme devoid of such guarantees. First, the nature of the condition must be understood in light of the surrounding social protection system and labour market policies in the early 1990s. Second, an overview of the political process resulting in the enactment of workfare provides insight into both the nature of the programme and the way in which it was later implemented, during its first years of operation.

The policy context

The main target group for workfare in Norway is young unemployed people. This section outlines the alternative programmes designed to cater for the needs of these individuals. Four areas of policy will be briefly outlined: social assistance; the wider social security system; a number of work and training schemes which combine to create a tertiary labour market; and finally, formal training.

Social assistance

In Norway, workfare is a part of Social Economic Assistance within the social assistance scheme. The right to assistance is enshrined in the 1991 Social Services Act. The purpose of this scheme is to provide a last safety net by ensuring that individuals in need have adequate resources and to help them to become self-supporting. Financing and the implementation of social assistance are the responsibility of the local municipalities. The programme is thereby separate from the remainder of social security, which remains a state responsibility. Local authorities determine eligibility and are to a great extent free to set the level of benefits, based on a judgement of the individual's need and the local cost of living. The Ministry of Health and Social Affairs sets only very general guidelines for the kind of expenses that should be included in the determination of eligibility and for benefit levels, thus leaving considerable discretion to the local authorities, and often to individual case workers. The minimum age for independent claims is 18. Students are not eligible for aid, except in the two months not covered by the state education grants and loans. Entitlement is based on the principle of domicile, which includes non-nationals provided that they are legally residing in the country. There are no time limits for assistance, and entitlement remains for as long as needs last and conditions are met.

Social assistance in Norway has a strong element of work testing. Claimants must seek and be willing to take work offered. Young people may be asked to participate in work training programmes organised by the labour market authorities. These programmes are, however, distinct from the new work requirement in three important ways. First, these schemes are not part of the Social Services Act. Second, the schemes are organised by, and benefits are paid out by, the local labour administration. Third, benefits are generally higher than social assistance benefits, and an incentive for participation is therefore in place. As we will see below, recent developments suggest, however, that the boundaries between the two sets of programmes is being reduced.

Unemployment benefits

In Norway unemployment benefit is the main source of income for people who are involuntarily out of work. The programme is part of the national social insurance system but, unlike the rest of this system, benefits are paid by the labour market administration. This is a state agency with local offices.

Benefit entitlement is determined according to earnings in the year prior to becoming unemployed. The income threshold for benefits is at present approximately 61,000 Norwegian Kroner. Benefits are related to earnings and the replacement rate is 65%. Moreover, benefits are awarded without the use of a means test. The duration of benefits is, at the moment, three years. After this a new period of ordinary work, or participation in a temporary employment programme is required in order to renew entitlement to benefits.

Among the losers in this relatively comprehensive and generous system are young people who fail to enter the labour market after the completion of education or training. They are either excluded from benefits, or receive only a small sum based on previous (part-time) earnings. As a result, this is the group of unemployed people most frequently dependent on the underpinning social assistance scheme.

Today, the main labour market constraint in Norway is lack of available labour. The situation was, however, different around the time of the enactment of the Social Services Act. In 1991, 5.5% of the workforce were unemployed. Among the workfare target group the situation was much worse still, 17% of 16- to 19-year-olds and 11% of 20- to 24-year -olds were unemployed at that time (the numbers include students seeking part-time employment) (Statistics Norway, 1994, 1998). Youth unemployment in general, and increasing dependency on social assistance in particular, was therefore a major concern at the period of enactment.

Tertiary labour market

Today, active labour market policies are advocated by organisations, such as the OECD, and the EU (see Chapter One). Norway has a history of such programmes dating back to the early 1980s. During a period of increased unemployment in the late 1980s, programmes were extended dramatically. Between 1988 and 1990, participation increased by 400% while unemployment increased by 90% (Torp, 1995). In 1993, 3% of the labour force participated in such programmes. Faced with problems of coordination of the then existing plethora of programmes and a continued need for new measures, it was decided that year to amalgamate the existing programmes into one new scheme called 'KAJA'. This abbreviation stands for "Competence, training for work and job creation for unemployed people". KAJA was meant to be a last-resort measure targeted at unemployed people who were in danger of being permanently excluded from the labour market. The groups covered include both recipients of unemployment benefits as well as people who receive social assistance either because they extended their entitlement or because they had no such entitlement in the first place. This means that KAJA was intended to be, and indeed functions as, an alternative to workfare organised by the local authorities. The distinction between the two programmes was also somewhat blurred by the fact that the local authorities found work for KAJA participants. The local labour market administration was in charge of selecting participants, and its central agency channelled funds to the local authorities for the creation of work places. The cooperation between the involved agencies was formalised in the form of a joint committee (Directorate of Labour, 1995). While KAJA functioned as a last-resort active labour market programme, workfare as a condition for the receipt of social assistance creates a last-resort scheme for those unable to make use of KAJA or alternative training programmes. While KAJA still exist, it is seldom used today. Instead social assistance recipients now have greater access to other ALMP programmes.

Together with various apprentice programmes, a wide array of measures targeted at young unemployed people were in operation at the time of the launch of the workfare measure in 1993. The situation in Norway is therefore one of an active labour market policy embracing almost, but not all of, the young out-of-work. Resulting from this, a Norwegian 'social division of training' was created between workfare on the one hand and active labour market programmes on the other.

Training and education

Following an extensive education reform in 1994, everybody is entitled to 12 years of education. This reform emphasises vocational training in an attempt to guarantee all youth access to further education. In principle, everybody is provided equal chances to higher education, regardless of sex, socioeconomic background or location. Most educational institutions are public and do not charge tuition fees. The state Educational Loan Fund provides loans and grants to students in high school and in higher education. Loans and grants are means-tested against the student's own and parents' earnings until the student reaches the age of 19, and the student's own income after this age. Loans and grants are given for 10 months a year, leaving the student to manage through work, parental support or social assistance for the remaining two months.

The educational reform of 1994 also contains a *youth guarantee*. All youths aged 16-19 are guaranteed access to either work, training or education. In addition, all unemployed people between the ages of 20 and 24 are given priority access to government training courses.

To sum up: the policy context into which workfare was introduced in 1991 featured a number of state programmes which combined to reduce the workfare target group to a small minority of young people who failed to make use of the higher echelons of social security, education or active labour market measures. In Norway, there is no tradition for central government to supervise the welfare targeted at the small minority falling outside state programmes. In a tradition dating back to the Poor Law, assistance has remained the financial and administrative responsibility of local government. As a part of this scheme, a detailed regulation would have introduced a breach with a strong tradition of local autonomy in Norway.

The political process leading to the enactment in 1991

This section considers early proposals for reform, the changing position of the Labour Party and the discussion in Parliament over the proposal for a workfare element.

Early proposals

An Oslo City Council committee made the first proposal for a work requirement, in 1990. With the statement "If society fails to put demands on people it deprives them of some of their self respect", the committee proposed a work requirement for all the able-bodied recipients (Oslo Kommune, 1990).

The first national initiative came with a proposal for an amendment to the then existing Social Care Act in 1991. Two representatives from the

Conservative Party proposed an addition to the conditions for aid which is identical to the wording of the new law enacted later the same year. The justification for the reform and the motives were, however, different. According to the proposal the new programme would further three objectives:

1. *The interest of the recipient:* participation would qualify the claimant for work and thereby avoid passivity and social exclusion;
2. *The interest of the local authority:* work in the public interest can be carried out without the danger of displacing ordinary work;
3. *The preventive consideration:* by requiring that recipients report to work 2-3 hours a day, those who are actually working will cease to claim the benefit to which they are not entitled. In this way 'work in the shadow economy' is avoided, the community saves money and societal solidarity and the support for the welfare state is strengthened (Dokument nr 8/ 31, 1990/91).

The Labour Party

Thus far the new 'work approach' of the Labour Party was not extended to include a support for workfare in social assistance. However, in the autumn of 1991 a key figure in the Party launched a debate that was indicative of a division within the Party along these lines. Rune Gerhardsen, the party's candidate for leader of the Oslo City government, published a book (which translates to kindism in Norwegian) (Gerhardsen, 1991) which sparked a heated debate. By applying this term, which is reminiscent of the welfare state critique imbedded in the term 'nanny-state' – that recipients are virtually treated as children – Gerhardsen aimed to raise moral issues concerning the division of responsibilities between the state and the individual. By arguing that making demands on the individual was an expression of solidarity, he aimed to take an issue thus far dominated by the political Right and to make it part of the values upon which the labour movement is based. In doing so, he evokes sentiments that have long been a part of the Norwegian Labour Party (Lødemel, 1997b; Terum, 1996). A strong emphasis on a work ethic has always been a key feature of the Labour Party in Norway. Gerhardsen's initiative provoked, however, considerable resistance within the Parliamentary party. The debate in the *Storting* concerning the new Act shows that his ideas were premature, and that the party was not ready to accept these views at the time.

The discussion in Parliament

The original proposal for a workfare element from the Conservative representatives did not succeed at first. Instead, the initiative was repeated in the deliberations over the proposal for a new Act to replace the existing Social Care Act in the fall of 1991. In the Social Committee, the Conservatives won the support of the Christian Democrats and the Agrarian Party. The then Labour Party's Minister of Social Affairs, Tove Veierød, focused on the difference between ALMP and workfare, and argued that instead of workfare, the best solution to solve the problem of youth unemployment was to be found in training schemes aimed at qualifying young unemployed people for work. The non-Socialist proposal was, in her view "limited to casual work without the element of systematic qualification" (Deliberations in *Storting*, 14.11.1991). The spokesman of the Social Committee (Alf E. Jakobsen), also from the Labour Party, similarly argued that work training and qualification was the responsibility of the Labour Market Authorities and that the social services should not get involved in the provision of employment for recipients of social assistance. According to him, such a solution would lead to a "further stigmatisation of those forced to apply for social assistance" (Deliberations in *Storting*, 14.11.1991).

A minority Labour government ruled Norway when the Social Services Act was enacted. In the vote the proposal was passed with the support of all the non-Socialist parties; only the Labour Party and the Socialists voted against. The wording of the condition was identical to that proposed by the Conservative members of Parliament a few months earlier although, as we have seen, the three objectives accompanying the early proposal had been reduced to one – the interest of the participant.

Later developments in the Labour Party suggest that the party had a divided view with regard to this condition, and that the support for the programme increased with time. There is also reason to believe that the Labour Party Minister of Social Affairs, Tove Veierød, at the time supported the introduction of workfare, but the ground was not yet paved in the Parliamentary party for such a reform (Lødemel, 1997a). Although no evaluation of the use of the workfare condition was conducted, the party gave official support to the work requirement at its national convention in 1995. Over a period of only four years a position which was originally seen as populist views expressed by one party member had changed to become official party policy.

At the time of enactment, the Labour Party was, however, forced to introduce a work requirement to which they objected. Rather than aiming at ensuring implementation in accordance with the objectives agreed upon in Parliament, the then Minister of Social Affairs chose to take an 'ostrich position' and give few specifications beyond passively referring to the views expressed by the Parliamentary majority. Rather than furthering compliance in implementation by issuing regulations, the Labour government in this way left to the local authority decisions on how to use the condition.

National objectives and local implementation

The first part of this chapter presented a picture of a scheme which is built on a clear objective, but which leaves great autonomy to the local authorities in designing the programme. Based on a national survey covering all local social services departments, this part presents the main finding regarding local implementation two years after the Act was put into effect (Lødemel, 1997a). In 1995, one third of the municipalities had used the work requirement at least once. These municipalities were not systematically different from the rest on key variables such as party political dominance, level of unemployment and social assistance expenditure. In view of the political struggle leading up to the enactment, it is interesting to find that Labour Party-lead local authorities were no less likely to use the condition compared to other, non-Socialist municipalities.

When asked about their objectives with the use of the work requirement, the leaders of the social services answered in close adherence to the objectives determined by Parliament and the Ministry. Only in a few cases were objectives such as saving on assistance expenditure, and getting jobs done for the municipality mentioned.

The survey questions concerning the actual implementation of the workfare condition revealed, however, a different picture. Five criteria for implementation in accordance with official objectives were identified in the overview above (The second criteria, working hours, relates to the fears of displacing ordinary work. The remaining criteria are drawn from policy maker expressions of how the condition is to be used in order to further the overarching aim of helping young people into work). Table 5.1 presents the answers of heads of social services in the 146 departments where the condition was applied.

With regard to working hours, cooperation with the labour authorities and the provision of training, a majority of social services departments were found to implement condition, the workfare in conflict with official criteria (Lødemel, 1997a). This finding is, however, not sufficient to conclude that the breach of individual criteria involves implementation in conflict with the over-riding objectives of the legislator. It is therefore interesting to look at the extent of breach with several criteria within the same office. Only a few offices implemented the workfare condition, in conflict with all five. On the other hand, an equally small number followed all but one criteria. The main picture is, however, that *more than* half of the offices used the work requirement in a way that was in conflict with at least three of the five criteria listed[1] (Lødemel, 1997a).

Did the social services departments pursue other objectives?

These findings give reason to discuss whether the majority of the local social services departments shared objectives other than those expressed by the legislator, and those expressed by themselves when asked about general aims with the use of workfare. We saw above that the original proposal for reform from Conservative MPs stressed the aim to discourage unnecessary claims and the objective of utilising the labour of the claimants in getting public works carried out. We also saw that the final official objectives did not contain these elements, and limited the aim of the programme to further the integration of young people. The hypothesis for the analysis was that *the non-compliance documented above could be interpreted as an adherence to the objective of reducing spending through discouraging claims* (Lødemel, 1997a). In order to test this hypothesis an analysis of the development of spending on social assistance in different local authorities was carried out. The key findings were: non-compliance with criteria often resulted in a harsh workfare regime with no training and long working hours in ordinary jobs and with strong sanctions for non-participation.

Table 5.1: Percentage of social services departments that implemented workfare in conflict with five criteria

Criteria	%
Age group: more than one third of participants over the age of 35	24
More than 15 working hours per week	67
No individually established number of working hours	41
Do not cooperate with labour market authorities	55
No training for participants	61

In some offices clients worked full time in ordinary jobs for more than a year with no payment beyond social assistance. Based on the level of benefits this amounted to an average wage, which was approximately a third of the pay for unskilled personnel doing the same job.

Based on the five criteria listed above, an index of 'harshness' was constructed. After controlling for a number of relevant variables, the following finding was statistically significant: *The growth in social assistance expenditure was lower in municipalities with 'harsh' programmes compared to those who implemented more in accordance with nationally established criteria.* Based on information from individual small communities where workfare was introduced harshly with an explicit aim of discouraging claims, the 'Lavangen hypothesis' was formulated. In the small northern town of Lavangen most of the young claimants disappeared after the social services departments introduced a programme with an explicitly preventive objective, and spending on social assistance was reduced by 65% in the first year. There is reason to believe that the stigma of social assistance is more strongly felt in small and transparent communities compared to larger towns and cities. A harsh system of workfare may compound this by making dependency on aid more visible, in particular in cases where all the young claimants are working together in the public parks as was the case in the town of Lavangen. The hypothesis was *that participation in a harsh scheme would be particularly incriminating in a small and thereby transparent community.* By comparing the use of workfare in large and small communities, two significant findings were: *the effect on expenditure after introducing workfare was greater in small compared with larger municipalities; the effect of 'harshness' was significantly greater in small compared to large municipalities.* Although the findings were statistically significant, they do not give ground to final conclusions about causality. The development of expenditure was only analysed for a limited period of three years. Also, it is not possible to establish the causal relationship between expenditure and nature of programme statistically; we cannot rule out that other factors, such as whether alternative administrative curtailments of eligibility influenced the outcome. In spite of these qualifications, the findings indicate that the introduction of workfare may curtail spending and that this is best achieved when implemented in a harsh way and thereby in conflict with the objectives established by central government. The low number participating also suggests that, when implemented harshly, workfare may have a preventive effect beyond the individual client compelled to work. Finally, the findings indicate that local authorities, often struggling with mounting expenditure, chose to use this local autonomy to introduce programmes more in adherence with the original proposal of the Conservative MPs than with the objectives laid down by the Parliamentary majority. By failing to give binding guidelines to the implementing agencies, the Labour government thereby facilitated a practice which in many cases was more in line with those found in the US than in other European countries (Chapter Nine).

Recent developments

The primary source for this chapter is a survey carried out in the fall of 1995, two and a half years after the Social Services Act took effect (Lødemel, 1997a). Over the last five years the situation in Norway has changed in several ways which impact on the way the work requirement is used.

Most importantly, new data and research evidence have brought attention to a set of programmes where workfare is implemented in a more organised way than that found in 1995. A survey carried out in 1998 found that 44% of local authorities operated so-called *municipal active labour market programmes* (Vik-Mo and Nervik 1999). There is no clear definition of this type of programmes. In the survey, it was defined as labour market related programmes where the local social services had the main responsibility for the planning and follow up (Vik-Mo and Nervik, 1999, p 181). The term 'programme' implies that the activity is organised and has some permanency (Moe, 1986, p 11) and that it involves other agencies than the social services alone (Moe, 1986, p 3). The municipal labour market programmes differ in the extent to which they use the workfare instrument to recruit participants. Among the local authorities implementing such programmes in 1998, 55% used the workfare condition sometimes or always (Vik-Mo and Nervik, 1999, p 88). The interesting information here is that a majority of the local authorities which offered labour market programmes to social assistance recipients did so without applying the workfare condition to compel recipients into participation. While we have no new evidence of the extent to which and how workfare is applied in towns without municipal programmes, the recent development suggests that a wider range of options, compulsory and non-compulsory are available to many clients today.

Starting in 1996 Statistics Norway provide data on the extent of participation in municipal programmes. That year, 7,400 recipients of assistance participated (Statistics Norway, 1997). These numbers were, however, reduced to 2,100 in 1999 (Statistics Norway, 2000a). The reduction may be caused partly by the fall in the number of unemployed recipients during this period, but it may also reflect greater difficulties in securing funding from the labour market authorities. In response to falling unemployment the ALMP programmes have been cut back (Kommunal Rapport, 2000). Unemployment is reduced from 5.9% in 1993 to 3.3% today (White Paper no 50, 1998/99 and Statistics Norway, 2000b). The favourable development on the labour market has also brought attention to the needs of social assistance of the long-term unemployed, among them many recipients of assistance. As the labour market has absorbed the majority of the unemployed, the remaining workless are, however, more often than earlier distant from work and more often in need of combined efforts in order to further the transition into work.

In order to provide new opportunities for this group the Ministry of Social Affairs recently introduced an initiative aimed at the work integration of long-term recipients of assistance. At the outset 10 local authorities receive state support for a four-year pilot to develop effective local programmes in cooperation with the labour market authorities (Ministry of Social Affairs, 2000). The Directorate of Labour recently expressed a desire to stimulate municipal programmes. Their then Director, Ted Hanisch, promised to contact the municipalities that still lack programmes with the view to further cooperation (Kommunal Rapport, 2000). The strengthened emphasis on cooperation is also expressed in two recent government documents (White Paper no 21, 1998-99 and White Paper no 50, 1998-99) and a new joint circular from the Ministry of Social Affairs and the Directorate of Labour (Ministry of Health and Social Affairs, 1997). In their deliberations over the recent White Paper on inequality, the Storting recently addressed policies targeted at long-term recipients of welfare. The majority of the Social Committee concludes that the need for improved delivery requires a reorganisation of the local services if successful coordination is not achieved (Innst. S. no 222, 1999-2000, p 53). The Committee furthermore proposes an extension of compulsory work or other activities by proposing that social assistance is replaced by a new 'qualification-wage' for refugees (Innst S. no 222, 1999-2000, p 65).

Conclusion and discussion

Unlike, for example, the schemes introduced in some states in the US, the discouragement of claims and the curtailment of spending is not part of the official objectives behind the Norwegian work requirement in social assistance. The low level of specification in the form of binding rules and guidelines from central government to the implementing agencies has, however, left the design of the programme to local government and social services departments. In doing so, the legislator has opened up the possibility of implementation in conflict with nationally agreed objectives. It was found that the majority of local authorities using the work requirement chose to design a different, less individually tailored and with a greater emphasis on work and, in effect, a much harsher form of workfare than intended by the legislator. Based on a finding that these municipalities achieved a curtailment in expenditure growth, it is likely that cost-cutting was probably one, if not the only objective.

The main responsibility for the outcome in implementation lies, in the view of this author, with central government. Without rules, guidelines and resources for implementation, many local authorities, often struggling with mounting expenditure, choose to use the new powers to discourage claims and perhaps also save money by displacing ordinary work with the labour of their social assistance clientele. In Norway, workfare was introduced as a residual programme under a close to universal umbrella of active labour market policies aimed at young unemployed people. Also, the majority of the unemployed enjoyed earnings-related unemployment benefits. Only those with little or no work history depended on social assistance. As a result, those least likely to succeed in the labour market participated. Together with the tradition of local autonomy in social assistance, this is probably the single most important factor in explaining the residual nature of the programme. The political situation at the time of enactment compounded the government's inability and unwillingness to give binding guidelines and thereby ensure that implementation was more in accordance with nationally set objectives.

In Norway the introduction of workfare contributed to a *social division of activation*. A comparison of workfare and the main active labour market programme for young people, at the time when the study was conducted, revealed a stark contrast in the way objectives were translated into rules and regulations. In the latter programme, which was targeted at the same group of people, participants were paid tariff wages, working hours were regulated, time was set aside for training and funds were allocated for operation and the partial subsidy for employers. In *The welfare paradox* (Lødemel, 1997b) I concluded that the residual nature of Norwegian social assistance compared to the UK scheme was best explained by differences in the size and composition of the target group. In that case, it was mainly the success of social insurance coverage that explained why assistance remained a system for the poorest and least deserving parts of the population. The study of workfare reveals a similar picture. In this case perhaps it is the success of active labour market policies which has yielded a similar result. Again, therefore, it is only apparently contradictory that the highly developed welfare state of Norway produced a system of workfare more in common with the systems under operation in many US states (see Chapter Eight) than with those developing in many other European countries.

The development after 1995 suggests that workfare in Norway is changing. While central government has remained passive in regulating the use of the workfare condition, it has contributed to the growth of more organised and tailored programmes at the local level. Although we still know little about the nature of the new initiatives, the social division of activation in Norway is now more complex than it was five years ago. More localities now than earlier practice a form of workfare which is closer to ALMP, while at the same better tailored to the needs of unemployed recipients of assistance. The fact that less than half of the municipalities have implemented their own programmes suggests, however, that the implementation in conflict with the official criteria and objectives described in this chapter still prevails. In order to improve this situation, more binding regulations an earmarked resources are required. At the same time in is necessary to encourage social initiatives and implementation which utilise the local labour market and good practices of cooperation between the different agencies which have goal of furthering the integration of the workless in work or other meaningful activities. The residual nature of social assistance, and later, workfare was conditioned by a strong separation of these systems from those of the insured. Perhaps the most promising aspect in the recent development of workfare and activation in Norway is that these boundaries seem to be reduced. The new municipal programmes may benefit from the resources and stronger regulation of ALPM while at the same time the case work and closer follow up of the social services may contribute to tailoring these programmes towards the needs of those among the workless who are most distant from the labour market. The current shortage of labour and the good prospect for the Norwegian economy suggest that the success of good programmes is closer at hand in Norway than in most of the countries considered here.

Note

[1] A different interpretation of objectives is provided by Vik-Mo and Nervik (1999). Here, the objective of rehabilitation is seen as the single most important criteria for compliance. In their view, local authorities may also pursue other objectives such as cost-cutting, corrective and preventive objectives. Based on a qualitative study of social services departments, their study concluded that although the implementation was in breach with other criteria, the content and effect of the use of workfare furthered rehabilitation of participants in four of the five departments studied (Vik-Mo and Nervik, 1999).

References

Dahl, E., Fløtten, T., Hagen, K., Hippe, I.M. and Lødemel, I. (1995) *Velferdssignaler*, Fafo-rapport nr 174, Oslo: Fafo.

Deliberations in *Storting* [*Stortingsforhandlinger*] 14.11.1991.

Directorate of Labour (1995) *Tiltaksboka*, Oslo: Arbeidsdirektoratet.

Dokument 8:31 (1991) *Forslag fra stortingsrepresentantene John G. Bernander og Thea Knutzen om endring i lov av 5. Juni 1964 nr.2 om sosial omsorg. Hjemmel til å stille krav om arbeidsytelse.*

Gerhardsen, R. (1991) *Snillisme på norsk*, Oslo: Schibsted.

Hvinden, B. (1994) *Divided against itself. A study of integration in welfare bureaucracy*, Oslo: Scandinavian University Press.

Industrial Tribunal (1993) *Decision no 23/1993.*

Innst. O. nr 9/1991-92.

Innst S. no 222, 1999-2000.

Kjellevold, A. (1995) *Sosialhjelp på vilkår*, Oslo: Juridisk Forlag.

Kommunal Rapport (2000) 5 October.

Lødemel, I. (1997a) *Pisken i arbeidslinja. Om iverksetting av arbeid for sosialhjelp*, Fafo-rapport nr 226, Oslo: Fafo.

Lødemel, I. (1997b) *The welfare paradox*, Oslo: Scandinavian University Press.

Ministry of Health and Social Affairs (1991) *Rundskriv*, p-5/91 17.7.1991.

Ministry of Health and Social Affairs (1993a) *Rundskriv, i 1/93 Lov om sosiale tjenester m.v.*

Ministry of Health and Social Affairs (1993b) *Letter from the Minister of Health and Social Affairs Grete Knudsen to LO 19.03.1993.*

Ministry of Health and Social Affairs (1997) Rundskriv H28/97.

Ministry of Health and Social Affairs (2000) Press Release, 17 July.

Moe, A. (1996) *Kommunale arbeidsmarkedstiltak,* Trondheim: NTNU.

Nathan, R.P. (1993) *Turning promises into performance. The management challenge of implementing workfare,* New York, NY: Columbia University Press.

Nervik, J. A. (1997) *Offentlig politikk og klientløpebaner Sosialhjelp og arbeidsmarkedstiltak – bidrag til selvforsørging eller ringdans i velferdsbyråkratiet,* Institutt for statsvitenskap, Oslo: Universitet i Oslo.

Oslo Kommune (1990) *Perspektivutvalget,* 16.10.1990.

Pinker, R. (1979) *Social theory and social policy,* London: Heinemann Educational Books.

Statistics Norway (1994) *Historisk statistikk,* Oslo: SSB.

Statistics Norway (1997) *Sosialhjelpsstatistikk,* Oslo: SSB.

Statistics Norway (1998) *Ukens statistikk,* nr 18, Oslo: SSB.

Statistics Norway (2000) *Arbeidskraftundersøkelsen,* Oslo:SSB.

Statistics Norway (2000a) *Sosialhjelpsstatistikk,* Oslo: SSB.

Statistics Norway (2000b) *Arbeidskraftundersøkelsen,* Oslo: SSB.

Terum, L.I. (1996) *Grenser for sosialpolitisk modernisering,* Oslo: Universitetsforlaget.

Torp, H. (1995) *Norway baseline study,* Oslo: Mimeo, ISF.

Vik-Mo, B. and Nervik, J.A. (1999) *Arbeidsplikten i Arbeidslinjen. Kommunenes iverksetting av vilkåret om arbeid for sosialhjelp,* Instituut for Sosiologi-og Statistend, NTNU.

White Paper no 21 (1998/99) *Rehabiliteringsmeldinga.*

White Paper, no 35/1994-95 *Velferdsmeldinga.*

White Paper no50 (1998/99) *Utjamningsmeldinga.*

SIX

When all must be active – workfare in Denmark

Anders Rosdahl and Hanne Weise

Introduction

Denmark is a small country (population 5.25 million) with an active population. Labour force participation is high (78% in the age group 16-66) – mainly due to the fact that Danish women have nearly as high a participation rate as men (73% compared to 82%, Danmarks Statistik, 1997). Nonetheless, a very large number of people of working age are provided for through public income transfer, via unemployment benefit, social assistance, early retirement pension and sickness benefit. In the period from the beginning of the 1960s to the mid 1990s the number of people receiving these benefits consistently increased alongside high and increasing unemployment (reaching more than 12% in 1994) before decreasing again (to about 6% in 1999)[1].

The main cause of high levels of cash transfer was the long period of high and increasing unemployment between 1974 and 1994. Developments in technology, new organisational forms and competitive working practices have led to a long-term trend towards increased demand for general and vocational qualifications as well as interpersonal skills. A consequence is that more and more people have found themselves judged unable to perform to required standards. In addition, increased labour market participation among women has led to an increased number claiming benefits related to lack of work.

In response to the increasing numbers of working age people receiving out-of-work state transfers, successive Danish governments have developed an 'Active Line' which links social and labour market policy. The underlying principle behind the Active Line is that 'workless' people in receipt of public income transfers should be participating in activities which bring them closer to the labour market, and which are beneficial to society as a whole. This line was increasingly emphasised throughout the 1990s.

In the past, 'active measures' (for example, training and publicly supported work) were offers or options that unemployed people and social assistance clients could take up if they chose to do so. However, increasingly, active measures have become both a right and an obligation for recipients. This is the essence of one form of *compulsory* active measure – here termed 'activation'. Currently, *all* clients must receive an activation measure after a standard period in receipt of unemployment benefit or social assistance. If such a measure is refused outright, public economic assistance is, in principle, suspended. Measures often, but do not always, include a work-based component. Payment levels in the form of either benefits or wages, vary depending on the measure. Sanctioning for non-compliance once within the scheme is only partial although refusal to participate prior to entry into a scheme can lead to a total sanction.

While strongly associated with debates around the 'rights and responsibilities' of individual recipients, the Danish Active Line, and activation itself, is unusual in two key respects. First, it is characterised by an understanding that the state *and* private enterprise have a responsibility to provide opportunities for inclusion. Second, as unemployment has fallen since the mid-1990s, activation policy has swung towards accepting the necessity of a long-term strategy towards inclusion in the labour market for highly marginalised individuals.

Officially, the primary purpose of activation is to bring people back into employment by developing their human capital. With decreasing unemployment since 1994 the target groups for activation have become 'weaker'; today, enhancing the general quality of life of participants is also a legitimate goal, with the idea that 'social activation' may help to reduce social problems. In principle, activation is a non-permanent situation for the individual participant. However, in practice, activation may continue for very long periods of time for some of the more disadvantaged groups, as they pass from scheme to scheme.

Work forms a significant proportion of activation offers, so that as activation has grown 'workfare' has become a more integral part of Danish labour market and social policy. The origins of compulsory activation can be traced to 1990 and the introduction of a 'Youth Allowance Scheme'. This required 18- to 19-year-olds who claimed social assistance to participate in activation in return for benefits. This scheme was later extended to 20- to 24-year-olds, and today the basic principle (activation in return for economic assistance) holds for all social clients after a set period of receipt.

It is likely that compulsory activation (and hence compulsory work) will become still more extensive in the future as a further extension of the principle that 'everyone with at least some work capacity to work should work'. This could even be extended so that early retirement or disability pensions are replaced with offers of work in circumstances adapted to individuals' reduced working capacity.

This chapter does not focus on forecasting but rather describes *current* Danish workfare policies – their causes, contents, developments and dilemmas. The chapter begins with a presentation of active measures generally, of which compulsory activation is the most important part. The remainder of the chapter focuses on compulsory activation.

Active measures

Active measures include measures targeted at people of employable age without work who, for whatever reason, have been unable to obtain work in the regular labour market and who receive some form of income transfer, for example unemployment benefit, social assistance or an early retirement pension. Reasons include reduced working ability resulting from health problems or a lack of suitable jobs. In some, but not all, cases participation in active measures is a precondition for receiving financial aid from the state.

1. *Work:* activity (often in cooperation with others) which leads to some product (either a physical or a service product). This work may be in ordinary public or private enterprises (in other words, with a wage subsidy), in voluntary organisations (for example, of a humanitarian kind) or in special institutions created for the purpose of activating certain groups (for example, specifically set up for social assistance recipients).
2. *Training/education:* activity involving organised learning under the supervision of a teacher. Training may take place in standard educational settings or through special courses created for specific categories of people without work.
3. *Activities of a social nature:* these include activities involving exchange of experience with other people in similar situations.
4. Some mix of the above.

To qualify as an active measure, an activity must take place within a formal organisation of some kind. Individual 'self-activation' (for example, taking care of one's own children, fishing, or digging the garden) is not accepted as an active measure. Usually active measures are part of a public policy programme financed wholly or partly by the State (represented at national government, local authorities and at county level). The activity is formally regulated. Regulation concerns: the purpose and type of measure; the implementing institutions; the target groups and conditions for participating; the allowance received by participants; the duration and hours of participation; for which groups participation is obligatory; and the consequences of not attending in terms of the right to benefits. The most important active measures are described in Table 6.1. Some of the more recently introduced measures, including 'flex jobs' and 'protected work', have been, as yet, little used. However, the present government aims to increase the use of these schemes.

A distinction needs to be made between active measures generally and activation more specifically. Only activation is compulsory, and hence 'workfare-like'. If recipients do not accept an activation offer, social assistance payments may be stopped for as long as an activation offer remains available. However, in contrast to workfare in an idealised sense, and in common with German 'Help Towards Work' policies, sanctioning is partial (see Chapter Three). If, once entered into the programme, a person does not subsequently take up an activation offer without valid reason, help is reduced in proportion to the number of hours absent. However, help can only be reduced by up to a maximum of 20%.

The measures described in Table 6.1 are a manifestation of the Active Line in Danish social and labour market policy, which has developed over the course of many years and been strengthened during the 1990s.

In recent years, the Active Line has enjoyed widespread political approval. The impact has been seen both in the legislative changes to traditional public policy programmes and in campaigns (initiated, for example, by the Ministry of Social Affairs). Recent surveys have shown that this line has legitimacy with long-term unemployed people as well as the wider Danish population (Bach, Larsen and Rosdahl, 1998).

Table 6.1: Active measures in Danish social and labour market policy

Name Introduced	Target group	Aim of measure	Contents of measure	Compulsory	Number of participants
Activation Late 1970s	People receiving unemployment benefit or social assistance.	To bring people back to regular employment, or to increase general welfare.	Typically some form of training or work – or a combination.	Yes	77,690 (average 1998)
Training leave 1994	Insured unemployed people aged 25 years or more.	To increase qualifications and employment chances (maximum period is 1 year).	Participation in public approved education. The leave for more than 4 weeks presupposes approval from the Public Employment Service.	No	13,824 (average 1998)
Rehabilitation Around 1960	People whose working ability is reduced due to physical, psychological or social factors and who are expected to be able to regain total or partial working ability, with the help of a rehabilitation programme.	To provide work in the regular labour market or in some special form of employment (for example a flex job).	Often some form of training, but may also include work (with a wage subsidy).	No	23,452 (total 1996)

Table 6.1: cntd.../

Name Introduced	Target group	Aim of measure	Contents of measure	Compulsory	Number of participants
Flex job 1998	People with permanently reduced working ability, who are not considered to be able to benefit from rehabilitation. People who are already employed (in ordinary employment) as well as those without work.	To provide permanent employment for people with permanently reduced working ability.	'Flex jobs' are created in ordinary workplaces (public or private enterprises). The wage is agreed collectively. The employer receives a wage subsidy amounting to 1/3, 1/2 or 2/3 of the relevant minimum wage – depending on the degree to which the working ability of the person employed is reduced. In principle, employment in a flex job is not temporary.	No	5,811 (participating 31 May 1999)
Protected work 1998	People receiving early retirement pension.	To provide permanent employment for the target group.	A wage subsidy is given when people are employed at ordinary work places according to this scheme. 'Sheltered employment' may also be of a collective nature, in other words take place in special institutions where people with mental disorders, or other disabilities are employed.	No	5,475 (participating 31 May 1999)

Table 6.1: cntd.../

Name Introduced	Target group	Aim of measure	Contents of measure	Compulsory	Number of participants
Employment under special conditions Late 1990s	People whose working ability is reduced.	To reintegrate or retain people in the work place, who have a high risk of long-term unemployment.	'Social chapters' have been introduced in many collective agreements. The purpose of these chapters is to make it possible for employers and employees to reach local agreements regarding special terms of employment for people whose working ability is reduced, due to age or other reasons. The special terms of employment may concern the contents of work, (a lower) wage and/or (reduced) working hours. No (public) wage subsidy needs to be involved.	No	3,659 (survey estimate: November 1998)

The Danish Active Line is based on following principles:

- Income support, especially for long periods, and especially for young people, has a number of negative social and psychological consequences. Instead of receiving 'passive' income maintenance, people should be 'active'.
- Active measures should help to integrate people into society and should contribute to enhancing the qualifications and employability of people without work.
- It is the responsibility of the individual to improve his or her qualifications, his or her working ability and his or her ability to be self-sufficient.
- It is the responsibility of society to provide the opportunities that make this possible.
- Society has a right to demand effort (for example, through participation in activation) from individuals receiving income transfer. The economic incentives implied in the levels of unemployment benefit and social assistance should promote 'activity' rather than 'passive' receipt. To summarise: 'If you receive economic assistance from society, you have to make the best effort you can in return'.
- Through active measures, people should be helped to obtain regular jobs in the regular labour market. It is important to prevent people of employable age from entering schemes in which they are more or less permanently provided for, solely through public transfer.
- Because finding regular work is more difficult for some people than for others, private enterprise in the regular labour market should be encompassing in its employment policies. Companies should be willing to hire people with reduced working abilities. There should be a place for 'weak groups'. In other words, private as well as public enterprises are expected to uphold a practice of social responsibility.

Right and obligation to activation

An average of nearly 30,000 social assistance recipients were undergoing activation in 1998 (Danmarks Statistik, 1999), making up just under two fifths of the total population participating in active measures. Activation has not always been obligatory. During the 1970s and early 1980s people tended to see it as a 'right', so that participants who had a right to an activation offer could and *did* demand one. However, particularly since

1990, the obligation aspect has been strengthened so that, while in theory recipients meeting the qualifying criteria may assert a right to a placement, local authorities can now demand participation of people who do not assert this right – and the latter scenario is more usual.

Activation schemes for insured and uninsured unemployed people (social assistance recipients) are administered by the Public Employment Service (PES) and by local authorities within a two-tier system. Insured and uninsured people are governed according to separate legislation (although there is some overlap), under the Ministry of Labour and the Ministry of Social Affairs respectively. The division of responsibilities between social policy (Ministry of Social Affairs and local authorities) and labour market policy (Ministry of Labour and the PES), is a point of contention.

There are 275 local authorities in Denmark, which are governed by political bodies elected every four years. Most authorities are very small (135 have a population below 10,000), some are medium-sized (119 have a population between 10,000 and 50,000), and a few are very large (21 have a population larger than 50,000) (Danmarks Statistik, 1998a). In contrast, the PES is organised into 14 regions under the Labour Market Authority, which comes under the Ministry of Labour.

Social assistance forms the 'lowest' security net in the social security system, designed for people who are unable to provide for themselves and who cannot be provided for in other ways. Entitlement presupposes some change in situation, for example, loss of work, divorce or illness, with the result that an individual is in need of help. Help may be passive (social assistance) or active (activation). It is a precondition of help that the applicant (or their spouse) does not have a 'suitable work offer'. An offer is suitable if the local authorities think that the person can manage the job. Pay relative to former employment is not relevant. People who receive social assistance must also take a 'reasonable' activation offer to enhance the possibility of their finding employment.

Individual authorities administer and part-fund social assistance and have some autonomy over methods of activation but there is no autonomy when it comes to the level of social assistance paid, or to the minimum level of payment to activated clients. Social assistance is means-tested. Help cannot be given if a person has assets (although small assets under 10,000 DKK (1,345 Euros) are not taken into consideration). This help is 'supplementary'. Where income from other sources is available, help is reduced accordingly.

For adults providing for children, social assistance amounts to 80% of maximum unemployment benefit and is worth 60% to non-providers aged 25 years or more. Young people (under 25) receive nearly 40% of maximum unemployment benefit if they live alone, but only about 20% if they are living with their parents. In addition to the basic assistance there are special provisions, for example for top-ups for housing costs where these are very high. Social assistance may be received for an unlimited time period. However, the assistance (including additional allowances) is never more than the maximum unemployment benefit, after six months of receipt.

On an administrative level, people receiving social assistance must fall into one of the following categories:

1 Unemployed:
   a) according to the general ILO criteria;
   b) would be unemployed if they were not currently undergoing activation.
2 Receiving social assistance for some other reason (including people who may be activated).

The local authority is obliged to ensure that people in category 1a are registered with the Central Unemployment Register (where insured unemployed people are also registered). These people are included as registered unemployed in Denmark's official unemployment statistics. They are registered in the PES files in the same way as insured unemployed people, and they receive the same counselling services as insured people. If a social assistance recipient does not take a job offer or is not present for counselling or information meetings in the PES without good cause then PES staff are supposed to inform the relevant local authority. The local authority should then consider whether the conditions under which social assistance is offered are being fulfilled. However, while the PES may make job offers to social assistance recipients, this agency is not responsible for providing active measures for non-insured people.

Municipalities fund half the cost of social assistance payments to clients in their area, so that the number of social assistance clients affects the local level of taxation. In the past, local authorities had a financial incentive to activate social assistance recipients. Through subsidised employment, recipients subsequently could become entitled to unemployment insurance, so that local authorities no longer had responsibility for their welfare (as is still the case in Germany; see Chapter Three). A law passed in 1994 put an end to this practice, so as to enhance the aim of permanent integration into the labour market rather than merely shifting the economic burden of the local authorities to the state.

Despite administrative divisions at the State level, and variation in practice at the level of local authorities, there is a sense in which activation for insured and uninsured recipients constitutes a single policy. The client groups overlap considerably. Many social assistance recipients are (defined legally as) unemployed and a number of long-term unemployed people receiving unemployment benefit could just as well be social assistance recipients.

Trends in activation policy

Initiatives for non-insured young unemployed people were intensified in the later half of the 1970s. In 1978[2] local authorities were obliged by the central government to set aside a certain amount of money per inhabitant to combat youth unemployment. The most important schemes included in this initiative were employment projects (now called individual job training), employment with a wage subsidy in private companies (now called job training), extraordinary apprenticeship places and training courses of various types.

The *Youth Allowance Scheme* (1990) introduced obligatory activation of 18- to 19-year-olds on a part-time basis for at least five months, with a vacation period of 14 days. The right to benefit was matched with an obligation to work. Activation took place after only two weeks on social assistance. The wage was a special low 'project-wage'. After completing five months activation, young people were able to return to 'passive' benefit receipt. The age group for this scheme was widened in 1992 to include 18- to 24-year-olds and the vacation period was extended.

As of January 1994, social assistance recipients aged over 25 are officially supposed to be activated after one year on social assistance; in fact a number of people aged 25+ had been activated by the local authorities before 1994 (Brogaard and Weise, 1997). The 1994 Labour Market Reform did not bring major changes for young unemployed social assistance recipients. However, in 1998 local authorities were obliged to activate all young recipients after three months on social assistance, including those with more severe social problems. The only exceptions were people with dependent children who were supposed to be 'activated' after a period of 12 months.

Prior to activation, individuals are offered counselling in the form of a guidance and introduction programme which lasts a maximum of six weeks. The subsequent obligatory activation period lasts between six and 18 months. If no work is found after a further three months of social assistance receipt, recipients under the age of 30 are entitled to (and are obliged to participate in) a new activation measure.

The development of the Danish Active Line can be viewed as a process by which those who define and administer legislation have felt their way forward, gained experience and made adjustments. The following gives a (simplified) picture of some political trends in the development of active policy during the last 10-15 years.

- First, the *extent* of initiatives has been increased, particularly with the activation of more people earlier in their period of unemployment. This has meant that activated people have comprised a growing group relative to registered unemployment.
- Rights to activation were first introduced for people entitled to unemployment insurance. As those rights have been extended to assistance recipients the *emphasis on obligation has increased.*
- A third trend is *increased emphasis on training* – which includes ordinary education courses. Unemployed people are able to undertake training, including introductory vocational courses. Subsidies are now provided for the establishment of apprenticeship places.
- A fourth characteristic is that the *allowances for some types of activation have been reduced.* In the 1980s, participants in employment projects were paid wages according to public sector collective agreements. Since 1990 participants have received a lower so-called 'project-wage'. The magnitude and conditions of allowances have increasingly been used as an instrument to influence the behaviour of unemployed people, including increasing their motivation to seek ordinary work.
- A fifth characteristic is increased emphasis on the responsibilities of local authorities to provide activation offers to assist clients. Authorities are now *obliged to provide guidance and to provide an offer.*
- Sixth, the recent fall in unemployment has meant that a larger proportion of social assistance recipients have social problems, as more employable people have been absorbed into the labour market. As a result, the focus of activation has shifted to *developing personal skills and motivation.*
- Last, but not least, *preventing long-term receipt* has become more important. Specified 'high risk groups' now receive priority early on in a period of unemployment.

Target groups for activation

According to the 1998 Act, obligatory activation holds for everyone receiving social assistance; people whose only problem is understood to be their lack of a job; and people with social problems in addition to unemployment. Exceptions to this general rule include:

- People who are sick, or who have a high probability of becoming sick if they are activated. The illness should be confirmed with a physician's statement.
- Pregnant women or women with children younger than six months.
- People with small children in cases where it is impossible (for the local authority or others) to provide childcare. Publicly provided childcare is generally available for children aged one and over.

Excepted individuals may still participate in Active Measures.

In general the local authorities may themselves decide whom they will activate, how they will be activated and for how long. However, national legislation includes some minimum demands, which the local authorities must fulfil.

Under 30-year-olds must be activated after a period of 13 weeks continuous receipt of (passive) social assistance. For unemployed people deemed to have no significant problems other than lack of work, the activation period is 18 months, unless the young person has a vocational qualification in which case the period is six months. Since most young social assistance recipients have no vocational qualification, the typical activation period is 18 months. Activation is for at least 30 hours per week, up to a maximum of 37 hours per week. People aged under 30 who are considered to have social problems in addition to unemployment, also receive 18 months of activation. However, the local authority has the discretion to prescribe considerably fewer hours of activation per week.

Over 30-year-olds are activated after one year of social assistance receipt. Local authorities decide the duration of activation and the number of hours per week. If activation is for periods longer than 12 months an activation-free period (or 'vacation') of one month must be included. Local authorities are not obliged to re-activate recipients aged over 30 following a first activation period.

Action plans for activation

Local authorities may use written 'Individual Action Plans' in an attempt to ensure a coherent form of help, and to take account of the background, the abilities and wishes of the activated person. The plan may specify an employment target, or may include more 'soft targets', such as improvement of the person's general life situation, or overcoming a drinking problem.

Social assistance recipients are expected to take a positive attitude towards determining their Individual Action Plan. The degree of influence they can exert is determined by the types of activation offers available within the municipality, by the way the local authority chooses to administer the programme, and by the aspirations of recipients themselves.

Activation offers

According to the legislation, local authorities *should* try to give clients a choice of offers. The variety of activation offers has gradually increased, and today they range from subsidised jobs to voluntary unpaid activities. Typical activation offers include the following:

1. *Short counselling and introductory courses.* Such courses are often given at the beginning of a period of social assistance receipt. The courses may contain information about activation offers and about rights and obligations. These courses are provided for the people local authorities consider to be in need of information regarding rights and, more particularly, responsibilities.
2. *Job training*, private or public. This takes the form of wage subsidy to employers which amounts to a little more than half of a typical minimum wage. Wages for people in job training are determined according to collective agreement, although in public sector job training there is a maximum level (85.10 DKK/hour, or 11.45 Euros). The usual minimum period with the same private employer is six months. The six months may be exceeded if the employer either offers training (corresponding to at least one twelfth of the total period of job training), or employs the unemployed person under normal conditions (without a subsidy) for a period of at least the same length as the job training period (the wage subsidy period).
3. *Individual job training.* In practice, individual job training for non-insured people largely consists of employment projects. These may be established by private employers or voluntary organisations, but more

often operate as local authority led, created work projects. Individual job training is targeted at people who face severe difficulty obtaining work under normal conditions. The work in such projects is 'additional' and must be of a type which otherwise would not have been performed as ordinary waged work. Production and marketing can take place only if this enhances the future employment prospects of the participants, in which case goods can be sold and sales achieved on the same terms as for ordinary enterprises producing the same products. The income in individual job training is equal to social assistance plus a small employment supplement.

4. *Specially adapted training courses.* Types of training include:
   - further education in day high schools;
   - extraordinary education in youth schools;
   - courses in community education colleges;
   - Danish language courses for immigrants and refugees.

5. *Special activation measures.* These consist of a mix of training and work, such as guidance and counselling and practical work training.

6. *Voluntary unpaid work.* Voluntary unpaid work plays a very minor role within activation. Activities are organised by voluntary organisations and associations in the area of culture, social work, environmental protection and sport. Voluntary activities are supposed to contain an employment or (further) training perspective.

7. *Adult education and further training.* People over the age of 25 who have been unemployed for six months (including activation periods), and who have poor employment prospects, may participate in further training.

All the activation offers described above count towards the activation period – so it is clear that in Denmark compulsory activation does not always mean 'work', let alone 'workfare'. The pay under activation corresponds to social assistance except for those in job training. In addition to this the local authority may decide to pay up to 1,000 DKK (135 Euros) per month (or 1,500 under extraordinary circumstances) to cover expenses related to activation, such as transport costs.

Activation: who gets what?

Research carried out in 1994 showed that in the early 1990s job training in the private sector was a common method of activating social assistance clients (Ingerslev, 1994). This route has been shown to be more effective than activation in other sectors (Ingerslev, 1992; Weise and Brogaard, 1997). More recently, as employment has increased, the pool of social assistance clients has become less skilled and less suited to job training. In addition, job training in the private sector has become more expensive to use. The resultant trend has been towards more and more use of *individual* job training as the main 'offer', the target group for which is the 'weakest' group. This appears to represent a trend towards *greater use of workfare*, as increasingly people have to work for social assistance level wages. In 1997, individual job training accounted for nearly two thirds of all activated people in work (Danmarks Statistik, 1998a).

The formal target group for individual job training is people who have problems finding ordinary work. While individual job training may take place in the regular labour market, this seldom occurs and places are more often in special projects alongside other recipients. The typical form of individual job training is an 'employment project' (the term was introduced when this type of activation was directed to young people in the late 1970s). In the 1970s the local authorities could not demand participation in such projects, and wages were set according to collective agreement. This meant that the young people participating in employment projects could be relatively well off, both compared to their situation while on social assistance and often also in comparison to regular work. However, allowances have since been reduced alongside an increase in the level of obligation.

There are two popular images of employment projects. The first is that much of the work is meaningless, because the projects are only created to keep (young) people busy. The second is that many projects include work that is interesting and fulfilling. It may be work with some artistic flavour, for instance in music, media or the theatre. Sometimes the work is combined with interesting training courses and a number of (young) people may prefer such projects to boring industrial work under a strict authoritarian regime. Many projects cooperate with training institutions of different kinds, the extent of this training element is unknown at present, but it is likely to be very important.

The duration of activation in individual job training is, on average, about five months (Danmarks Statistik, 1998b). Currently there is no clear representative picture of the content of this type of activation. However, a 1996 survey of about 550 leaders of activation projects (Weise and Brogaard, 1997) found an average of 16 participants per project. According to the project leaders the aim of one third of the projects was to 'enhance the personal qualifications' of activated people. The aim of the remaining projects was primarily to bring the people into regular employment. Two thirds of the projects produced a physical product (for example, children's clothes) or a service product (for example, theatre, film, café, garden or cleaning work).

Workfare or activation?

The term 'active' only came to be applied to policies in the late 1980s. Participation in job training or subsidised work has been an option for many insured unemployed people since the late 1970s, when such measures were linked to the right to continuous receipt of unemployment benefit. Active social and labour market policies have nearly always had an element of workfare within them, since participation in activation has often been a condition for receiving benefits. Until 1990 however, the workfare element of the schemes was less explicit. Only with the introduction of the Youth Allowance Scheme did refusing to participate automatically mean that a person became ineligible for social assistance. The Youth Allowance Scheme was the first scheme in which failing the 'work test' had such severe consequences. Under the Youth Allowance Scheme activation started almost immediately after registering for benefit, unlike previous programmes.

The Youth Allowance Scheme changed the rules of social assistance so that it became possible to end the support if a person refused an *activation offer*. The ordinary job offer was no longer considered to be an effective work test, as labour demand fell and offers became more scarce. While the Youth Allowance Scheme changed the letter of the law, there was a greater change in interpretation. It became legitimate to question whether a young person really was unemployed or just was claiming social assistance because it was an easy way to finance a summer vacation. These were central aspects in the debate in the media at the time.

One aim of Youth Allowance was to stop the inflow into long-term social assistance. The scheme was thought to work in two ways:

A. by preventing people who could provide for themselves from claiming social assistance, or from claiming for a long period. The idea is that the activation requirement deters people who can find jobs, or who can support themselves by other means (such as through their parents), from claiming assistance in the first place; and
B. by helping unemployed people into jobs or education through improved qualifications or through direct help with job placements.

Where did the ideas that lie behind the Youth Allowance Scheme come from? Many forces were pushing youth unemployment policy in that direction. Changes in the labour market resulted in an increase in the numbers of young people affected by unemployment, and local municipalities developed their own strategies to cope with these changes. To an extent the Youth Allowance Scheme can be seen to be the culmination of many local responses to a lack of employment and education possibilities. Local authorities began to use workfare as a work-test tool and as a means of separating the 'deserving' from the 'undeserving' in a period when it was becoming increasingly acceptable to say that unemployment in some cases was 'voluntary'.

Activation and local authority strategies

While all local authorities have a strong financial incentive to minimise the number of clients within their boundaries, they have taken different approaches to activation. Two main strategies have been used:

- *Immediate activation* – to deter potential benefit claimants (type A strategy, above). Activation of 'strong' clients in non-attractive projects can be used as a 'work-testing' tool, to make 'strong' clients seek employment elsewhere.
- *Help into jobs or education* – for example private job placements, with or without a wage subsidy (type B strategy, above). Placements in private jobs often lead to permanent employment, but are usually only possible for 'strong' social clients. Until the practice was ended, this was also used as a strategy for 'weak groups' to enable them to be passed into the insurance system.

In general, municipalities used the Youth Allowance Scheme to defer entry into social assistance. Activation requirements were enthusiastically and extensively applied in most municipalities.

Both strategies work very well for 'strong' social clients in periods of high unemployment, such as in the second half of the 1980s. At such times, 'weak' clients become less visible and do not pose an immediate problem. The result is that the policies appear to be successful.

There appears to be no correlation between the type of strategy that was used and the political persuasion of the local authority. Municipalities with both Left- and Right-wing majorities used each strategy. While the activation idea was founded in the Right wing of the political spectrum, the apparent effectiveness of the policy in cutting municipal spending has affected the practice of Left-wing authorities.

Activation and ideology

During 1986 and 1987, when the Danish economy was booming, bottlenecks began to appear in many areas of the labour market and paradoxically unemployment was high. In general terms, the situation was held to be caused by a lack of relevant qualifications among unemployed people. Nonetheless, questions about a lack of efficient jobsearch and an unwillingness to take jobs that were different from the last job held with respect to location, pay and trade began to be asked (Det Økonomiske Råd, 1988; Bach, 1987). In the late 1980s it became more acceptable to discuss whether the behaviour of unemployed people could be changed by using economic incentives.

While youth unemployment was relatively high, few educational opportunities were available at this time. Young unemployed people in Denmark without any further education are not entitled to unemployment benefit and so fell back on social assistance. An increase in youth unemployment meant an increase in the number who claimed social assistance.

In 1988, when the Youth Allowance Act was first proposed, rhetoric focused not only on the high levels of youth unemployment, but also on middle-class children who, after finishing high school, claimed social assistance during the summer. This behaviour came to be seen as immoral and undermining because these young people did not have any social problems. Both issues played an important role in influencing the direction of the debate – and helps to explain why the resultant policy is both punitive and ameliorative.

The Youth Allowance Act was first proposed by the Liberal Democrat Minister of Social Affairs in a Right-wing minority coalition government (Folketingets Forhandlinger). In order for the Act to pass, the Liberal Democrat government needed votes either from the extreme Right or from the Social Democrats (and other Left-wing parties). Politicians on the extreme Right refused to support the proposition because they felt that the 'project wage' was too high, and did not offer enough incentives to jobsearch. On the other hand, Social Democrats would not support the initiative because the unions were very much against part-time activation, and it was felt that the immediate activation would result in activating people waiting to start a job or education programme (and hence be a waste of resources). Social Democrats also felt that five months of activation were not enough, and that there would be a need for ongoing or repeated activation.

The Left believed the scheme should only target the young people with severe labour market problems. The Right believed the primary aim should be restricting passive benefit: even a short period of passive benefit was felt to be potentially harmful to young people because of stigmatisation. The result was that Youth Allowance was initially rejected. While the general idea attracted support, there was strong disagreement about how the scheme should operate.

Six months later, an economic incentive for local authorities to supply full-time activation was included in the proposal, and it was stressed that people who needed it should be reactivated. The proposition was put before Parliament a second time and was passed, with votes from all parties except the extreme Right. At present, a large majority supports the idea of workfare, and some of the reservations Social Democrats had about part-time employment and immediate activation have subsided.

The expansion of activation in the 1990s was partly due to an increased desire to work-test a wider range of clients associated with a strong belief in the danger of idleness. However, while the Danish workfare policy began deterring entry into the social system (type A strategies), it has changed and now also concerns itself with helping the social clients out of the system (type B strategies). There are still harsh immediate requirements, but there is also a focus on the quality of activation offers.

The future: expansion beyond unemployed clients

Since 1994 unemployment in Denmark has fallen from 12% to 6%. Many social clients and unemployed people with high levels of human capital found jobs. The result has been that a relatively greater proportion of those who remain unemployed have problems other than unemployment. People who have been 'hiding in the system' and who are not ready for the labour market, now form the bulk of the client group.

The obligation since 1994 for social clients with broader social problems to be activated has proved to be difficult to implement (Brogaard and Weise, 1997; Weise and Brogaard, 1997). Employment-based activation programmes are often redundant for this group, because many clients are in such a difficult situation that they are unable to participate. Evaluation evidence shows the lowest employment effects for activation are for the group who have been receiving social assistance for the longest period

(Weise and Brogaard, 1997). Staff in most municipalities believe that activation of this group does not bring them any closer to the regular labour market. Rather, activation is supposed to have a positive effect on their everyday life, in that it may prevent a further development of social problems.

It is clear that activation with an immediate labour market goal does not work very well for the weakest groups. Labour market measures targeted at the weaker groups produce different outcomes when compared to the same measures targeted at those whose only problem is unemployment. There are indications (Weise and Brogaard, 1997) that the weakest groups do not react to economic incentives. If they receive a low wage in activation, they do not increase jobseeking, as the more resourceful clients do. These clients remain in activation because they have no alternative.

Integration or reintegration into employment is a very long and expensive process, because it often means starting education at a basic level. Increased use of social activation, where the goal is to improve quality of life and not labour market performance, may be the main option for the future.

Notes

[1] Fewer than 200,000 people of working age received public transfers in 1960 compared to just under a million in the mid-1990s (people on Activation and Training Leave schemes are included in these figures, Smith, 1998a).

[2] The Extra-Ordinary Local Authority Employment Measures Act.

References

Bach, H.B. (1987) *Lønmodtageres arbejdskraft mobilitet,* Socialforskningsinstituttet, Publikation 169.

Bach, H.B., Larsen, J.A. and Rosdahl, A. (1998) *Langtidsledige i tre kommuner,* Socialforskningsinstituttet 9, København.

Brogaard, S. and Weise, H. (1997) *Evaluering af kommunal aktivering,* Socialforskningsinstituttet 7, København.

Danmarks Statistik (1997) *Statistiske Efterretninger: Arbejdsmarked* 18, Registerbaseret arbejdsstyrkestatistik, 11.7.1997.

Danmarks Statistik (1998a) *Statistisk Årbog 1998*, Københaun.

Danmarks Statistik (1998b) *Statistiske Efterretninger: Arbejdsmarked*, Arbejdsmarkedspolitiske foranstaltninger 1997, 14, 19.5.1998.

Danmarks Statistik (1999) *Nyt fra Danmarks Statistik*, 29.4.

Det Økonomiske Råd (1988) *Dansk Økonomi*, juni, København.

Folketingets Forhandlinger: Div år.

Ingerslev, O. (1992) *Resultater af Herning Kommunes beskæftigelsesindsats*, Amternes og kommunernes forskningsinstitut.

Ingerslev, O. (1994) *Succes eller fiasko? – Effekten af den kommunal besftigelsesindsats i 26 kommuner*, Amternes og kommunernes forskningsinstitut.

Smith, N. (1998) *Det effektive, rummelige og trygge danske arbejdsmarked?*, i: Arbejdsmarkedspolitisk Årbog 1997, København.

Weise, H. and Brogaard, S. (1997) *Aktivering af kontanthjælpsmodtagere*, Socialforskningsinstituttet, 21, København.

SEVEN

Steps to compulsion within British labour market policies

Heather Trickey and Robert Walker

Introduction

Facing an out-of-work population increasingly reliant on social assistance provision, successive British governments over the last 20 years have implemented a range of supply-side labour market policies to tackle unemployment. These demonstrate a trend towards increased use of compulsory activity and, latterly, compulsory work activity, which has come to be an accepted feature of policies directed to unemployed people. The social democratic New Labour government has developed this trend in two key respects. First, through introducing a universal policy of mandatory activity for young unemployed people in receipt of unemployment assistance, and second, through extending the reach of activating social policies to a range of 'workless' groups not previously within the scope of mainstream labour market programmes.

Unemployment and 'worklessness'

The size and structure of the UK labour market has changed radically in the last 30 years. An upward trend in employment rates was accompanied for much of the period by rising unemployment. Employment continued to rise throughout the 1990s and by 1998 had reached an historic high with an employment to working-age population ratio of 71.2% (OECD, 1999). Meanwhile, labour force participation among 15- to 64-year-olds remained more or less constant at around 76%, and unemployment fell from its recessionary high of 9.7% in 1994, to 6.2% in 1999.

These changes reflected a process of de-industrialisation, with a decline in manufacturing employment, concentrated especially in the traditional industrial regions, and a growth in the service sector. Between 1984 and 1989, 80% of employment growth was in non-manual occupations (White and Forth, 1998) and this trend has continued. Moreover, while the employment rates of the best qualified remained constant in the two decades to 1997, they fell by 12% for those with intermediate vocational qualifications and by 18% for those without qualifications.

The extent of the growth in so-called flexible employment is disputed (Meadows, 1999; Walker et al, 1999), but it is clear that people *returning to work* from unemployment tend to enter the more unstable sections of the labour market. While many people who become unemployed rapidly return to work, the jobs available to them – particularly to those who have been without work for some time – are disproportionately unskilled, short term and poorly paid (White and Forth, 1998). Only 22% of the jobs taken by people moving off benefit are full time and permanent (Gregg and Wadsworth, 1995). Meanwhile, there has been a decline in the prevalence of the nine-to-five working day. About a quarter of UK employees are employed part time compared with a fifth in 1981, and over half work hours that vary from week to week. Six per cent of jobs are temporary. While this is well below the European Union (EU) average of 11%, the number has increased by over 40% since 1990 (HM Treasury, 1997).

Unlike most other European countries, UK unemployment is lower among *women* than *men* (in 1998, 5.3% and 6.9% for women and men respectively) (OECD, 1999). Female unemployment also proved less sensitive than male unemployment to movements in aggregate demand during the recession and recovery of the early 1990s (Central Statistical Office, 1997). This is explained by a much lower participation rate (58%, compared with nearly 84% for men). Participation rates are particularly low among lone mothers, with a much lower proportion of lone mothers participating than is the case in many European countries (Bradshaw et al, 1996). The overall proportion of lone mothers in work has actually *decreased* since 1979, when just under half were working, to 41% in 1996. Approximately 40% of lone mothers are 'economically inactive' and caring for their children, with a further 10% in education (Rowlingson and McKay, 1997).

A third of unemployed people are unemployed *long term* (12 months or longer). Although unemployment overall has fallen sharply, the decline in long-term unemployment (one year plus) has been much slower. The ratio of long- to shorter-term unemployment is associated with the stage in the economic cycle, typically declining at the start of an economic downturn and increasing towards the end. However, the ratio for men fell from 49.6% in 1995 to 38.4% in 1998 while that for women fell from 32.3% to 24.6%.

The evidence shows that people with limited qualifications, skills, and work experience and people in poor health are more likely to become long-term unemployed (Trickey et al, 1998). Again, rates are higher for men (38.4% of unemployed men compared to 24.6% of women). A disproportionate number of the people in the UK who experience long spells of unemployment are aged 55 or over. Calculations for 1994 showed that the majority of people who became unemployed after this age were unlikely ever to work again (Shaw et al, 1996). Moreover, the proportion of men of this age who are outside the labour market has more than doubled from 14% in 1977 to 37% today. If the same proportion of men over 54 were employed or looking for work as 20 years ago, the recorded unemployment rate would be nearly a million higher (HM Treasury, 1997).

Short-term unemployment is particularly concentrated among younger people. In the UK, and especially since the introduction of New Labour's welfare reform policies, 'younger people' have come to be defined as people aged under 24, which is the definition used here. The *traditional* youth labour market (until recently this referred to the labour market for 16- to 19-year-olds) has never recovered from the dramatic deflation which it experienced in the early 1980s. This resulted in a lengthening of the school-to-work transition as the task of finding unsubsidised employment became particularly problematic for 16- to 17-year-old school leavers (Maguire, 2000). The rise in the number of school leavers who fail to find employment or to take up training places is an area of concern for the government (Social Exclusion Unit, 1999).

Unemployment for both prime age workers and for workers aged 55 plus fell in the UK between 1990 and 1998, while youth unemployment rose slightly from an already high base of just over 10% to over 12%. Rates are higher among young men than young women (13.8% compared to 10.5% in 1998). Similarly, labour market participation rates among younger people in the UK remain high having dropped from 78% to just under 70% (OECD, 1999). Levels of unemployment among young people in the UK reflect high rates of *inflow* into unemployment rather than long average durations, and the inflows of young people are more closely related to changes in labour demand than is the case for older unemployed people.

A proportion of young people is insufficiently skilled for the majority of available jobs. The mismatch between the demand for skilled and semi-skilled labour and the available labour supply is particularly marked among young people entering the labour market. Despite the increasing size of the higher education sector (30% of young people go to university or a higher education institution (Dearing, 1997)) and the numbers taking advanced qualifications, about 8% of young people leave school without any qualifications.

In the UK, the number of people of working age who do not work as a result of *sickness or disability* has increased by 1.5 million over the last 20 years. There is a positive *geographical* link between moves into Incapacity Benefit and unemployment; in some northern regions of England and in South Wales sickness claimants account for more than 15% of the male workforce. This suggests diversion of long-term unemployed people onto sickness-related benefits in areas of high unemployment – a component of the 'hidden unemployed' population (Beatty et al, 1997).

In 1993-94, 64% of households with a sick or disabled adult received no income from work. Over a quarter (27%) of such households received all of their income from benefits, compared to 10% of households in the general population. Four fifths of adults who had a disability and lived alone reported having a gross household income of under £200, compared to two fifths of the whole population (Rowlingson and Berthoud, 1996). In addition, a substantial minority (just under a quarter) of unemployed claimants report a health condition that they believe affects the type of work that they can do (Trickey et al, 1998). Such people are substantially more likely than other claimants to spend long periods as unemployed and a disproportionate number of them eventually move on to Incapacity Benefit. People with disabilities often have comparatively few skills and limited work experience.

The UK has a high proportion of what the government has termed 'workless households' – that is, households where no adult is in *paid* employment. About one in six families with at least one adult member of working age are deemed 'workless', compared with 9% in 1979. In part this is because although the employment rate among women with partners in work has increased, non-working men and women are also increasingly partnered. Individuals are twice as likely to find work if their partner is already working (HM Treasury, 1999a). This disparity has often been cited as evidence of the disincentive effects of Britain's means-tested unemployment-related benefits. While this may be so, there is also evidence that people often share the poor employment prospects of their partners (Elias, 1997). Moreover, traditional one-earner couples are more susceptible to unemployment than dual-earner families.

Unemployed people and social security

At £93 billion in 1997-98, spending on social security accounted for just under a third (32%) of all public expenditure and exceeded the budgets of the next two largest policy areas, health and social services (17%) and education (12%) put together (DSS, 1997a). Moreover, the proportion of public expenditure accounted for by social security increased from under a fifth (18%) in 1971 and from just 14% in 1949. By far the largest item within social security is pensions, which account for 44% of the total. Most of the remainder is attributable to spending on benefits for the long-term sick and for family support. Spending on unemployment-related benefits accounted for only 9% of the social security budget in 1997-98. The government believes that benefit reductions might be readily made in this area by reducing the number of claimants.

Within the system of social security provision, the division between social assistance recipients and people who receive state-run insurance (or contributory) benefit, is much less marked than elsewhere. Rather, to a greater extent than elsewhere, clients are *distinguished according to reason for claiming* – in particular, people who receive financial help as a result of unemployment are subject to very different rules from those who receive help primarily for other reasons.

The systems of benefit delivery for contributory, non-contributory and means-tested state assistance are *integrated* and highly *centralised*. In both cases, delivery and terms and conditions are the responsibility of national government, through the Secretary of State for Social Security who heads the Department of Social Security (DSS). With the exception of Housing Benefit, (a means-tested benefit payable to help meet the cost of renting), and Council Tax Benefit (a rebate on local property tax), local authorities have no role in the administration or payment of benefits. Moreover, even in these cases local authorities merely act as agents of central government, operating within tightly defined limits.

Claimants have *well-established rights* to benefit. Contributions are made through Social (National) Insurance (NI) and are generally not earnings-related but similar in level to means-tested benefits, although the most important, Retirement Pension, contains earnings-related components. Benefits are administered through an executive agency of the DSS, the Benefits Agency (BA). A certain element of income, including some earnings and child maintenance payments may be disregarded. *In-work assistance* is available for low income families with children through Working Families Tax Credit (formerly Family Credit). A similar form of in-work support (Earnings Top Up) has been piloted for adults without children and the government's long-term aim is to introduce an employment tax credit (HM Treasury, 1999a), replacing the adult component of Working Families' Tax Credit and possibly expanded to cover some families without children. From 2003 the government plans to parcel together child additions in out-of-work benefits (Income Support and Jobseeker's Allowance), in-work tax credits and the new children's tax credit to create a single payment of support relating to children – an integrated child credit.

Developments in conditionality and entitlement: pre-New Labour

Unemployed claimants have always had to be available for, and to actively seek, work, and to be willing to accept 'reasonable' job offers. However, in common with other OECD countries, recent UK governments have re-emphasised the 'work-test' rules and the conditional nature of entitlement for people claiming assistance during periods of involuntary unemployment. At the present time these work-test rules do not apply to groups claiming other forms of assistance, including lone parents and people claiming on the grounds of sickness or disability. This is because, until very recently, these groups had been widely considered to be unavailable for, or unable to, work.

The tenure of Lord Young as Secretary of State for Employment in the mid-1980s was associated with a marked shift away from earlier Conservative policies that used work experience programmes and early retirement to remove individuals from the official unemployment register. Instead, legislative changes to social security during the latter half of the 1980s and early 1990s both *tightened benefit eligibility and strengthened benefit conditionality*. Conditionality was emphasised, and measures were introduced to encourage people to leave benefit: these included compulsory 'Restart' interviews after six months unemployment; short, mandatory, re-motivation programmes, jobsearch programmes and longer (usually voluntary) work experience programmes. Many of these measures, or their successors, have remained under New Labour, providing a policy environment that underpins the government's welfare reform strategy.

Meanwhile, as the Conservative government's Secretary of State for

Social Security during the late 1980s, John Moore had introduced the term 'welfare dependency' into the British political lexicon and began to give the term 'welfare' negative rather than positive connotations. Subsequently, Peter Lilley, Secretary of State until the 1997 election, succeeded in securing media consensus that expenditure on benefits was too high and that social security fraud was a major problem even if one confined to the activities of a minority of claimants. In this, Frank Field (Labour), who was then Chair of the House of Commons Select Committee on Social Security and who became Minister for Welfare Reform on Labour's coming to power, supported Lilley.

Policy changes in the 1980s were particularly dramatic for *16- to 17-year-olds*. As the employment possibilities for this group fell in the early 1980s, the government introduced a nationwide training scheme for young people in the form of the *Youth Training Scheme* (in 1982). The Youth Training Scheme, and its successor *Youth Training* (introduced in 1990) aimed to provide participants with vocational qualifications, to meet the need for higher skills, to combine training with work experience and to offer extra help to those who had not found employment towards the end of their training. These schemes came to be viewed as being of little value for many participants, failing, in some places, to provide quality training. They were open to abuse from employers who were able to use the government subsidised schemes rather than employ young people directly (Raffe, 1988; Coles, 1995). More recent attempts to improve the quality of training for young people have included the introduction of Modern Apprenticeships (1995) and National Traineeships (1997). These are discussed below.

Meanwhile, the *1988 Social Security Act* removed Income Support from 16- to 17-year-olds other than 'special groups', such as lone parents, discharged offenders and disabled students. School leavers who failed to find employment were expected to supplement their incomes through participation in work-based, government supported training provision. This withdrawal of benefit was linked to a guarantee to provide training places to young unemployed people registered as seeking work. However, the number of places did not match demand and many young people ceased to 'sign on', and thereby declare themselves as 'seeking work', because no benefit was payable for doing so.

Entitlement rules for disability benefits were also tightened during this period. The 1988 Act removed 'extra payments' and reduced benefit premiums for many disabled people, and reduced the numbers eligible. Concern about the growing numbers of people claiming Invalidity or

Sickness Benefit led to their being replaced with *Incapacity Benefit* in April 1995 – which defined eligibility criteria more tightly in an attempt to limit assistance to those 'genuinely' unable to work.

In April 1996 *Project Work* was piloted for long-term unemployed people (more than two years). This consisted of 13 weeks intensive jobsearch followed by 13 weeks mandatory work experience – usually in manual community work. The scheme was considered to mark a 'new departure' in introducing compulsory work linked to benefit, and was dubbed by critics as 'workfare by any other name' (Working Brief, 1995/6). The scheme was found to be successful in removing people from the claimant register, although findings regarding success in placing people in work were much more ambiguous. Nonetheless, Project Work received high level government backing and it was announced that the scheme was to be implemented nationally even before the pilot evaluation period was complete. It was clear that one objective behind the expansion of Project Work was to 'weed out' those who (because they dropped off the register) were assumed not to want a job. Meanwhile, voluntary community work schemes, which pre-dated Project Work, were scrapped, despite some encouraging findings (Murray, 1996).

Qualitative analysis of interviews with Project Work participants and staff found "widespread and persistent opposition to the idea that people should be forced to work in order to continue receipt of benefit" (Ritchie and Legard, 1999). In addition, both staff and participants complained of too little choice over job placements and limited training experience. Concern about the consequences of sanctioning appeared to be stronger among older people with family responsibilities.

In October 1996 a new benefit, *Jobseeker's Allowance* (JSA) was introduced with the intention of simplifying the system of benefit delivery and re-emphasising conditionality within a more coercive regime. Novak (1997) noted that the ease with which the change to JSA was introduced served to highlight the shift in policy stance which had occurred within the Labour opposition over the preceding years. Essentially the new benefit introduced four key changes.

1 The previous dual system of contributory Unemployment Benefit and non-contributory Income Support was replaced by a *single benefit* for unemployed people, further blurring the boundaries between contributory and non-contributory benefits. JSA does retain a contributory component, although this only lasts for up to six months

(as opposed to 12 months under the old unemployment benefit system). The majority of people on JSA claim the means-tested allowance.

2 *Contracts* were introduced in the form of 'Jobseekers' Agreements'. These define for the individual unemployed person (henceforth to be known as a jobseeker) what Employment Service agency staff can expect from them in terms of 'actively seeking' and 'availability'.

3 *Conditionality* was strengthened through the introduction of the 'Jobseekers' Direction'. The sanction regime was changed with the introduction of JSA to make it clearer and sharper (Bottomley et al, 1997). Employment service staff were now permitted to require that individuals take measures to improve their chances of employment as directed. The direction is backed by threat of benefit sanction. Measures might entail attending a course to improve skills or motivation, or taking steps to present themselves acceptably to employers.

4 Benefits Agency and Employment Service staff were *co-located at Jobcentres*. These are the local offices of the Employment Service, which is an executive agency of the Department for Education and Employment (DfEE). Unemployed people claiming benefit are obliged to visit the Jobcentre fortnightly, when staff should review their jobsearch activity, and provide advice. An extended 'Restart Interview' is obligatory after six months.

Meanwhile, the range of available motivational packages continued to grow. In all, some 42 *welfare-to-work programmes* were running in the UK prior to the 1997 change of government (Gardiner, 1997). Gardiner used a broad definition of 'welfare to work', namely "any policy intervention that encourages or facilitates a transition from benefits to paid employment", including benefits paid to the unemployed (for example JSA) which have a conditionality of jobsearch attached. Most of the programmes reviewed were connected with education, training or jobsearch assistance. In addition, there were in-work benefits, assistance with job-related costs and incentive schemes for employers. According to OECD estimates, spending on *Active Labour Market Policies* (which excludes conditional benefit payments) as a proportion of all spending on labour market policies increased from 27% of spending in 1994 to 31% in 1997 (OECD, 1999).

New Labour's welfare reform

The landslide election victory of May 1997 gave Labour the parliamentary majority needed to implement the 'reform' of welfare that was a central plank of their election manifesto. This was presented as part of a project to 'modernise' Britain and to make public administration more effective in "meeting the challenges of a different world" (Blair, 1997). However, the measures implemented under previous Conservative administrations, particularly the introduction of Project Work and JSA, were necessary precursors to the employment strategies that New Labour implemented under the current government. John Major's 'Dole to Dignity', via JSA and Project Work (John Major, 1996, quoted in Murray, 1996), has been modified and extended to become New Labour's 'Welfare-to-Work'. Importantly, New Labour has continued to favour a supply-side approach. This promotes training and flexibility as a solution to unemployment and rejects traditional Keynesian macroeconomic thinking. It has "advanced the coercive elements" of employment policy under the previous government in an attempt to remove an assumed group of 'voluntary' claimants from the register (Tonge, 1999, p 217).

Reform and rhetoric

The rhetoric within which New Labour's welfare reform programme has been packaged has tended to oscillate between fighting a 'dependency culture' and even an 'underclass' on the one hand, and solving the problem of 'social exclusion' on the other. The Labour Party's 1997 manifesto uses implicitly the language of 'underclass' with an emphasis on mutual obligations (Deacon, 1998), a theme echoed in speeches given by Tony Blair both before and after the General Election (Walker and Howard, 2000). Despite this, in government New Labour has so far tended to focus on 'social exclusion' (which often means 'exclusion from work'), and 'poverty' and to steer away from the language of 'dependency' in official documents. The ideological thrust behind the welfare reform programme is that the majority of unemployed people are only too eager to escape social exclusion and 'benefit dependency' through work, but face a number of structural barriers in doing so. In other words, that (pre-New Labour, at least) dependency was often caused by the system rather than by the individual. Nonetheless, from the start the language has been noticeably 'tougher' in application to younger people, who have been given 'no fifth option' of remaining in 'passive' receipt of JSA beyond six months.

In March 1998, some nine months after coming to power, the social security reform policies that had been introduced or announced were given coherence by the publication of a consultative document or Green Paper. *New ambitions for our country: A new contract for welfare* set out the "three key problems with the pre-existing system":

1. Worsening inequality and social exclusion, especially among pensioners and children, despite rising spending on social security.
2. Barriers to paid work, including financial disincentives.
3. Fraud that was taking money out of the system and away from genuine claimants.

Points 2 and 3 serve to exemplify this tension between a characterisation of a proportion of unemployed recipients as deserving of help, and others characterised as 'undeserving' or fraudulent. Point 1 reveals that, regardless of which version has greatest credence, the welfare reform policies were embedded within another important agenda of tackling the 'problem' of rising expenditure.

The reform package

The welfare reform package comprises three policy strands, identified with three, oft-repeated 'soundbites' of policy-speak: 'welfare to work', 'making work pay' and providing 'work for those who can; security for those who can't [work]'. The package builds on former British programmes, as well as borrowing and adapting ideas from other, particularly English-speaking, nations. US incentive and disincentive measures, including the introduction of 'workfare' schemes and in-work benefits, are widely acknowledged to have been particularly influential (Deacon, 2000; Walker, 1999), as have been the Australian 'Working Nation' reforms (Finn, 1997).

Welfare to work

The first strand consists of active labour market policies directed at people who are currently not in employment. A family of *New Deal*, work-orientation, schemes constitute the most important of these. These are described in more detail below, but are 'new' in three senses. First, they build on former schemes, including Project Work, to extend compulsory, *workfare-like* activity to a greater range of unemployed people than ever before – through 'New Deal for Young People', and 'New Deal for Over 25s' which is directed towards long-term unemployed people. Secondly, to a greater extent than ever before, they explicitly target work orientation strategies to people traditionally considered to be outside the labour market – through 'New Deal for Lone Parents', 'New Deal for Disabled People' and 'New Deal for Partners of the Unemployed'. Finally, the schemes have been introduced with an unprecedented level of political and financial investment.

The New Deal schemes were initially funded by a politically popular one-off windfall tax on the 'excess' profits of the privatised utility companies. This tax generated £5,200 million. The greatest portion of the funds was directed towards the New Deal programme for 18- to 24-year-olds (£2,620 million), despite the greater number of long-term unemployed people, who received only £450 million (HM Treasury, 1998). A commitment for New Deal to continue to be funded and budgeted for within the government's spending programme was announced as part of the 2000 Spending Review (HM Treasury, 2000a).

The expansion of the government's Welfare-to-Work strategy has continued with the introduction of *ONE* which, announced in March 2000 (DSS, 2000), is to be supported by a new agency for people of working age that blends the function of the Benefits Agency and the Employment Service. This comprises a 'single gateway' through which nearly all benefit claimants of working age are channelled, an idea which has been drawn from similar developments in the Netherlands and in Australia. The intention is to "forge an entirely new culture" within the system of benefit delivery, by breaking down the differences between claimant groups, and to promote a work orientation among all claimants (HM Treasury, 1999a). From April 2000 (subject to legislation) *all* new claimants in pilot areas have been required to take part in a work-focused interview. There are now plans to roll this Act nationally in 2002 along with a new Working Age Agency, which will combine the function of the Employment Service and Benefits Agency for people of working age (HM Treasury, 2000b).

Making work pay

Studies of welfare-to-work measures implemented under the last government concluded that a move into paid work does not necessarily imply that households move out of benefit dependency, or out of poverty in either the short or longer term (for example, Millar et al, 1997). Hence, the second strand of the welfare reform, *making work pay*, comprises a package of policies intended to ensure that economic barriers to work, or unemployment traps, are removed. The most important of these policies is the *Working Families' Tax Credit* (WFTC), which is based on the US Earned Income Tax Credit (EITC) and was introduced in October 1999. WFTC replaces Family Credit for low-income workers with dependent children. It increases the level of support, makes more transparent the financial advantages of work by paying through the wage packet and supposedly removes the stigma associated with claiming in-work benefits. Other measures include a minimum wage, introduced in April 1999 (this excludes under 18s and is set at a lower rate for trainees and for people under 22 years old), and a National Childcare Strategy (DfEE/DSS, 1998) which aims to make childcare more accessible and affordable. Parallel reforms of the benefit system for disabled people include a Disabled Person's Tax Credit (DPTC) and measures to increase access to work, through increasing the limits on the amount of work which disability benefit recipients can undertake without losing their benefit and extending the length of 'trial periods' (DSS, 1998).

Working Families' Tax Credit appears to be only the first step in a more fundamental reform of the benefit interface between welfare and work. Under proposals outlined in late 1999 (HM Treasury, 1999b), rates benefit and tax credits for children are separated from those for adults. This is to be achieved by parcelling child additions, paid under existing benefits and in-work support credits, with the new Children's Tax Credit into a single integrated child credit. (The Children's Tax Credit is Labour's replacement for the very long-standing Married Person's Tax Allowance which from 2001 will be paid to lower rate payers with children. This will create a single payment of means-tested support relating to children, which will be paid alongside universal Child Benefit.)

The forms of state support affected include JSA (contributory and means-tested unemployment benefit), Income Support (social assistance for lone parents and some disabled people), WTFC and DPTC. Jobseeker's Allowance and Income Support will in future be paid only on behalf of the claimant and any adult dependants. In analogous fashion, Working Families' Tax Credit will be replaced by an employment tax credit which will be paid solely on behalf of adults and may be extended to those who do not have dependent children.

Security for those who cannot work

The third strand of Labour's welfare reform package involves providing *security for those who cannot work*. This group chiefly includes people who are outside of the standard working age bracket (retired people and children) or who cannot work because of physical or mental disabilities, or because of heavy caring responsibilities. Crucially, this group is smaller than traditionally defined due to the expansion of the target population for welfare-to-work through the New Deals for lone parents, disabled people and partners, and through the ONE programme. Significantly, the 1998 Green Paper on welfare did not mention "those who are unable to work because there are *no jobs available*" (Deacon, 1998).

Many of the policies introduced to support those who cannot work have been couched as measures to promote social inclusion and include strategies to bring about closer working relationships between government departments. Child Benefit has been increased and restructured alongside the longer-term strategy announced to unify financial support for children; the Labour government has established the objective of eradicating child poverty within 20 years (HM Treasury, 1999b). The government has also introduced a number of area-based schemes, such as New Deal for Communities, Employment Action Zones, Education Action Zones and Health Action Zones. These focus resources on localities of exceptional deprivation with the aim of enhancing local services, improving the social infrastructure and tackling the root causes of deprivation. An annual poverty audit has been launched setting out success criteria against which the performance of policy is to be assessed.

Current compulsory work measures

Despite the proliferation of work-focused schemes, jobseekers, and particularly *young* jobseekers, constitute the target group for *compulsory* work initiatives. Table 7.1 describes the main work-focused programmes available for jobseekers in each age group, as well as for other benefit recipients. The main 'workfare' elements are summarised. There is a 'moderate to high' component of workfare for school leavers on National Traineeships and for 18- to 24-year-olds on the New Deal; both schemes require work instead of benefit, but provide training that leads to a qualification. The scheme for older unemployed people includes a 'moderate' workfare element – participation is compulsory, but consists either of work in the regular labour market (at a 'going rate for the job'),

Table 7.1: Main British work-focused schemes for out-of-work groups, by target group

Group	Labour market status Summer 1998	%	Main work-focused programme	Strategy (for out-of-work population)	Workfare element?
Age <16	–	–	None	Education. Some 'additional' work permitted.	**None** – Compulsory education.
Age 16–17	Employment Unemployment 6-12 mths	48.1 20.6 13.2		Focus is on further education. If the young person studies full time, all parents receive continued state support through Child Benefit, and parents of those who are out of work continue to receive a benefit premium. Education Maintenance Allowance is currently being piloted: this may constitute direct cash payments to young people in full-time education.	**None** – Funding for education guaranteed where place offered. **But** – no standard benefit alternative for jobseekers– discretionary payments only. No national minimum wage.

Table 7.1: cont.../

Group	Labour market status Summer 1998	%	Main work-focused programme	Strategy (for out-of-work population)	Workfare element?
			National Traineeship (NT) 31,700 participants (1998-99)	Intended to provide majority of participants with 'employed status' and training. Possible to make the transition to a Modern Apprenticeship. Participants achieve a qualification (NVQ2).	**Moderate to high** (depending on placement). Route most likely to be taken where no 'employed status', wage minimum is by local arrangement at roughly £45 per week.
			Modern Apprenticeship (MA) 135,700 participants (1998-99)	Provides majority of participants with 'employed status' and training at a higher level than a National Traineeship. Participants achieve a qualification (NVQ3).	**Low to moderate** – No benefit alternative. Usually high quality training and 'going rate for the job'. Where no 'employed status', wage minimum is by local arrangement at roughly £45 per week. Vast majority of participants have employed status.
Age 18-24	Employment	67.5	Jobseeker's Allowance	Strong conditionality on job-seeking. Strong work-testing.	**Low** – Requirement to take 'reasonable' offers. 'Jobseeker's Direction' may be issued to require compulsory participation in training.
	Unemployment	11.9			
	6-12 mths	16.8	(then) New Deal for Young People (after six months)	Tailored advice and support for work (and some non-work) issues. (Then back to Jobseeker's Allowance)	**Moderate to high** (depending on trajectory). Compulsory participation in: subsidised work (paying at least minimum training wage); or education/training (at benefit levels); or, secondary labour market work (near benefit pay).
	12-24 mths	18.4			
	>24 mths	8.3			

Table 7.1: cont.../

Group	Labour market status Summer 1998	%	Main work-focused programme	Strategy (for out-of-work population)	Workfare element?
Age 25–50	Employment <35	78.4	Jobseeker's Allowance	Strong conditionality on job-seeking. Strong work-testing.	**Low** – Requirement to take 'reasonable' offers. 'Jobseeker's Direction' may be issued to require compulsory participation in training.
	Employment >35	80.9			
	Unemployment	5.1			
	U/e>6 months	15.6	(then) New Deal for Over 25s (after 18 months)	Tailored advice and support for work (and some non-work issues. (Then back to Jobseeker's Allowance).	**Moderate** – Compulsory participation in: subsidised jobs (paying at least minimum training wage); or education/training (at benefit levels).
	U/e>12 months	34.0			
	U/e>2 years	22.2			
Age: 50–60 (f) 50–65 (m) (50+)	Employment	65.8	Jobseeker's Allowance	Intended to include strong conditionality on jobseeking and strong work-testing.	**Low** – Strong conditionality on jobseeking, strong work-testing.
	Unemployment	4.5	(then, voluntary) New Deal for Over 50s (after six months)	Available to people who are economically inactive as well as registered unemployed. Personal advice including help with job search. Employment credit direct to participant– allowing participant to take a job at a lower wage.	**Low** – Strong conditionality on jobseeking, strong work-testing.
	U/e>6 months	12.9			
	U/e>12 months	52.2	(then) New Deal for Over 25s (after 18 months)	As described above. (Then back to Jobseeker's Allowance)	**Moderate** – as described above.
	U/e>2 years	35.6			

Table 7.1: cont.../

Group	Labour market status Summer 1998	%	Main work-focused programme	Strategy (for out-of-work population)	Workfare element?
Age: 60+ (f) 65+ (m)	Employment Unemployment	7.6 2.8	None	Retirement. State pension plus Income Support, or other occupational/ private pension arrangement.	**None**

Special groups	Main work-focused programme	Strategy	Workfare elements
Lone parents	New Deal for Lone Parents	Work-focused interviews Income Support and Child Benefit (lone parent premium frozen from 1998).	**Very low** – compulsory interviews.
Disabled people	New Deal for Disabled People	Work-focused interviews. Disability Living Allowance.	**None**
Partners of unemployed people	New Deal for Partners	As for jobseekers in the same group. No individual benefit (premium on partners benefit).	**Variable** – depending on family status and membership of groups listed above.

Source: Labour Market Trends, November 1999. UK ILO unemployment rate = 3 month average June-Aug 1998, denominator = all in relevant age group;

UK employment rate = 3 month average June-Aug 1998, denominator = all in relevant age group;

Modern Apprenticeships and National Traineeships = 1998-99, England and Wales only.

or education and training at benefit levels. Participation in programmes is not currently compulsory for other groups. Programmes for these groups can be said to have a low, or very low, workfare element.

Young people aged 18-24

The New Deal for Young People is the government's flagship welfare-to-work policy, and follows from a pre-election manifesto pledge to move 250,000 young people from benefit into work. The New Deal for Young People is applied universally to jobseekers aged 18-24 who have been in receipt of assistance for six months. Some 'special groups' of claimants, considered at risk of long-term unemployment or in need of extra support, may enter the New Deal early. Exemptions are extremely rare.

The explicit aim of the New Deal is to find participants permanent, unsubsidised unemployment, rather than to merely move them out of a passive claiming status. At least in terms of official design, the New Deal can be thought of as having a greater focus on integrating participants rather than preventing claims for benefit. According to the Employment Service's 'Operational Vision, which outlines the *aims* of the New Deal, the policy is designed to:

1. "Give [young unemployed people] a greater chance to take control of their lives, recognising that work is the foundation for independence and a sense of self-worth.

2. "Utilise their talents and energy to equip them with the skills to compete for future jobs.

3. "Contribute to the regeneration of local communities, not just through the move from welfare to work and the provision of training, but directly through the environmental and voluntary work undertaken by young people on the New Deal.

4. "Focus resources to help people move from welfare to work, and so assure those working and paying taxes that their contributions are being used creatively to tackle one of the biggest problems in society."

Figure 7.1: Pathways through the New Deal for young people

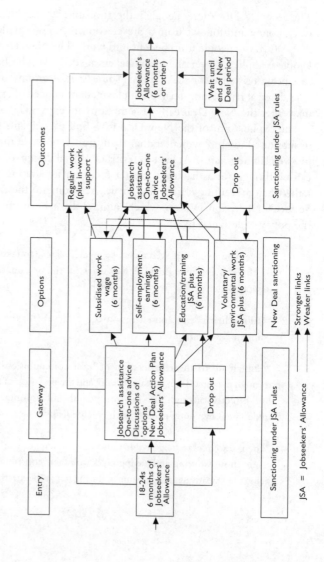

While the focus is on work as a primary goal, the emphasis on training and skills development demonstrates that 'activation' is an important intermediate objective. The main routes through the New Deal process are described in Figure 7.1. (for detailed descriptions of the New Deal see DfEE [1997] and CPAG [2000]). The programme has three main components: after six months of unemployment participants enter a *gateway* period of intensive jobsearch; this is followed by an *options* period, which usually lasts for six months (or a year if in education or training). Options include education and training, subsidised jobs, voluntary and environmental work and self-employment. If unsubsidised work has not been found after this time, participants enter a *follow through* period of further intensive support.

Participants are referred for gateway support on reaching the six months limit. The gateway lasts for up to four months, depending on whether the participant is ready and *willing* to be referred to an option. During the gateway period claimants continue to sign on, and to be 'available for' and 'actively seeking' work. This period is intended to avoid providing unnecessary assistance to those who would have found work anyway through 'intensive help'. The government target is for about 40% of gateway participants to find unsubsidised jobs without entering the options stage. Each New Deal participant is assigned a *Personal Advisor* who introduces the participant to the New Deal and begins the process of drawing up an *Action Plan,* which is supposed to set "realistic and achievable job goals" (CPAG, 2000).

Strictly speaking, the gateway stage of the New Deal has no compulsory elements. The guidance stresses the 'voluntary' and 'participatory' nature of the New Deal programme and states that young people should not be forced into options in the early stages of gateway. However, young people who are judged to "wilfully and persistently" refuse opportunities (for instance through refusal to attend a New Deal interview) may be issued a Jobseeker's Direction and stand to lose two or four weeks of benefit as a sanction. The effectiveness of the gateway, in terms of people finding employment, has shown to be related to case-load size. Clients who need greater levels of support are prone to over-run the gateway period. (Tavistock Institute, 1999a).

The focus within gateway was shifted at the end of 1998 to re-emphasise job placement in the light of evidence that only a minority of clients were actively engaged in job-search rather than taking courses or preparing for options. Even so, differences in the delivery of gateway persist with variations in the range of provision offered (Hasluck, 2000). It is also the case that many clients remain in gateway for longer than the target period. This may reflect the need for remedial training and also the desire to place people in work while in gateway. In addition, there have been delays in people joining gateway.

Once gateway is complete, the options *are* compulsory. *New Deal sanctions* may be used for failure to attend and for those who leave options early or who are dismissed from an option for misconduct. The sanction period is two or four weeks loss of benefit, depending on whether the claimant has previously received a sanction.

The options are as follows:

- *Subsidised work:* participants are employed, treated according to the terms and conditions experienced by other employees and registered for tax purposes; they are eligible for a number of in-work benefits. The wage that they receive, which is the 'going rate for the job' must at least equal the subsidy paid to the employer by the Employment Service. Employers sign an agreement to provide training, and to offer a job at the end of the subsidy period if the participant shows "*necessary aptitude' and 'commitment*". Employers are not permitted to displace existing employees and are not allowed to make a cash profit from the subsidy. Preliminary evaluations have shown that employers have experienced some disappointment with regard to the quality and volume of New Deal clients referred to them (for example Walsh et al, 1999).
- *Self-employment:* young people can receive assistance to draw up a business plan and receive training. Participants receive an allowance plus a grant of up to £400 paid in fortnightly instalments, plus up to six months advice from training providers.
- *Work in the voluntary sector/environment task force:* this constitutes the most 'workfare-like' option within the New Deal. Voluntary sector environment task force options are targeted towards people who have basic qualifications but are not considered 'job-ready' and those who have a specific interest in gaining specialised work experience in the voluntary sector. The precise work undertaken within these options varies from location to location according to provider. Participants receive their benefit plus a small subsidy, which they may take in the form of a wage.
- *Full-time education/training:* the full-time training and education option is for people with no basic qualifications. Working towards higher qualifications is permitted only in circumstances where this is likely to "*result in immediate employment*", but, in practice, this option is often

used to facilitate better qualified clients taking courses. Participants receive an allowance equivalent to their Jobseeker's Allowance. Some suppliers have doubts about the ability of certain young people to cope with a structured learning routine (Tavistock Institute, 1999a).

There are no precise criteria for allocating clients to particular New Deal options. Officially, the options have parity and placement decisions are based on the discussion of the needs and aspirations of each individual during the gateway period. Nonetheless, decisions are clearly also influenced by local variation in availability. Qualitative evaluation has shown that clients' knowledge about the range of available options varies from location to location and that they have a marked preference for subsidised employment and for full-time education or training and other options (Woodfield et al, 1999).

There are no options that solely involve work and none that do not involve contact with the labour market. Options focus to different extents on gaining *work skills* (both job-specific skills and 'soft' skills that enable those with limited experience to adapt to the world of work) and on *training*. Participants in the full-time education/training option are guaranteed a minimum of four weeks work experience within their option. Other options include the equivalent of at least one day a week education or training towards an approved qualification. Nonetheless, evaluation suggests that the training element within the 'subsidised work' option is not always strong, and that individuals on the full-time education option sometimes do not receive work-experience (Woodfield et al, 1999).

With the introduction of the New Deal the government has emphasised the desirability of "*delivery through partnerships*" (DfEE, 1997b). The government has been particularly keen to gain the involvement of private companies, both in delivering options and in managing areas of the overall New Deal programme. Employer coalitions have been set up to advise on increasing employer participation, and private sector organisations have been contracted to take over the bulk of the delivery of the New Deal in 10 pilot areas.

The government has also stressed the scope for local variation and discretion although the largely centralised 'top-down' system of delivery and control of social security in the UK has *not* been substantially challenged by this initiative. Within the DfEE, the Employment Service retains lead responsibility for the overall design and coordination of programmes.

Over 25-year-olds

The New Deal for Over 25s, directed to long-term unemployed people follows the same three phase model as the New Deal for Young People with a general gateway, options and follow-through. However, most people must have been unemployed for 18 months to become eligible and the range of options is much smaller. Where available, participants may take up subsidised jobs, and changes to the benefit rules have been made to improve access to education and training.

As a 'poor relation' of the New Deal for Young People, the New Deal for Over 25s has been relatively less successful in moving unemployed people into work. Only 8% of school leavers found jobs compared to 26% of 18- to 24-year-olds (Working Brief, 1999). As well as facing the skills deficit experienced by younger clients, older clients face other barriers including age discrimination, the benefits trap, and family responsibilities (Tavistock Institute, 1999b). It is also possible that slack labour demand, in areas of high unemployment, constitutes a more substantial problem for long-term unemployed people than for younger people who have only been unemployed for six months (Working Brief, 1999).

The mismatch between the funding for the New Deal for Over 25s relative to that for the New Deal for 18-24s has been highlighted (Working Brief, 1999). The fact that older long-term unemployed people adapt less well to changes in the economic climate, and that this group is now much larger than the 18- to 24-year-old target group, has led to calls for attention and cash to be redirected.

The 1999 November pre-budget report (HM Treasury, 1999b) announced a strengthening of the New Deal for over 25s, "building on the principles of the New Deal for 18-24s and bringing the rights and responsibilities for those aged 25 and over closer into line with those for young people". The scheme is to be implemented in April 2001 and the plan seems to be to offer the same options as for 18-24 year olds with the same pattern of enforcement (Brown, 2000). Currently a range of pilot schemes for people aged over 25 are being evaluated.

In recognition of the difficulties experienced by older people who are out of work, a voluntary *New Deal for over 50s* was launched nationally in April 2000. This is available to claimants and their partners after six months of claiming, and includes a subsidy paid direct to the unemployed person that guarantees an income of £170 a week for those returning to work and an in-work training package.

School leavers aged 16-17

The central thrust of government policy for young people aged under 18 continues to be to encourage the development of a skilled labour force through participation in full-time education beyond the age of 16. The Labour government is emphasising the importance of providing high-quality in-work training. Over the last decade the proportion of 16-year-olds in full-time education rose by 5% to 85%, while the proportion of 17-year-olds grew by 12% to 78% (DfEE, 1999). However, the increase in participation in full-time education has not always been matched by increased levels of achievement (Maguire, 2000).

Because jobseekers under the age of 18 do not generally receive JSA, they do not fall under the umbrella of the New Deal. Outside of mainstream education a hotchpotch of arrangements, much of which pre-dates the New Deal, exists. Currently two work-based training schemes, *National Traineeships* (NTs) and *Modern Apprenticeships* (MAs), constitute the main forms of provision. Both schemes place young people directly with employers, and both are designed to allow individuals to achieve a vocational qualification. Modern Apprenticeships are aimed towards young people who are able to achieve a higher level qualification than those on NTs, although it is possible to use NTs as a stepping stone to MAs. Both schemes are supposed to make a break with previous unpopular youth schemes by giving participants 'employed' status (so that they are not considered to be 'trainees') and in most cases a 'going rate for the job'.

Modern Apprenticeships are popular with young people, who consider them to be a source of high-quality training and work experience, although Gardiner (1997) notes that they may be helping those least in need of assistance. Employers believe MAs to be an improvement on earlier schemes, providing better qualified staff and a more appropriate training programme (Howarth and Stone, 1999). National Traineeships have also proved generally popular with participants although there is concern about low pay and the failure of participants to be accorded employee status while on the scheme (just under a third do not receive 'employed' status). Employers in some sectors express doubts about the relevance of the 'key skills' which clients have to obtain for accreditation (Everett et al, 1999).

In the absence of Unemployment Benefit for people aged under 18 who do not remain in post-compulsory education, and are unable to secure employment, participation in government supported training provision provides the only legitimate way of securing income. Such training, even when it fails to materialise due to lack of supply or lacks effectiveness as a result of poor quality, may become a form of 'workfare' – serving the purpose of keeping young people busy until they reach the age at which they become entitled to unemployment-related benefits.

Challenges to the expansion of compulsory work

Political opposition to Labour's New Deal was initially muted due, in part, to a growing consensus about the desirability of welfare-to-work strategies. Such criticism as there was primarily pointed to groups that were omitted and a lack of detail about policies to provide security for people unable to work. More recently the Conservative opposition has criticised the New Deal as being an overly expensive remedy for unemployment and has itself proposed a 'can work, must work' guarantee which would remove benefits from all unemployed people who refuse an offer of work.

Evaluation continues to highlight internal areas of difficulty. However, concern about welfare reform also relates to more general and normative considerations. These include the emphasis which welfare-to-work and the New Deals place on supply-side solutions to unemployment and 'worklessness', and the focus on paid work as a desirable goal for all and as a solution to poverty.

Supply-side focus

Like most recent welfare-to-work policies, the New Deal has essentially a supply-side focus, which aims to improve the employability and work-readiness of those out of work, in some cases including re-skilling to match the unemployed to an altered labour market. Some have argued that in order for such policies to be effective they must be implemented within a labour market with sufficient and appropriate job availability. Lister (1998) notes that the Green Paper reasons that the government has a duty to *"provide people with the assistance they need to find work"*, but no duty to ensure that there is paid work to do. The point has been made that the success of workfare programmes in US states like Wisconsin may be related to the buoyancy of the local labour market (for example Cook, 1997). Thus, 'economic slowdown' is considered a threat to the efficacy of the UK welfare to work programme.

A related point is that the New Deal scarcely acknowledges the *geography* of unemployment, and that the concentration of all the main New Deal target groups in areas of high unemployment may cause a form of adverse selection, whereby the programme is least effective in areas of greatest need. Turok and Webster (1988) warn of a situation whereby Employment Service staff attempt to push all five target groups into an already overcrowded market and note the lack of factual information about the spatial concentration of target groups and its relation to job availability. Employment Action Zones, which extend New Deal to those of *all ages* who have been unemployed for a year or more in selected areas of high unemployment, may serve to exacerbate the problem in these areas.

Work focus

The employment focus of New Deal has led some people to argue that 'work' should not become the only badge of full citizenship. This increases exclusion for those out of work and out of the labour market in other – unpaid – forms of work, including caring for children or disabled relatives (see, for example, Lister, 1998). As the government has attempted to extend employment-based policies to groups that have not traditionally been considered part of the labour market, it has become evident that there is by no means universal consensus as to who should be obliged to work and who should not. The work-focused gateway for all claimants of working age (ONE) makes attendance at a work-focused interview compulsory for all people of working age. Compulsory job search has not been extended as yet to disabled people or lone mothers; however, there is increasing debate about whether lone parents should be expected to work once their youngest child reaches secondary school age.

Summary

Measures to strengthen conditionality and tighten eligibility pursued by previous Conservative governments have largely been carried forward under New Labour, with a renewed emphasis on the reciprocal nature of the rights and responsibilities of unemployed claimants. However, the focus of reform has widened to include the out-of-work population more generally, and new initiatives have been characterised by an emphasis on training and broader human capital development.

Work-for-benefit policies piloted under the last Conservative government have been adapted and extended with a particular focus on young people. Through the New Deal, 18- to 24-year-olds may be compelled to participate in what is mis-termed 'voluntary' or community work for little more than their benefit for a period of six months. However, training towards a formal qualification is an integral part of the deal, as is a programme of intensive advice, and, in principle, young people may choose the option of enrolling on an educational course (where suitable), or taking up subsidised work (where an employer can be found). As yet, work-for-benefit measures are not widely used for other groups, although people aged over 24 years who have been unemployed for 18 months may be compelled to participate in education or subsidised work.

For under 18-year-olds, who are usually excluded from Jobseeker's Allowance, a mix of work and training provides a means by which young people can gain an income. However, young people who fail to participate in training, education or employment, and who are otherwise ineligible for an income, are increasingly a subject of policy concern.

While young unemployed people are still the core target group for compulsory policies, the focus is shifting to other groups, who may be more difficult to engage. The mixture of hassle and help to find work targeted at older unemployed people has intensified with the extension of the New Deal for Over 25s and the introduction of a New Deal for Over 50s. The development of New Deals for other groups and a 'single gateway' to benefits extends this formula to all benefit recipients of working age.

References

Beatty, C., Fothergill, S., Gore, T. and Herrington, A. (1997) *The real level of unemployment*, Sheffield: Centre for Economic and Social Research.

Blair, A. (1997) 'The will to win', Speech given on the Aylesbury Estate, Southwark, 2 June.

Bottomley, D., McKay, S. and Walker, R. (1997) *Unemployment and jobseeking: A national survey in 1995*, DSS Research Report no 62, London: The Stationery Office.

Bradshaw, J., Kennedy, S., Kilkey, M., Hutton, S., Corden, A., Eardley, T., Holmes, H. and Neale, J. (1996) *The employment of lone parents: A comparison of policy in 20 countries*, London: Family Policy Studies Centre.

Brown, G. (2000) 'Prudent for a purpose: working for a stronger and fairer Britain', Budget Speech, London: Hansard, 21 March (available at http://www.hm-treasury.gov.uk/budget2000/speech.html).

Coles, B. (1995) *Youth and social policy*, London: UCL Press.

Cook, D. (1997) 'From welfare to work and back again', *Choice in Welfare*, No 39.

CPAG (2000) *Welfare Benefits handbook*, London: CPAG.

Deacon, A. (1998) 'The Green Paper on Welfare Reform: a case for enlightened self interest', *Political Quarterly*, vol 69, no 3, pp 306-11.

Deacon, A. (2000) 'Learning from the US? The influence of American ideas upon New labour thinking on welfare reform', *Policy & Politics*, vol 28, no 1, pp 5-18.

Dearing, R. (1997) *Higher education in the learning society: Report of the National Committee*, National Committee of Enquiry into Higher Education, London: HMSO.

DfEE (1997a) *Design of the New Deal for 18-24 year olds*.

DfEE (1997b) *New Deal: Delivery through partnerships. National design consultations.*

DfEE (1999) *Participation in education and training by 16-18 year olds in England: 1988 to 1998*, First Statistical Release, SFR12/1999.

DfEE/DSS (Department for Education and Employment) (Department for Social Security) (1998) 'A framework and consultation document (National Childcare Strategy)', www.open.gov.uk/dfee/childcare.

DfEE Press Release (1998) '£6.8 million to aid New Deal voluntary sector', 126/98, 10 March.

DfEE Press Release (1998) 'Private sector to deliver New Deal in Forth Valley and Exeter and East Devon', 157/98, 26 March.

DSS (Department for Social Security) (1997) *Social security overview*, London: DSS, Welfare Reform Focus.

DSS (1998) *Green Paper: New ambitions for our country. A new contract for welfare*, London: HMSO.

DSS (2000) *Prime Minister unveils modern agency to provide 21st century service to people of working age*, London: DSS Press Release 00/70.

Elias, P. (1997) *The effect of unemployment benefits on the labour force participation of partners*, Warwick: Institute for Employment Research.

Everett, M., Trinh, T. and Caughey, A. (1999) 'National traineeships: An evaluation of the development and implementation phase', DfEE, *Labour Market Trends* (November).

Finn, D. (1997) *Working nation: Welfare reform and the Australian job compact for the long-term unemployed*, London: Unemployment Unit.

Finn, D., Murray, I. and Donnelly, C. (1996) *Unemployment and training rights handbook*, London: Unemployment Unit.

Gardiner, K. (1997) *Bridges from benefit to work*, York: Joseph Rowntree Foundation.

Gregg, P. and Wadsworth, J. (1995) 'A short history of labour turnover, job tenure and job security, 1975-93', *Oxford Review of Economic Policy*, vol 11, no 1, pp 73-90.

Hasluck, C. (2000) *The New Deal for young people, two years on*, Sheffield: Research and Development Report, ESR41.

HM Treasury (1997) *The modernisation of Britain's tax and benefit system. Number one: Employment opportunity in a changing labour market*, Pre-Budget Report Publications, London: HM Treasury.

HM Treasury (1998) *Budget 98, The Working Families Tax Credit and work incentives: The modernisation of Britain's tax and benefit system*, London: HM Treasury.

HM Treasury (1999a) Pre-Budget Report November, *Stability and steady growth for Britain*, London: The Stationery Office.

HM Treasury (1999b) 'Supporting children through the tax and benefit system', *The modernisation of Britain's tax and benefit system*, 5, London: HM Treasury.

HM Treasury (2000a) *Spending review 2000*, London: The Stationery Office.

HM Treasury (2000b) *Budget Report*, London: The Stationery Office.

Howarth, S. and Stone, S. (1999) 'Modern apprenticeships: four years on', *Labour Market Trends*, Feb, pp 75-81.

Labour Market Trends, November 1998.

Lister, R. (1998) 'New Labour, new welfare: setting the scene', Paper presented to the West Midlands LPU conference, 23 April, Birmingham.

Maguire, S. (2000) *Employers' diminishing demand for young people – Myth or reality*, CRSP Working Paper 2296, Loughborough: CRSP, Loughborough University.

Meadows, P. (1999) *The flexible labour market: implications for pensions provision*, London: National Association of Pension Funds.

Millar, J., Webb, S. and Kemp, M. (1997) *Combining work and welfare*, York: Joseph Rowntree Foundation.

Murray, I. (1996) 'Project work goes nationwide', *Working Brief*, November Issue, pp 4-8.

Novak, T. (1997) 'Hounding delinquents', *Critical Social Policy*, vol 17, no 50, pp 99-109.

OECD (Organisation for Economic Co-operation and Develoment) (1999) *Employment outlook*, Paris: OECD.

Raffe, D. (1988) *Education and the youth labour market: Schooling and scheming*, London: Falmer.

Ritche, J. and Legard, R. (1999) *The first project work pilots: A qualitative evaluation*, DfEE Research Report no 30.

Roberts, K. (1995) *Youth and employment in modern Britain*, Oxford: Oxford University Press.

Rowlingson, K. and Berthoud, R. (1996) *Disability Benefits and employment*, DSS Research Report no 54, London: HMSO.

Rowlingson, K. and McKay, S. (1997) *The growth of lone motherhood: The pursuit of economic independence and individual happiness*, CRSP Working Paper 285 (Draft), Loughborough: Centre for Research in Social Policy.

Shaw, A., Walker, R., Ashworth, K., Jenkins, S. and Middleton, S. (1996) *Moving off income support: Barriers and bridges*, DSS Research Report no 53, London: DSS.

Social Exclusion Unit (1999) *Bridging the gap: New opportunities for 16-18 year olds not in education, employment or training*, London: Social Exclusion Unit.

Social Trends (1997) Table 4.23 in Chapter 4 'Labour market'. data from the Labour Force Survey, *Social Trends 27*, ONS, London: The Stationery Office.

Tavistock Institute (1999a) *New Deal for young unemployed people: National case studies of delivery and impact*, Employment Service Report no ESR30.

Tavistock Institute (1999b) *Case study evaluation of New Deal for the long-term unemployed*, Employment Service Report No ESR31.

Tonge, J. (1999) 'New packaging, old deal? New Labour and employment policy innovation', *Critical Social Policy*, vol 59, no 19, 2, pp 217-32.

Trickey, H., Kellard, K., Walker, R., Ashworth, K. and Smith, A. (1998) *Unemployment and jobseeking: Two years on*, London: The Stationery office.

Turok, I. and Webster, D. (1988) 'The New Deal: jeopardised by the geography of unemployment?', *Local Economy*, vol 12, no 4, pp 309-28.

Walker, R. (1999) 'The Americanisation of British Welfare: a case-study of policy transfer', *Focus, Journal of the Institute for Research on Poverty*, University of Madison-Wisconsin, vol 19, no 3, pp 32-40 (to be reprinted in the *International Journal of Health Services*).

Walker, R., Goodwin, D. and Cornwell, E. (1999) *Work patterns in Europe and related social security issues: coping with the myth of flexibility*, Paper presented at the Annual Conference, European Institute of Social Security, Lemosos, Cyprus, 6 October.

Walker, R., with Howard, M. (2000) *The making of a welfare class? Benefit receipt in Britain*, Bristol: The Policy Press.

Walsh, K., Atkinson, J. and Barry, J. (1999) *The New Deal gateway: A labour market assessment*, Employment Service Report no ESR24.

White, M. and Forth, J. (1998) *Pathways through unemployment: The effects of a flexible labour market*, York: York Publishing Services.

Woodfield, K., Turner, R. and Ritchie, J. (1999) *The New Deal for young people: The pathfinder options*, Employment Service Report no ESR25.

Working Brief (Dec 1995/Jan 1996) 'Workfare by any other name marks new departure', *Working Brief*, 70, p 1.

Working Brief (May 1998a) *New data disguises demand for work*, London: Unemployment Unit.

Working Brief (May 1998b) *Nine out of 10 jobless under 18s without an income*, London: Unemployment Unit.

Working Brief (1999) 'Fixing the 25+ New Deal', *Working Brief*, November, p 2.

EIGHT

Making work for welfare in the United States

Michael Wiseman[1]

Introduction

Over the past 30 years the core US social assistance programme for families with children has been transformed from a focus on the alleviation of need to emphasis on the obligation of adults wanting aid to prepare for and actively seek employment. This transformation accelerated in the 1990s. It is associated with significant decentralisation of governing authority and further distancing of the American welfare model from the principle of relief from poverty as an entitlement of citizenship. The reforms in place as the decade closes – often termed 'workfare' – enjoy considerable political support among American voters. They are widely believed to have contributed substantially to the remarkable reduction in public assistance use the US has experienced since 1994. These changes have drawn attention from citizens in other countries, notably in Europe, Australia, and New Zealand. Responses range from viewing what is happening in the US as a fundamental threat to social democracy to seeing the emerging system as a model worth careful study, if not emulation.

Traditionally, the term workfare has been reserved for transfer schemes that make receipt of cash assistance or other benefits conditional on performing public service jobs. In the new American schemes, the work in workfare is generally defined more broadly to include mandatory participation in a variety of activities intended to accelerate movement from benefit to self-support. This chapter reviews the incidence and character of workfare obligations in the US at the end of the decade – the *work* of this new workfare.

The American social assistance system

The point of departure for this excursion to workfare-watch is a short review of American social assistance programmes. The US is a federal system, and the country's social assistance system is constructed from a number of building blocks. Assignment of responsibility among the various levels of government differs across these components. The result is that the assistance available, and the obligation associated with that assistance, depends in part on where a poor person lives, and very much on age and family circumstance.

The six programmes

As is true for many other developed countries, in the US the absolute number of programmes providing benefits to persons with limited income is large – 81 means-tested antipoverty programmes, ranging from Medicaid to special immigrant assistance (Burke, 1997). Six major programmes deliver the lion's share of the benefits, however, accounting for almost three quarters of all national outlays for low-income assistance in the federal fiscal year 1998. These are:

• The Earned Income Tax Credit (EITC)

The EITC is an earnings subsidy provided to low-income workers with child dependants; a small benefit is available for workers aged 25-64 who do not have children. The core benefit is part of the national income tax code, and the $33 billion cost is fully federally funded. Ten states supplement the federal benefit.

• Temporary Assistance to Needy Families (TANF)

TANF provides cash grants to low-income families with children. The size of the grant varies by family size, location, and income; it is paid for by a combination of federal and state funds, with more than half of the $17 billion cost paid by Washington. With some exceptions, adults are required to participate in work or work-related training activities.

• Food stamps

Food stamps are provided to low-income households for food purchase. Unemployed adult recipients without childcare responsibilities are required to seek work. Total benefit costs ($17 billion in 1998) are roughly the same as for TANF.

• General Assistance

General Assistance is available to some needy persons ineligible for TANF or Supplemental Security Income (SSI). Funds are provided from local or state government revenues with no federal contribution. Work requirements for general assistance are common. State outlays in 1998 amounted to less than $2 billion.

• Supplemental Security Income (SSI)

SSI is a uniform national cash grant available to needy aged, blind and disabled persons. As is also true for the EITC, some states supplement the federal SSI benefit. There is no activity requirement for SSI. SSI benefits amount to about $25 billion.

• Medicaid

Medicaid covers the cost of medical care for low-income families with children, pregnant women, and aged, blind, and disabled persons. Medicaid funds come from both federal and state governments. The federal share varies across states but always exceeds half of all costs. This federal 'match' for state contribution is based on state per capita income. Medicaid benefits cost the federal and state governments over $116 billion in 1998.

The total federal budget for fiscal year 1998 was $1,652.6 billion, and the six major programmes accounted for about 9% of federal outlays. The federal poverty standard for a family of three in 1998 was $13,133; families with an annual cash income less than this amount are officially poor (although the standard varies by family size and differs slightly for persons living in urban and rural areas). Benefits from the six major programmes are not confined to those who meet the federal poverty standard, but most benefits go to persons in families with incomes less than twice the poverty level. In 1998, people in families with children accounted for about half of all people in the US. There were 37.4 million families of this type. Of the families with children, 16% were poor by the federal standard. Children in such families accounted for 19.2% of all children.

Since these names – TANF, EITC, and so on – mean little to outsiders, the implications of the programmes are best illustrated by translating the theory into what one experiences on the ground. Consider, for example, what happens to a lone parent who seeks assistance. A single mother seeking assistance goes to the local office of the state social services agency. She is required to provide information on her income, assets and, if she is not receiving child support from the father of her children, the particulars necessary for establishing a court order for such payments. Based on this information and the size of her family, she receives a monthly cash grant from the income support programme, TANF, and food stamps. She also receives a card (from the Medicaid programme) that authorises health care providers to bill the state for common medical services she and her children might require. If she is working, the food stamps and TANF benefits are reduced according to the amount of earnings she has. This reduction is offset in part by a refundable tax credit (EITC) that is most often collected when she files her income tax return at the beginning of the year following earnings . If she is not working (and, in some cases, if she is working only part time), workfare obligations are applied (as described later in this chapter). If she or one of her children is disabled, she may also apply for Supplemental Security Income, a national programme. This benefit generally results in reduction in TANF and food stamps.

Key features

Four points are particularly relevant to drawing workfare-related distinctions between European and American social assistance systems:

• *None of these benefits is explicitly linked to job loss.*

In the US there is no means-tested unemployment benefit like the German *Arbeitslosenhilfe*. It is possible for persons receiving unemployment insurance (UI) benefits to receive food stamps and, in some cases, TANF payments. However, food stamp benefits will be reduced by $30 for every dollar of insurance benefits, and TANF payments will in general be reduced by even more. For those covered, UI benefits last up to 39 weeks in states with high unemployment rates, and a few states provide benefits for 52 weeks. Once benefits are exhausted, needy workers must seek assistance under the common rules of the programmes of the six major means-tested programmes. Long-term unemployment is not a direct focus of American workfare effort, because long-term unemployment per se does not qualify a person for benefits. Between 1990 and 1996, only about one third of all unemployed individuals in the US received unemployment benefits (Vroman, 1998).

- *The American social assistance system is structured like a nest, with a federal rim and a state/local bottom.*

Base benefits for three of the major programmes – food stamps, SSI, and the EITC – are nationally uniform, but states are permitted to supplement both SSI and the EITC, and some states do. The food stamps benefit is much like cash, although it is still in most places paid with vouchers. By 2002 all states will be making food stamps benefit payments using an electronic benefits system, which has access procedures in grocery stores and will make them virtually indistinguishable from standard bank debit cards. For the food stamp programme, funding is federal, but determination and benefit calculation are handled at the local level. For TANF, in contrast, both eligibility standards and benefit amounts are established by states.

- *The state/local core differs by family type; young single individuals are generally ineligible for benefits.*

TANF is available only to families with children. This is the programme that replaces what was called, until the beginning of the 1997 federal fiscal year, Aid to Families with Dependent Children (AFDC) (where data in this chapter span the transition, reference will be made to AFDC/TANF). If adults or children in such families are disabled, they may receive SSI, but payments for non-disabled family members will come out of TANF. Individuals without children are eligible under certain circumstances for food stamps and the EITC, but basic cash assistance is available for people in this group only if they live in a state or locality which offers general assistance. In 1998, only 18 of the 51 states (including the District of Columbia, treated here as a state) offered cash assistance to able-bodied adults without children (Gallagher et al, 1999). Thus, a second target of European workfare interest, young school leavers, is virtually excluded from social assistance in the US.

- *The assistance a poor person receives depends very much on where that person lives, especially if not working.*

In October 1997, the basic TANF benefit for a family of three (like the lone parent with two children used above for illustration) varied from just 15% of the federal poverty standard in Alabama (one of the states with lowest benefits) to 52% in California (one of the highest). Since the federal food stamp benefit is conditioned on TANF, food stamps reduce this variation. With food stamps included, the range is from 44% of the federal standard in Alabama to 77% in California. As a result of EITC, with 20 hours of work at the minimum wage ($5.15 per hour in 1997), family income rises to 83% of the poverty standard in Alabama and 114% in California. Full-time work reduces this span from 111 (Alabama) to 134 (California). Thus, work brings convergence in incomes.

To sum up this overview, the American social assistance system is a combination of programmes, some of which are operated with near-uniformity nationwide, and some of which exhibit considerable place-to-place variation. The most significant connection between work obligation and assistance appears in TANF, and it applies to adults with children. (While work requirements are common in general assistance, general assistance programmes are very small.) Because food stamps and the EITC are nationally uniform, there is less state-to-state variation in combined benefits for working poor people than there is in assistance for those without earnings.

During the 1990s, interstate variation in basic benefits has grown. In addition, changing federal policy has permitted greater state and local choice in procedures for welfare intake and in the obligations enforced as a condition associated with benefit access. These changes are the subject of the next section.

Origins of the new workfare

By the end of the 1990s, the most celebrated feature of the American social assistance system was the decline in the number of families receiving assistance. Figure 8.1 plots the number of families receiving AFDC/TANF benefits from 1980 through 1998. The chart identifies four milestones in the recent progress of workfare in the US: (a) the Omnibus Budget Reconciliation Act of 1981 (OBRA), which carried the Reagan administration's welfare reforms; (b) the Family Support Act of 1988 (FSA); (c) relaxation of standards for state welfare experiments by the Clinton

Figure 8.1: AFDC/TANF national caseload (1979-98)

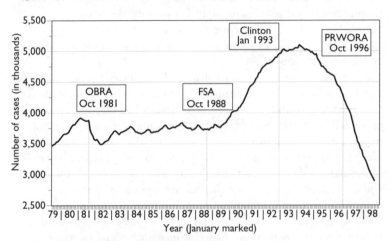

Key: OBRA: Omnibus Budget Reconciliation Act
FSA: Family Support Act
CLINTON: Clinton Waiver Policy
PRWORA: Personal Responsibility and Work Opportunity Reconciliation Act

administration beginning in 1993; and (d) the Personal Responsibility and Work Opportunity Reconciliation Act of 1996 (PRWORA). The interest in this chapter is how these milestones are associated with the transformation of welfare to workfare and the extent to which this change in policy has affected the caseload (that is, the number of families receiving assistance). In particular, we are interested in the link between the workfare transition and the precipitous caseload decline that began in 1994.

Conditioning assistance on work has a long history in the US. Josephine Shaw Lowell, author of *Public relief and private charity* (1884) and founder of the American 'scientific charity' movement of the late 19th century, thought that a work test – famously "chopping wood or breaking stone" – was essential to the successful operation of a charitable enterprise (Katz, 1996, p 74). Since the late 1960s, political support for linking assistance to work or other efforts to increase self-support has grown. Four factors contributed to this political development.

First, like their predecessors in the scientific charity movement, the political elite as well as some scholars became concerned about growth of a 'culture of dependency' founded on the guaranteed income provided by social assistance and, in particular, by the AFDC programme. Somewhat paradoxically, this concern grew despite evidence that many AFDC recipients received benefits for only a few years; the discovery of such 'movers' seemed to increase concern about the behaviours of those who stayed. The result was expanding interest in more activist intervention to encourage self-support.

Second, there has been a social change. As originally conceived, Aid to Dependent Children (later changed to Aid to Families with Dependent Children) was intended as a bridge benefit principally to support the children of workers who died before accumulating sufficient work history to provide claim to survivors' benefits under Social Security. Most mothers, especially mothers with pre-school children, worked at home. The growth in general labour force participation by women, including those with young children, has weakened the case for providing assistance without obligation, even for lone parents.

Third, both experience and analysis have raised doubts about the effectiveness of relying upon financial incentives alone to move adults from cash benefit into the labour force. In the 1970s, creation of financial incentives to work was the focus of much reform effort. Benefit reduction rates were adjusted to ensure that movement by recipients from dependence on benefit to work produced a net increase in income – in other words, made work 'pay', and this was heralded as a positive development. While it is true that lowering the benefit reduction rate creates positive incentives for welfare recipients who are not working to take jobs, the same changes – by raising the number of working families who are recipients – can reduce labour supply for those who are already or would otherwise be in the labour force. This conundrum, well known to students of income maintenance policy, leads to a search for other incentives. Time-consuming work requirements, by reducing the benefit of the 'leisure' offered by social assistance, add to incentives for moving to self-support.

Fourth, beginning in the early 1980s, changes both in law (the Omnibus Budget Reconciliation Act of 1981; see Figure 8.1) and in administrative policy increased the latitude granted states in linking AFDC benefit to work and training obligation. The result was a series of state experiments with work-related innovations. The outcomes of these experiments served both to encourage politicians inclined to raise the work requirements for social assistance and to place on the defensive those opposing such obligations. Moreover, as is discussed next, the experiments set a precedent by relaxing the restrictions of the AFDC entitlement.

Workfare 1980s style

The Omnibus Budget Reconciliation Act of 1981

Aid to Families with Dependent Children was originally established as an entitlement. That is, all families that met basic qualifications for assistance under a federally approved state plan had a benefit claim that could be pursued, if necessary, in court. The enabling legislation, the Social Security Act of 1936, permitted the income eligibility standards applied and benefits offered under state AFDC plans to vary from state to state. Also, certain programme features – notably providing aid to two-parent families, a provision added to the law in 1961 – were state options, not requirements. Nevertheless, once a feature was made part of the state's plan, it had to be provided uniformly to all the state's residents – a facet of the law called the 'uniformity provision'.

In 1967, Congress established a Work Incentive Program (WIN) that required certain adult AFDC recipients to register for work with local offices of the national employment service. In California, the then Governor Ronald Reagan attempted in the early 1970s to push beyond WIN and experiment with a California Work Experience Program (CWEP) that was basically work for benefits (Levy, 1978). Reagan campaigned for the presidency in 1980 in part on the basis of his record as a welfare reformer in California, and once in office he sought to include a *Community* Work Experience Program (still CWEP) as a state option for AFDC. Congress responded in the Omnibus Budget Reconciliation Act of 1981 (OBRA) by authorising states to require mandatory job search, job training, and/or CWEP participation for adults in certain circumstances (lone parents with pre-school children were among those exempted).

The uniformity provision posed a problem for implementation of the OBRA job search/work experience requirements. The more complicated the planned procedures for raising the obligatory components of assistance, the more difficult would be uniform state-wide implementation. The solution pursued by states wishing to increase work obligations was to take advantage of another provision of the Social Security Act, just as Governor Reagan had done in California in the previous decade. These states petitioned the federal government for waivers of the uniformity requirements to support experimentation with work and obligation reforms on a limited basis within their state. (Back in 1962, Congress had granted the Secretary of the Department of Health and Human

Services authority to permit such variation if the larger objectives of the Social Security Act were served.)

These early 1980s innovations were never widespread, and fewer than half the states were involved. The programmes were, in general, simple, most commonly involving agency–managed job search, followed by training or CWEP jobs of short duration. Recipients required but unwilling to participate were subject to loss of some, but not all benefits – sanctions were typically applied only after a lengthy process of counselling and adjudication (Greenberg and Wiseman, 1992). In light of subsequent developments, the significant features of the OBRA demonstrations were: (a) some sort of standard sequence of activities; (b) an obligation supported by modest sanction; and (c) the power of the state to enforce requirements for only some subsets of potentially eligible recipients. The presence of an activity sequence was particularly important, because this made welfare-to-work activities look like traditional case-work: the object of the system was not just to combat need with cash but to assess barriers to self-support and prescribe procedures intended to overcome them. Obligation merely made the prescription mandatory.

One of the conditions for federal approval of state waiver requests has long been that states promise to evaluate the effects of the approved change. Given that resource limitations or other considerations made many states unwilling to apply changes motivated by OBRA immediately to all potential eligible candidates, it was possible to consider assigning participation obligation at random. This procedure would then provide the basis for a 'classical' demonstration evaluation, in which outcomes for those assigned by chance to the state's welfare-to-work demonstration are compared to outcomes for those who (also by chance) were not assigned. Evaluations of the initial OBRA demonstrations began to appear in 1986. Many were done by the same firm, the Manpower Demonstration Research Corporation (MDRC). MDRC vigorously promoted both random assignment and its own analyses of the outcomes.

The results generally showed that such exercises had small but positive effects on employment and earnings and, in some cases, reduced assistance use (Gueron and Pauly, 1991). That such effects were detected through what was labelled 'rigorous' evaluation added to public perception of the credibility of the outcomes (Wiseman, 1991). Moreover, the experiments produced no evident hardship; indeed, participants appeared to welcome them. What was often lost in the discussions of the outcomes of these OBRA demonstrations was the problem of scale. For the most part, the demonstrations were small, falling far short of including the entire potential population of eligible candidates in any state, and the level of activity actually achieved for participants tended to be very low. This suggested, of course, that higher rates of activity could produce even more favourable outcomes.

The Family Support Act

The initial evaluations of these state experiments contributed to the political momentum leading to passage of the Family Support Act of 1988 (FSA) (Wiseman, 1991). The FSA established a new welfare-to-work programme, called Job Opportunities and Basic Skills (JOBS). It also broadened federal authorisation for imposition of job search, training and work requirements; mandated inclusion of needy two-parent families; required states to develop an 'employability plan' for each participant; challenged states to raise the proportion of recipient adults fully involved in job search, training, and work; and defined permissible sanctions for those failing to comply. The FSA offered agencies the option to translate the employability plan into an agreement specifying recipient obligations under the plan and the supporting services and activities to be provided by the state. This option reflected then current thinking that softened the workfare obligation in a sense by linking the obligation of individuals to obligations of government. When President Ronald Reagan signed the new legislation, the FSA was considered a major event in American social policy history.

Whatever the expectations when the FSA was made law, in general, states failed to take advantage of the resources it made available or to acknowledge reciprocal obligation. In part this reluctance arose because the FSA called for some state fiscal contribution to delivery of the new system. The programme's ambitious scale may also have been a factor: it was one thing to implement small-scale demonstrations with modest interventions; it was quite another to increase the number of hours of required activity and to involve, as the FSA encouraged, a much higher percentage of each state's entire caseload. By August 1996 only six states required a JOBS agreement that obligated government (Committee on Ways and Means, 1998, p 472). The JOBS participation requirements were never effective; state-reported data on JOBS activity were considered so unreliable that they were printed in a Congressional summary of welfare programmes with a cautionary note (Committee on Ways and Means, 1996, p 427). In addition to these issues, state administrative attention was diverted to focus on a rapid increase in the number of families receiving benefit (see, again, Figure 8.1).

Into the 1990s

By 1990, work-oriented welfare reform was moribund in most states. Some states, most notably Wisconsin, began to seek new waivers of federal requirements to pursue policies at variance with even the FSA provisions (Wiseman, 1993, 1996). In late 1991, the Bush administration chose to encourage more such demonstrations, seeing them as a useful means for forming alliances with the nation's (mostly Republican) governors as the nation headed into a presidential campaign in which welfare reform was an important issue.

Bill Clinton campaigned for his first term as president in part on a platform that emphasised more obligation in welfare. The greatest media attention was directed toward a proposal for 'time-limited' welfare, in which new applicants for assistance were allowed only two years of benefit. Payments thereafter were to be linked to participation in community work experience or training activities. This was the scheme that was to become part of the Clinton administration's failed reform legislation, the Work and Responsibility Act of 1974.

Once inaugurated, as his administration began work on what was to become the work and responsibility proposal, President Clinton chose to grant states essentially free rein. The consequence was a dramatic expansion of state participation in the demonstration process. In 1992, some 17 states had waivers for welfare reform initiatives (Wiseman, 1993). By 1996, the Clinton administration had granted permission to 43 states (including additional waivers to many on the 1992 list) to alter their AFDC programmes in ways that deviated from federal law (US DHHS, 1997).

Many of these changes involved increasing the range of obligations associated with public assistance receipt and the speed and severity of penalties applied to adults (and, in some instances, the families of adults) who failed to meet such obligations, including participation in welfare-to-work programmes. Indeed, 37 of the state programmes approved by the Clinton administration allowed states to apply more rigorous sanctions to noncompliant recipients, in contrast to only seven of the waivers in effect or approved by the end of 1992 (Wiseman, 1993, Tables 1 and 2; US DHHS, 1997, Table I.B).

The changes also reflected a retreat from interest in education and training as part of the welfare-to-work process. Attention had always been paid to the 'barriers' to employment that assistance recipients face, but by the late 1980s evidence began to appear that what counted more than training was job taking. Thus, the most successful programmes – notably those in Riverside, California and in Wisconsin – seemed to emphasise a labour force attachment over a human capital development strategy for recipients. The labour force attachment strategy promoted quick job placement, even at low wages, in the expectation that 'work first' is the best way to build (or forestall loss of) work habits and skills. In contrast, human capital development strategies focused on education and training as a precursor to the type of employment with wages adequate for self-support. Results from a Saturation Work Initiative Model demonstration in San Diego published in 1988 (with follow-up in 1989) seemed to indicate that, beyond skills, what really led to improvement in employment rates was administrative effort at raising time spent by unemployed recipients in jobseeking or other activities oriented toward quick placement (Hamilton and Friedlander, 1989).

The logic of the labour force attachment model encouraged the movement of people into work without beginning benefit receipt at all. The ideology behind it was reinforced by the presumption, common among many politicians and indeed the public, that the system, not the people in it, was the source of many of the behavioural problems identified with America's underclass. Thus, diversion of families from assistance was itself a positive outcome, and demonstrations increasingly involved application of job search and other work-related requirements to people when they first applied for welfare. Wisconsin's diversion initiative, initiated in 1994, was called 'Self-Sufficiency First'.

Policy at mid-decade

The explosion of activity generated by the Bush–Clinton waivers fostered a public perception that states were capable of productive and work-oriented intervention in the lives of assistance recipients. A four-part consensus began to emerge:

- Assistance should be linked to efforts to achieve employment and greater self-support for those capable of working.
- This work emphasis was best realised by establishing at benefit initiation a plan for attaining employment and implementing that plan through some form of case management.

- Emphasis on job placement was at least as important as skills development as a strategy for moving recipients to self-support, and the earlier applicants were made aware of the importance of job placement, the better.
- States knew what they were doing.

Beginning in 1994, this perception of state competence was reinforced by declines in the number of families receiving assistance. States that had been most active in changing the system and most focused on labour force attachment, such as Wisconsin, seemed to have produced the earliest and most substantial caseload turnaround (Wiseman, 1999a). Movement by politicians toward legislating more obligation and a stronger work focus was clearly also propelled by the polls. Not only did the states seem able to do workfare, but the public wanted it. In early 1996, Public Agenda, a respected non-profit organisation, reported the results of a major national survey of public opinion on welfare reform (Farkas et al, 1996). The results reflected the general complexity of public opinion about social assistance and its recipients, but the work message was clear. Public Agenda concluded that "Americans want a welfare system that requires work from the very beginning – community service for anyone receiving benefits and a transition to paying jobs as quickly as possible" (18). Almost six in 10 Americans interviewed (57%) said that requiring 'recipients to do community service in exchange for benefits' was absolutely essential. 85% said they would be satisfied if recipients were 'required to do something in exchange for their benefits – even if was just raking leaves or cleaning roads' (18).

'Work from the very beginning' was not part of the Clinton administration's Work and Responsibility Proposal. Instead, the upshot of this convergence of state experience and public opinion was the Personal Responsibility and Work Opportunity Reconciliation Act of 1996, commonly referred to by the unpronounceable acronym PRWORA.

The Personal Responsibility and Work Opportunity Reconciliation Act

PRWORA ended AFDC and replaced it with a block grant to states for Temporary Assistance to Needy Families – the TANF programme referred to above as the core income support programme in the current US system. Five features of this complex legislation are central: (1) the shift to block grants, (2) the expansion of state latitude, (3) time limits, (4) loss of entitlement, and (5) the performance requirements.

Block grants

Federal assistance to states for provision of AFDC benefits was matching and open-ended. Matching means that the federal government pays a fixed share of benefit costs and administrative expenditures. Open-ended means that once a state plan is established and approved, the federal government continues to pay its share no matter how many eligible families are identified. The federal share – called the match rate – ranged from 50% in the states with the highest per capita incomes to almost 90% in those with the lowest. From many states' perspective, this meant that, practically speaking, welfare was cheap. There was also little incentive to control costs, because any saving accrued, for example by promoting movement to self-support, went largely to the federal government.

PRWORA committed the federal government to maintaining the grant made to each state for its TANF programme at that state's highest welfare expenditure level established in the three years prior to 1996. Since, as Figure 8.1 indicates, caseloads in most states by 1997 were well below the levels established for the block grant baseline, PRWORA produced a financial windfall. However, at the same time, the legislation created a powerful incentive to reduce outlays, since every dollar saved could now be translated into state tax relief. In economists' terms, while resources were ample 'at the margin', welfare was no longer cheap – indeed, the price of increments in welfare outlays increased in most states by at least 50%, and in some by as much as 500%. What was true of the cost of *increments* in social assistance outlays (they went up) was true also of the fiscal dividend from *decrements*: block grants make welfare reduction pay.

The contradictory impact of this change was initially offset by further augmentation of the resources provided by PRWORA with funds from a variety of other welfare-to-work programmes, and the legislation itself includes state maintenance of effort requirements intended to forestall cut-backs. The restrictions are quite weak, however, and many options exist for circumventing them.

Expansion of state latitude

States are no longer required to obtain federal approval for many of the innovations adopted in the early 1990s. The ability of states to require work-related activity on the part of both applicants for, and recipients of, social assistance increased, as did states' ability to sanction those failing to comply.

State latitude was expanded not only for setting recipient obligation but also for setting eligibility criteria. For example, the PRWORA rules eliminate certain restrictions on benefits to two-parent families and allow states to substantially alter many other restrictions on access to assistance, including standards for allowable assets such as automobiles and savings accounts. The new rules also allow states to add work incentives to benefit calculation; most states have responded by making the treatment of earnings for working recipients more generous (Gallagher et al, 1998).

Time limits

States may not use TANF funds to provide aid to a family that includes an adult who has received 60 months of TANF benefits. However, states are allowed to exempt up to 20% of their caseload from this time limit, and nothing precludes use of their own state revenues for assistance to families after the federal time limit has been reached. States must require parents and other caretakers to engage in 'work activities' after 24 months of aid and, unless the state opts out, to participate in community service after two months of aid. States can exempt parents with children under the age of one, and a number of other exemptions can also be made as long as states achieve certain work participation rates. Thus, while the time limits introduced by PRWORA have drawn considerable attention, in practice they are likely to be applied to very few cases. States do have the option of imposing shorter time limits, and some have done so.

End of entitlement

No feature of recent US developments contrasts more dramatically with European social assistance concepts than the PRWORA provision that eliminates the right of categorically eligible families to obtain cash assistance. "This part shall not be interpreted to entitle any individual or family to assistance under any state programme under this part", the law says, and 'this part' is the section of the bill (401(b)) that replaced AFDC with TANF.

The significance of this provision lies largely in the latitude it implies for sanctioning for non-performance. With one exception, recipients are given no federal recourse if they claim requirements are inappropriate or sanctions unjustified (Kaplan, 1999, p 2). (The exception is that states are directed to provide specific protections to parents with children under the age of six who are unable to obtain childcare.) The practical consequence has been to permit more aggressive sanctioning of recipients who fail to comply with work requirements. What the FSA termed an employability plan became an individual responsibility plan "that sets forth *obligations* of the recipient and *describes* services to be provided by the state" (Committee on Ways and Means, 1998, p 500; italics added).

Under JOBS, mandatory participants who failed to comply with activity (job search, training, CWEP) requirements faced a series of sanctions, including the removal of the adult from the unit's benefit calculation for a specified period. The sanction for the first violation lasted until the affected recipient came into compliance, the second for at least three months, and the third and subsequent violations for at least six months each. Under waivers and after PRWORA passage, sanction rules were generally made more severe by either extending the length of the sanction period or increasing the size of the benefit reduction. Only six states kept the sanctioning procedures established by the FSA in place. All the others tightened them. Thus, under TANF, sanctions are greater than under AFDC, they are applied more swiftly, and there is less legal recourse against them, although most states retain some adjudication procedures for clients who wish to appeal.

PRWORA eliminated the right to TANF benefits, but not rights to food stamps, Medicaid, the EITC, or SSI. As discussed below, this differentiation is a source of conflict in federal/state relations and a source of administrative problems for some states. Subsequent legislation permitted states to freeze food stamp benefits at rates associated with full TANF payments, so that the financial consequences to recipients of reduced TANF benefits would not be offset by increases in food stamps, as implied by the federal food stamps benefit calculation formula.

Participation requirements

Reflecting the unsettled state of American federalism, PRWORA was schizophrenic in its approach to welfare reform. On the one hand, as indicated above, many restrictions on state social assistance plans were reduced or eliminated. On the other, some new restrictions were added, such as time limits. From the workfare perspective, the most significant of the new requirements involve activity. PRWORA requires states to achieve certain standards of recipient involvement (participation) in 'work activities', and these standards rise over time.

The legislation distinguishes the standards required for one adult in two-parent families (the second parent is exempt) and those imposed on lone parents and the few two-parent TANF families in which one adult is disabled. Remember that all TANF families are, by definition, receiving some type of cash assistance. In each case, PRWORA specified for the years 1997-2002 a required participation rate and a procedure for assessing participation. The participation rate is the proportion of adults in the indicated family category that must meet the standard for the indicated fiscal year. The standards are defined in terms of hours per week in certain types of work activities. In 1997, on average 25% of single parents were to be participating for at least 20 hours per week in any of nine work activities. Permissible activities included unsubsidised employment, subsidised private sector employment, subsidised public sector employment, work experience ("if sufficient private sector employment is not available"), on-the-job training, job search and job readiness assistance, community service programmes, vocational training (for no more than 12 months), and provision of childcare services to individuals participating in a community service programme (Brady and Snow, 1996). The required participation rate rises to 50% by 2002, with then 30, instead of 20, hours required to count for participation. Initially, virtually no general educational activities count as participation; the legislation relaxes this restriction slightly in later years of the programme. The participation requirements imposed by PRWORA upon two-parent families are much tougher. For this group the required participation rate for the non-exempt parent rises from 75% in 1997 to 90% in 2002, and through the five year period 35 hours per week of activity are required for meeting the participation standard.

The details of the PRWORA participation requirements can be a bit overwhelming, but several aspects are interesting. The first thing to note is that, at least initially, the required participation rates are not high. Indeed, they are probably considerably lower than what outsiders might presume is occurring as a matter of course, given media images of what 'workfare' is supposed to mean. Note also that activity can mean many things, including private sector employment. Further, the distinction between subsidised employment and work experience is important. In subsidised employment schemes, TANF benefits are used to repay employers for recipient wages, and participants who get these jobs are subject to all normal requirements and benefits of the American workplace, including tax withholding, mandatory social security payments, and, at low wages, the EITC. Work experience and community service programmes, in contrast, apply to work required in return for cash benefit. While human capital development is a permitted use of time under the participation requirements, the opportunities are initially quite limited and are relaxed only gradually. The federal participation standard clearly puts first emphasis on work and efforts related directly to work.

The participation standards are straightforward in principle. In practice, accumulation of the data necessary to assess whether or not states are meeting the standards is an arduous task, and one that is well beyond the capabilities of the management information systems used for most state TANF programmes (Nathan and Gais, 1998; Wiseman, 1999b). Two years after PRWORA's passage, "significant data transmission, data format, and data quality problems" still prevented the US Department of Health and Human Services (DHHS) from reporting TANF participation (US DHHS, 1998, section II, 1).

PRWORA included one qualification to the specified participation standards that has proved extremely important. States were allowed to reduce future targets for participation by any caseload reductions achieved between 1995 and each of the five years of the PRWORA horizon (1998-2002). Thus, while a sort of incentive (what Europeans would call 'activation') is promoted by the participation and activity standards, the strongest incentives in PRWORA appear to be all in the direction of reducing caseloads. Such reductions now save more money than would have been the case under AFDC and alleviate the burden of achieving the participation goals as a bonus. Elimination of entitlement and expanded latitude for sanctions provide additional tools for bringing caseloads down.

Recent experience: a tale of a city, two states, some other places, and the country

How has this discretion been used? How does workfare American-style appear in action? Despite the various reporting requirements mandated by PRWORA, only the fuzziest of pictures is currently available on what is actually happening. For outsiders wishing to benefit from American experience this is a particular problem, for surely the transferable lessons lie in the details, the how-to-do, if workfare is really being done. This section pursues details in three locations. Its point of departure is a more general picture of the assistance process.

As has been pointed out elsewhere (Wiseman, 1999b), managing a welfare-to-work process is a substantial task. Among other things, monitoring activity and elapsed time on assistance requires far better record keeping by social assistance agencies than was ever done before PRWORA. As a result, it is quite difficult to assemble information either on the disposition of cases as they open or the distribution of recipients at any point in time across the various states and activities. Rather than attempt a national survey, this chapter focuses on sample data from operations in New York City and the states of Wisconsin and California. Governments in each place have pursued quite different reform strategies.

New York City

Like AFDC, TANF is the responsibility of states, and in most states local social assistance offices are agencies of state government. In some, however, responsibility for administration is devolved to counties. New York City is a consolidated city/county government that operates TANF through its Human Resources Administration (HRA). Because of its size and the visibility of everything that occurs in the nation's largest city, the city's TANF programme has attracted much attention and much criticism. In an article published in December 1998, a *New York Times* reporter described the city's HRA in this way:

> The overwhelming mechanics of [the welfare-to-work] effort now fall, under a compressed calendar, to an agency typically introduced by the word 'troubled'. Starved of supplies as basic as paint and paper clips, its caseworkers, who number in the thousands, are used to a bureaucratic wasteland where anything that can go wrong, will. They are rigidly clerical and chronically discontent. And they are now being charged with nothing less than reordering of the lives of the underclass. (DeParle, 1998, p 53)

Transformation of this system was signalled by relabelling the city's 'Income Support Offices' as Job Centers, undertaking a massive review of the capability of adults in the city's recipient caseload for employment, and aggressively promoting development of work experience positions both within city government and among non-profit social services organisations. Perhaps surprisingly in light of the anaemic character of general assistance elsewhere in the country, the basis for work expansion in the city was a Work Experience Programme (WEP) originally established as part of the city's general assistance programme, called Home Relief (HR). The New York WEP is now the nation's largest workfare programme; it continues to involve both HR and TANF recipients.

TANF recipients in WEP work 20 hours weekly unless their grant divided by the minimum wage cannot support 20 hours. Applicants who fail to obtain employment during a 30-day application period and recipients who are determined by their caseworkers to need work experience are given a WEP assignment. Assignments are not time limited, although attempts are made to reassess clients after six months to determine whether they need additional services (Cohen, 1998, p 6). New York applies a partial benefit reduction sanction for persons who do not comply with workfare requirements. The sanction amount is moderate in comparison to that of many states, but the city is very aggressive in applying it in instances in which, for example, recipients fail to make scheduled interviews for employability assessment.

Important features of New York City's TANF/WEP programme are revealed by investigating the status of the 278,000 Home Relief and TANF cases open in August, 1999. The department distinguishes between cases with adults judged 'engageable', in other words, potentially capable of work, and cases that, for one reason or another, do not fit this category. Cases judged unengageable include, among others, families without recipient adults, cases in which adults receive SSI, cases with adults who are temporarily incapacitated, and cases in which single adults are caring for children less than three months old. This identification removes approximately one quarter of cases from workfare eligibility.

Of the 204,000 cases that the department considered at least potentially engageable, more than half (109,000) were not in fact active. Some 24,000 had not yet been called in for assessment. Appointments have been made or assessments are otherwise in process for 31,000. Fully one quarter of those judged engageable – 54,000 were either under sanction or have in some way failed to meet the department's activity standards and are involved in administrative adjudication.

This leaves approximately 95,000 people classed as engaged. Engagement includes a sizeable number of people involved in 'other participation', which includes some students, people involved in training and directed job search, people needed for home care-taking, and some adults receiving substance abuse treatment. Roughly 30,000 were in regular jobs, for which the TANF/HR benefit provides supplementary income (treatment of earnings in New York's TANF system is quite generous). The remainder includes 33,000 in WEP plus 5,000 in residential substance abuse treatment, which from the city's perspective counts as engagement.

HRA classifies its placements as involving office services, maintenance services, or human community services, and it contracts with both other city agencies and non-profit organisations for job creation and participant management. In August 1999, WEP jobs were almost equally divided between TANF and HR recipients, but the two groups were distributed much differently across city and non-profit agencies. HR recipients are much more likely to work in the parks department; while TANF recipients are more likely to be assigned to smaller departments and agencies.

The use of community work experience participants in so many government jobs has created controversy over displacement. A series of articles in the *New York Times* in early 1998 concluded:

> The Mayor says workfare participants have not taken the places of regular city employees. But, in seeming violation of state welfare law, many participants, especially those cleaning city office buildings or working as clerks and receptionists, are doing work once performed by civil servants. In some cases, they are working side by side with civil servants, doing the same tasks. (Finder, 1998, p 1)

The issue of displacement is still largely unresolved in the city; challenges to current policy have slowed growth of placements in government and increased efforts to involve non-profit agencies in developing work positions for recipients.

In its zeal to use its administrative powers to transform its welfare system into an employment system, New York has repeatedly encountered problems generated by the difference in discretion granted states under TANF, which has no entitlement, and the related programmes for food stamps and Medicaid, which do. The city provides access to all such benefits under one 'Job Centre' roof; this promotes the work first message. In at least the initial stages of the current reform effort, city workers failed in some instances to inform applicants of benefits to which they are entitled without satisfying the job search and other requirements of TANF. And Job Centre case workers tended to emphasise only those aspects of the Centres that concerned job search and welfare-to-work activities.

Complaints prompted an investigation by the US Department of Agriculture. An advocacy group, the Welfare Law Centre, filed a federal class action suit against the City in December 1998, arguing that Job

Centre procedures illegally discouraged needy people from applying for food stamps, Medicaid, and cash assistance. Plaintiffs were granted an injunction. The city filed a corrective policies and procedures plan intended to make it clearer to prospective applicants that they could file an application for food stamp and Medicaid benefits on their first visit to a Job Centre. Job Centre staff were instructed to inquire about emergency needs and provide expedited food stamps and cash assistance where appropriate (Welfare Law Centre, 1999).

The New York data provide important points for reflection for outsiders. First, consider scale. No state has more workfare-engaged recipients than does New York City, yet the total actually involved in jobs in August 1999 was only slightly more than 30,000, barely 10% of the adults on benefit. Second, the numbers (and indeed most anecdotal accounts, including the lawsuit testimony) suggest that in workfare as practised here it is process that counts more than work for welfare itself. The number of persons reported to be in the sanctions process, for example, is far greater than the number of persons actually working for benefit. Activation in this model involves both setting requirements for recipients and moving those hoards of the 'rigidly clerical and chronically discontent' to carry out the process. Third, the fact that the data reported here are readily available says something about the department's own activation. Very few social assistance agencies in the country have management information systems capable of producing anything like the management reports used in this description, and the reports available provide far more detailed information than has been cited here.

Wisconsin

The strategy followed by New York City in transforming its assistance system, while radically ambitious, is in practice incremental. WEP for general assistance was not new, nor is the possibility of applying work tests for welfare applicants and aggressively sanctioning non-compliance. In a system as large as New York's, little else is possible, and, as the opening quotation in the New York description (p 230) indicates, most observers initially questioned the feasibility of even modest change. For historical as well as substantive reasons, Wisconsin has pursued much more radical reform. As a result, Wisconsin has probably attracted the greatest national and international attention of any jurisdiction for its welfare reform efforts. Wisconsin Works, nicknamed W-2, is the culmination of a long series of experiments. It is certainly the boldest of the post-PRWORA programmes.

New York's strategy has been to attempt to engage all employable TANF applicants and gradually to accomplish the same with its backlog of recipients. Wisconsin, in contrast, closed its AFDC/JOBS programme and substituted a system in which, at least nominally, cash benefits are available only through some form of employment (Wisconsin Department of Health and Social Services, 1995; page references that follow relate to this source). The heart of the new system is an intake process that attempts immediately to divert applicants to employment and, failing that, to involve them immediately either in work experience positions – Community Service Jobs – or W-2 Transition activities intended specifically to address barriers to regular employment. Those moved directly to employment retain means-tested access to subsidised health insurance and childcare. There is no state general assistance programme in Wisconsin.

The W-2 programme has four tiers of support (rungs on the ladder up to self-sufficiency) for adults with children plus off-tier classifications for adults in special circumstances. In addition, approximately 11,000 cases are outside the work obligation track (nonengageable, in New York City terms) because they involve children under care of relatives other than their parents. Persons who seek assistance first meet with a Financial and Employment Planner (FEP). It is the job of the FEP to help needy applicants "think through their best options to provide for the economic security of their families" (p 34). Those meeting eligibility standards are directed to one of the rungs in the self-sufficiency ladder. Some applicants move into unsubsidised employment – the highest ladder rung. Applicants initially unable to find unsubsidised employment are either accommodated in 'trial' subsidised jobs in private or public organisations or placed in community service jobs (CSJs). The bottom rung, W-2 Transition, is "for those legitimately unable to perform independent self-sustaining work even in a community service job" (p 9). The programme is structured so that movement upward on the ladder raises income, and duration of tenure in each category save W-2 Transition is strictly limited. The overall lifetime limit on cumulative participation in any W-2 activity is five years, with some options for extension.

W-2 includes three off-ladder placements. A lone parent with a child 12 weeks old or less who meets the various other requirements for W-2 employment positions will be assigned to 'Caretaker of an Infant' status and given the same grant as is attached to CSJ classification until her child is three months old. At this point the parent is reassigned to a ladder category. Mothers who are less than 18 years old may receive FEP services, but they are not themselves eligible for cash benefits. Otherwise, minor parents are expected to live with their own parents or with other adult custodians. Adults responsible for minor parents are themselves eligible for W-2 or Kinship Care benefits, depending on their relationship to the minor. Women who are pregnant and have no other dependent children may also receive FEP services, but they are not eligible for TANF assignment until their child is born. Such women are eligible for Medicaid and, if income is sufficiently low, food stamps.

Wisconsin Works is operated by a variety of organisations, both public and private, with which the state contracts for delivery of the programme. The nation's largest urban area, Milwaukee, is divided into six districts served by five contractors, two of which are for-profit organisations. Each agency is responsible for developing trial, community services, and Transition positions and routing applicants into them. The community service and W-2 Transition positions are 'work experience' positions. They do not pay wages; rather, recipients receive grants of $673 per month in Community Service Jobs (CSJs), $628 in W-2 Transitions. For every hour the participant fails to work or do an assigned work-related activity, the grant is reduced by $5.15. The W-2 system imitates employment in that the basic grant, like wages, does not vary with family size. Food stamps do, however.

As was true for New York City, subsidised private sector employment – the trial job component of W-2 – is rare. The reasons seems to be that employers do not consider the benefits of government wage subsidy to be worth the administrative burden created by such jobs, and developing and monitoring such positions is considerably more difficult than arranging community work experience positions.

In general, W-2 Transition and CSJ employment placements are in non-profit organisations. Little information is available on the degree of success of W-2 agencies in actually achieving 'full employment', that is, full-time occupation in activities, of people in the CSJ or W-2 Transition categories. Since W-2 contractors are paid on fixed-price contracts, failure to move persons into self-support reduces profits (for for-profit agencies) or surplus for other purposes (for non-profit agencies).

Sanctions data indicate, at least indirectly, that the contractors have achieved a substantial degree of activity. Wisconsin has a 'graduated' sanction. When a client fails to participate in a scheduled activity, the next grant payment is reduced by $5.15 for each hour missed. In the absence of sanctions, recipient payments should be, as indicated above, $673 in the CSJ category, $628 in the W-2 Transition category. When actual payments are less than that for participants who are enrolled all month, it means that sanctions have been applied. During the last half of 1998, on average 36% of CSJ and 12% of W-2 Transition participants were experiencing some sanction each month. In March 1999, the most recent month for which data were available at this writing, sanctions affected 34% of the W-2 population. These sanctions were frequently steep. The median sanction in March was $350, implying that the median sanctioned adult had failed to participate in over 67 hours of required activity. In the last half of 1998, 6% of adults typically were subject to full sanction each month. In such cases, no TANF payments were received, but food stamp benefits were retained at levels associated with the basic TANF grant without sanctions.

Little is known about the circumstances of families that are sanctioned. Press coverage has been substantial, and critics have argued that the combination of active diversion policies plus sanctioning has increased homelessness in Milwaukee. But this connection is far from certain; increased evictions may reflect general tightening of the city's labour markets in the context of a booming state economy.

Like New York, Wisconsin is exceptional in its degree of activism and success in gleaning useful management information from its operations support system. The extent of sanctions raises serious questions about the consequences of the strategy for family, and especially children's, well-being. While the state has mounted multiple investigations of the status of families that have left public assistance (Wisconsin Department of Workforce Development, 1999), no systematic study of the situation of sanctioned households has yet been done.

California

New York City and Wisconsin provide two examples of activist obligation-oriented welfare policy in which recipient obligations are asserted through required activities, including community work experience. Both are using work experience to meet or exceed PRWORA participation goals. However, TANF work requirements may also be satisfied by moving recipients into private employment. California has taken this route by expanding the income range over which recipients can continue to receive some TANF cash assistance. For reasons to be detailed below, the long-run viability of this strategy is uncertain.

The California caseload is the largest in the nation, accounting in 1998 for almost one quarter of all TANF cases nationwide. The average monthly TANF caseload in 1998 was 718,000 cases, of which 17% were two-parent families and therefore subject to the highest PRWORA participation rate requirement. (California has the highest incidence of two-parent TANF families among the states.) While innovations in some of California's counties – notably Los Angeles, Riverside, and San Diego – have received much attention, the degree of participation of recipients in welfare-to-work activities has been far lower than seems generally appreciated.

Take Riverside, for example. A recent national study of welfare to work activities under JOBS provides some sense of the levels of activity attained under the pre-TANF programme, even though the activity measure used was far less rigorous than that applied by PRWORA (Hamilton, 1997). In this investigation welfare recipients in three sites – Atlanta (Georgia), Grand Rapids (Michigan), and Riverside (California) – were assigned at random to a control group receiving essentially no services and two 'treatment' groups. The treatment options were: (a) a Labour Force Attachment track which promoted immediate job search and placement; and (b) a Human Capital Development track which placed greater emphasis on education or training. Work experience was an available option under both tracks. Not only was activity lowest in the Riverside site, but Riverside was least likely of the three locations to involve participants in work experience. What seems to have been important in Riverside (and in the other sites for the demonstration) was not participation in welfare work. Rather, it was an activist intervention that challenged recipients to look for work and used sanctions liberally when recipients failed to perform up to contract standards.

Under CalWORKS, the state's TANF programme, all counties now have a welfare-to-work programme. Anecdotal evidence suggests that rates of recipient participation in activities other than unsubsidised employment remain very low (Klerman, 1999). Sanction rates, in contrast, are substantial in many counties. The sanctions are generated by the failure of recipients to attend scheduled 'job club' meetings that are intended to promote early job placement.

Despite low levels of administered activity in CalWORKS, the state has managed to satisfy the federal participation standard not by promoting work experience or training but by combining welfare with unsubsidised work. Since 1993, a central aspect of California's welfare strategy has been to reduce benefits, but to offset the consequences of this strategy for families by making work 'pay'. The state does this by simultaneously reducing the level of benefits *and* the rate at which the remaining payments decline as earnings increase. This policy, originally permitted in AFDC under waivers granted by the Bush administration, has been carried over to CalWORKS. Even with a series of reductions, the state's basic benefit is relatively generous, and movement to even part-time work produces substantial benefit. Sentiment in the state, especially given the change in administration from Republican to Democratic in the November 1998 election, is also to ignore time limits for working cases. Recent data show a pronounced increase in the incidence of employment among welfare cases; in 1998, 34% of TANF cases in the state had earnings outside welfare (California Department of Social Services, 1999, p 42), up from less than 10% in 1994. Thus, California's strategy is to increase the incidence of work within the caseload but to emphasise neither diversion nor rapid movement of cases from the rolls. Community work experience is virtually non-existent.

This strategy may be creating problems for the future. The work incentives that allow some families to combine work and welfare are not available to all since, as in AFDC, the 'disregard' of income applied in calculating benefits is not applied in assessing CalWORKS eligibility. As a result, the state is creating an ever-increasing class of low-income working poor households that are privileged over many families in otherwise similar circumstance solely by the fact that at some earlier point they achieve TANF eligibility. A similar inequity, created by work incentives in AFDC and harshly criticised by Ronald Reagan, led to time-limiting of such incentives in the Omnibus Budget Reconciliation Act of 1981. In America, welfare policy is cyclical.

Other locations

There are as yet no national data on the distribution of activities by TANF participants, although some early data suggest that enrolment in work experience activities is increasing. In a study of seven states, the US General Accounting Office found that between 4% and 31% of TANF participants who were in work activities by 1997 were in community service and work experience, as compared to between 0% and 3% in the same states in 1994 (US General Accounting Office, 1998). As in the national welfare-to-work tabulations reported earlier, the activity standard applied in making these counts was not as rigorous as that required by PRWORA.

Conclusions: what workfare in America means today

For reasons already discussed, this overview is idiosyncratic. It has focused on three high-benefit states, with a smattering of information from other locations. The basic message is that, aside from Wisconsin, there is not much work in American workfare. What seems to be the case is that the core of American workfare is the message that work, even at low wages, is better than welfare, and welfare without work will be a hassle. It is not the 'job you can't refuse'; it's the *appointment* you can't refuse. Getting this message across has not required that every assistance recipient be given a community work experience job. Nevertheless, in both New York City and Wisconsin, the jobs have been an important part of the process package. While actual activity rates in Wisconsin are not known with precision, it is certain that they are higher than in New York, where rates are still higher than elsewhere in the country.

Sanctions play a very important role in workfare in New York City and in Wisconsin, and it appears the incidence of sanctions is growing in California. This conclusion is consistent with the outcome of more formal studies. A recent econometric study of caseload dynamics by the White House Council of Economic Advisors, for example, finds that state-to-state variation in sanction policies is significantly correlated with caseload trends. Those states with the most severe sanction policies (for example, states that eliminate all TANF benefits for families with sanctioned adults) have experienced the largest declines (Council of Economic Advisors, 1999, p 18). The Council's analysis attributes 36.2% of the decline in the TANF caseload from 1996 to 1998 to policies facilitated by the new law, 7.8% to reduction in unemployment, 9.6% to an increase in the nation's minimum wage, 1.4% to state reductions in cash benefits and the remaining decline (45%) to 'other' factors. If almost half of the recent caseload decline evident in Figure 8.1 cannot be reliably linked to either nominal policy or economic trends, caution is advised for those who would swallow the sweeping generalisations offered by politicians and pundits.

States have so far been rescued from the PRWORA activity requirements by a combination of caseload decline and mixing welfare with unsubsidised employment. Prior to PRWORA, small projects made big news, and in public discourse it became common to claim that what was accomplished in waiver-based demonstrations or other initiatives was common across entire states. PRWORA created a standard for activation that, on its face, seems modest – only half of lone parents on benefit by 2002, just 30% in the first year of the programme's operation. But the reality is that most locations come no where near this level.

As discussed earlier, state participation requirements were reduced a percentage point for every percentage point reduction in the caseload between the year under consideration and the caseload in federal fiscal year 1995. Thus, while the required participation rate for fiscal year 1998 is 30% for lone parent families, a caseload decline of 18% between fiscal year 1995 and fiscal year 1997 (roughly the national decline over that period) would reduce the required rate to 12%. In August 1999 the Department of Health and Human Services announced that, given this latitude, all 50 states had achieved the 'adjusted' targets (US DHHS, 1999). The overall participation rate was 35%. A careful reading of the Health and Human Services report reveals more. While 35% of adult recipients nationally met the TANF requirements, the share of employed recipients was 23%. The proportion of recipients who were working – which includes employment, work experience, and community service – reached 27%. The implication: in typical months in 1997, only 4% of adults nationwide were involved in work experience or community service jobs – 'workfare' as commonly considered. What really made the difference, then, was the increased incidence of employment – an increase that is generated in part 'mechanically', by raising the maximum level of earnings a family may have and continue to receive some benefit.

The rapid decline in the AFDC/TANF caseload has produced considerable media concern and a raft of surveys of welfare 'leavers', that is, interviews with former recipients conducted 6-12 months following termination (Brauner and Loprest, 1999). Such studies could be useful, but from an outside perspective, they miss a lot of the point. What would be more useful, and what is still generally unavailable, is information on the status of those families diverted from assistance and the circumstances of families undergoing sanction.

Note

[1] The research assistance of Eve Shapiro and Sarah Staveteig is gratefully acknowledged, as is general project assistance provided by Mike English and Tracy Roberts.

References

Brady, H.E. and West Snow, B. (1996) *Data systems and statistical requirements for the Personal Responsibility and Work Opportunity Act of 1996*, Berkeley, CA: University of California Data Archive and Technical Assistance.

Brauner, S. and Loprest, P. (1999) 'Where are they now? What states' studies of people who left welfare tell us', *New Federalism Issues and Options for States Series A*, no A-32, Washington, DC: Urban Institute.

Burke, V. (1997) *Cash and non cash benefits for persons with limited income: eligibility rules, recipient and expenditure data, FY1994-FY1996*, CRS Report for Congress 98-226 EPW, Washington, DC: Congressional Research Service, The Library of Congress.

California Department of Social Services (1999) *Temporary assistance for needy families: Characteristics survey, federal fiscal year 1998*, Sacramento, CA: The Department.

Cohen, M. (1998) 'Work experience and publicly funded jobs for TANF recipients', *Welfare information network issue notes*, vol 2, no 12.

Committee on Ways and Means (1996) *1996 Green Book: Background material and data on programmes within the jurisdiction of the committee on ways and means*, Washington, DC: US Government Printing Office.

Committee on Ways and Means (1998) *1998 Green Book: Background material and data on programmes within the jurisdiction of the committee on ways and means*, Washington, DC: US Government Printing Office.

Council of Economic Advisors (1999) *The effects of welfare policy and the economic expansion on welfare caseloads: An update*, Washington, DC: The White House.

DeParle, J. (1998) 'What welfare-to-work really means', *New York Times Magazine*, 20 December, p 50.

Farkas, S., Johnson, J., Friedman, W. and Bers, A. (1996) *The values we live by: What Americans want from welfare reform*, New York, NY: The Public Agenda Foundation.

Finder, A. (1998) 'Evidence is scant that workfare leads to full-time jobs', *The New York Times*, 12 April, p 1.

Gallagher, J.L., Gallagher, M., Perese, K., Schreiber, S. and Watson, K. (1998) *One year after federal welfare reform: A description of state Temporary Assistance for Needy Families (TANF) decisions as of October 1997*, Washington, DC: The Urban Institute.

Gallagher, J.L., Uccello, C.E., Pierce, A.B. and Reidy, E.B. (1999) 'State general assistance programmes, 1998', *Assessing the New Federalism Discussion Paper 99-01*, Washington, DC: The Urban Institute.

Greenberg, D. and Wiseman, M. (1992) 'What did the OBRA demonstrations do?', in C.F. Manski and I. Garfinkel (eds) *Evaluating welfare and training programmes*, Cambridge, MA: Harvard University Press, pp 25-75.

Gueron, J.M. and Pauly, E. (1991) *From welfare to work*, New York, NY: Russell Sage Foundation.

Hamilton, G. and Friedlander, D. (1989) *Final report on the saturation work initiative model in San Diego*, New York, NY: Manpower Demonstration Research Corporation.

Kaplan, J. (1999) 'The use of sanctions under TANF', *Welfare Information Network Issue Notes*, vol 3, no 3, pp 1-12.

Katz, M. (1996) *In the shadow of the poorhouse: A social history of welfare in America* (revised), New York, NY: Basic Books.

Klerman, J.A. (1999) 'The pace of CalWORKs implementation', Testimony, California State Legislature, Santa Monica, CA: RAND. URL: http://www.rand.org/CalWORKS

Levy, F. (1978) 'What Ronald Reagan can teach the United States about welfare reform', in W.D. Burnham and M. Wagner Weinberg (eds) *American politics and public policy*, Cambridge, MA: Massachusetts Institute of Technology Press, pp 336-63.

Nathan, R.P. and Gais, T.L. (1998) *10 early findings about the newest federalism for welfare*, Albany, NY: Nelson A. Rockefeller Institute of Government.

US DHHS (Department of Health and Human Services) (1997) *Setting the baseline: A report on state welfare waivers*, Washington, DC: US Department of Health and Human Services, Office of the Assistant Secretary for Planning and Evaluation.

US DHHS (1998) *Temporary Assistance for Needy Families (TANF) Programme: First annual report to Congress*, Washington, DC: US DHHS Administration for Children and Families.

US General Accounting Office (1998) *Welfare reform: States are restructuring programmes to reduce welfare dependence*, Washington, DC: The Agency.

Vroman, W. (1998) 'Effects of welfare reform on Unemployment Insurance', *New Federalism Issues and Options for the States, Series A*, no A-22, Washington, DC: The Urban Institute.

Welfare Law Centre (1999) 'New York City implements major changes in manner in which applications for Food Stamps, Medicaid, and Cash Assistance are processed', http://www.welfarelaw.org/nycimp.htm, New York: Welfare Law Centre.

Wisconsin Department of Health and Social Services (1995) *Wisconsin works*, Madison, WI: The Department.

Wisconsin Department of Workforce Development (1999) *Survey of those leaving AFDC or W-2 January to March 1998*, Madison, WI: The Department.

Wiseman, M. (1991) 'Research and policy: a symposium on the Family Support Act of 1988', *Journal of Policy Analysis and Management*, vol 10, no 4, pp 588-666.

Wiseman, M. (1993) 'Welfare reform in the States: the Bush legacy', *Focus*, vol 15, no 1, Spring, pp 18-36.

Wiseman, M. (1996) 'Welfare reform in the United States: a background paper', *Housing Policy Debate*, vol 7, no 3, pp 1-54.

Wiseman, M. (1999a) 'In midst of reform: Wisconsin in 1997', *Assessing the New Federalism Discussion Paper 99-03*, Washington, DC: The Urban Institute.

Wiseman, M. (1999b) 'A management information model for new-style public assistance', *Assessing the New Federalism Discussion Paper 99-10*, Washington, DC: The Urban Institute.

NINE

Comparing workfare programmes – features and implications

Heather Trickey

Introduction

The introductory chapter to this book defined workfare programmes or schemes as those which '*require people to work in return for social assistance 'benefits'*. Contributors who, in Chapters Two through Eight, have sought to describe the most 'workfare-like' programmes in operation in each of the seven countries have used this definition as a starting point. This chapter considers differences and similarities in these programmes.

In order to simplify comparison, the focus in this chapter is on just *one* example of a workfare programme from each country. The programmes chosen represent the purest current form of workfare in that country – the programmes which exhibit the strongest 'compulsory element', the greatest 'work-relatedness', and which are most clearly targeted at social assistance clients. A more representative picture of the range of related policies in operation in each national setting is obtained through reading Chapters Two through Eight.

Programmes chosen to represent the six European countries are: RMI-based insertion (France); Help Towards Work (Germany); the Jobseeker's Employment Act (JEA) for young people (the Netherlands); local authority schemes resulting from the 1991 Norwegian Social Services Act (Norway); activation (Denmark); and, the New Deal for Young People (the UK).

In Germany, France and Norway national legislation is reinterpreted locally to such a degree that a different programme might be considered to exist in each locality. To accommodate this, an 'overall' picture of the programme (or set of schemes) is given from a national viewpoint and the extent of intra-national variation is indicated. Three programmes for claimants of Temporary Assistance for Needy Families represent the US (New York City, Wisconsin and California); these are described in Chapter Eight. The programmes compared here are not representative of the totality of programmes in each country – the three US programmes represent three of the most developed forms of workfare in the US.

This list does not include any of the 'opt-in' programmes for young people who are not otherwise entitled to state support, such 'opt-in' programmes have been described in chapters on French and British workfare (Chapters Two and Seven). While there is a sense in which these can be understood provide a very stark choice for potential participants, as there is no benefit alternative, they are difficult to compare to programmes which have a stronger relationship to social assistance.

The sections which follow consider differences between programmes in terms of their aims and ideological underpinning; their target groups; their administrative framework; and the extent to which they diverge from the 'ideal-type' workfare model. Patterns of variation are then discussed in order to establish whether distinct 'types' of workfare can be distinguished. The final section considers the issues that arise from the set of common problems which compulsory work programmes face.

Aims and ideology

The definition of workfare used here is neutral with regard to the purpose of the programme and to ideological context. It is useful to compare aims and ideological underpinnings as these may be thought to influence the design of the programmes (for example, see Torfing, 1999).

The programmes have common roots. Lack of employment ('worklessness') experienced by population sub-groups is a common concern within all seven nations despite a range of labour market circumstances. Changes in the size and composition of unemployed and inactive populations; growth in the number of social assistance claimants; and, an associated rise in social assistance expenditure can be *everywhere* identified as key motivating factors for the introduction of active labour market policies, including workfare (Heikkilä, 1999). Active labour market policies have been taken forward in the context of a growing international consensus that these are prime tools in targeting specific labour market disadvantage (for example, see OECD, 1994; EC, 1999a; EC, 1999b; and Chapter One).

In addition to economic considerations, the use of workfare is underpinned by common ideological objectives related to changes in the way the relationship between paid work and citizenship is understood and described. These have been made manifest in rhetoric through the concepts of 'social exclusion' and 'dependency' – insofar as they refer to exclusion from the labour market and 'dependency' on social assistance – and to changes in the contract of 'rights and responsibilities' between claimants and the state (Halvorsen, 1998; Chapter One). The names of the programmes themselves provide a first clue to ideological differences. Compare, for example, the focus on the individual in 'Personal Responsibility and Work Opportunity' (US) with the focus on society in the term 'insertion' (France); and then, the deliberate attention drawn to the contract between individual and state in the term 'New Deal' (UK).

There is a great deal of ambiguity surrounding the use of the terms 'dependency' and 'exclusion'. This can be seen as being deliberate and advantageous to policy makers who need to sell workfare to a range of audiences. Differences in emphasis can allow policy makers to tailor their presentation of objectives to suit the different concerns of a target group member or a taxpayer (or both at the same time). The ease with which workfare has been adopted by parties of different political persuasions may be, in part, due to the susceptibility for explanations to change with audience and over time. Nevertheless, differences in the ideological underpinning of the programmes can be seen in the extent to which they seek to address individualised dependency as opposed to social exclusion resulting from structural causes.

This section describes variation in emphasis on cost–cutting, on preventing individualised dependency, on removing social exclusion, and on re balancing rights and responsibilities.

Cost-cutting

Despite the common reasons for the rise in social assistance claims and common concerns about social assistance expenditure (Ditch and Oldfield, 1999; Hanesch, 1999; Chapter One), the relationship between wider macroeconomic concerns and programme objectives is not straightforward. Indeed, pinning down the specific aims of workfare programmes is problematic. Controlling social assistance expenditure is an ambition common to policy makers in all seven nations considered here, however, this is usually expressed as part of a more general direction of policy rather than an explicit aim of a specific workfare programme. Reducing net social assistance expenditure is a relatively long-term ambition for the British, Dutch and Danish programmes, which are highly individualised and resource intensive (Table 9.1, column 1). An accounting distinction is made between expenditure on so-called 'passive' programmes which require limited activity from the participant towards improving employability or flexibility and 'active' programmes, which involve stimulating participants to improve their chances of finding work, and subsequently remaining and progressing in the labour market[2]. Most of the workfare programmes discussed in earlier chapters focus on a short-term goal of reducing what is seen as 'passive' expenditure (even if this occurs via more expensive 'active' routes) and a long-term goal of developing human capital to the extent that this will result in fewer claims.

French insertion policies most clearly exemplify an actual and explicitly planned increase in expenditure – since Insertion programmes have been introduced alongside a national minimum income scheme[3] (Chapter Two). By contrast, in the US the cost-cutting agenda clearer, and underlined by the fact that workfare has been introduced alongside welfare time limits (Chapter Eight). Similarly, many of the 'with-contract' German Help Towards Work schemes are explicit in their primary aim of reducing local authority expenditure – moving people into the primary labour market is just one means to the end of lifting clients from local assistance into the nationally funded social insurance pool (Chapter Three).

Preventing individualised dependency

Preventing individual sources of 'dependency', including rational (or economic) dependency, psychosocial dependency (or poor expectations) and cultural dependency (or non-work focused life-styles) is a concern for architects of all workfare programmes (Chapter One). As discussed in Chapter One, the presumed existence of these forms of dependency constitutes the justification for compulsion. There are, however, clear differences in the extent to which such dependency is prioritised as *the* problem to be overcome. The focus of rhetoric on individualised roots to dependency is more important for the Norwegian workfare schemes (described in Chapter Five) and for the US programmes (Chapter Eight) than it is elsewhere (Table 9.1, columns 2 and 3)[4] although this varies considerably between localities in these countries. For most of the programmes considered in this book, the objective of reducing individualised dependency is seen as being pertinent for only a proportion of the group targeted.

Combating exclusion

Structural barriers to work constitute a lack of transferable skills, qualifications and experience, meaning that the unemployed person is not able to fill available posts – termed 'exclusion unemployment' in France (Chapter Two). This may involve a lack of 'soft skills' – including time keeping or self-presentation – or a lack of formal education or qualifications. The focus is on improving supply-side competencies, but the problem is understood as one of a mismatch between supply and demand rather than one of individuals choosing to remain dependent.

Within Europe, the demise of traditional Keynesian thinking, and the more recent rise of a 'Third Way' ideology within social democracy, is associated with the interpretation of worklessness as resulting from supply-side skills deficiencies (for example, see Giddens, 1998). Workfare programmes that set out to resolve such problems aim to develop skills and experience within the labour supply population, through developing human capital or promoting flexibility among their target populations. The introduction and extension of activation in Denmark, the Jobseeker's Employment Act (the Netherlands), and the New Deal programmes (UK) are associated with the aim of overcoming skills and experience deficits (Table 9.1, column 4). For example, the New Deal for Young People aims to equip young people "with the skills to compete for future jobs" (ES, 1997a).

The compulsory work measures are not restricted in their focus to the supply-side concerns. Relatively poor macroeconomic conditions have led to an emphasis on demand-side solutions to worklessness. This demand-stimulation function occurs most explicitly in East German cities where workfare is used as a means of supporting job creation programmes in the public sector to meet unmet needs, but is also an important component of French insertion programmes (Table 9.1, column 5).

Rights and responsibilities

The balance of emphasis on individual versus structural dependency and on a supply- versus demand-side focus is reflected in rhetoric, concerning the balance of rights and responsibilities between the individual social assistance client and the state.

The first thing which comparison reveals is that the 'correct' point of balance between what claimants have a right to, and the duties which they have a responsibility to undertake, is an abstraction. The official determination of the point of balance is entirely in the hands of policy makers, with support from a wider electorate, and is determined by cultural, historical and temporal differences in what is expected, and from whom. The fact that the new workfare policies have been introduced *at all* demonstrates that a claimant's 'responsibilities', at least, are open to change.

One way of comparing programme differences in the balance of rights and responsibilities is to consider whether clients have a 'right' to participate in a workfare programme, to match their responsibility to comply (Table 9.1, column 6). In principle, Danish and French social assistance clients have a right to *some form of* activation or insertion respectively. RMI (France) is supposed to confer a 'double-right' (to a minimum income and to an insertion programme). Nonetheless, it is important to note that, despite the rhetoric, in France this 'right' cannot be realised due to a shortage of placements (Chapter Two). For people eligible for the New Deal (UK) and the Jobseeker's Employment Act (the Netherlands) the situation is rather more ambiguous. The programmes are supposed to apply to everyone, but this is not an explicit 'right'. Finally, it is clear that participants are not *entitled* to participate in Norwegian workfare, German Help towards Work, and US programmes resulting from the 1996 Personal Responsibility and Work Opportunity Reconciliation Act (PRWORA).

Another way of comparing rights is to consider the extent to which, overall, provision for affected groups is intended to be extended or curtailed alongside the introduction of workfare. At one extreme the introduction of workfare in the US is linked to the 'end of entitlement' for a whole group of claimants (see Chapter Eight). Elsewhere programmes set out to 'give more' overall (although this is not always the case in the Norwegian and German programmes) in terms of human capital development, but combine this with reinforced responsibilities (Table 9.1, column 7).

In principle, the French schemes (and particularly RMI) are more focused on rights than the other programmes considered here. The French Republican ideal, which states that 'exclusion' is the responsibility of society as a whole rather than the excluded individual, explicitly underwrites them. The right to work is enshrined in law (but cannot be fulfilled), and the social integration of people constitutes a 'national imperative'. Indeed, while some policy makers believe that high levels of youth unemployment are linked to cultural and psycho-social factors, such as criminality and drug addiction, as well as to structural factors such as low labour demand, officially this is still a problem which society as a whole has to solve.

Intra-national variation in aims and ideology

As an added complication, official aims of workfare as articulated and registered at the national level may show considerable divergence at the level of local implementation (hence the variable scores in Table 9.1). This is particularly the case where the level of local autonomy over the policy is great. This is an important factor for the Norwegian workfare schemes, where broad national guidelines that the work requirement be used to help people find work in the regular labour market were often ignored by local municipalities in favour of using the measure as a work-testing tool (Chapter Five). In France, a government circular clarifying that the insertion component of RMI constitutes a right, rather than an obligation, has similarly been interpreted differently at the level of implementation (Chapter Two). German Help Towards Work programmes serve different objectives according to the agendas of different local authorities (Chapter Three).

Summary: aims and ideology

In summary, programmes that require compulsory activity from people in need of social assistance are being implemented and justified within a wide range of ideological settings; from French Republicanism to Anglo-American liberalism. In most cases they combine dual objectives of preventing dependency and tackling social exclusion to promote integration.

Workfare programmes are associated with an ambition to accommodate changes in the job market by targeting 'active' policies towards recipients. However, there is both cross-national and intra-national variation in the extent to which workfare is predicated upon a belief that the target population is exhibiting undesirable 'dependency' type behaviours as opposed to being victims of structural mismatches between supply and demand. It follows that there is variation in the extent to which workfare is used to enforce recipients' 'responsibilities' rather than to provide a service to bridge structural gaps. The result is that the workfare programmes compared here incorporate both demand-side measures (job creation/wage subsidisation), and supply-side measures (to increase flexibility and job mobility) in tackling unemployment.

Broadly, a scale from 'most integrative' (focus on structural problems and reinforcing rights) to 'most preventive' (on dependency and reinforcing responsibilities) would run from French insertion at one extreme to US state post-PRWORA programmes at the other.

Table 9.1: Aims and ideological underpinnings

Name of programme	1 Cost-cutting	2 Tackle dependency: economic model	3 Tackle dependency: psycho-social/cultural models	4 Tackle exclusion/dependency: skills and experience deficit	5 Tackle exclusion/dependency: low labour demand	6 Programme as a 'right'?	7 Overall: rights to benefit curtailed¹? Provision extended?
DN Activation	Moderate	Moderate	Moderate	High	Low	Yes	Rights to benefit remain. Provision extended.
F Insertion	Low	Low	Moderate	Low–High (varies)	Low–High (varies)	Yes (insufficient places)	Rights to benefit extended. Provision extended.
GD Help Towards Work	Moderate-High (varies)	Moderate	Moderate	Low–High (varies)	Low–High (varies)	No	Rights to benefit remain. Provision extended in some cases.
NL JEA – Young People	Moderate	Moderate	Moderate	Moderate	Low	Ambiguous	Rights to benefit remain. Provision extended.
N Schemes resulting from the 1991 Social Services Act	Moderate-High (varies)	Moderate-High (varies)	Moderate-High (varies)	Low-Moderate (varies)	Low	No	Rights to benefit remain. Provision extended in some cases.
UK New Deal – Young People	Moderate	Moderate	Moderate	Moderate	Low	Ambiguous	Rights to benefit remain. Provision extended.
US State programmes resulting from the PRWORA (based on California, New York City and Wisconsin)	Moderate-High	High	High	Low-Moderate (varies)	Low	No	Rights to benefit curtailed. Provision extended.

Preventive → Integrative

Individual focus → Structural focus

Supply focus   Demand focus

¹ Although benefit now conditional on participation in the programme.

Different target groups

Because social assistance is a 'last-resort' measure, social assistance populations tend to include comparatively large numbers of people with multiple barriers to work. These include people with numeracy, literacy, and language problems as well as groups who are known to have greater difficulties in entering the labour market for other reasons, including older people, people from ethnic minorities, disabled people, and people with long-term health problems (for example, see Mckay et al, 1997).

Differences in the role of social assistance within the seven countries are important. The workfare target population is necessarily circumscribed by the underlying structure of the social assistance population itself, resulting in some important differences. Beyond this, the composition of the target group is a consequence of policy makers selecting 'work-able' groups *within* the social assistance population that they particularly wish to target with compulsory work measures. This section compares workfare programmes in terms of the social assistance clients they are targeted at, the stage in receipt at which they intervene, and the proportion of the defined target population they actually affect. Table 9.2 summaries information about the target populations.

Who? Which groups?

Important cross-Atlantic differences in target group exist (Table 9.2, columns 1 and 2). In the US, the primary target population for workfare is TANF recipients, who are predominantly lone parents. In Europe a large number of people claim social assistance primarily because they have been unable to find work. The focus in Europe (to date) has been on people who would describe themselves as 'unemployed' under ILO criteria, rather than those who would describe themselves as unable to work due to health problems or caring responsibilities. Workfare exists as an extension of a pre-existing requirement to be available for work, and is built on pre-existing legislation regarding seeking work and taking job offers (Chapter One). This difference between the US and Europe is important, as strategies designed for one group may not be directly transferable to other populations. Nonetheless, it is worth noting that early US workfare programmes were introduced for recipients of 'General Assistance' (the social assistance cash benefit that some states provide for non-TANF claimants – Chapter Eight).

Table 9.2: Target group

Name of programme	1 Benefit group	2 Age group	3 Exclusion criteria	4 Period of benefit receipt prior to participation in compulsory activity	5 Early entrants	6 Scope of programme with regard to target group
DN Activation	Social assistance (similar programme for insured groups)	None – but differential entry dates	Poor health/ pregnancy/ mothers of young children	13 weeks or 52 weeks	Yes: 26 – 30 years enter early at 13 weeks	Universal
F Insertion (RMI)	Social assistance (minimum insertion income)	>25	None	Any length of time or never	Yes: those aged 26 – 30 who are not eligible for unemployment insurance	Quasi-universal
D Help Towards Work	Unemployment-related social assistance (sometimes also unemployment insurance)	Any	No	Any length of time or never	No	Usually selective (sometimes universal)
NL Jobseeker's Employment Act – Young People	Unemployment-related social assistance *and* unemployment insurance	16-23 years	Physically and/or mentally disabled. Women with young children	0 – 1 year (older people may enter a version of the programme after one year)	No	Universal (the programme is selective in application to older people)

Table 9.2: contd.../

N	Schemes resulting from the 1991 Social Services Act	General Social Assistance	None: broadly 'young people'	Disabled/lone parents with young children	Any length of time, or never	No	Selective
UK	New Deal – Young People	Unemployment-related social assistance	18 – 24 years	Exceptional	6 months (older people may enter a version of the programme after 18 months)	Yes: defined groups with special needs	Universal
US	California: CalWORKS	Temporary Assistance for Needy Families	Any	Families without recipient adults, adults receiving a federal disability benefit, adults temporarily incapacitated, adults caring for children aged under 3	0 months	N/A	Quasi-universal
	New York City: Work Experience Program	Temporary Assistance for Needy Families *and* Home Relief (Social Assistance)	Any	As above	0 months	N/A	Quasi-universal
	Wisconsin: Wisconsin Works	Temporary Assistance for Needy Families	Any	As above, but exemption occurs only if child aged under 3 months	0 months	N/A	Quasi-universal

Young unemployed people are the clear focus of European workfare programmes[5]. Changes in the structure of the labour market have caused young people, and particularly poorly skilled young people, to experience increased difficulty in finding work. As a result, average periods of transition from compulsory education to employment have extended. The designation 'young person' varies from country to country but, reflecting the extended transition period, extends well into the 20s, ranging from age 23 and under in the Netherlands to 30 and under in Denmark.

Three justifications are made for compulsory work for benefit level pay for young unemployed people. First, the new programmes act as a replacement for, or extension of, youth training programmes (as in Denmark, France, parts of Germany, the Netherlands and the UK), so that compulsion is considered justifiable in the same way that compulsory education for younger age groups is considered justifiable. Second, the issue of adequate remuneration for labour input is less pertinent for young people. Most young people, with limited work experience, will have been used to earning less than older unemployed people, and have lower expectations. Transitional financial support from families is also often assumed to exist. In many countries a lower minimum wage officially reflects (and reinforces) the lower value attached to the work of young people. Finally, policy makers in all the European countries considered here seem more willing to consider the experience of 'passive' social assistance receipt to be corrupting for young people as they generally have little labour market experience. 'Dependency' early in a labour market career is seen as damaging to the development of a work ethic.

In Denmark, the Netherlands and the UK, compulsory programmes tend to have been introduced first for young people and subsequently extended to other groups of recipients. Programmes for young people have greater priority than programmes for other groups in terms of funding and political drive. Younger people enter programmes after shorter periods of claiming. In Norway, where programmes and target groups are less clearly specified, social workers are guided to target the workfare instrument towards 'young people'. German Help Towards Work schemes are exceptional among the European workfare approaches in not being originally geared to young people, although the focus has now shifted to younger groups.

Long-term unemployed people have become the second target group for European workfare programmes, as concern about young people has begun to subside and to be replaced with a desire to 'do something' about high unemployment among other groups. 'Dependency' is generally considered to be less pertinent for older people, although still present. The barriers to work that members of this latter group experience are more often considered to have a structural root, resulting from a mismatch of skills and experience, or even an insufficiency of labour demand. The result is that programmes *specifically* for long-term unemployed people (as opposed to younger people) in the Netherlands and the UK have a greater focus on combating structural exclusion than individualised dependency. They are less well resourced, but also contain less comprehensive quid pro quo 'work for benefit' measures (see Chapters Four and Seven for programmes for older unemployed people in the Netherlands and the UK). Similarly, activation is applied in a less 'workfare-like' form to older Danish recipients (Chapter Two).

In Europe at least, people who have primary reasons for claiming social assistance other than unemployment are, as yet, largely excluded from workfare programmes. People with caring responsibilities or disabilities, are seen as being more difficult to integrate into the labour market and consequently the use of compulsory measures has traditionally been seen as less justifiable. However, as 'passive' claiming has increasingly come to be seen as a problem which needs to be solved, so the boundaries between 'work-able' and 'non-work-able' groups are being blurred. Criteria for transition to disability benefits, for example, have been tightened (see the discussion of the background to workfare programmes in the Netherlands and the UK).

Whole groups of claimants, previously understood to be exempt from seeking paid employment, are coming to be seen as potentially economically active. Two striking examples of this kind of 're-designation' are covered in the previous chapters. The first is the 1996 US reforms, which re-designated lone parents as a group who should be seeking work in the regular labour market (Chapter Eight). The second is the 1998 Danish Social Assistance Act, which extended compulsory activation (although not necessarily work) to *all* recipients (Chapter Six). The introduction of the British 'ONE' programme (in 2000) – which includes 'work-focused' interviews for all social assistance claimants – also represents a step in this direction (Chapter Seven).

When? Timing of interventions

This section considers the timing of interventions. One motivation for workfare intervention is evidence that (other things being equal) longer periods of unemployment are associated with reduced chances of re-entry to the labour market (for example, Trickey et al, 1998). There are a number of reasons why this might be so, including a re-enforcing effect of employer's unwillingness to employ long-term unemployed people. It has also been argued that long-term unemployment is itself responsible for 'sclerosis' of job-finding potential – for example, as existing skills and qualifications become less relevant or as jobseekers become disillusioned with jobseeking (Layard, 1999). Finally, when reducing moral hazard is a key policy objective, even a short period of 'passive' recipiency may be considered undesirable.

Programme architects struggle with a trade-off between allowing claimants to remain on benefit too long before intervening and avoiding the 'dead-weight' problem. Where the objective is to find a claimant work in the primary labour market, the 'dead-weight' problem comprises the risk of 'wasting' resources on claimants who would have found 'real' work without a workfare intervention. This issue has greater significance for more resource intensive programmes. In less resource intensive programmes, such as the Norwegian workfare schemes, dead weight is not perceived as a problem. The reason for focusing on long-term recipiency here is primarily to prevent 'dependency'. The danger of 'dead-weight' is compounded by the possibility that the chances of a proportion of claimants getting a regular job may actually diminish as a *result* of participation in the programme (for example, Aucouturier, 1993, cited in Chapter Two). This may occur either because they lose time and freedom to seek a job, because participating is demotivating to the participant, or because the experience of participating reduces a participant's marketability to employers.

In order to avoid 'dead-weight', programmes tend to be targeted towards claimants who are not expected to find work within, what policy makers consider to be, an acceptable period. Judgements regarding an 'acceptable period' and an optimum point for intervention depend upon the balance of objectives which policy makers hope to meet and resource constraints. In reality, even given a firm set of objectives and unlimited resources, the optimum point is likely to vary from individual to individual. Programmes use two main methods of avoiding 'dead-weight', which are not mutually exclusive:

1. By prescribing a specified length of time before a person becomes eligible for workfare. The scientific basis for decisions about points of intervention is not always clear – although longitudinal studies which consider the relationship between length of unemployment period and

chances of finding work can assist here (Leisering and Walker, 1998). In Denmark, the Netherlands and the UK younger recipients enter programmes at an earlier stage than recipients in other age groups. By contrast in Norway, the timing of intervention is left to the discretion of an individual social worker. In France and Germany, depending on how insertion and Help Towards Work programmes are implemented at the level of departments and local authorities, the point of intervention may be imposed by the administration or result from negotiation with the client. In the Netherlands all clients are assessed, and suitability for intervention is determined according to set criteria. Some attempt to take account of the special needs of individuals at greatest risk of being 'excluded' can be made through allowing people to queue-jump (enter the programme early), on the basis of specified characteristics (Table 9.2, column 5).

2. By providing intensive case-management support to divert people from claiming or remaining on benefit before they are placed in a compulsory programme. This method is most strongly adopted in the US (particularly see New York City, Chapter Eight), but is also the function of the 'gateway' in the British New Deal programme, and the 'rights and responsibilities' courses in the Danish activation programme.

What proportion? Universal versus selective programmes

This section describes the proportion of people within prescribed target groups who are affected by the introduction of workfare policies. The programmes reviewed here can be differentiated according to how tightly they define their target groups (Table 9.2, column 6). Danish activation, the British New Deals and the Dutch JEA for young people are 'universal', in the sense that the obligation to participate in compulsory activity is designed to relate to every member of the target population meeting the inclusion criteria. Target groups are well defined – according to benefit, duration of claim and even age of the recipient. The US state programmes and the French insertion programme can be described as 'quasi-universal', in that they impinge on every eligible client, although not all clients become participants in a work or training activity. In California, New York City and Wisconsin, only the pre-workfare interview stage is applied to all TANF recipients. In France, while RMI 'insertion' contracts are supposed to apply to all recipients (and leaving aside the fact that this does not happen), these need not specify compulsory activity.

In contrast, 'selective' programmes are designed to encompass only a proportion of the 'in scope' target group. Of the programmes compared here, these include the Norwegian workfare schemes and most of the German Help Towards Work programmes.

Taking a selective rather than universal approach to target groups has important consequences for strategy. This is because universal programmes apply to a wider range of recipients within their target groups (who therefore encounter a greater range of barriers to work). Selection is one way of specifically targeting people who are less easily described by firm age or 'duration of claim' criteria. It may be used to target people *within* a social assistance population on more qualitative grounds. For example, in Norway it is used with regard to people who are believed to be in particular need of awakening to the 'connection between the responsibility of the individual and entitlements' (Chapter Five).

The discretion which administrators have to include or exclude individuals into the workfare programme can have positive or negative consequences for social assistance recipients. Administrators and social workers may use it to decide not to involve people who are likely to 'fail' within the existing system – for example, German social workers may decline to offer places to people where they think the result will be sanctioning (Chapter Three). However, selection is usually associated with localised funding and a lower level of investment in the workfare programme as a whole. As a result, it is often used to target more disaffected recipients (as in Norway), or to push 'easy wins' (as in France and Germany) – where there is a higher chance of a return on investment.

Summary: target groups

In summary, there are very important differences in primary target groups between Europe and the US. Within Europe, the focus is on young unemployed people. Danish activation stands out as the programme most intended to extend to people whose main reason for claiming is not unemployment. Programmes differ as to whether they are applied universally or more selectively to their target populations. The most 'universal' programmes are the Danish, Dutch and British programmes, with the German and Norwegian programmes being the most selective.

Administrative framework

Differences between 'universal' and 'selective' programmes are related to other differences in the way that schemes are administered. This section describes the differences between the programmes in terms of their administrative framework. In part, variation results from differences in the way that social assistance is delivered[6]. However, in Denmark and the Netherlands in particular, workfare programmes are less guided by such underlying differences. The main distinction made here is between workfare programmes that are centralised and decentralised.

Centralised versus decentralised framework

Programmes that apply universally to defined target populations across the country are able to do so because they are funded and controlled centrally, and can therefore be standardised (Table 9.3, column 1). Where local bodies control (or part-control) funding, they may determine the extent to which programmes are implemented. A greater degree of centralisation also results in greater intra-national standardisation, as central government has an interest in ensuring that funds are spent in a manner consistent with a national strategy (Chapter Ten). As a result, programmes are more codified, hence there is less room for administrative discretion, for instance, over sanctioning policy or the range of available placements (Table 9.3, column 2). Historically, central governments have had responsibility for administering social security for insured population groups, while local authorities have had responsibility for maintaining uninsured populations. As a result, programmes for social assistance clients that are centralised (the British, Dutch and Danish programmes) show a greater degree of overlap with active labour market programmes for insured clients (Table 9.3, column 3).

The separate systems of administration and provision for insured and uninsured social security claimants, which exist in all the countries except the UK[7], provide the structure for the introduction of new active labour market policies and are carried forward into separate systems of active labour market provision. In all seven countries, historically, benefits for insured and uninsured clients have been administered through separate government departments, focusing on labour market integration versus social protection respectively. This division has been eliminated in the UK, but remains in the other countries compared here. In Denmark and

Table 9.3: Centralised versus decentralised programmes

Name of programme (or collection of schemes)	1 National – local[1]	2 Codified- discretionary[2]	3 Unified- segregated[3]
DN Activation	2	2-3	2-3
F Insertion	2	2	2
D Help Towards Work	2	2	2
NL JEA – Young People	3	3	3
N Schemes resulting from the 1991 Social Services Act	1	1	1-2
UK New Deal – Young People	4	3	4*
US State programmes resulting from PRWORA	3	3	1*

* But no comparable insured group in the US or the UK (in the UK unemployed people are not eligible for insured benefits after six months, prior to this the benefits are more or less unified: hence score = (4)).

[1] Degree of central (National / Federal) control over funding and main components of delivery. (1) = least control, to, (4) = most control.
[2] Level of discretion held by individual administrator / social worker over inclusion, placement strategy and sanctioning. (1) = greatest, to, (4) = least
[3] Extent of distinction within the programme between clients receiving insurance-based benefits and clients receiving assistance benefits. (1) = programmes for insured clients are nearly always completely separate from this programme, (2) = this programme may overlap with programmes for insured groups – though this varies from locality to locality, (3) = this programme overlaps with a programme for insured clients who enter through a different doorway, (4) = there are no distinctions between insured and uninsured clients according to the design of this programme.

Norway the distinction has become less clear as ALMPs have become more localised.

The workfare programmes described in the chapters on France and Norway pertain more or less exclusively to social assistance clients. In Germany the level of overlap with programmes for insured clients is in most cases quite low. In the US there is no comparable 'insured' population to TANF recipients – but unemployed and general assistance recipients receive entirely separate treatment. As a rule, of the programmes considered here, those that are locally funded and segregated tend to be more 'preventive' in their outlook, and less geared to providing a client-focused service, although this varies from region to region. This is particularly the case where local or state authorities are looking to make savings in administration costs as well as on benefit pay-outs (as is usually the case in Germany, Norway and the US).

Intra-national variation

In general, greater levels of segregation between programmes for insured and uninsured groups mean a higher level of local responsibility and control over the funding, objectives, target groups and content of programmes for social assistance clients than for insured unemployed claimants, hence much greater variation in practice. Such variation is related to administrative factors (Denmark, Germany, Norway), as well as the political beliefs of local legislators (France).

National governments tend to consider that such local variability is counter to the ambition of labour market integration. As a result, the introduction by national governments of compulsory activity policies for assistance clients has been associated with a trend towards merging provision for insured and uninsured groups, and bringing assistance clients into contact with programmes traditionally reserved for insured groups. The Dutch JEA and Danish activation programmes display a high degree of programme coordination, so that the same compulsory programmes can, in theory, apply to insured and uninsured clients (although in practice, as in Denmark, the quality of placements may differ).

Attempts to coordinate the activities of relevant government departments have tended to prove problematic – particularly in France where the administrative system for assistance clients is exceedingly complex. In Denmark, Norway and the Netherlands the introduction of the activation, 'workfare' and JEA programmes respectively were accompanied by a direction for relevant departments and executive agencies to work more closely together, although, in some cases, achieving this has been more difficult (Chapters Four, Five and Six).

Summary: administrative framework

In summary, there are important similarities and differences between the programmes with regard to their degree of centralisation. The British New Deal, Dutch JEA, and Danish activation programmes are more centralised than the rest; Norwegian workfare and German Help Towards Work programmes are most decentralised. Differences in the level of centralisation are related to the extent of intra-national variability in programme delivery (this is greatest where the programmes are least centralised).

Divergence from work-for-benefit

The extent to which programmes diverge from the idealised workfare model outlined in Chapter One is a reflection of the extent to which their architects define the causes of worklessness differently, and, so, seek to accommodate the varied circumstances of individual clients. Different strategies are a reflection of differences in underlying ideological aims, and in attempts to respond to the heterogeneous needs of target populations. This section describes three methods used to accommodate heterogeneity:

1. Selecting suitable clients from within a wider target population.
2. Tailoring placements to individuals within the programme.
3. Applying discretion with regard to sanctioning policy.

Method 1 involves restricting the use of workfare to a narrower and less clearly defined group of clients. Methods 2 and 3 involve divergence from the idealised 'workfare' model defined in Chapter One.

Selecting suitable clients

Selectivity is discussed above. This is a feature of decentralised programmes, and is related to scarcer resources and to more localised funding bases. Traditionally in Norway and Germany selective schemes have focused on 'work-testing' (underpinned by an ideological objective of removing 'rational dependency'). More recently they have been used in France and Germany to 'cream off' the members of the target population who are thought most likely to move out of social assistance (and into work) following participation (Chapters Two and Three). In Norway, in localities where new coordination programmes are in place these are used to offer different opportunities for 'job-ready' uninsured people.

Tailoring placements to individual clients

All seven countries include a range of 'activation' placements (to use the terminology of the Danish programme), of which work-for-benefit level pay is just one possibility. Such placements include non-work activities which are nonetheless considered socially valuable because they are underpinned by a normative assumption that 'an 'active' life is better to live than a 'passive' one' (Hvinden, 1999).

As an alternative to 'passive' receipt, or to absolute removal of financial assistance, there are five main means by which social assistance clients are 'activated' through the programmes reviewed here. These are:

- work-for-benefit (or near benefit) level pay;
- subsidised work placements in the regular labour market or temporarily supported self-employment;
- created public jobs for collectively agreed or standard minimum wages;
- education (or vocational training); and
- social activation.

These are not straight alternatives, and are often combined. For example, German 'vocational training' within the Help Towards Work programme may involve a mix of 'created public jobs' and 'education'; and Danish 'special activation measures' mix guidance with work training. Rosdahl and Weise (Chapter Six) list seven possible types of Danish activation 'offer', but essentially they are made up of combinations of the five options above. Table 9.4 shows the main methods of activation used within each 'benefit-based' programme.

From the viewpoint of the participant, the rate of pay, and the form that the payment takes, provide key means of distinguishing between more or less 'real' jobs, as well as of assessing the more or less workfare-like aspects of multi-trajectory programmes. The difference between 'work-for-benefit' and 'created public jobs' concerns conditions of employment (labour rights and wage levels) and is one of degree. Both are distinguished from 'subsidised work', in which the state supports only part of the income of the participant.

The range of placements on offer also vary in the extent to which they seek to develop human capital through the use of education and training rather than seeking to place participants directly into the labour market. In addition, some seek to overcome more severe barriers to employment through 'social activation'.

Table 9.4: Placement types

	N Activation	F RMI	D Hilfe zur Arbeit	NL JEA – young people	N Norwegian Social Services Act	UK New Deal for Young People	US CalWorks	US Work Experience Program	US Wisconsin Works
Work-for-benefit (or near-benefit) pay	X	X	X	X	X	X	X	X	X
Subsidised work in the regular labour market	X	X	X	X	X	X	X	X	X
Created public jobs for 'regular' wages	X	X	X						
Education and training	X		X	X		X	X	X	
Social activation	X			X					
Universal/selective[1]	U	Q-U	S	U	S	U	Q-U	Q-U	Q-U

[1] Universal/selective: See Table 9.2: Target group; U = Universal, S = Selective, Q-U = Quasi-universal.

Work-for-benefit placements

Programmes vary enormously in the extent to which their most work-for-benefit-like placements approximate to the idealised model of 'workfare' as opposed to a world of 'real' work:

1. Within most of the programmes considered here, there is no straight 'for benefit' arrangement, only arrangements that approximate to 'for benefit'. Participants generally receive a sum in addition to their benefit. Depending on the original level of benefit received, Dutch municipal work participants may considerably improve their income as a result of participation. More usually, however, the extra amount is small and provided in order to compensate for travel and other expenses incurred as a result of participating. However, it may also be presented as an 'earned' reward (as for UK New Deal participants undertaking environment task force or voluntary work options – see Chapter Seven).
2. Participants may actually receive a 'wage' rather than a 'benefit' (for example, this occurs for municipal work participants in the Netherlands, and is an option for UK environment task force/voluntary work participants). This is supposed to give participants a feeling of being in work, as it creates a dependency on an employer rather than on social assistance provision.
3. There are differences in the length of the work requirement. In Norway the work period is open-ended, although a case decision by the Industrial Tribunal found that long-term work could result in displacement (Chapter Five). Elsewhere it is much shorter (for example, under New Deal in the UK it lasts six months) although work periods may be repeated.
4. Participants may work alongside regular employees rather than in segregated work outside of the regular labour market. In the Netherlands most of this work takes place in regular workplaces, elsewhere the situation is usually more mixed, and in Norway the work usually takes place in segregated work schemes.
5. Participants are usually supposed to carry out 'additional' or non-displacing work, often leading to a tension between providing meaningful activity and not disrupting the labour market. As a result, many programmes sidestep this rule to different extents. In the Netherlands, for example, Dutch policy makers accept that the Jobseeker's Employment Act will result in some level of displacement.

Where alternatives to work-for-benefit exist, this placement type is justified as: (i) a disincentive to benefit; (ii) to remove people who can find work or otherwise support themselves; *and*, (iii) as a 'work-experience' tool for people who have comparatively greater difficulty in securing a job.

Subsidised work placements

Most contributors argue that subsidised work does not really qualify as 'workfare'; or, at least, only in the 'market workfare' sense that people are forced to take jobs where employers pay less than the market rate (Grover and Stewart, 1999). This is because while participation is compulsory, the formerly unemployed participant receives a regular wage for the work. Elsewhere they have been distinguished from other activation measures because of their focus on engaging employers and stimulating labour demand (Bosco and Chassard, 1999). Spies and van Berkel (Chapter Four) describe such placements as a compulsory 'work-regime' as opposed to a 'workfare-regime'. Because they insert people directly into waged work, such placements are regarded by both administrators and by clients as providing a 'higher tier' of provision for social assistance recipients with fewer barriers to work.

Through using subsidised placements, programme architects aim to overcome exclusion resulting from a deficit of experience. Subsidised work placements assume, first, some capacity within the ordinary labour market to accommodate special needs, and, second, that a subsidy is sufficient to entice employers to accommodate workers whom they would not normally employ. The fact that clients have not found work up until that point means that, *if the system is operating as it is designed*, people who take this route into employment have barriers to independently securing unsubsidised work. Because the intention is that participants will quickly build up the necessary experience to carry out the work without a subsidy, the period of direct subsidy to the employer is usually quite short (about six months in the Netherlands and the UK). As a variant of subsidised work, the New Deal for 18- to 24-year-olds (UK) also subsidises self-employment for a limited period.

The system falls down if employers hire employees where they would previously have hired unsubsidised employees, or where existing employees are dismissed to make way for cheaper replacements. Evidence from subsidised work and training schemes indicate that this is a serious pitfall for programmes that provide an incentive to employers (see discussion in Chapters Two and Seven). Governments use a range of safeguards to limit such substitution (see, for example, safeguards under the JEA listed in Chapter Four). The second major pitfall for subsidised work placements is that employers become disillusioned with the programme. This occurs when participants fail to live up to expectations of employers (a problem in the early days of the New Deal in the UK) or when the administrative hassle of buying into the programme is off-putting (as, for example, in the New York and Wisconsin TANF programmes).

Created public work placements

'Created public work' constitutes a complete job subsidy. This type of placement is used to overcome deficiencies in skills and experience as well as shortfalls in labour demand. It is, therefore, particularly important in high unemployment areas in parts of France and Germany. In a sense, created jobs constitute an extension of public sector employment. Employees have the same employment rights as other public sector employees, although contracts are on a temporary basis (usually lasting one year in Germany). There is, however, an inherent conflict between creating temporary jobs and meeting society's unmet needs; work is usually funded on a temporary basis, and the more employable clients move on (Chapter Two).

Non-work placements: education and social activation

Non-work placements exist either because programme architects believe that work is not a possibility for participants in the short term, and/or because they believe that the best interests of society are served by developing participants' human capital through education and training, although initiatives to promote the development of 'soft skills' and through initiatives to sort out acute barriers to work. Recipients placed in social activation are compelled, as a condition of benefit receipt, to participate in some kind of non-work activity primarily designed to improve personal skills, motivation and readiness for work. Spies and van Berkel (Chapter Four) suggest that such activities contribute to a 'tightened welfare regime' but do not constitute 'workfare' as such.

Education may be used either as a short-term remedial tool to get clients back into the first job they can take, or as part of a longer-term strategy to build up human capital. Within the British New Deal, the official purpose is the former and the education and training 'option' is supposed to focus on basic qualifications. Language training performs a similar function in other parts of Europe and is commonly used for new immigrants. In contrast, within Danish activation, 'education and training' may constitute a longer-term investment in human capital and can involve participation in ordinary education (Chapter Six). Similarly, Help Towards Work placements are used to allow young East Germans to complete their vocational training according to the 'dual system' of work plus education, in the context of scarce demand for trainees (Chapter Three).

Negotiating placements

Where administrations create more than one type of placement opportunity, these form an acknowledged or unacknowledged hierarchy as viewed by both recipients and administrators – with subsidised or 'created' jobs at the top. This is unsurprising, as these constitute 'real' work, and come with 'real' pay and conditions. 'Creaming' – picking off easier-to-employ individuals for the more work-like options – occurs everywhere. In Germany the 'gradient' is explicitly described within social assistance legislation (Chapter Three, Figure 3.1). In the Netherlands there is a deliberate hierarchy from 'training and social activation' at the bottom, through 'municipal employment', to 'subsidised work' at the top (Chapter Four, Figure 4.1). These are seen as 'phases' that cumulatively build up participants to the point where they can take unsubsidised jobs. By contrast, in the UK the alternative options are supposed to have parity – and each placement type is independently supposed to support moves into unsubsidised work.

In principle, whether in the short or longer term, all the programmes work towards supporting transitions to unsubsidised employment. However, to different extents administrating organisations tacitly accept that, for some people, a move into work is unrealistic. The experience of French employment programmes is that clients who have little hope of finding regular work are cycled within 'exclusion trajectories'. The programme may fulfil the functions of providing social welfare and ensuring that individuals are participating. This is most clearly the case in Denmark, as activation policy has expanded to net a wider group of recipients with more complex social disadvantages. The tougher ideology underlying the US state programmes, and tighter target populations for Norwegian workfare (selective) and for the UK New Deals (unemployed people only) mean that improving general welfare outside of the context of finding work is not yet an important part of the strategy of these programmes.

Table 9.5: Negotiating placements

Name of programme	1 Use of advisor-client negotiation[1]	2 Use of advisor – client contracts[2]	3 Assistance to meet special 'barriers' organised through negotiation[3]
DN Activation	3	2	Yes
F Insertion	2	3	Varies by area
D Help Towards Work	2 (varies)	1-2 (varies)	Varies by area
NL JEA – Young People	3	3	Yes
N Schemes resulting from the 1991 Social Services Act	1 – 2 (varies)	1 – 2 (varies)	Varies by area
UK New Deal – Young People	3	3	Yes
US California: CalWORKS	2	3	Yes
New York City: Work Experience Program	2	3	Yes
Wisconsin: Wisconsin Works	2	3	Yes

[1] By design: (1) No negotiation, (2) Consultation where alternatives available, (3) Intention that a range of alternatives *should* be available in order that suitable placements can be made in consultation with the client.
[2] By design: Contracts to specify client's responsibilities and plan of action: (1) seldom used, (2) often used, (3) always used.
[3] For example, housing problems, addiction problems.

Different mechanisms are used to assign recipients to placements (Table 9.5, column 1). Where programmes are selective (French RMI, German Help Towards Work, Norwegian workfare), an assessment by a case or social worker is used to inform a decision as to whether a recipient should enter the programme at all. In the Dutch, Danish and British universal programmes, and in the quasi-universal programmes of California, New York City and Wisconsin, an assessment is a component of the programme itself and some sort of negotiation process is entered into (Table 9.5, column 1). However, there is great variation in the extent to which participants can make a free 'choice', or to which they are allowed, at an initial stage, to refuse offers. Facilitating individuals to choose placements is part of the official design of Danish, Dutch and

British programmes, although inevitably the range of alternatives are greater for some than for others. For individuals who are judged by themselves or by administrators to be less than 'job-ready', the existence of alternatives – different types of community work, different forms of social activation, different training courses – becomes very important in giving a sense of choice.

Dutch participants are 'measured' (according to qualifications, work history, and barriers to work), and this is supposed to determine suitability for the different levels of the JEA programme. Elsewhere the process is less explicit, although all universal (and quasi-universal) programmes include a discussion with individuals so that action plans and 'contracts' can be drawn up to suit the specifics of individual situations (Table 9.5, column 2). Universal programmes also use the negotiation process to identify special barriers to work (Table 9.5, column 3), so that these can be acted upon. However, the Danish and French experience is that sticking to such plans and enforcing contracts become more problematic for clients who have many barriers to work.

Discretion in sanctioning individual clients

Failure to attend work-for-benefit placements, or non-work placements, is subject to sanction in all countries (individuals who fail to attend subsidised or created jobs generally risk losing their employment in the same way as ordinary employees). For most programmes, compulsion applies to all clients to whom an offer is made[8], although not necessarily in the first instance (surveys of German 'Help Towards Work' show high rates of refusal which do not necessarily result in sanctioning). However, the severity and extent of sanctioning varies from programme to programme (Table 9.6).

Sanctioning does not always result in full removal of benefit. In Wisconsin, sanctioning is proportionate to the number of hours not 'worked' on a scheme. Once registered within the Danish activation programme, participants are only ever sanctioned for up to one fifth of their full benefit. Under the German Help Towards Work programme, only a quarter of a recipient's benefit is initially removed – although the sanction increases until the individual complies. German recipients who have dependants have a proportion of their benefit protected on behalf of their family. In most countries (but not in the US or in France), sanctioned recipients may apply for discretionary hardship payments from the administrating agency.

Table 9.6: Sanctioning

Scheme	1 Sanction: initial failure to participate	2 Sanction: subsequent failure to attend	3 Hardship fund available to which sanctioned clients can apply	4 Type of sanction	5 Level of discretion usually available to administrator
DN Activation	100% until compliant	20% until compliant	No	Partial (until compliant)	Low-Moderate (varies)
F Insertion (RMI)	100% until compliant	100% until compliant	No	Full (until compliant)	High
D Help Towards Work	25% in the first instance, up to 100%, until compliant	25% in the first instance, up to 100%, until compliant	One time discretionary payments available	Partial (until compliant)	Low-High (varies)
NL JEA – Young People	100% for one month, then renewed sanction or benefit reduction until compliant	100% for one month, then renewed sanction or benefit reduction until compliant	Discretionary hardship payments	Full (time limited)/ or full then partial (until compliant)	Low
N Schemes resulting from the 1991 Social Services Act	100%, until compliant	Discretionary withdrawal, until compliant	Discretionary hardship payments	Full (until compliant)	Moderate-High (varies)
UK New Deal – Young People	100%, two weeks renewable, four weeks in second instance	100%, two weeks renewable, four weeks in second instance	Discretionary hardship payments if deemed to be in a 'vulnerable group'	Full (time limited)	Low
US CalWORKS (California)	Partial	Partial	No	Partial (until compliant)	Low
Work Experience Program (New York City)	Partial	Partial	No	Partial (until compliant)	Low
Wisconsin Works (Wisconsin)	Complete	Proportionate to hours not participating	No	Proportionate (until compliant)	Low

Programmes vary in the amount of discretion that they afford administrators over sanctioning. As might be expected, greater discretion over other aspects of the programmes is more frequently found in decentralised than centralised programmes. The rate of sanctioning is also very different. Sanctions are more aggressively applied in the three US examples than in Europe; in New York City the number of people undergoing sanctions exceeds the number in workfare; and, in Wisconsin 6% of the caseload is under sanction. There appears to be a greater reluctance to sanction within European programmes, the consequences may nevertheless be severe. Within the Dutch JEA programme, warnings are given and partial sanctions may be applied before benefit is removed completely. Nonetheless, there is evidence that sanctioning policy in the Netherlands has led to 'drop out' among those already at greatest risk of exclusion (Chapter Four). There is anecdotal evidence that concern about the consequences of sanctioning may have affected a national initiative to toughen up the sanctioning rules for participants in the German Help Towards Work programme, as social workers are reluctant to offer placements to people who they think may refuse (Chapter Three).

Summary: divergence from work-for-benefit

Programmes show considerable divergence from an idealised workfare model. Indeed, 'work-for-benefit placements' are not used for many clients, and when they are used they include features which move them away from a 'work-for-benefit' exchange. Work-for-benefit options are more likely to be experienced by clients with greater difficulties in securing work. Some programmes (Danish, Dutch, British, and Californian) include 'education and training' or 'social activation' as alternative means of provision for such clients. In addition, the Danish, Dutch, British and US programmes include a 'case management' process, in order to tailor the programme to the individual clients. However, of these four sets of programmes, the Danish activation programme is distinguished from the rest in its emphasis on a long-term strategy and on human capital development, whereas the US programmes have greatest emphasis on providing routes for early re-entry into the labour market.

Types of workfare?

The preceding sections have outlined programme differences in aims, target populations, administrative framework, and divergence from an idealised workfare model towards greater emphasis on a human capital development approach and on 'tailored' programmes. This section demonstrates the extent to which differences in these factors co-vary – and to which recognisable 'types' of workfare can be identified. Explanations for co-variance are explored further in Chapter Ten.

One group of programmes might be labelled 'European centralised programmes' – represented here by activation (Denmark), the Jobseeker's Employment Act for Young People (the Netherlands) and the New Deal for Young People (UK). The remaining programmes are less easily grouped. The German and Norwegian programmes are similar in that they are decentralised, although the German programme shares many of the features with the European centralised programmes, including a tendency towards greater universality. The French and US programmes are striking (and different from each other) in that they have ideological roots which are not reflected elsewhere.

European centralised programmes

The Danish, Dutch and British programmes are underpinned by an ideology which supports 'integrative' as well as 'preventive' aims. The relationship between administrative framework and ideology is illustrated by the clustering of these programmes in the top right corner of Figure 9.1, centralised and integrative. These centralised programmes have a broader target population, are more visible, and so aim to appeal to a broader electorate. A key factor is their 'universal' rather than 'selective' status. While in these countries the taxpaying public may accept that *some* people choose not to work, they are less likely to accept that this is the cause of worklessness for the vast majority of the target population. As a result, architects of these *'European centralised programmes'* acknowledge a wide range of 'causes' of worklessness (Table 9.1).

The centralised programmes tend to have a wide range of placement options available, including options which emphasise 'human capital development' as well as 'labour market attachment' (Figure 9.2). In Figure 9.2 the most centralised programmes are situated within the top right hand corner of the figure; centralised, and with an emphasis on human resource development. This reflects a strong funding base enabling more resource intensive forms of assistance. These centralised compulsory work programmes form a strong part of *the* national strategy for overcoming worklessness. Because they recognise a wide range of *causes* of worklessness, they employ a broad range of strategies to negate these causes.

Because they are nationally standardised and highly codified, centralised programmes tend to have rigorous sanctioning policies – permitting little discretion to individual administrators over sanctioning (Figure 9.3). In Figure 9.3 the *European centralised programmes* are situated within the bottom right hand corner of the figure; centralised, and with fairly well defined sanctioning policies that permit little room for discretion.

Of the three *centralised European programmes*, Danish activation is more integrative than the rest, and places a stronger emphasis on human resource development. This may be due to two factors. First, the target population for the Danish activation programme is broader than for the Dutch and British programmes for young people, and includes a higher proportion of non 'job-ready' individuals. Second, the Danish activation programme has grown out of a rights-based voluntary scheme (Chapter Six).

Other programmes

The more decentralised policies are less easily typified. Nonetheless, in localities where the German Help Towards Work programme is more centralised, the programme is often also more integrative, more human resource development oriented and more formalised with regard to sanctioning policy. The most decentralised programme – Norwegian Workfare – also demonstrates the relationship between centralisation and other factors; being a decentralised, broadly preventive-oriented programme with a strong focus on labour market attachment objectives. Administrators have a high degree of discretion over sanctioning policy (Figure 9.3).

Given that the US programmes are often presented as a model for workfare delivery, the differences between US and European centralised programmes are important. The US programmes described here combine a moderately centralised approach with an emphasis on: preventing claims rather than integrating clients; on labour market attachment rather than human resource development; a limited range of short-term solutions; and strong sanctioning policy. The difference is certainly linked to the strong individual-focused ideology behind US welfare policy making.

In striking contrast, as a result of the republican ideology of French social policy architects, French insertion policies stand out in the strength of their emphasis on the structural causes of unemployment and on the responsibility of society to solve the problem of 'worklessness'. In principle, at least, sanctioning plays a very limited role.

Summary: types of workfare

European centralised programmes diverge markedly from an ideal-type 'workfare' definition with regard to strategy, but low levels of divergence with regard to enforcing compulsion than more decentralised programmes – however, these relationships are not straightforward. Torfing's term 'offensive' (see Chapter One) might be used to describe these programmes, although Torfing was actually seeking to distinguish Danish workfare from US and pre–New Deal British programmes (Torfing, 1999).

European centralised programmes are not associated with countries sharing a common history with regard to either social security or social assistance provision. A possible explanation for this is that in Europe workfare policies have only recently come to be considered a major factor within social assistance provision. Compulsory work policies have expanded during the 1990s, alongside the more general expansion of active labour market policies. Attempts to synthesise traditional social-democratic and neo-classical approaches to labour market policy have been made. In this sense the introduction of workfare policies may represent something of a paradigm shift within social assistance provision. The fact that many workfare policies are currently undergoing rapid transition suggests that the groupings presented above are likely to alter over a short period of time. A fuller discussion of possible explanations for the development of different types of programmes in different countries is given in Chapter Ten.

Discussion – implications for the future

Workfare measures are understood to increase outflows from benefit receipt via two mechanisms. First, they are understood to operate as a 'sorting' tool, whereby people who are already working (and claiming fraudulently) or not really looking for work (when this is a condition of receipt) can be excluded from receiving assistance. Second, they are understood to coerce people into a situation where they can develop work opportunities and build up human capital, thus allowing them to improve their chances of integration within the regular labour market. Systematic comparison reveals that a range of programmes and approaches, which acknowledge

Figure 9.1: Administrative framework and aims

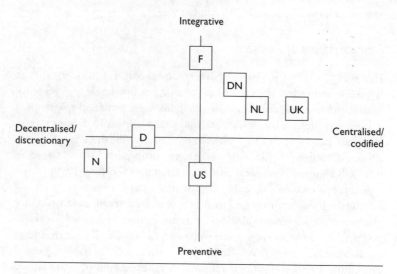

Key:

The figure does not draw on measurable or scientific data and should be seen as illustrative of the relationsships desribed in the chapter.

Y-axis: overall qualitative assessment of ideological underpinnings based on Table 9.1 from integrative-preventive.

For ease of presentation programmes are denoted by the initial letters of the country in which they operate. This Figure is supposed to illustrate the positioning of individual *programmes* and should *not* be taken to represent the totality of compulsory work programmes within each country.

DN – Activation
F   – RMI-based insertion
D   – Help Towards Work
NL – Jobseeker's Employment Act for young people
N   – Local authority based workfare schemes following the 1991 Social Assistance Act
UK – New Deal for Young People
US – State programmes following from PRWORA, *but,* represented by programmes for TANF recipients operating in California, New York City and Wisconsin

Figure 9.2: Administrative framework and strategy

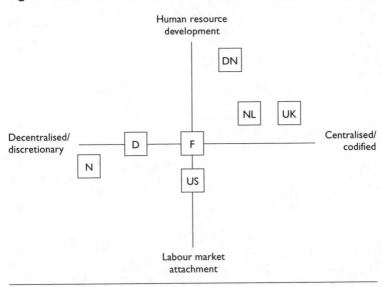

Key:

The figure does not draw on measurable or scientific data and should be seen as illustrative of the relationsships desribed in the chapter.

Y-axis: overall qualitative assessment of ideological underpinnings based on Table 9.1 from integrative-preventive.

For ease of presentation programmes are denoted by the initial letters of the country in which they operate. This Figure is supposed to illustrate the positioning of individual *programmes* and should *not* be taken to represent the totality of compulsory work programmes within each country.

DN   – Activation

F   – RMI-based insertion

D   – Help Towards Work

NL   – Jobseeker's Employment Act for young people

N   – Local authority based workfare schemes following the 1991 Social Assistance Act

UK   – New Deal for Young People

US   – State programmes following from PRWORA, *but,* represented by programmes for TANF recipients operating in California, New York City and Wisconsin

Figure 9.3: Administrative framework and sanctioning policy

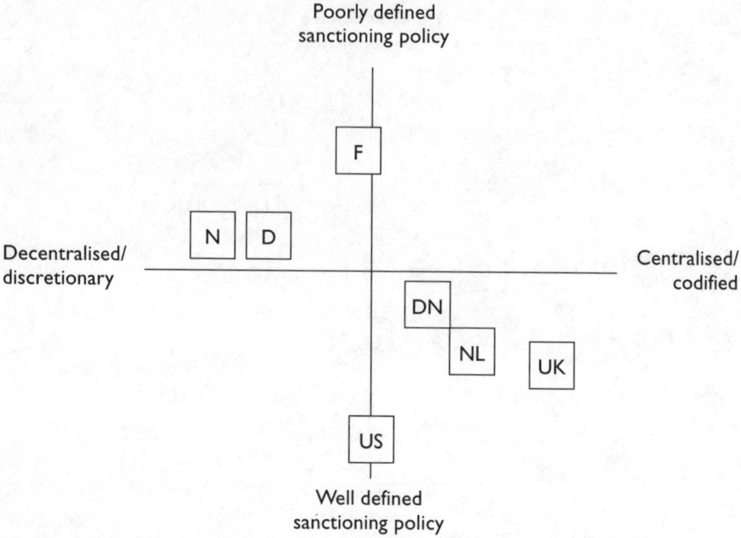

Poorly defined
sanctioning policy

Decentralised/
discretionary

Centralised/
codified

Well defined
sanctioning policy

Key:

The figure does not draw on measurable or scientific data and should be seen as illustrative of the relationsships desribed in the chapter.

Y-axis: overall qualitative assessment of ideological underpinnings based on Table 9.1 from integrative-preventive.

For ease of presentation programmes are denoted by the initial letters of the country in which they operate. This Figure is supposed to illustrate the positioning of individual *programmes* and should *not* be taken to represent the totality of compulsory work programmes within each country.

DN   –   Activation
F   –   RMI-based insertion
D   –   Help Towards Work
NL   –   Jobseeker's Employment Act for young people
N   –   Local authority based workfare schemes following the 1991 Social Assistance Act
UK   –   New Deal for Young People
US   –   State programmes following from PRWORA, *but,* represented by programmes for TANF recipients operating in California, New York City and Wisconsin

and employ a combination of these two mechanisms, represent 'workfare' as defined in this book.

Given the attractiveness of 'workfare' to a range of ideological positions and political parties and the congruence of this policy form with a range of objectives it is likely that compulsory programmes for people in need of financial assistance will continue to be expanded. As expansion occurs, compulsory programmes are increasingly used to target recipients who have greater and greater barriers to work. The result of redesignating groups as 'work-able' and of tightening work-testing criteria is that programmes now encompass people who in an earlier era would have been considered unable to (or incapable of) work.

As the programmes expand to include a wider proportion of the social assistance population, target populations become increasingly heterogeneous. This can result in policy makers acknowledging a greater range of interpretations of the causes of worklessness, and hence implementing a greater range of strategies to deal with the problem. In consequence, at least in Europe, as workfare policies expand, the perceived value of workfare as a primarily diversionary tool appears to be diminished. The descriptions of policy development in the chapters at the core of this book demonstrate a strong trend towards the second mechanism – developing human capital and employment opportunities – within the framework of compulsion that is associated with 'social exclusion' based justifications for intervention (Chapter One). This involves moving away from the 'ideal-type' work-for-benefit workfare model outlined in the definition at the start of this chapter, so that rather than looking at workfare programmes we begin to map the development of a broader range of compulsory policies for social assistance recipients. In Europe this is demonstrated by the development of programmes which are increasingly centralised, codified and individualised. Similarly, although these developments are not the focus of Chapter Eight, the shift away from purely diversionary tactics is also represented by the new interest in intermediate labour market strategies in the US (Johnson and Goldenberg, 1999). Among the European countries, the localised Norwegian workfare schemes featured particularly strong discretionary characteristics. However, recent developments suggest that here also the trend is towards greater integration with ALMPs for insured groups and toward a more human resource development focus (Chapter Five).

Despite their appeal, compulsory programmes face a common set of problems that emanate directly from the fact that they are compulsory, work-based, and increasingly targeted at a population facing formidable barriers to work. Employment within the primary labour market is extremely difficult for multiply disadvantaged groups to achieve. If compulsory participation in active labour market programmes is to be increasingly understood as facilitating a long-term route for groups facing severe barriers to employment, two key considerations emerge from the comparison of programmes described within this book. The first relates to the surrounding package of measures designed to assist the target group; the second to the quality and appropriateness of the programmes themselves.

Both considerations involve recognition of the difference between a state level contract, balancing what the state is doing for social assistance recipients in general and what is required of social assistance clients as a group – and an individual level contract, between clients and individual social assistance officers around a particular agreement. This distinction is not generally acknowledged. Currently, as far as most programme participants are concerned, the front line worker in a programme or social assistance office, represents the state, and it is this person with whom an 'agreement' or 'contract' is brokered. The policy environment within which the compulsory programme is embedded will generally have a larger impact on individuals' chances in the labour market than the workfare programme itself. 'Personal advisors' responsible for delivering programmes have little or no control over broader initiatives which improve or diminish individuals' chance of finding work. In addition, an individual advisor/social worker is generally unable to provide any guarantee to individual clients about the quality or the effectiveness of the programme they provide.

In terms of the broader relationship between the overall responsibilities of the state to social assistance recipients as a group, workfare programmes are only one tool in the box of available policy strategies. As a match to the responsibility which recipients have to seek regular work, the state has the following duties:

- First, the state's broader policy framework (from macroeconomic policy to housing, transport, law and order policies) should support a well functioning labour market; otherwise the purpose of policies that enforce jobseeking becomes less clear.
- Second, the state has a responsibility to ensure that a coherent overall social policy strategy exists, which ensures that the interaction between tax and benefit systems supports moves into work for individual clients rather than creates unemployment and/or poverty traps. If the

responsibility to seek work (and to engage in programmes which enhance the chances of finding work) expands to groups of people who would not traditionally have been expected to seek work, this includes ensuring that an improvement in living standards due to working is apparent to people with additional costs resulting from working. For example, this would include additional costs resulting from the need to accommodate disabilities, health problems and/or childcare provision.

• Third, concentrating on the perceived defects of individuals does nothing to counteract failures within the labour market in terms of employers' reluctance to employ people from certain groups – including disabled people (Meager et al, 1999), older people (McKay and Middleton, 1998) and people from certain ethnic minority backgrounds (Social Exclusion Unit, 1999)[9]. Compulsory work measures need to be supported by the introduction of policies to tackle wider structural and cultural issues, including employer discrimination. In other words, they should be underpinned by a social model of unemployment which considers all barriers – individual, cultural and structural – faced by clients (Oliver and Barnes, 1998).

At the narrower level of the contract between individual programme participants and the state, the relationship between the quality and appropriateness of compulsory programmes and an individual recipient's responsibility to participate needs to be clarified. Compelling clients to participate in programmes that are unproven in terms of their effectiveness is morally and economically suspect. This book does not explicitly set out to consider empirical evidence for effectiveness, or to disentangle reasons for differences in outcomes[10]. Nonetheless, research evidence from at least three of the seven countries – Denmark, the UK and US – suggests that compulsory programmes have had some aggregate impact on falling caseloads and on moves into work (Weise and Brogaard, 1997; Chapter Eight). Programme effects in these countries have been supported by improvements in overall labour market performance. Clearly under some conditions, compulsory programmes can be successful in increasing the overall numbers of people moving into work. By contrast the available evidence from German Help Towards Work evaluations and from evaluations of French programmes suggests that these have been less effective – at least in terms of moving participants into unsubsidised regular employment. However, such programmes may contribute to other, sometimes unstated, objectives. For example, as Enjolras et al suggest

(Chapter Two), the reason that workfare programmes for French under 25-year-olds continue to be used may be because they provide a form of income support for this group. Similarly, in Leipzig (Chapter Three) they provide a means of creating employment in an area of demand shortages.

Evaluations of workfare programmes typically use aggregate outcome indicators determined by available quantitative information. However, from the perspective of an individual client, overall programme success measured by aggregate falls in social assistance rolls, or even by increases in the number of participants who move into work, cannot justify the use of compulsory methods with them personally. From a participant's perspective, to measure success in this way is to ignore the plight of those who are not helped by the scheme – who have entered a contract resulting in diminished autonomy over how they spend their time on the understanding that participation is meant to improve their circumstances. 'Workless' individuals who do not gain from a compulsory programme, either through improved work chances or in some other way, are worse off through participation. From the perspective of the State, the objective of preventing exclusion may be at odds with the use of compulsion if it leads to increased drop out or to an endless series of work experience programmes for groups who initially had a lower chance of labour market integration.

In all programmes where a range of placement opportunities exists, a social division of workfare inevitably mirrors the selectivity of the regular labour market. More job-ready clients, who have a better chance of being accepted by employers, are likely to be 'creamed off' and provided with placements that have a greater approximation to the 'real' labour market. While the European centralised programmes appear to offer a greater range of opportunities, the fact that they are more strongly codified with regard to sanctioning means that there is a firmer limit to the compromises that can be made to accommodate individual needs than elsewhere. On the other hand, greater codification can clarify the rights of participants. Intermediate trajectories, employed particularly by the centralised European programmes, provide means of trying to accommodate heterogeneity. However, they have the potential to result in people who are less employable experiencing 'exclusion trajectories' or 'sink options' and of being recycled within programmes which bring them no closer to sustained employment. Within more decentralised programmes, the least employable groups in greatest need of assistance – people with multiple disadvantage, living in areas of lower labour market demand – may simply be ignored by the programme.

Case management, increasingly employed within programmes in all seven countries, potentially provides another means of meeting the needs of groups with complex living situations. However, compulsion means that tensions inevitably occur between the social work and policing roles of programme administrators. The trade-off between the pressure to meet targets such as moving people off benefit or even into work, and the requirement to provide a tailored programme, is unresolved, and most problematic for administrators working with clients who confront many barriers to finding employment. Research from the Netherlands (Chapter Four) reveals that compulsion can result in further marginalisation and an exacerbation of the problem of social exclusion. Where the primary aim of the programme is to reduce expenditure, 'drop out' may not be considered a problem in the short term. However, this does not take into account the knock-on effects, which may result from the need to spend in other areas (for example, on health or law enforcement).

The evidence that does exist suggests that although workfare programmes may show an overall effect resulting from implementation, for some people the transition to work may take a long time. Despite the use of intermediate trajectories and case management approaches, architects of existing programmes appear to take an unrealistically homogenous approach to their target populations. Research with groups for whom the programme appears to 'fail', in the context of a clearer policy position with regard to improving the employment/life-style opportunities of extremely disadvantaged groups, would lead to clearer conclusions about the appropriateness of employment outcomes as realistic and/or ideal objectives for sub-groups of clients. In particular, such research could consider the value of intermediate outcomes and different target periods for regular employment in relation to the 'hardest to help' groups. Even in countries where evaluation is relatively widespread, there is limited information about what happens to clients who have been sanctioned, which means that the consequences of the complete removal of benefit can often only be assumed.

The reasons for 'drop out' and marginalisation are largely unknown, as are the processes that support inclusion and integration of sub-groups with many barriers to work. Such understandings can only be fully gained through good qualitative evaluation (see, for example, Spies, 1996). If the lessons of 'good' and 'bad' compulsory programmes are to be learned, this kind of research will need to be used as a complement to outcome research. Of the formal evaluations of programmes considered in this book, the UK New Deal programme is the programme which clearly sets out to mix evaluation methods in this way (ES, 1997b).

As Rosdahl and Wiesse point out (Chapter Six), as employment has risen, leaving a relatively residualised out-of-work population, the Danish activation programme has turned to non-labour market outcomes as indicators of success. The value of such outcome measures, from the point of view of participants and policy developers, would appear to be an important topic for evaluation. In addition, the impact of compulsory programmes in promoting or detracting from other ways in which people can make a contribution to society could be investigated more fully.

Finally, the lack of clarity about entitlement to programmes in many countries suggests that there needs to be greater transparency about the rights of claimants with regard to the availability and indeed the quality of the programme. This would match the clarity that already exists regarding the responsibilities of individual clients. The power imbalance, whereby the acceptable standard of provision is determined by policy makers may need to be addressed – perhaps by involving service users themselves in decisions around determining what constitutes an 'acceptable' outcome for a set level of input, and around determining acceptable levels of programme quality. Such involvement would help drive policy towards a situation where rights and responsibilities are more explicitly balanced from the perspective of the individual and whereby 'successful outcomes' are considered to be 'successful' by both programme administrators and programme participants.

Notes

[1] The term 'programmes' is used throughout this chapter for ease of reading.

[2] The OECD makes a distinction between 'active' and 'passive' measures. The definition of 'active' is very broad – including public employment and services administration, labour market training, measures for disadvantaged young people and youth training measures, subsidised employment schemes and vocational and sheltered work measures for disabled people (OECD, 1999).

[3] In addition, French Insertion programmes have been introduced to supply workfare places to young people who are not otherwise eligible for financial assistance where no such work training programme previously existed (these are 'opt in' policies).

[4] However, perhaps less obvious is that, even 'opt-in' programmes for people not otherwise entitled to benefit, such as the French Youth Employment programmes (Chapter Three) and the British Youth Training programme (Chapter Seven), are associated with these interpretations of the problem of 'dependency'. The very fact that these policies have no benefit equivalent underlines a determination that target group members should not be allowed to depend on an alternative non-work source of income.

[5] Although in France young people are not covered by RMI. High rates of youth unemployment undermine traditional presumptions of family support. Youth insertion programmes have provided a more acceptable policy solution to the financial needs of young people than extending minimum income entitlement.

[6] For discussion of differences, see Eardley et al, 1996a and b. Also see Chapters Two through Eight for descriptions of delivery arrangements.

[7] In the UK differences between insured and uninsured benefits have been eroded to such an extent that distinctions between the treatment of insured and uninsured unemployed people are negligible beyond a short period of non-means-tested entitlement. Because the period of insurance-based receipt *is* so short, the New Deal policies fail to directly affect insured clients.

[8] Although officially in France the right to RMI is supposed to be divorced, participation in 'insertion' and in some places the German Help Towards Work scheme is implemented as a voluntary programme.

[9] As one example, in the UK the reasons why Afro-Caribbean young men suffer severe disadvantage in the labour market *in spite of* educational success (Berthoud, 1999) need to be considered alongside policies developed to assist young people generally, including the New Deal.

[10] The research group is currently reviewing evidence for effectiveness in each of the seven countries.

References

Aucouturier, A.L. (1993) 'Contribution à la mesure de l'efficacité de la politique de l'emploi', *Travail et Emploi*, DARES, n 55, 1/1993.

Berthoud, R. (1999) *Young Caribbean men and the labour market: A comparison with other ethnic groups*, Joseph Rowntree Foundation Report no 69, York: York Publishing Services.

Bosco, A. and Chassard, Y. (1999) 'A shift in the paradigm. Surveying the European Union discourse on welfare and work', *Linking Welfare and Work*, Luxembourg: European Foundation for the Improvement of Living and Working Conditions.

Ditch, J. and Oldfield, N. (1999) Social Assistance: recent trends and themes', *Journal of European Social Policy*, vol 9, no 1, pp 65-76.

Eardley, T., Bradshaw, J., Ditch, J., Gough, I. and Whiteford, P. (1996a) *Social Assistance schemes in the OECD countries. Volume 1. Synthesis report*, DSS Research Report 46, London: HMSO.

Eardley, T., Bradshaw, J., Ditch, J., Gough, I. and Whiteford, P. (1996b) *Social Assistance schemes in the OECD countries. Volume 11. Country reports*, DSS Research Report 47, London: HMSO.

EC (European Commission) (1999a) *Employment in Europe*, Brussels: European Commission.

EC (1999b) *Joint employment report*, Brussels: European Commission.

ES (Employment Service) (1997a) *Operational vision*, UK Employment Service.

ES (1997b) *New Deal: Objectives monitoring evaluation*, UK Employment Service.

Giddens, A. (1998) *The Third Way: The renewal of social democracy*, Cambridge: Polity Press.

Grover, C. and Stewart, J. (1999) 'Market workfare: Social Security, social regulation and competitiveness in the 1990s', *Journal of Social Policy*, vol 28, no 1, pp 73-96.

Halvorsen, K. (1998) 'Symbolic purposes and factual consequences of the concepts of 'self-reliance' and 'dependency' in contemporary discourses of welfare', *Scandinavian Journal of Social Welfare*, vol 7, pp 56-64.

Hanesch, W. (1999) 'The debate on reforms of Social Assistance in Western Europe', *Linking Welfare and Work*, Luxembourg: European Foundation for the Improvement of Living and Working Conditions.

Heikkilä, M. (1999) 'A brief introduction to the topic', *Linking Welfare and Work*, Luxembourg: European Foundation for the Improvement of Living and Working Conditions.

Hvinden, B. (1999) 'Activation: a Nordic perspective', *Linking Welfare and Work*, Luxembourg: European Foundation for the Improvement of Living and Working Conditions.

Johnson, C. and Goldenberg, A. (1999) *Designing publically funded jobs to meet community needs*, Washington, DC: Center on Budget and Policy Priorities.

Layard, R. (1999) *Tackling unemployment*, Basingstoke: Macmillan.

Leisering, L. and Walker, R., (eds) (1998) *The dynamics of modern society: Poverty, policy and welfare*, Bristol: The Policy Press, p 320.

McKay, S. and Middleton, S. (1998) *Characteristics of older workers*, DfEE Research Report RR45.

McKay, S., Walker, R. and Youngs, R. (1997) *Unemployment and jobseeking before Jobseeker's Allowance*, DSS Research Report 73, London: HMSO.

Meager, N., Bates, P., Dench, S., Honey, S. and Williams, M. (1999) *Employment of disabled people: Assessing the extent of participation*, DfEE Research Report RR69.

OECD (Organisation of Economic Co-operation and Development) (1994) *The OECD jobs study*, Paris: OECD.

OECD (1999) *Employment outlook*, Paris: OECD.

Oliver, M. and Barnes, C. (1998) *Disabled people and social policy: From exclusion to inclusion*, London: Longman

Social Exclusion Unit (1999) 'Jobs' (Policy Action Team 1).

Spies, H. (1996) 'Workfare: emancipation or marginalisation?', in M.P.M. de Goede, P.M. de Klaver, J.A.C. van Ophem, C.H.A.Verhaar and A. De Vries (eds) *Youth: Unemployment, identity and policy*, Aldershot: Avebury, pp 191-212.

Torfing, J. (1999) 'Workfare with welfare: recent reforms of the Danish welfare state', *Journal of European Social Policy*, vol 9, no 1, pp 5-28.

Trickey, H., Kellard, K., Walker, R., Ashworth, K. and Smith, A. (1998) *Unemployment and jobseeking: Two years on*, London: The Statuionery Office.

Turok, I. and Webster, D. (1998) 'The New Deal jeopardised by the geography of unemployment', *Local Economy*, vol 12, no 4, pp 309-28.

TEN

Discussion: workfare in the welfare state

Ivar Lødemel

Introduction

The main objective of this book has already been achieved. As a first systematic comparison of workfare programmes across several nations, the book has mapped variation among programmes in the seven countries studied and the main comparative findings are presented in Chapter Nine. Although future studies may arrive at descriptions and comparisons that deviate from the ones presented here, the material presented solidly builds on evidence about policy design and the aims of programmes expressed in legislation and statements from key policy makers in each of the seven countries. We shall now leave this solid ground in order to speculate on how the impact of the introduction of workfare can be assessed, and how the differences and similarities found among the seven programmes outlined in this book can be explained.

This chapter consists of three parts, each devoted to a question or an issue introduced in Chapter One. First, the extent to which the introduction of workfare programmes involves a change in social assistance towards either providing *more* or providing *less* to those targeted among the social assistance clientele. Second, the extent to which the evidence presented suggests a convergence of policies, or if the main picture is one of diversity. Finally, it explores different hypotheses which provide tentative explanations for the differences found between programmes.

In order to make the discussion feasible, this chapter focuses on one aspect of variation in the workfare programmes. This is the content of the programmes, described in Chapter Nine as *strategy*. This includes the selection of participants and the extent to which programmes individually tailor placements to the situation of each participant by offering options other than work alone. Variation in strategy was described as ranging from Human Resource Development (HRD) to Labour Market Attachment (LMA). In the first two parts of the chapter variation in the strategy of programmes is used to assess the change of the social assistance contract – described here as the more–less equation – and the extent of convergence. In these two parts, strategy is therefore considered mainly as an independent variable. In contrast, the third part discusses possible reasons for variation in strategy. The structure of this chapter is illustrated in Figure 10.1.

A change towards more or less?

In Chapter One, we argued that the introduction of workfare programmes involves a change in the contract of social assistance. Because workfare introduces a new condition to the provision of social assistance, the right to aid is curtailed. In this sense, workfare leads to a reduction of entitlement – or *less*. In spite of this curtailment of rights, the application of workfare may, however, have the potential to provide new resources to participants and thereby improve their chances for labour market integration; an expressed aim of all programmes. Where workfare programmes are designed in this way, the change in the contract of assistance may be towards giving *more*.

Figure 10.1: Overview of Chapter Ten

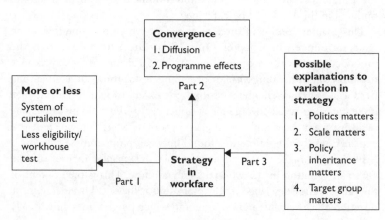

The distinction between an HRD and an LMA approach is used here to give a comparative assessment of the extent to which the introduction of workfare can be described as a change in the contract of social assistance towards *more* or *less*. In Chapter Nine the distinction between LMA and HRD was used to assess deviation from the idealised workfare model described in our definition of workfare (Chapter One). The following discussion presupposes that workfare according to this idealised model (work in exchange for benefits) implies a curtailment in the contract of social assistance, and that an LMA-approach comes closest to this ideal type. Workfare close to an LMA-approach is therefore considered as having a greater chance of providing *less*.

Because, as the name suggests, the HRD-approach focuses more on the development of human resources and opportunities, programmes closer to this approach are considered here to have a greater potential for providing *more*. This presupposes a wider understanding of rights than simply as entitlement to economic support. Social assistance everywhere provides economic support with the aim of helping improve people's lives and to help them become self-reliant. In other words, even if the new obligation to work is a curtailment of existing rights, the new opportunities provided to participants may improve their chances for labour market integration. While we equate *more* with a HRD-approach, an alternative analysis which includes outcomes from participation may find that, for many participants, 'less can be more'. For example, in a tight labour market which is able to also offer jobs to people with few skills, and at wages that enable them to achieve an improved standard of living. In this part we assess, first, the more–less equation across programmes and, second, the extent to which the introduction of workfare programmes may have altered the contract of social assistance in each of the seven nations.

When we compare strategies across nations, one group of programmes shares a strong HRD approach (Chapter Nine, Figure 9.2). These are the programmes found in Denmark, the UK and in the Netherlands. Because these programmes are also more centralised in delivery than the other four, they have been described as centralised European programmes. The strategies chosen suggest that these programmes – in particular the Danish programme – offer their participants *more* than is provided to participants in other countries. The programmes in Germany and France have an approach somewhere between LMA and HRD. The description of programmes in Chapters Five and Eight suggest that programmes in

Norway and the US offer their participants *less* in terms of the development of human resources.

To assess whether workless recipients of assistance in each nation get more or less as a result of participating in a programme, both the strategy of the new workfare programme and the nature of the initial social assistance scheme need to be considered. For ease of analysis, we focus the discussion on the 'less' side of the more–less equation and consider the extent to which the introduction has involved a curtailment in the participant's right to income maintenance. Workfare programmes can be used as a means of checking or conditioning entitlement to social assistance. Prior to the introduction of workfare, six of the seven countries considered in this volume had entitlement to means-tested cash benefits in place, although, in France, the RMI programme combined entitlement with a workfare condition from the outset in 1989. In principle, an unconditional right to assistance can only be achieved in a system of a guaranteed minimum income. However, to date, such a guarantee is only found in Alaska (Halvorsen, 2000).

All seven countries conditioned the entitlement to social assistance to different extents and by different methods. The methods applied to check entitlement have been described as *instruments of curtailment* (Midré, 1992, see also De Swaan, 1988). Such instruments have been an integral part of transfer programmes throughout the history of statutory relief. Two main forms can be identified: the suppression of benefit levels and the imposition of various forms of social control. In the Poor Laws of the 19th century, the combined principles of *less eligibility* and the *workhouse test* were applied to curtail entitlement to statutory relief[1]. The less eligibility principle addressed financial incentives by ensuring that benefits were always below the lowest wages in the economy; the workhouse test ensured that the pauper had to give away their freedom and make their labour available to the authorities as a condition for the receipt of aid. We use the terms 'workhouse test' (social control) and 'less eligibility' (low level benefits) in the following discussion.

Albeit usually less draconian in their application, current-day variations of curtailment in social assistance can be described with reference to these two forms (Bradshaw and Terum, 1997; Lødemel, 1997). The study of social assistance within OECD countries referred to earlier (Eardley et al, 1996; Gough et al, 1997) can be used to illustrate the different balance between the two forms of curtailment in the social assistance schemes of each of the seven nations. The extent to which 'less eligibility' is applied can be illustrated by the level of benefit in relation to average earnings[2]

(Gough et al, 1997, p 32). Of the countries considered here, the highest levels of benefits were found in the Netherlands and Denmark, followed by Norway. Germany, France and the UK had similar, but lower benefit levels. The lowest levels were found in the US.

More than other forms of curtailment (such as strict means tests, social work intervention or a strong requirement to seek and take work offered) workfare is more similar to the 'workhouse test' in that it conditions entitlement on activity, thereby limiting the freedom of the recipient and, it may be argued, by re-introducing work in return for financial support. The use of the 'workhouse test' as a method of curtailment in social assistance, can be illustrated by the extent to which national schemes provided benefits as a right. Based on data on the administration of social assistance, Eardley et al (1996) constructed an *exclusion index*[3]. This was used to assess the extent to which the national schemes matched the ideal of a citizenship right to social assistance (Gough et al, 1997, p 35). A low exclusion score is used to suggest a low level of curtailment in the form of social control. The country closest to a citizenship right to social assistance was the UK. The Netherlands and, perhaps surprisingly, the US also featured low levels of social control, followed by France and Denmark. The two countries which deviated the farthest from a citizenship right to social assistance were Germany and Norway.

The social assistance data of Eardley et al (1996) were collected in 1992, making their study well suited to illustrate the situation prior to the introduction (or expansion) of workfare programmes. If we combine the two sets of data we find that Denmark and the Netherlands were the two countries with lowest levels of curtailment in their social assistance schemes (in the early 1990s). These two countries therefore appeared to apply neither benefit levels nor social control as instruments to curtail spending. In France and Germany benefits were average, while a relatively high exclusion rate suggests that curtailment may have been achieved here by the use of social control[4]. In Norway benefit levels were relatively high, while a high degree of exclusion suggests that the extent of curtailment was similar to that found in the German and French schemes. In the UK recipients received below average level benefits, while the right to aid was extensive. In a situation similar to that in the UK, in the early 1990s social assistance in the US was characterised by low level benefits combined with an above average citizenship right to aid.

While the social assistance schemes in France, Germany, Norway, the UK and the US all featured strong levels of curtailment, they appeared to apply either the 'workhouse test' or the 'less eligibility' principle rather than combining the two. This may suggest that where benefits were low (for example in the US) the need for social control was felt less strongly compared to countries where benefits were relatively high, as in Norway.

The extent of curtailment in social assistance prior to the introduction of workfare suggests that, if similar strategies were pursued in workfare programmes, there would be a very different impact on the more–less equation for social assistance recipients targeted by workfare. However, as described above, the workfare programmes considered differed substantially in strategy. By comparing the situation in social assistance in the early 1990s to the later strategy of workfare, we can give a first assessment of the change in the contract of social assistance for the target group of workfare programmes.

Two of the European centralised programmes, the Jobseeker's Employment Act in the Netherlands and activation in Denmark, may have resulted in similar changes in the social assistance contract. While the social assistance contract changed from a citizenship right to generous benefits in 1992 towards an increase in the 'workhouse test' after the introduction of workfare, the relatively strong HRD-approach taken by these programmes suggests that the citizenship approach to welfare remains fairly strong. In other words, in the social assistance schemes in the Netherlands and Denmark, the new curtailment can be seen to be matched by new opportunities. The high degree of universality in the application of workfare programmes also suggests that their introduction impacts more on the social assistance schemes of these two nations than elsewhere. However, two further factors suggest that workfare programmes in these two nations may be developing in different ways. In Denmark, the recent extension of activation to include people with little prospect of labour market integration can be viewed as a further strengthening of an HRD-approach. In the Netherlands, the introduction of workfare has been accompanied by a decrease in the level of social assistance benefit (Chapter Four). This suggests that, although the social assistance scheme has maintained a lower than average level of 'workhouse testing', policy makers may have reduced attractiveness and expenditure by focusing on the alternative form of curtailment ('less eligibility'). While programmes in both countries have been designed within an HRD-approach to workfare, Danish activation may have gone furthest in developing workfare with the potential to give participants more than before its introduction.

While the UK New Deal programme has much in common with Danish activation and the Dutch Jobseeker's Employment Act, the change of the social assistance contract has been different and stronger in the

UK. Here, compulsory participation in New Deal is today (as was social assistance in 1992) combined with relatively low level out-of-work benefits. It can be argued that the stronger conditionality resulting from compulsion involves a greater change in the contract of assistance when benefits are low. Accepting this, one might conclude that, in spite of a relatively strong HRD-approach, it is less clear that the introduction of workfare programmes in the UK represents a change in the contract of assistance towards providing *more*.

In France, the simultaneous introduction in 1989 of general social assistance and workfare as one package makes it difficult to disentangle the impact of workfare on the assistance contract. The fact that prior to 1989 the target group of workfare was not entitled to financial aid indicates that the introduction of RMI may have involved a change towards more. Recipients have been offered both a new entitlement *and* a new opportunity to participate. As Chapter Two demonstrated, the universal character of insertion is reduced in implementation and only seven out of ten RMI recipients had signed an insertion contract in the mid-1990s. Depending on the strategy followed in local implementation, the less than universal application of insertion in RMI may have the potential of being either *more* or *less*. We found that the strategy of RMI-insertion to be positioned between HRD and LMA on the scale (Chapter Nine, Figure 9.2). Where insertion represents a new opportunity (HRD), the result of selective application may be that fewer people benefit from these opportunities than those established by law. Where insertion is used selectively to curtail rights (LMA) rather than to offer new opportunities, the result may be that more people have benefited from the new RMI entitlement without experiencing strings attached.

In Germany the Hilfe zur Arbeit programmes contain elements of both HRD and LMA depending on where they are implemented. The fact that the expansion of workfare took place within a social assistance scheme which was average in generosity and with a stronger than average 'workhouse test' suggests that the expansion of workfare is a change towards *less*. However, the amount of local variation in implementation implies that whether the change is towards less or more may also vary. For participants in the contract programmes, the increased curtailment of an LMA-approach may be balanced by a particular German version of providing 'more': after the completion of a one-year workfare contract, participants are entitled to unemployment insurance and participation in ALMP (Chapter Three). In this way participants may benefit in the longer run from both higher level benefits and programmes more in line with an HRD approach.

In Norway, the introduction of local workfare schemes with a strong LMA-approach further accentuates the use of the 'workhouse test' as the most common method of curtailment in social assistance. There is no indication that the relatively generous benefits have changed in a way that alters Norway's position compared to other countries. Because of substantial local variation in implementation, the more–less equation differs, however, from locality to locality. While our impression is that in Norway the introduction of local authority-based workfare appears to have been a change towards less for participants who are not able to make use of the opportunities offered by ALMP, the selective use of workfare by local authorities suggests that the majority of recipients are not directly affected by this change (Chapter Five)[5].

Taken together, the three US programmes appear to have a stronger LMA-approach to workfare than any of the European programmes. While the Norwegian programme is closest in strategy, the social assistance schemes in the two countries differ substantially. In the US, a corrective and preventative form of workfare was expanded within a social assistance scheme which had a relatively weak 'workhouse test', but had the lowest levels of benefits among the seven nations considered in this book (see also Gough et al, 1997, p 32). That in itself indicates a movement towards *less*. Accompanying changes in social assistance since 1992 strengthen this conclusion and also suggest an increasing US 'exceptionalism' in workfare and social assistance. With the end of entitlement to AFDC in 1996, the US is the only country studied which has not only combined the two forms of curtailment in a harsh way, but, in principle, has taken this further than the practice of the 19th-century Poor Laws. In the 19th century 'less eligibility' and the 'workhouse test' were imposed as an *alternative* to ending entitlement. The recent introduction of compulsory work in exchange for food and lodging, rather than cash benefits, in New York for example (Bernstein, 1999), strengthens the impression that the US has gone furthest in using workfare as one of several instruments to achieve a change in the contract of social assistance towards providing *less* than it did at the beginning of the 1990s.

The discussion thus far has focused on variations in strategy. A separate factor which influences the more–less equation is the extent to which compulsion 'sticks' are matched with 'carrots' in the form of additional benefits or pay on top of the standard social assistance benefit. If such additional payments are applied in LMA programmes more than in programmes with an HRD approach, this would alter the picture presented so far. As Chapter Nine documented, such payments can be found in all seven countries. However, it is only in the UK and the Netherlands that such additions are an entitlement for all or some of the participants. Because the programmes in these two countries feature a strong HRD-approach, the inclusion of this factor suggests that differences in the more–less equation between HRD- and LMA-approach programmes may be strengthened. Depending on the level of additional benefits provided, the inclusion of 'carrots' may also alter the assessment of the more–less equation of social assistance in the UK[6].

In conclusion, while the introduction of workfare involves a strengthening of the 'workhouse test', in the social assistance schemes of each of the seven countries, the extent to which this involves a change towards *less* differs. In countries where a low level of curtailment in social assistance is followed by HRD-focused workfare (Denmark and the Netherlands), the change of contract is perhaps best described as a change towards new opportunities rather than altering the more–less balance. In countries where pre-workfare curtailments in social assistance were stronger, the more–less equation differs depending on both strategy in workfare and the form of curtailment previously used. In Norway, for example, an LMA approach strengthened an already strong 'workhouse test' while the level of benefits remained high. By contrast, a similar LMA approach in the US programmes involved a turn towards the 'workhouse test' while the tradition of curtailment through 'less eligibility' was strengthened at the same time.

Does the introduction of workfare programmes involve a convergence of national social assistance schemes?

The idea that welfare states would become more similar, or converge, as they developed, was first put forward in the 1950s. Among others, Wilensky (1975) developed the 'convergence thesis' further, maintaining that the welfare state is an integral part of modern capitalist society and that nations at similar levels of development will feature similar arrangements. Critics have argued that this assertion ignores the role of politics and over-emphasises similarity over difference (see for example Mishra, 1977; Castles, 1981). While the importance of politics dominated academic discourse in the 1980s and early 1990s, discussions about convergence have recently returned to the centre of the academic social policy discourse.

Often, the claim for convergence is associated with vague notions such as 'globalisation'. This is central to the so-called "new convergence theory" (Mabbett and Bolderson, 1999, p 48). The central premise is that in a globalised world "all market economies are subject to competitive constraints on state welfare activity"; Mabbett and Bolderson, 1999, p 48). The introduction of workfare programmes may be a part of one policy development associated with this theory – the "curtailment and targeting of cash transfers" (Mabbett and Bolderson, 1999, p 49). Where workfare is used on a large scale, as in Denmark and the UK, its introduction may, however, equally be described as an increased public investment in welfare, even if the long-term objective is cost containment through reduced dependency. This question will not be pursued further here.

Rather than addressing causal mechanisms, we are concerned with a more limited measure of convergence. Øverbye quotes Seeliger who provides a useful definition of convergence:

> To classify the relative direction of policy developments in two countries (eg countries A and B) we need to have one measurement for each country at one point in time ($t1$) and a second pair of measurements at a later point in time ($t2$). Becoming more similar (convergence) presupposes objective – ie measurable – differences in $t1$. Between $t1$ and $t2$ country A, country B or both countries must have initiated measures that have reduced the difference measured in $t1$. (Øverbye, 1998, p 208)

Seeliger also makes a distinction between two different levels of convergence. If a country adopts a policy when previously there was none, and another country had the same policy in place at $t1$, this is described as 'nominal' convergence (Seeliger, 1996, p 289). In this book, the introduction of workfare is viewed as a new policy, and the extent of nominal convergence is made with reference to differences in $t1$ (the early 1990s) and $t2$ (the present day) in the seven countries. In order to discuss the extent of the second level – 'qualified' convergence – it is necessary to apply a "set of scaled measurements" (Seeliger, 1996, p 289). Because workfare is a part of, or attached to, social assistance, our limited discussion of qualified convergence focuses on the extent to which the introduction of workfare has altered key characteristics of national social assistance schemes. Before we turn to such 'programme effects' of workfare, we will first consider the extent to which the spread of workfare results from the diffusion of ideas across nations.

Convergence resulting from diffusion across nations

Diffusion has been described as a process by which innovations spread from one social system to another (Rogers and Floyd Shoemaker, 1971, p 13). Diffusion can occur either through dispersing ideas across social systems, or though using lessons learned in one system to design policies in another system (Kuhnle, 1984, pp 91-3). The discussion here focuses on the diffusion of *ideas* among nations as this is more pertinent to our findings discussed below. This form of diffusion may be either hierarchical or geographical (Kuhnle, 1984). The recent introduction of a workfare-style programme in South Korea may serve as an example of hierarchical diffusion. Here, the introduction of new programmes to deal with the shocks to the labour market following the 1998 financial crisis was influenced by the advice of the World Bank (Lødemel and Dahl, 2001: forthcoming). While we will point to the possibility of hierarchical diffusion resulting from the influence of the OECD and the EU for the countries considered here, the emphasis will be on the geographical diffusion of ideas. Because the spread of workfare is often linked to developments in the US, we will focus on the extent to which diffusion from the US to the six European countries is supported by our evidence. We have not been able to study these processes in great detail, and we can therefore only provide tentative interpretations which may be useful for future studies.

The introduction of compulsory programmes in very different welfare states is a sign of *nominal* convergence. At the beginning of the 1990s, only the US and Germany had in place workfare programmes as defined here. A decade later, the five other countries discussed had introduced such programmes. In spite of expressed differences in the understanding of the causes of worklessness, in political orientation, and the scale of the problem, the choice of compulsory rather than voluntary programmes shows that dependency is perceived to be a problem in all seven countries. As Chapter One demonstrated, in the US, this understanding of social problems is both more strongly expressed, and has been an important part of the social policy discourse for a longer period, than in the European nations considered here. Despite this move towards a shared understanding, the discussion above shows that strategies of implementation are very different and have had very different effects on the social assistance contracts in each country.

The fact that the programmes considered here were all either introduced or greatly expanded within only one decade, suggests that this convergence may have resulted from a rapid diffusion of ideas across nations. During this decade policy makers in all seven countries shifted their focus towards a greater emphasis on the obligations of the recipients of assistance.

The importance of timing and diffusion is that policy makers are influenced by the prevailing spirit at the time when new policies are decided. Research into the comparative history of welfare has identified several periods when similar ideas have developed in one nation and then spread internationally. A distant example is the Poor Law policies which were introduced as a reaction to the mercantilist emphasis on entitlement and on substituting low wages in Britain in the early 19th century. Those new policies inspired the change towards a more repressive system of relief on both sides of the Atlantic (see for example De Swaan, 1988; Katz, 1986). The cross-Atlantic spread of ideas in the first century of statutory welfare (from 1850 to 1950) can be described as predominantly going from East to West (see for example Rodgers, 1998). However, in the 1950s and 1960s ideas that were first developed in the US had a marked influence on Europe, this time in areas closely related to social assistance. During this period the case-work approach to social work found fertile ground in Europe where the early postwar understanding of social problems as structural problems (Titmuss, 1956) had been replaced by an emphasis on individual causes and, in many cases, pathological interpretations of worklessness and other social problems (Jackson and Valencia, 1979; Lorenz, 1994).

The uneven impact on European social assistance of this last example of diffusion may be attributable to differences in the timing of policy changes. The UK, for example, abolished its Poor Law in 1948, and introduced an entitlement-based scheme influenced by a structural understanding of poverty. In Norway, the first modern social assistance scheme was enacted in 1964, and was heavily influenced by a pathological understanding of poverty using case-work as the chosen solution (Lødemel, 1997). The present move towards obligations and responsibility may be viewed as another change in the understanding of poverty and social problems, resulting in a new prevailing spirit at the beginning of the 21st century (Chapter One).

The intensity of legislative activity in seven nations during such a short time period, suggests that globalisation resulting from economic interdependence, information technology, the ease of travel and so on (Midgley, 1997), has resulted in faster diffusion today than was possible only a few decades ago. Commenting on the development of social insurance as recently as 1973, Heclo concluded that:

> ... despite what is declared to be an accelerating rate of diffusion in
> technical innovation, the rate of diffusion of these social innovations
> appear to have changed little in the last century. Between 50 and 80
> years is the likely diffusion time for all such programs. (1973, p 11)

The combination of the development of a new understanding of
worklessness and its appropriate solutions, and the rapid diffusion of these
ideas may have facilitated a greater convergence of policies than was
considered possible only a few decades ago. In contrast, the diffusion of
case-work ideology in the 1950s and 1960s may have resulted in less
convergence because the ideas spread at a slower pace, and policy makers
reacted more slowly, eventually legislating in times of different
understandings of the causes of and remedies for social problems.

As with the spread of case-work ideology, the spread of workfare is
also often considered to be a diffusion of ideas from the US to Europe
(Hanesch, 1998, p 73). This Americanisation of ideas and lessons has
been more central to the debates in Britain than elsewhere in Europe.
While some observers in Britain claim that Labour's Welfare to Work
programme is inspired by developments in Scandinavia, and Sweden in
particular (for example Giddens, 1998, p viii), others argue that the
influence of the US is more important (Ditch and Oldfield, 1999; Peck,
1999; Walker, 1999; Deacon, 2000; Dolowitz et al, 2000, among others)[7].
The evidence presented in this book suggests that if diffusion from the
US has had an impact in Europe, it is likely that this influence may have
facilitated a convergence in the understanding of worklessness, and a
corresponding re-balancing of rights and obligations in the provision of
welfare. Diffusion may therefore provide a good starting point for future
studies of nominal convergence in this policy area.

However, our main finding is that, regardless of this limited convergence,
countries pursue different strategies in the design of their workfare
programmes. This suggests, first, that understandings other than
dependency have guided the design of programmes and, second, that the
cross-Atlantic diffusion has been a proliferation of *ideas* about the need
to re-balance rights and obligations, more than an application of *lessons
learnt* from US programmes. In those European programmes (in Norway
and, to a lesser degree, in Germany) which share an LMA approach with
the three US programmes, explanations for their similarities can probably
be found in the national context of the programmes. We will address
some of these factors in the final part of this chapter. Future studies may
find that the three countries with European centralised programmes,

together with France, have been more influenced by diffusion from the EU and the OECD than from the US. While the EU has influenced the focus on the problem of social exclusion, the OECD and, later, the EU have both promoted policies which combine 'carrots' and 'sticks' with the view to promoting more active social and labour market policies (Chapter One).

Recent developments suggest that EU influence on policies targeted at young unemployed people in the member states is increasing. The 1998 Employment Guidelines (European Commission, 1998, see also Chapter One) have been followed up by so-called National Action Plans where member states set out how they will achieve agreed objectives. One of the objectives in the Employment Guidelines is of particular relevance: "every unemployed young person is offered a new start before reaching six months of unemployment, in the form of training, retraining, work practice, a job or other employability measure" (European Commission, 1998, p 4). A new system of coordination (in EU documents termed 'open coordination') involves, among other things, the use of 'benchmarks' as a basis for evaluating national success in achieving the aims of the guidelines.

The convergent developments found here in the UK, Denmark and the Netherlands, may be associated with those countries' efforts to achieve the aims of these guidelines. The much more active approach of the UK to EU social policy following the change of government in 1997, suggests that the UK is now more open to participation in policy making on a European level. Moreover, the UK has played an instrumental role in working out the tools for implementing the Employment Guidelines. The introduction of 'benchmarking' is, for example, a UK export. Although France and Germany have traditionally played an important role in EU policy making, these two large countries are at the same time less open to change in their national traditions of welfare. In contrast, the Netherlands and Denmark are both small nations that have a history of greater openness to foreign and international ideas. While we have insufficient information to test an assumption about EU-induced convergence in this area, this offers an interesting topic for future research.

Convergence resulting from programme effects

In order to discuss whether the spread of workfare programmes has resulted in *qualified* convergence, we need to focus on the extent to which workfare has impacted on the different social assistance schemes of which it has become a part. Because this is not a study of social assistance per se, the discussion is limited to the information we have available to us on the aspects of social assistance that are most likely to change as a result of the introduction of workfare. While the term 'programme effect' is usually associated with 'path dependency' rather than convergence, it is used here to discuss the impact on social assistance of shared characteristics of workfare programmes.

The first part of this chapter considered how the move towards compulsion resulting from the introduction of workfare has impacted on the contract of social assistance. There are two further aspects which are inherent in all workfare programmes and which are likely to have a direct impact on the national social assistance schemes. These are the combination of case-work with the provision of financial aid (cash and care) and the fact that the implementation of workfare programmes is always subject to local variation.

Perhaps the major distinguishing cross-national factor in social assistance schemes has been the extent to which the provision of financial assistance is separated from case-work interventions (Jones, 1985). Without exception, the implementation of workfare programmes involves case-work. Whether the case-work is carried out by those who allocate the benefits or by separate agencies, cash is tied to care and, in turn, both are tied to some form of control due to the conditional nature of workfare.

National social assistance schemes are also distinguished by the extent to which they are centralised in terms of regulation. Workfare programmes, on the other hand, are always implemented at the local level leading to variation resulting from local differences in programme design, in the problems addressed, and in the range of placement options available (Chapter Nine). Variations in the extent of cash-care multi-functionality and in the degree of centralisation in social assistance schemes at the beginning of the 1990s (Chapter One) suggest, therefore, that these convergent trends have had different impacts on the national social assistance schemes. Similar workfare programmes may exert very different influences depending on the characteristics of the social assistance schemes to which they are now attached.

The extent of convergence resulting from programme effects can be summarised as three different developments. The greatest convergence, perhaps resulting in *qualified* convergence, consists of social assistance schemes that were dissimilar and have become more similar after the introduction of workfare. A second group consists of schemes that were different and continue to have different characteristics and are *non-convergent*.

The third group consists of schemes that were similar and are now dissimilar; this can be described as a divergent development. We will consider these in turn.

The three countries with European centralised programmes – Denmark, the Netherlands and the UK – represent the clearest case of convergence in social assistance, here viewed as a possible *qualified* convergence resulting from the introduction of workfare. This follows from their shared HRD-approach to the design of workfare programmes and the differences in their social assistance schemes prior to the introduction of workfare (Chapter One). Denmark and the Netherlands had in place similar social assistance schemes which were less centralised and combined cash and care to a greater extent than the UK scheme. However, the *workfare* programmes in all three of these countries are distinguished by being more centralised than elsewhere (Chapter Nine, Figure 9.2). While New Deal is the most centralised programme of the seven countries considered here, it is more subject to local variation than the highly centralised social assistance found in the UK in the early 1990s. If future studies find that the social assistance schemes of these three countries converge, it is likely to be the result of further centralisation in Denmark and the Netherlands and a turn towards a more *de*centralised and cash–care multifunctional assistance scheme in the UK. This suggests that an HRD-approach *centralises* local assistance schemes and *decentralises* those which were highly centralised prior to the introduction of workfare.

A possible convergence can also be found among the two countries with the strongest LMA-approach to workfare – Norway and the US – which had very different social assistance schemes in the early 1990s. In the US, the AFDC scheme was centralised and the provision of cash was not generally conditioned on case-work interventions (Eardley et al, 1996, p 118). With the expansion of workfare and other accompanying changes as described above, social assistance for workfare recipients in the US is both more decentralised and increasingly tied to case-work interventions. In Norway, the administration of social assistance was local, and the provision of aid was cash–care multifunctional. The impact of workfare on these two aspects of social assistance was therefore limited. While the Norwegian schemes remain unchanged in these two dimensions, there *is* evidence of change in the US programmes. This suggests that an LMA approach is closely linked to *decentralised* cash–care multifunctional social assistance schemes, and is likely to decentralise a previously centralised system. Signs of a move towards an HRD approach in Norway and that this development may *centralise* Norwegian workfare programmes further indicates a close link between central delivery and HRD (Chapter Five).

Perhaps an example of the second development path, social assistance in France and Germany has changed less than others since the expansion of workfare in the 1990s. The schemes in these two countries have both been described as belonging to a "dual social assistance regime" (Gough et al, 1997, p 36), and as being separated by a distinction of a "corporatist regime" in Germany and a "latin regime" in France (Lødemel and Schulte, 1992, pp 533-4). We found that the strategy pursued within the RMI and the Hilfe zur Arbeit was similar, although the French programme had more centralised delivery than the German programme. This reflects the different degree of centralisation in the overall social assistance schemes of the two nations (Lødemel and Schulte, 1992). Moreover, because both countries combined the provision of financial aid with case-work in social assistance, the introduction of workfare is not likely to have impacted on these two aspects of the French and German social assistance schemes.

Perhaps the clearest sign of *divergence* in national social assistance schemes is demonstrated by the developments in Denmark and Norway. At the beginning of the 1990s social assistance in Denmark was described as belonging to a Nordic model of decentralised and residual social assistance (Lødemel, 1992). Later comparisons suggest a change towards a scheme more akin to that found in the Netherlands, for example (Bradshaw and Terum, 1997; Gough et al, 1997). The development of a European centralised programme in Denmark may therefore be a sign of a further departure from the Nordic model of social assistance.

In concluding this discussion of convergence, the rapid spread of a new emphasis on matching entitlement to obligations in the provision of social assistance may have been facilitated by the diffusion of ideas from the US to policy makers in the six European countries studied. Diffusion is therefore a possible explanation for the *nominal* convergence described here. However, if we look beyond the introduction of compulsory participation at the extent of possible *qualified* convergence, our findings suggest that the cross-Atlantic diffusion of ideas has not been matched by the import of US-style programmes in Europe. This is perhaps best exemplified by the UK where the influence from the US has received the greatest political and academic attention. Further studies into the diffusion of workfare programmes may find it more fruitful to look at intra-European processes of policy transfer. The identification of a cluster of similar programmes in Denmark, the Netherlands and the UK may provide an interesting case for future studies of geographical[8] diffusion.

The impression that there is divergent development between the programmes of the two English-speaking countries considered here is further strengthened when we looked at the programme effects of introducing workfare. Among the seven nations considered, the impacts of these changes were greatest in the US and the UK. In spite of widespread assumptions about the diffusion and the shared turnaround in the administration of social assistance, these two countries pursue very different strategies in their workfare programmes. This suggests that similarities in the degree of centralisation and in the extent to which cash and care are separated in social assistance delivery – often regarded as key distinguishing criteria in comparisons of such schemes – may not result in a convergence in the content of the new workfare programmes. The strong divergence of the two programmes in the Nordic model reiterates this. However, the possible *qualified* convergence between the social assistance schemes of the UK, Denmark and the Netherlands has resulted from both a shared strategy to workfare and new similarities in the administration of social assistance.

Because the workfare programmes target only a proportion of social assistance recipients, the new convergent changes in administration caused by the programmes may not have greatly altered the social assistance regimes as they have been described in the mid-1990s. Our findings indicate, however, that the previously centralised schemes are now more local, less entitlement based and more cash–care multifunctional. With the possible exception of the Dutch and Danish schemes, the introduction of workfare may therefore be part of a convergence towards a model of a local and cash–care multifunctional social assistance previously associated mainly with the Nordic countries (Gough et al, 1997). However, our discussion in the first part of this chapter suggests that this need not result in the emphasis on control and the problems of stigma associated with social assistance in Norway in particular (Gough et al, 1997, p 37).

The deviation from previous similarities and the variation in social assistance can perhaps be best summed up as *new diversity* (Enjolras and Lødemel, 1999). If this is the case we need to reassess the social assistance typologies (or regimes) as they were described in the 1990s.

Jessop (1993) has predicted a convergence towards a 'Schumpetarian workfare state' and considers the spread of workfare as defined here to be an important part of this convergence (see Chapter One). If we accept Jessop's description of wide-ranging changes in 'the model of regulation', which involves a departure from the welfare states as we have known them, it should not come as a surprise that diversity is the result. There is little to suggest that the 'Schumpetarian workfare state' (Jessop, 1993) should engender more similarities than those systems of welfare existing under the former Keynesian or Fordist models of regulation. We will therefore explore possible explanations for the similarities and dissimilarities found by focusing on the national context of programmes.

Tentative explanations for variation and similarity

So far in this chapter, we have focused on how the introduction of workfare in general, and the strategy pursued in programmes in particular, may have impacted on the contract of social assistance and other (distinguishing) characteristics of the social assistance schemes into which workfare is introduced. Our discussion about the extent of convergence arrived at the conclusion that the diffusion of ideas, while able to partly explain the spread of workfare, does not add to our understanding of why countries have pursued different *strategies*.

There are at least four factors which may add to our understanding of why the seven countries have pursued different strategies in the design of their workfare programmes. The first two considered here are derived from the ideological positions and concerns generally associated with the introduction of workfare programmes (discussed in Chapter One). These are an ideological shift towards a re-balancing of rights and obligations, concerns about high unemployment and about increases in social expenditure in terms of numbers of recipients and spending. Chapter Nine documented that these ideological positions and concerns were among the factors which facilitated the introduction or expansion of workfare programmes in all seven countries considered in this book. While similar ideological positions and similar concerns would suggest convergence, the discussion above found 'new diversity' to be the more common result. This therefore necessitates an assessment of cross-national differences in the strength of these ideological positions and in the scale of the problems addressed by the programmes. The third factor we need to look at is the importance of the characteristics of the welfare structure into which the programmes are introduced. While this has been alluded to earlier in this chapter, we are now treating social assistance and the wider policy context as independent variables. Finally, we introduce a fourth factor by assessing the relevance of the group targeted by the workfare programmes.

From these factors we can develop four hypotheses that offer plausible explanations to the variations in programme strategies. The first hypothesis

– *politics matters* – is inspired by the research tradition which emphasised politics to explain the development of welfare (for example, Castles, 1981; Korpi, 1983; Esping Andersen, 1985). When used here, the emphasis is on differences in ideological or normative positions. While politics emphasises the role of political parties, the inclusion of the term 'ideology' implies that a re-balancing of rights and obligations may have wider ideological implications. The second hypothesis – *scale matters* – proposes that increases in the scale of transfer programmes in each country facilitated the introduction of workfare, and that the scale of these problems influences the strategy of programmes. The third hypothesis – *policy inheritance matters* – emphasises continuity over change. This is inspired by authors who claim that, when changes in policy are introduced, it is the pre-existing arrangements that condition the way policies are shaped (see for example Rose and Davis, 1994; Pierson, 1996). The discussion of the fourth hypothesis – *target group matters* – is inspired by the research traditions which focuses on the size and composition of 'risk groups' as a key factor in explaining the nature of welfare policies (for example, Baldwin, 1990; Schneider and Ingram, 1993; Lødemel, 1997). In the discussion of the four hypotheses, the aim has been to assess the extent to which variation in strategy *fits* assumptions that can be drawn from the hypotheses. This is followed by a discussion of the relevance of each factor, or hypothesis, for each of the seven programmes included in this book.

The purpose of this discussion is to offer an initial interpretation of the plausibility of each of these hypotheses with a view to motivating further comparative research. Given the design of this study, it is not possible to *explain* cross-national differences between programmes. Contributions from researchers in different countries have focused on description rather than explanation. Where explanations have been given, these are related to country-specific factors. A more thorough inquiry into these questions would require in-depth studies of political processes, including the role of different actors.

Hypothesis 1: Politics matters

More than other forms of social security, social assistance is imbedded in normative assumptions about the proper balance between the rights and responsibilities of citizens. Distinctions are often made between deserving and undeserving people (Golding and Middelton, 1981; Lødemel, 1997). Usually such labels are related to the behaviour and lifestyles of recipients (Bradshaw and Terum, 1997). Throughout the history of these programmes and the Poor Laws before them, able-bodied workless people have been at the core of debates about rights and responsibilities. Because workfare programmes are usually designed to target the able-bodied sections of a social assistance population, differences in the understanding of the causes of worklessness and the 'correct' remedies prescribed are likely to bring normative issues to the forefront of discussions about which strategy to pursue in using compulsory work for recipients.

Two contrasting ideological positions, or political discourses (Levitas, 1998), may result in differing aims for and strategies pursued in the programmes (Chapter One). Whereas a focus on the problem of dependency may lead to programmes favouring prevention and work-testing (or *less*), an interpretation of the problem of joblessness as resulting from a social exclusion calls for integrative measures, if necessary, by means of compulsion, with a view to providing '*more*' to recipients. The literature review in Chapter One highlighted an Atlantic divide in political discourses relating to worklessness. In the US, a dependency discourse dominates, while in Europe – particularly in France – social exclusion is more often perceived as the main problem.

One way to assess the importance of ideology in relation to workfare is to compare the relationship between (on the one hand) the *aims* of and (on the other hand) the *strategy* pursued in different programmes. When strong ideological positions (aims) are matched with a corresponding strategy, this suggests that the ideology has impacted on the way in which programmes are used. Differences in aims are described in Chapter Nine (see Figure 9.1) where French and US programmes are positioned closest to the extremes. The preventive underpinnings found in the US programmes corresponds with a dependency-oriented objective and, conversely, the integrative underpinnings of French policies suggest that a focus on social exclusion in wider political discourse manifests itself in French policy aims. In both nations, the dominant political parties share the same ideological position, nonetheless, differences in emphasis between the political parties can be detected. In France, for example, the parties on the Right facilitated the exclusion of single people under the age of 25 when RMI (as the country's first general social assistance scheme) was introduced in 1989. As the fear of dependency was a key motivator of this choice, it can be argued that France has since (at least partly) avoided a dependency debate about social assistance by excluding this group.

In the US the Republican majority in Congress pressured the Clinton administration to enact a particularly harsh measure to combat the perceived problem of dependency: the end of entitlement (Chapter Eight).

The focus on the problem of dependency is, however, one that is shared by the two dominant US parties. The choice of single parents as the main target group for workfare in the US is partly a reflection of the structure of the social assistance system. It also reveals a divide between policy makers on either side of the Atlantic about which target group is perceived to be most problematic from a dependency perspective. When single parents are targeted for active measures in Europe, this is usually on a voluntary basis, as in the New Deal for Lone Parents in the UK for example (Chapter Seven)[9].

While strong ideological positions in the US and in France find expression in the aims of the workfare programmes, further analysis of the relevance of politics requires consideration of the extent to which these aims are followed up in the *strategy* of the programmes (Chapter Nine, Figure 9.2). In the three US states, strong aims are translated into a strong LMA approach, thereby suggesting that ideology and politics are particularly important here. By contrast, the strategy of the French RMI appears to diverge from its expressed aims in implementation. This suggests that, contrary to the arguments of earlier observers (such as Morel, 1998), the French social exclusion discourse may be stronger in rhetoric than it is in substance. While the *aims* of the French programme are more integrative than those found for the three European centralised programmes, the *strategy* pursued in Denmark, the Netherlands and the UK is closer to an HRD approach than that found for RMI. It should be noted, however, that one reason for the position of the RMI strategy is that it is less universally applied than the European centralised programmes.

In Norway, as in the US, prevention of dependency featured highly among the aims expressed by policy makers. This is perhaps surprising to observers who are aware that Norway has a strong tradition of integrative programmes for unemployed people. In Norway, it was a Right-of-Centre majority in parliament that made the minority Labour government introduce a workfare option as part of the revised social assistance scheme in 1991. Later developments show, however, that in Norway and elsewhere in Europe, social democratic parties are changing their positions with regard to workfare. It took, for example, only three years before the Norwegian Labour Party changed from its original opposing position and supported the measure. Interestingly, in Norway, it was a non-socialist coalition government that recently called for a "softer and less corrective work-approach" than that pursued by the previous Labour government in the late 1990s (White Paper No 50, 1998-99).

A move towards stronger support for compulsion is also a key feature of other European social democratic parties that adhere to 'third way' policies. In Britain an early workfare programme, introduced as a pilot by the former Conservative government in 1996, met fierce opposition from the Labour Party. In 1997, the New Labour government changed tack, making compulsory participation in work and other activities a cornerstone of their New Deal for young unemployed people. However, the British Labour Party introduced a workfare programme which was less corrective and more in line with an HRD approach than the programmes of its predecessor. Similar moves towards a greater acceptance of compulsion within social democratic parties can be found in Germany, the Netherlands and Denmark.

The change towards an acceptance of compulsion among European social democrats may explain the spread of workfare in the European countries considered here. The move towards 'third way' policies in these countries does not, however, add to our understanding of differences in strategy. While the parties in the Netherlands and Denmark both support HRD-programmes, the situation is, as we have seen, different in Norway and Germany. Recent re-orientations here suggest, however, that the present Norwegian and German Labour governments may be becoming more like the social democratic parties in the other European countries considered here.

In summary, with the exception of the US (and, to a lesser extent, Norway), strong ideological positions with regard to aims are *not* reflected in the strategy of the programmes. This suggests that to understand the differences in policy we need to take factors other than politics and ideology into account.

Hypothesis 2: Scale matters

Economic pressure may be one reason why national policy makers diverge from their political position with regard to aims and strategy. As an example of this, the municipal government of Leipzig (an industrial city in the former DDR) enacted a large-scale workfare programme which combined job creation with strong sanctions for non-compliance. The realisation that public works could be used to improve the infrastructure of the city, combined with a staggering 40% unemployment rate, facilitated the necessary support from the (local) social democratic party for a policy that, at the time, would not have been condoned by the national party[10].

High levels of unemployment, increases in the number of people receiving assistance and resulting expenditure on transfer programmes were, in each of the seven countries, key motivations for reform (Chapter Nine). An initial look at the evidence presented in this book suggests, however, that the decision to introduce or expand workfare bears little relation to this factor. Policy makers in each of the seven countries have all opted for workfare in spite of substantial differences in the economy and the labour market. This finding supports the hypothesis that ideology plays a central role, possibly through the diffusion of ideas.

It is possible, however, that variation in the scale of the problems addressed by workfare is more closely related to the strategy pursued in programmes. Programmes with the strongest HRD approach were found in Denmark, the Netherlands and the UK. At the time when the current programmes were enacted, Denmark had relatively low levels of unemployment, the Netherlands had the lowest among the seven countries, while the UK had relatively high levels of unemployment. Also, the expenditure on social assistance in 1992 differed substantially between these three nations. The UK had the highest expenditure among the seven countries, followed by the Netherlands, while Denmark had the third lowest level of expenditure. Of the two countries with the strongest LMA approach to their programmes, Norway had the lowest level of expenditure and the second lowest level of unemployment when workfare was enacted. Similarly, the US had the third lowest level of expenditure and the second lowest level of unemployment among the seven nations[11].

These findings suggest that, while an HRD approach appears to be associated with a larger than average scale of problems, there is a clearer link between an LMA approach on the one hand and low unemployment and low social assistance expenditure on the other. In the discussion of the first hypothesis we concluded that strong political or ideological positions were only reflected in the strategy of programmes in the US and, to a lesser degree, in Norway. While this may be interpreted as an expression of an independent role of politics or ideology as a factor which influences strategy, the material presented here suggests that this causal relationship needs to be qualified. In the US and in Norway it is possible that the (unexpected) similarity in ideology (expressed as aims) may have resulted from a similarity in the scale of the problems addressed. If this is the case, the scale of the problem is an independent variable which impacts on ideology and which, in turn, impacts on the strategies pursued in the programmes.

An initial interpretation of why the size of the problems addressed may have this effect can be found by looking at the impact of low unemployment on the prospect of labour market integration. A low level of unemployment suggests a tight labour market with job opportunities for more people, including those with few skills. In this situation an LMA approach (which focuses more on direct labour market attachment) may be seen as a more sensible route than an HRD approach given that the final aim of both approaches is labour market integration. This interpretation would imply that ideology is less important.

At the same time, a tight labour market suggests that people who have been unable to enter the labour market may experience more problems than unemployed recipients of social assistance in countries where unemployment is high. If this is the case, those who remain unemployed in a tight labour market would be in greater need of a programme which emphasises the development of skills and other human resources. This interpretation would strengthen the importance of ideology in explaining the LMA approach of programmes in the US and in Norway.

Hypothesis 3: Policy inheritance matters

The existing structure of laws, programmes and established administrative divisions of responsibility represents the 'glue' of the welfare state, often limiting the scope of possible options for change. Rose and Davis (1994) argue, for example, that, more than anything else, policies inherited from the past control policy making at present. Similarly, the present upsurge in claims of policy convergence resulting from globalisation is countered with reference to the importance of 'path dependency' (Pierson, 1996). This section therefore considers the structure of welfare provision into which workfare was introduced. According to a policy inheritance or 'path dependency' hypothesis it is likely that the new workfare programmes are moulded by these existing structures and traditions.

An assessment of the relevance of policy inheritance requires two questions to be answered. The first is the extent to which new policies represent a continuation of, or a departure from, the social assistance policies to which workfare is now attached. In order to assess the explanatory importance of policy inheritance, we need to look at whether deviation from this inheritance, where this is found, is the result of political choices.

Inheritance in social assistance

With the exception of Germany and the US, where workfare programmes have a longer history, the programmes in the other five countries are all of recent origin (Chapter One). Therefore, while workfare in most of these countries is a new policy and thus a departure from the policy inheritance of modern social assistance[12], the extent of policy inheritance can be assessed by considering the strategies pursued in these programmes.

It is common to relate new developments in welfare to the welfare state model of individual nations. The most often referenced typology of total welfare state models today is that of Gøsta Esping-Andersen. He distinguished between 'three worlds of welfare': 'social democratic', 'conservative' and 'liberal' (Esping-Andersen, 1990, 1999, see also Chapter One). The evidence presented in Chapter Nine suggests that the strategy underlying specific workfare programmes does not directly reflect the character of welfare regimes. For example, Torfing's (1999) description of Danish 'workfare' as being especially 'offensive' (described here as an HRD approach) is upheld by this evidence, but his assertion that this is an expression of social democratic welfare may need some qualification.

The extent to which strategy in workfare programmes mirrored the social assistance scheme to which it became attached has been addressed earlier in this chapter where we have treated key characteristics of the social assistance schemes as dependent variables. The aim there was to assess the extent of change in the contract of social assistance after the introduction of workfare (pp 296-303) and possible convergence in social assistance as a result of the introduction of workfare (pp 303-13). Let us first consider the extent to which programme strategy results in similar groupings to those found in a typology of national social assistance schemes.

On the basis of a comprehensive study of OECD countries, Gough et al (1997) developed a typology dividing the nations into eight different social assistance regimes (Chapter One, Table 1.2). Five of these are represented among the countries covered in this book. In the European centralised programmes, social assistance in Denmark and the Netherlands is described as belonging to a 'citizenship-based residual' regime. British social assistance is described as a separate 'integrated regime'. German and French social assistance are grouped together as 'dual social assistance regimes' (characterised by different programmes for defined groups supplemented by general assistance programmes). The US is described as a 'public assistance state', and Norway as providing 'decentralised discretionary relief'. This typology of social assistance groups countries differently to how one might arrange them if looking at their workfare strategies.

The typology of assistance regimes developed by Gough et al (1997) is based on a large number of criteria, combined as expenditure on social assistance and numbers of beneficiaries, programme structure (degree of centralisation, discretion and the use of means testing) and outcomes including benefit levels. Some dimensions of social assistance are, however, more relevant to strategy in workfare programmes than others. The degree of centralisation in terms of funding and delivery proved particularly important in the study of Gough et al. The relevance of this factor is supported in other comparative mappings of social assistance and in the typologies resulting from these (see for example Lødemel and Schulte, 1992). The comparison in Chapter Nine showed that the strategy of workfare programmes was, in most of the countries, closely related to the degree of centralisation and codification in the delivery of programmes (Chapter Nine, Table 9.3, see also Figures 9.1 and 9.2). Both local/ discretionary and central/codified social assistance systems have introduced workfare without substantially altering these characteristics of the social assistance scheme into which it is incorporated.

This suggests a greater co-variation between social assistance and workfare programmes than between the wider welfare regimes and workfare. This is not surprising as it has already been observed that social assistance regimes bear limited relation to the total welfare regimes of Esping-Andersen and others (Gough et al 1997; Lødemel, 1992, 1997). This does not, however, necessarily imply that policy inheritence is always a decisive factor in determining the strategies of programmes.

The evidence presented in the first part of this chapter shows that, in two countries in particular, the introduction of workfare involved a stronger deviation from previous social assistance schemes than what was found elsewhere. In the UK this involved a shift from an entitlement-based scheme towards greater conditionality. While a similar change was observed in the US, unlike in the UK, the change resulted in an LMA approach and correspondingly greater changes in the access to financial aid.

The discussion of possible convergence resulting from programme effects (in the second section of this chapter) found both continuity and departures from previous social assistance traditions. The two nations with the clearest continuity were Germany and Norway. In the German scheme this may be the result of expansion of existing workfare in the 1990s, rather than its introduction as a new approach. The Norwegian scheme continued a localised system with strong levels of control into workfare programmes with limited national intervention and an LMA approach. This suggests that in these two countries, more than in the other five, the administration of, and strategy pursued in, workfare may result from policy inheritance. While both the UK and the US programmes diverged from previous traditions in social assistance, the US programmes deviated further from previous traditions than did programmes in the UK. Although the expected programme effect of decentralisation was found in the social assistance schemes of both countries, this was stronger in the US. In Denmark and the Netherlands the introduction of workfare involved a divergence from previous traditions of social assistance as well as from the effects expected from the introduction of workfare. So far we can conclude that policy inheritance appears to be important in the German and Norwegian programmes, thereby suggesting a strong 'path dependency' in these two countries.

Change without choice?

We have identified four programmes (in the US, the UK, Denmark and the Netherlands) which appear to diverge more from policy inheritance than elsewhere. However, this finding is not sufficient to exclude policy inheritance as an explanatory factor – in the words of Rose and Davis "Inheritance does not deny change; it is possible to have change without choice" (1994, p 21).

To assess this divergence from inheritance further, we need to consider other policies which may have impacted on the strategies pursued in workfare programmes. Workfare is part of wider developments, often described as a move towards 'activating policies' (Chapter One). The material presented in this book has demonstrated that, in many cases, it is difficult to distinguish between workfare and the set of programmes targeted mainly at the insured (ALMP). This suggests that, albeit to varying degrees, the strategy of workfare is influenced by developments in ALMP. Although it can be argued that workfare, where case-work and individual tailoring is applied, may be a better instrument to further the integration of people who are distant from the labour market, we continue on the assumption that, generally, ALMP is closer to an HRD approach than workfare. This follows from a greater emphasis on training in addition to or instead of work, higher benefits and more options within ALMP programmes.

ALMP programmes may influence the strategy of workfare in at least two ways. Where programmes for the insured and the uninsured are integrated, we may find an element of 'trickle down' from this higher tier (ALMP) to the lower tier of workfare. When this occurs, workfare participants may benefit from the stronger HRD approach generally found in these programmes. In addition, when ALMP is also available to the uninsured, this influences the size and the composition of the target group of workfare. While we will return to this second aspect in the discussion of the last hypothesis, the prospect for a 'trickle down' effect depends on the extent of integration between these two sets of programmes (and the development of ALMP).

The workfare programmes varied in the extent to which they were integrated with programmes for the insured (Chapter Nine, Table 9.3, column three). The European centralised programmes show substantial overlap with ALMP. The highest degree of overlap was found in the Netherlands and the UK, while Denmark had a medium-to-high level of integration of ALMPs and activation for the uninsured. Among the seven programmes, Hilfe zur Arbeit and RMI were average in the extent of their integration, while the local Norwegian schemes and the three US programmes were the most segregated.

The countries with the greatest integration between ALMP and workfare were also among the countries where we found the greatest departure from the tradition of social assistance (the UK, Denmark and the Netherlands, see pp 319-21 above). Moreover, the degree of integration is closely related to the strategy employed within the programmes. Integrated programmes are closer to HRD, and segregated programmes closer to an LMA approach. Seen in isolation, this suggests that the strategies of programmes in these three countries may be influenced by a trickle down from ALMP to workfare, and that the departure from policy inheritance in social assistance was facilitated by an integration between ALMP and workfare. This interpretation is strengthened by analysis of the development of the US programmes. These programmes were also among those which diverged strongly from past inheritance and, here, the LMA strategy was developed in a programme segregated from ALMP.

The reasons for variation in the extent of integration may, however, be different. A preliminary indication can be found by considering the extent to which ALMP is developed. At the time when most of the programmes considered here were either introduced or expanded, the development of ALMP differed substantially among the seven nations (Chapter One, Table 1.1, column 12, 1995). Norway and Denmark had the most extensive ALMP programmes in place. France, Germany and the Netherlands were in an in between position, while the UK and the US were the laggards in development of ALMP at that time.

In the US, ALMP is probably irrelevant in this context. The extent of ALMP was very limited and, for the target group of workfare, there were no programmes in place to which workfare could be attached. In the UK the integration may have been caused by a combination of a poor development of ALMP and a disappearing distinction between the insured and the uninsured following the reduction in the coverage of insurance for the unemployed. Workfare in the UK therefore caters to a much larger target group than elsewhere, including both people who are close to, and people who are distant from, the labour market. If the departure from policy inheritance is important in the UK case, this is likely to result as much from the choice to disband social insurance for the unemployed and the decision to develop ALMP beyond rudimentary coverage, as from a choice to develop an HRD strategy for the uninsured. In the two remaining programmes with a marked departure from policy inheritance this departure appears to result more from choice. In the Netherlands and, in particular, in Denmark a relatively extensive ALMP was in place when workfare was introduced. It appears to have been a politically-motivated decision to integrate workfare with these programmes, thereby perhaps achieving a trickle down effect.

Hypothesis 4: Target group matters

This hypothesis begins with the assumption that there is a causal relationship between the chosen strategy and the characteristics of the target group for programmes. First, we introduce two concepts which are useful for understanding how broad and narrow target groups relate differently to strategy. Second, we summarise the relevant information from this book about variation in target group of programmes and the strategy of these programmes.

Two functions of target group

Contributions from two related research traditions may aid our understanding of how strategy is differently related to broad and narrow target groups respectively. The first tradition focuses on the breadth of 'risk groups' covered by welfare programmes (for example Baldwin, 1990; Øverbye, 1998) and is particularly useful for understanding the relevance of broad target groups. Baldwin's study of social insurance highlights this general point. He challenged the view that the strength of the labour movement explains the universal and relatively generous form of social insurance found in the Nordic countries. In his view, the explanation is found in the fact that social insurance here catered to wider "risk groups" (Baldwin, 1990, p 289), including the rural peasant population, urban industrial workers and the middle classes, and that the majority of poor people in the Nordic countries benefited from "clinging to the coat-tails of the advantaged" (1990, p 298). These, mainly elderly and disabled, people were provided unilateral transfers within the broad 'people's insurance' systems. In contrast, the few people *not* included were often perceived as suffering from social problems rather than a lack of income.

Recipients of different schemes within social security experience different rights and are subject to different attitudes from both the general public and policy makers. An important distinguishing feature in social security is that, while social insurance is based on a *bilateral* form of exchange, with benefits provided in return for contributions, social assistance is a *unilateral* form of transfer, from the state to people in need. Where benefits are provided on the basis of need only, the giving of aid is more akin to a 'gift relationship' (Titmuss, 1970) than a reciprocal exchange. The provision of aid is therefore more dependent on the wider public's willingness to give to others, whether this is motivated by altruism or by solidarity (see for example, van Oorschot, 2000). While such normative issues have always proved important to the development of social assistance (Terum, 1996; Lødemel, 1997), the introduction of workfare has brought these to the centre of the policy discourse in all the countries considered here (Chapter One). We continue on the assumption that the choice of strategy is closely related to the groups targeted and the attitudes of policy makers towards these groups.

Evidence from the history of social assistance suggests that differences in the size and composition of recipient groups is linked to different attitudes and, as a result, associated with different policies. My own research into the history of social assistance in the UK and Norway may serve as an example. In the 1960s policy makers in both countries shared normative views about marginal groups, such as the able-bodied poor for example, and how best to balance rights with obligations and social control. The different developments of social assistance, with British schemes emphasising entitlement and Norwegian schemes focusing on discretion and control, were explained by the extent to which the schemes were designed for marginal groups only (Norway), or a wider segment of the population (Britain) (Lødemel, 1997).

The proximity to social insurance is also important for participants of workfare. This time both training programmes for the insured and the transfer programme itself are relevant. The extent of the integration of social assistance and social insurance, in terms of clientele and administration, has been found to impact on the characteristics of the social assistance scheme (Lødemel, 1997). In Baldwin's terms, a high degree of integration suggests a wider risk group, including both marginal people and those who are closer to the labour market. Similarly, an assumption may be that the extent to which workfare programmes are integrated in a more or less shared benefit scheme and with activating measures for groups other than social assistance recipients, impacts on the strategy of those workfare programmes. To paraphrase Baldwin, the uninsured participants in workfare may benefit from 'hanging on to the coat-tails' of insured unemployed people.

The second tradition – theories about the social construction of target populations (for example, Schneider and Ingram, 1993) – is particularly useful for understanding the relationship between strategy and target populations which are narrow and distant from the labour market. The normative foundation for workfare combined with the unilateral form of exchange may lead policy makers to base their decisions on prejudice or mistaken perceptions instead of a factual description of the recipients of social assistance. When this is the case, the *perception* (Lødemel, 1997, pp 160-71) or *social construction* of target groups (Schneider and Ingram, 1993) is more important to the shaping of policies than are the actual character of these groups. We found for example, that assumptions of widespread dependency has been refuted by empirical evidence (Chapter One, pp 18-22). In spite of such evidence, perceptions of dependency are a key motivating factor for introducing workfare programmes, albeit to different degrees (see Hypothesis 1 and Chapter One). Social constructions are stereoptypes of particular groups of people that have been created by, for example, politics, culture, socialisation, history, the media, literature and religion (Schneider and Ingram, 1993), and these can be both positive and negative. Negative constructions would include images such as "undeserving, stupid, dishonest and selfish" (Schneider and Ingram, 1993, p 335).

In their use of this theory, Schneider and Ingram argue that some social groups are more exposed to a "value-based cultural image" – the basis for the social construction of target populations (Schneider and Ingram, 1993, p 335). This is determined both by "the power of the target population itself – its propensity to mobilize for action" and the extent to which they are considered "deserving" (Schneider and Ingram, 1993, pp 335-6). Groups which are both powerless and which are also seen as undeserving are more likely to be subject to a cultural image which may result in negative social constructions. We can also see the possibility for positive social constructions within workfare, for example, where youth unemployment is widespread, and the risk is shared across social classes. This may give rise to a structural understanding of the problem and result in an HRD strategy. However (in my view), constructionist theory adds to the model provided by Baldwin, particularly where groups are narrow and where there is the likelihood of negative constructions. Following from this theory, a programme that selectively targets people who are distant from the labour market is more likely to be associated with negative social constructions such as dependency. When this is the case, an LMA approach is the likely outcome. The relevance of these contributions is that unemployment among uninsured people is perceived differently depending on its scale and the policy context in which programmes for these people are designed. In the concluding discussion, we will return to this issue by considering the role of politics and policy inheritance in the decision making of the seven countries with regard to the target group of their workfare programmes.

Variation in target group and in strategy

Chapter Nine documented important variation in the target groups of programmes in the seven countries (Table 9.2). The comparison revealed a strong cross-Atlantic difference. While the US programmes mainly targeted single mothers, the main target group in all six European programmes were young unemployed people. The extent to which all or only parts of the target group were affected by the compulsory programmes revealed a more diverse picture. Universal and selective programs are distinguished by the proportion of the target group that is affected by the introduction of the workfare programmes (Chapter Nine, Table 9.2, column six). The three European centralised programmes are described as 'universal'; the French and the US were categorised as 'quasi-universal', while the Norwegian and German programmes were described as 'selective' (although in some areas of Germany workfare is universally applied). While universal programmes include people with different skills and who are at different distances from the labour market, selective programmes target people who are generally more distant from the labour market.

The distinction among different "types of workfare" (Chapter Nine, pp 279-81) showed that strategy and the target group of programmes were closely related. The European centralised programmes combined broad target groups with an HRD approach. RMI in France was described as quasi-universal and contained elements of both HRD and LMA. The selective programmes in Germany and Norway were closer to an LMA approach. Among these, the Norwegian programmes were both the most selective and featured the strongest LMA approach. The exceptions here are the three US programmes, which were quasi-universal combined with a strong LMA approach.

In the discussion to follow, interpretations are given of how the 'target group' and the other three factors considered may have influenced the strategy of programmes in the seven countires.

Discussion

In the previous parts of this chapter the discussion has been limited to highlighting important aspects which need to be considered in order to assess the relevance of each hypothesis, and to provide information about how each programme varied on key aspects relevant to each hypothesis. We now turn to assess the explanatory value of each of these. As we will see, while each of the first three hypotheses contributes to our understanding, the question of how this has resulted in the choice of a particular strategy remains unanswered. This discussion will be based on the assumption that the nature of the target group is the most important lens through which we can see the relevance of each of the other three factors. Figure 10.2 illustrates the explanatory framework followed here.

The clearest and most unsurprising finding is that strategy embodied within a workfare programme is closely related to the characteristics of the social assistance scheme into which it was introduced. While broad country-by-country typologies of social assistance do not co-vary in terms of the workfare strategy adopted in each country, policy inheritance relates to two aspects in particular: the extent of centralisation and the degree of entitlement to benefits. HRD and LMA approaches are associated with centralised delivery and localised delivery respectively. Of the programmes considered in Chapter Nine only Danish activation and the three US programmes did not follow this pattern. However, these two countries emphasise the importance of the group targeted. Danish activation is characterised by a strong HRD strategy – the requirement

Figure 10.2: Explanatory framework

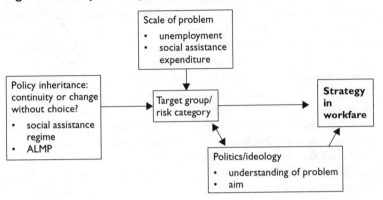

to participate is matched by the right to an offer of participation. As this is also applied to wide categories of recipients, workfare is more universally applied here than elsewhere.

In the discussion of programme effects resulting from the introduction of workfare, we have argued that the introduction of workfare was likely to decentralise social assistance schemes which were highly centralised. This followed from the observation that, in comparison to the provision of cash assistance which is highly centralised in some countries and a local responsibility in others, workfare is always implemented at the local level. Three countries in particular (the US, Denmark and the Netherlands) did not follow this pattern. While the three US programmes were relatively centralised, albeit on a state level, the design of these programmes was closer to an LMA strategy than the other programmes considered. Policy makers in the Netherlands and Denmark designed programmes with a strong HRD strategy in spite of their tradition of relatively decentralised social assistance schemes. Contrary to expectations, the introduction of workfare in these two countries has contributed to a centralisation of social assistance, at least for the target group of workfare.

The strategy embodied in the Wisconsin, New York and Californian programmes suggests that neither universal application nor centralisation necessarily result in an HRD strategy. The programmes here are more centralised and more universal than the other LMA programme studied – workfare in the Norwegian Social Services Act. However, the group targeted in the three US programmes was significantly different to that found in the European nations. In the absence of a national general assistance scheme, single parents constitute the main part of the clientele considered available for work[13]. Perhaps because this group is universally seen as being dependent (Fraser and Gordon, 1994), an LMA strategy is applied universally. In this case the existing tradition of central control, now increasingly on a state level, is used to further local compliance with this strategy. In Denmark the introduction of workfare has involved a centralisation of social assistance[14]. This politically-motivated centralisation may have proved instrumental in Denmark's further departure from the Nordic approach of localised and social control-oriented social assistance.

The relationship between the degree of centralisation, target group and strategy suggests that, when three national programmes were found to be similar in terms of strategy, they may have arrived at that point of convergence for different reasons. In the UK, policy inheritance from income maintenance and a comparatively late move towards more active labour market policies have facilitated a centralised, broad-based HRD strategy. In the Netherlands and, in particular, Denmark workfare is part of a politically-motivated move away from previous social assistance traditions.

Moreover, although this discussion has illustrated that the composition and size of the target group is strongly related to strategy, the causal relationship may differ. Where this appears to result from policy inheritance and recent developments in ALMP (as in the UK, Germany and Norway), our evidence suggest that the nature of the target group impacts on both aims and strategy. The evidence from the Netherlands and Denmark may indicate that the target group for these two programmes results more from political choice (ideology matters) than from tradition (policy inheritance).

We can summarise this discussion by providing a tentative interpretation of how, and why, the seven programmes studied in this book have arrived at the strategy pursued.

Throughout the discussion in this chapter the French RMI programme has proved difficult to place. This is because of three reasons: first, that this scheme did not exhibit a clear LMA or HRD strategy, second, that it was average in the degree of centralisation and, third, that workfare was introduced as part of the package when RMI (as the country's first general social assistance scheme) was enacted. Large scale unemployment in the target group may have facilitated a structural understanding of these problems, thereby contributing to the emphasis on social exclusion and resulting strong integrative aims. Perhaps the clearest finding here is that these aims were not reflected in the strategy of programmes. This indicates that these ideological underpinnings have influenced programmes less than has previously been suggested. This may be because the strong centralisation in the provision of cash benefits has not been followed up in the provision of insertion opportunities. Other aspects of policy inheritance are less important here than elsewhere. In addition to an absence of a social assistance inheritance, alternative programs (ALMP) were poorly developed and the chances of a 'trickle down' effect on workfare were therefore limited. On the other hand, the large scale of unemployment among the target group may have reduced the likelihood of a 'negative social construction' of the target group. Similarly, the poor development of ALMP, together with unemployment benefits set at the same level as RMI for large proportion of the unemployed may have contributed to an understanding of the workfare target group as part of a wider risk group. The lack of fulfilment of the guarantee of an insertion contract must be understood as an unwillingness or inability by local departments to organise and finance programmes, and thereby meet their obligations to the state and to recipients.

The fact that the German programme was introduced much earlier than the other six programmes (1961), and that it has recently been expanded rather than introduced anew, suggests that, in Germany, policy inheritance is an important explanatory factor. The inter-relationship between workfare and ALMP may have cemented the character of workfare and broader activating policies. Unlike Norway, where, in principle, all unemployed people have access to ALMP, access for social assistance recipients is secured in Germany by participating in one form of workfare. Those selected for participation in these 'contract' programmes must remain in work for one year for a transfer to state programmes to be achieved. Because successful completion of this contract involves a substantial saving for the local authorities (because the responsibility for both benefits and training is then transferred to Federal government), it is in the interests of local authorities to 'cream' participants who are closer to the labour market. As a result, we find a strong social division of programmes, within towns which organise both contract and non-contract programmes, and between towns which have either both in place or where only non-contract programmes are applied. With the exception of the former DDR, workfare has received less political attention in Germany compared to the other countries considered here. In spite of the greater attention given in the East, the much larger scale of the problem addressed has so far, here as elsewhere in Germany, resulted in expansion rather than re-direction. Notwithstanding a turn towards 'third way' policies in the current social democratic-led government, and the scale of youth unemployment, Germany has so far been 'immune' to the wide-ranging re-balancing of rights and obligations found in other nations with similar problems. This may partly be due to the fragmentation of responsibility between different levels of government and, perhaps, an apparent dependency on the country's own traditions rather than the adoption of ideas and lessons learnt from abroad.

The Netherlands, together with Denmark, is the country in which politics appear to have a strong impact on the strategy pursued in workfare programmes. Here, therefore, policy inheritance appears to have had limited influence as the development represents a departure from previous traditions of social assistance. Moreover, ALMPs were quite poorly developed in the mid-1990s and have, therefore, not exerted a decisive influence on workfare. On the contrary, the development of workfare, and its close integration with expanding programmes for the insured has contributed to a sharp increase in the totality of active measures targeted at the unemployed. The relatively small scale of the problems addressed strengthens the impression that a structural understanding of the problem results mainly from political orientation. Further, the universal coverage of programmes combined with the strong integration with programmes for the insured unemployed may have created a broad risk group and a corresponding avoidance of 'negative constructions' of the target group.

In Norway, the local workfare schemes represent a continuation of the history of a localised, relatively generous social assistance scheme exhibiting strong social control of recipients. The wider context of workfare has added to the importance of policy inheritance as a decisive factor. Among the seven countries, ALMP programmes were more extensive in Norway than elsewhere. The fact that recipients of social assistance were eligible to participate in these labour market programmes designed for the insured impacted on workfare in two ways. First, in this situation local authority workfare plays a residual role, selectively targeting people who are both distant from the labour market and who have failed to benefit from the opportunity to participate in ALMP or achieve entry into a tight labour market (which has ample job opportunities for people with few skills). As a result, it appears that a 'negative social construction' of the target group has been created, which has led to emphasis on corrective measures rather than investment through an HRD approach. This implies that, in Norway, policy inheritance is the main independent variable, which in turn impacts on the target group and on political decisions about strategy.

Danish activation represents perhaps the clearest case of an independent role played by politics. The choice of universal coverage of programmes and an HRD approach represents both a departure from policy inheritance and the expected programme effects associated with the introduction of workfare. Unlike neighbouring Norway, an already developed ALMP was here more integrated with workfare, thereby further facilitating a broad risk group and therefore avoidance of a 'negative social construction' of the target group. The recent extension of programmes to also include people with little prospect of labour market integration strengthens the impression of Denmark as a country which goes beyond an emphasis on work and thereby addresses the wider problems associated with social exclusion.

In spite of the high political profile surrounding the introduction of New Deal in the UK, and the fact that its introduction involves a departure from the key characteristics of pre-workfare social assistance, our evidence still suggests that policy inheritance, rather than politics, may offer a better explanation for the strategies pursued in workfare programmes. In the words of Rose and Davis (1994) the recent development in the UK could be described as a version of policy inheritance: "change without choice". Three factors may have facilitated this outcome. First, social assistance has been more centralised in the UK than in any of the other six countries. Compared to a localised system, a scheme under strong central government control is more easily changed by central government. Second, the unitary form of government "centralising choice in Whitehall and reducing local authorities' scope for choice" (Rose and Davis, 1994) may add to the prospect for politically-motivated change. While this may aid our understanding of the dramatic departure from the dominant "instrument of curtailment" (p 298) in social assistance and can therefore be seen as an outcome of political change, the strategy pursued is best understood to have been formed by the scale of the problem, inheritance and policy context. In addition to the relatively large scale of the problem, the tradition of universally applied polices (which is associated with centralisation) and the marginalisation of unemployment insurance have created a broad target group. As a result, the re-balancing of rights and obligations, however dramatic, may have been contained by this broad risk group. Because the broad drive for ALMPs includes groups with some political weight, this may have contributed to an avoidance of a negative social construction. If the UK had followed the US in strategy (as some observers claim that they have), this would have applied to a very different target group, and would therefore have been a more difficult (if desirable) political project. It remains to be investigated, though, if the hierarchy of options in New Deal represents a 'social division of activation' or if marginal groups have benefited from 'hanging on to the coat-tails' of unemployed people who are closer to the labour market.

The three US programmes have a similar departure to the UK from a rights-oriented social assistance with relatively low benefits, to social control with the introduction of workfare. In other aspects, the experience in these three states is exceptional in our overall findings and the departure from policy inheritance appears to be more politically motivated in the US than it is in the UK. There are five main reasons why this departure resulted in a LMA strategy. First, and most important, the target group is different from those found in Europe. In the European programmes single parents' participation in programmes is either voluntary, or they are not singled out as a target group at all. Although we have not pursued this aspect further, this highlights a strong trans-Atlantic difference in how single parents are viewed, and its implication adds an important gender dimension to workfare in the US. Moreover, the workfare discourse in the US is much more racialised than it is in Europe (Deacon, 2000). Second, the widespread assumption that dependency is the main problem of this group, rather than lack of income, work opportunities and childcare, further strengthens the trans-Atlantic difference, and shows an ideological dimension to the political choice of an LMA strategy in workfare programmes. Third, the focus on dependency and the associated negative social construction of the target group is further facilitated by the policy context of workfare. This results both from a poor development of ALMP and from changes in other areas of social assistance. Most importantly, among these changes is the strong reduction in the coverage of General Assistance which, in most US states, excludes single workless people (the main target group in the six European programmes) from more than rudimentary entitlement to aid. Fourth, these three states have experienced a tight labour market, with job opportunities available for people with low skills. This has resulted in a relatively small-scale problem, and has strengthened an individual rather than a structural understanding of worklessness. Fifth, because the target group here are parents, the high labour market participation among mothers in two-parent households in the US has also contributed to this negative social construction. These factors have all facilitated a pendulum swing from entitlement to obligations rather than a re-balancing of these two aspects of the contract between the state and people in need.

Conclusion

The authors of this book have made an attempt to survey an unchartered area for comparative studies. We needed to define workfare in order to select programmes and make comparisons, however, our evidence shows that the idealised definition of workfare only applies to some of the programmes considered. While this covers only a part of the options available to social assistance recipients, it has enabled us to do two things. First, through our focus, we have been able to address the change of the contract of social assistance for the most vulnerable groups among the social assistance clientele. Second, by studying deviation from the idealised model, we have been able to study the boundaries between workfare and related programs. As these were found, more often than not, to be blurred, our advice for future comparatists interested in the current move towards more activating policies is to take a broader view and include other forms of activation – voluntary as well as compulsory. As this study has demonstrated, the options available and the extent to which workfare programmes are integrated with other activating programmes impacts on what workfare involves for the individual workless social assistance recipient.

This discussion has also highlighted two different developments which may impact on the way workfare will develop in the future. On the one hand, the clientele targeted by workfare is likely to be more distant from the labour market in the future (Chapter Nine). At the same time, a tendency towards a stronger HRD approach in most of the countries studied, may suggest that future programmes will be better tailored to the needs of these groups.

On both sides of the Atlantic we are witnessing a redirection of welfare provision with the aim of furthering labour market integration. At the moment we can distinguish between two different experiments taking place. In Europe – particularly among the European centralised programmes – the experiment involves a move away from entitlement to unconditional aid and, perhaps, towards a new kind of entitlement more suited to the risks and changes in modern society (Leisering and Walker, 1998). In the US the experiment is more dramatic. By combining an *end* to entitlement and an accompanying emphasis on 'hassle' rather than help (Chapter Eight), the US is perhaps the first nation to follow the advice of Malthus and others more than two centuries ago: if welfare is the root of poverty and dependence, the best solution is to do away with welfare (Malthus, 1998 [1798]). It will take time and long-term evaluations will be necessary before we can assess the success of either experiment. Our hope is that this first attempt to survey these programmes will inspire policy makers and students of social policy in their efforts to shape and to understand these important re-orientations of welfare.

Notes

[1] This combination was first institutionalised in the British New Poor Law in 1834. Partly resulting from diffusion and lesson learning, this approach was followed, albeit with modifications, in other Western European countries and the US (for European developments, see for example De Swaan, 1988, for US developments, see for example Katz, 1986).

[2] This is calculated as disposable incomes of social assistance recipients as percentage of disposable incomes of the same household types where the head is earning average male earnings: average of six household types after housing costs. The highest levels were found in the Netherlands (73) followed by Denmark (66), Norway (57), Germany (44), France (43), UK (42) and the US (Pennsylvania 29, Florida 27, New York 19) (Gough et al, 1997, p 32).

[3] This was based on information about the degree of centralisation in delivery, the extent of discretion, earnings disregards, treatment of assets and the resource unit (Gough et al, 1997, p 30). The index did not, however, consider the impact of work requirements in the countries where this was already in place. Among the seven countries considered here the lowest exclusion score was found in the UK (19), US (27), Denmark and the Netherlands (29), Germany (32) and Norway (42).

[4] In France, the workfare condition was already introduced at his point. Also, in Germany, Hilfe zur Arbeit was in place, but applied less extensively than in the late 1990s (Chapter Three). The situation in the US was similar to that in Germany in this respect (Chapter Eight).

[5] Even where workfare is used selectively, it may have a wider impact. As was demonstrated in Chapter Five, the introduction of workfare programmes has had a preventive effect by sending a message to potential claimants that the contract of social assistance had changed.

[6] The relevant importance of additional payments can only be compared by considering local implementation in the five countries where this is not part of the official design of programmes. This is considered in a report resulting from

our implementation study of workfare in the six European countries considered here (Lødemel and Stafford, 2001: forthcoming).

[7] Ditch and Oldfield (1999) and Glennerster (1999) also attach importance to wider contacts between policy makers in Britain and the English-speaking countries of Australia, New Zealand and Canada, and a resulting diffusion of policy ideas from these countries to Britain. This may result from previous similarities in policies, the role of Commonwealth organisations, and, perhaps, a shared language. If similarity in language and other cultural factors have contributed to the development of 'networks' for learning and diffusion, future studies may find that the 'families of nations' approach (Castles, 1993) may provide a better starting point than 'welfare regimes'.

[8] Olsen (1999) has found few cases of diffusion from Denmark to the UK in their preparation of New Deal. Interestingly, however, one of her interviewees from the Trade Union Congress (TUC) told her that evidence from Denmark (that workfare could be much more than compulsion only) was instrumental in facilitating the TUC's support for the New Deal (p 93). Glennerster argues that the British re-orientation in policies addressing the relationship between welfare and work is a "distinctive approach that is neither exclusively American nor European" (1999, p 4).

[9] In three of the European programmes considered in Chapter Nine – the Danish, Dutch and Norwegian programmes – 'mothers of young children' are explicitly excluded from the obligation to participate. In the three US programmes, the Californian and the New York programmes excludes parents with children under the age of three, while the Wisconsin programme only excludes parents with children less than three months old (Chapter Nine, Table 9.2).

[10] Information provided by the administrative head of the programme during visit in Leipzig in July 1999.

[11] For data on expenditure on social assistance see Chapter One, Table 1.1. The data on unemployment levels is taken from OECD (2000). At the time of enactment (or expansion in the US, Germany and Denmark), the levels of unemployment were: Denmark 6.4%, France 9.3%, Germany ranging from approximately 8-9% in the period 1993-1999, the Netherlands 4.2%, Norway 5.2%, UK 6.9%, US 5.6%.

[12] We choose not to consider the compulsory work programmes of the Poor Laws (last applied on a large scale during mass unemployment in the 1930s) as part of policy inheritance. These programmes existed within different transfer schemes

and targeted different groups to the modern workfare programmes (Lødemel and Dahl, 2001: forthcoming).

[13] Workfare was first used in General Assistance and, in the United States, where it is still applied, workfare is still a central component today. Also, the major non-cash programme – Food Stamps – is now contingent on participation in workfare (Cammissa, 1998).

[14] Social assistance in Denmark was described s belonging to a Nordic model by Lødemel and Schulte (1992). After local discretion was reduced in the early 1990s, Gough et al (1997) described it, together with Sweden, as a system more similar to that found in the Netherlands.

References

Baldwin, P. (1990) *The politics of social solidarity class bases of the European welfare state 1875-1975*, Cambridge: Cambridge University Press.

Bernstein, N. (1999) 'City warns about shelter requirements at heated hearing', *New York Times*, 4 December.

Bradshaw, J. and Terum, L.I. (1997) 'How Nordic is the Nordic model? Social assistance in a comparative perspective', *Scandinavian Journal of Social Welfare*, no 6, pp 247-56.

Cammissa, A.M. (1998) *From rhetoric to reform? Welfare policy in American Politics*, Oxford: Westview Press.

Castles, F. (1981) 'How does politics matter? Structure and agency in the determination of public policy outcomes', *European Journal of Political Research*, vol 9, pp 119-32.

Castles, F. (ed) (1993) *Families of nations: Patterns of public policy in Western democracies*, Aldershot: Dartmouth Publishing Company.

Dahl, E. and Pedersen, L. (eds) (2001: forthcoming) *Does workfare work? Systematic review of workfare evaluations in six European countries*, Oslo: Fafo Institute for Applied Social Science.

Deacon, A. (2000) 'Learning from the US? The influence of American ideas upon New Labour thinking on welfare reform', *Policy & Politics*, vol 28, no 1, pp 5-18.

De Swaan, A. (1988) *In care of the state*, Cambridge: Polity Press.

Ditch, J. (1999) 'Full circle: a second coming for social assistance?', in J. Clasen (ed) (1999) *Comparative social policy concepts, theories and methods*, Oxford: Blackwell Publishers.

Ditch, J. and Oldfield, N. (1999) 'Social assistance: recent trends and themes', *Journal of European Social Policy*, no 1, pp 65-76.

Dolowitz, D.P., Hume, R., Nollis M. and O'Neil, F. (2000) *Policy transfer and British social policy: Learning from the USA?*, Buckingham: Open University Press.

Eardley, T., Bradshaw, J., Ditch, J., Gough, I. and Whiteford, P. (1996) *Social assistance schemes in OECD countries: Volume 1: Synthesis Report*, Department of Social Security Research Report No 46, London: HMSO.

Enjolras, B. and Lødemel, I. (1999) 'Activation of social protection in France and Norway: new divergence in a time of convergence', in D. Bouget and M. Palier (eds) *Comparing social welfare systems in Nordic Europe and France*, Paris, MIRE.

Esping-Andersen, G. (1985) *Politics against markets: The social democratic road to power*, Princeton, NJ: Princeton University Press.

Esping-Andersen, G. (1990) *The three worlds of welfare capitalism*, Cambridge: Polity Press.

Esping-Andersen, G. (ed) (1996) *Welfare states in transition: National adaptions in global economies*, London: Sage Publications.

Esping-Andersen. G. (1999) *Social foundations of postindustrial economies*, Oxford: University Press.

European Commission (1998) *From guidelines to action: The national action plans for employment*, Brussels: DG V.

Fraser, N. and Gordon, L. (1994) 'A genealogy of dependency: tracing a keyword for the US welfare state', *Signs: A Journal of Women in Culture and Society*, vol 19, no 2, p 310.

Giddens, A. (1998) *The third way: The renewal of social democracy*, Cambridge: Polity Press.

Glennerster, H. (1999) 'Which welfare states are most likely to survive?', *International Journal of Social Welfare*, vol 8, no 1, pp 2-13.

Golding, P. and Middleton, S. (1981) *Images of welfare: Press and public attitudes to poverty*, Oxford: Basil Blackwell.

Gough, I., Bradshaw, J., Ditch, J., Eardley T. and Whiteford, P. (1997) 'Social assistance in OECD countries', *Journal of European Social Policy*, vol 7, no 1, pp 17-43.

Halvorsen, K. (2000) 'Garantert minsteinntekt – svaret på velferdsstatens utfordringer?', *Nordisk sosialt arbeid*, vol 3, pp 130-8.

Hanesch, W. (1998) 'The debate on reforms of social assistance in Western Europe', in M. Heikkila (ed) *Linking welfare and work*, Dublin: European Foundation for the Improvement of Living and Working Conditions.

Heclo, H. (1973) *Modern social politics in Britain and Sweden*, New Haven, CT: Yale University Press.

Himmelfarb, G. (1998) 'Comment', in A. Guttman (ed) *Work and welfare*, Princeton, NJ: Princeton University Press.

Hvinden, B. (1999) 'Activation: a Nordic perspective', in M. Heikkila (ed) *Linking welfare and work*, Dublin: European Foundation for the Improvement of Living and Working Conditions.

Ingram, H. and Schneider, A. (1991) 'Target populations and policy design', *Administration and Society*, vol 23, pp 333-56.

Jackson, M.P. and Valencia, B.M. (1979) *Financial aid through social work*, London: Routledge and Kegan Paul.

Jessop, B. (1993) 'Towards a Schumpetarian workfare state? Preliminary remarks on post-Fordist political economy', *Studies in Political Economy*, vol 40, pp 7-39.

Jones, C. (1985) *Patterns of social policy: An introduction to comparative analysis*, London: Tavistock Publications.

Katz, M.B. (1986) *In the shadow of the poorhouse: A social history of welfare in America*, New York, NY: Basic Books.

Korpi, W. (1983) *The democratic class struggle*, London: Routledge and Kegan Paul.

Kuhnle, S. (1984) *Velferdsstatens utvikling: Norge i komparativt perspektiv*, Oslo: Universitetsforlaget.

Leibfried, S. (1992) 'Toward a European welfare state? On integrating poverty regimes into the European Community', in Z. Ferge and J.E. Kolberg (eds) *Social policy in a changing Europe*, Frankfurt: Campus and Westview, pp 245-79.

Leisering, L. and Walker, R. (eds) (1998) *The dynamics of modern society*, Bristol: The Policy Press.

Levitas, R. (1998) *The inclusive society?*, London: Macmillan Press.

Lorenz, W. (1994) *Social work in a changing Europe*, London: Routledge.

Lødemel, I. (1992) 'Sosialhjelpa i europeisk inntektssikring', *Sosiologi i dag*, no 2, pp 57-72.

Lødemel, I. (1997) *The welfare paradox: Income maintenance and personal social services in Norway and Britain, 1946-1966*, Oslo: Scandinavian University Press.

Lødemel, I. and Dahl, E. (2001: forthcoming) 'Public works programmes in Korea: a comparison to active labour market policies and workfare in Europe and the US', in *Financial crisis and labour market reforms in Korea*, Seoul/Washington, DC: Korea Labour Market Institute/World Bank.

Lødemel, I. and Schulte, B. (1992) 'Social assistance – a part of social security or the Poor Law in new disguise?', *Yearbook*, Leuven: European Institute of Social Security.

Lødemel, I. and Stafford, B. (eds) (2001: forthcoming) *The implementation of workfare in six European countries*, Oslo: Fafo Institute for Applied Social Science.

Mabbett, D. and Bolderson, H. (1999) 'Theories and methods in comparative social policy', in J. Clasen (ed) *Comparative social policy: Concepts, theories and methods*, Oxford: Blackwell Publishers.

Malthus, T. (1998 [1798]) *An essay on the principle of population*, Amherst: Prometheus Books.

Midgley, J. (1997) *Social welfare in global context*, Thousand Oaks, CA: Sage Publications.

Midré, G. (1992) *Bot, bedring eller brød? Om bedømming og behandling av sosial nød fra reformasjonene til folketrygden*, Oslo: Universitetsforlaget.

Mishra, R. (1977) *Society and social policy*, London: Macmillan.

Morel, S. (1998) 'American workfare versus French insertion policies: an application of Common's theoretical framework', Paper presented at Annual Research Conference of the Association for Public Policy and Management, New York, 29-31 October.

Olsen, L. (1999) 'En komparativ analyse af de ungdomsarbejdsløshedspolitiske netværk i Danmark og Storbritannien– med særlig henblik på spørsmålet om diffusjon', Postgraduate dissertation, University of Copenhagen.

Øverbye, E. (1998) *Risks and welfare: Examining stability and change in 'welfare' policies*, Oslo: NOVA.

Peck, J. (1998) 'Workfare: a geopolitical etymology', *Environment and Planning D: Society and Space*, vol 16, pp 133-60.

Peck, J. (1999) 'Workfare in the sun: politics, representation, method in US welfare-to-work strategies', *Political Geography*, vol 17, pp 535-66.

Pierson, P. (1996) 'The path to the European integration – a historical institutionalist analysis', *Comparative Political Studies*, vol 29, pp 123-63.

Rodgers, D.T. (1998) *Atlantic crossings: Social politics in a progressive age*, Cambridge, MA: Harvard University Press.

Rogers, E.M and Floyd Shoemaker, F. (1971) *Communication of innovations: A cross-cultural approach*, New York, NY: The Free Press.

Rose, R. and Davis, P.L. (1994) *Inheritance in public policy: Change without choice in Britain*, New Haven, CT: Yale University Press.

Seeliger, R. (1996) 'Contectualizing and researching policy convergence', *Policy Studies Journal*, vol 24, no 2, pp 287-306.

Schneider, A. and Ingram, H. (1993) 'The social construction of target populations: implications for politics and policy', *American Political Science Review*, vol 87, no 2, pp 334-47.

Terum, L.I. (1996) *Grenser for sosialpolitisk modernisering*, Oslo: Universitetsforlaget.

Titmuss, R. (1956) 'War and social policy'.

Titmuss, R. (1960) *Problems of social policy*, London: HMSO.

Titmuss, R. (1970) *The gift relationship: From human blood to social policy*, Oxford: George Allen & Unwin.

Torfing, J. (1999) 'Workfare with welfare: recent reforms in the Danish welfare state', *Journal of European Social Policy*, no 1, pp 5-28.

van Oorschot, W. (2000) 'Who should get what and why? On deservingness criteria and the conditionality of solidarity among the public', *Policy & Politics*, vol 28, no 1, pp 33-48.

Walker, R. (1999) 'The Americanisation of British welfare: a case study of policy transfer', *International Journal of Health Services*, vol 29, no 4, pp 679-97.

Wilensky, H. (1975) *The welfare state and equality*, Berkley, CA: University of California.

Index

A

activating labour market policies, Netherlands 114, 127-8
activating states 15
activation 13-14, *25*, 26, 31, 268-9, 322
  France 41
activation (Denmark) xvi-xvii, 32, *161*, 249, 300, 328, 332
  action plans 172
  administration 265-6, *266*, 267
  combating social exclusion 253
  compulsion 162
  convergence 303, 310, 312
  curtailment 300
  divergence 311
  as European centralised programme 279-80
  evaluation 177-9, 287, 290
  ideology 177-8, *256*, *282*, 317, 333
  local authority strategies 176-7
  negotiating placements 275-6, *275*
  offers 172-3
  placement types 172-5, 269, *270*, 274, 278, *283*
  policy trends 169-70
  rights and responsibilities 11, 166-9, 254
  sanctioning 276, *277*, *284*
  social assistance contract 300
  strategies 300, 323, 329-30, 332-3
  target groups 171, *258*, 264
  timing of intervention 263
  universal programme 263, 264, 300
  who gets what 173-5
  or workfare 175-6
Active Labour Market Policies (ALMPs) xiv, 13-15, 23, 26, 255, 290, 322-4
  Denmark 160, 161-2, *163-5*, 165, 166, 323
  expenditure *25*
  France 323-4
  Germany 323-4
  and HRD approach 323
  motivating factors 250
  Netherlands 323-4
  Norway 133, 139, 145-6, 149, 153-4, 155-6, 323
  UK 189, 191-2, 324
  US 324
  see also workfare
Active Line (Denmark) xvi, 159-60, 162, 166, 170
Active Social Policy Act 1998 (Denmark) 32
administration 128, 265-8
  and aims *282*
  Denmark 167
  France 42, 46-7
  Germany 90-1
  Netherlands 124
  Norway 142-3
  and sanctioning *284*
  and strategy *283*
  UK 185, 189, 192
  US 234
Aid to Families with Dependent Children (AFDC) (US) 219, 221-2, *221*, 223, 242, 302, 310
aims-based approaches 4-5
Alaska 297
Algemene Bijstandswet (ABW) (Netherlands) 108
Amsterdam Treaty 14
Assistance in Special Situations (Germany) 76
Australia 191

B

Baldwin, P. 324-6
Bane, M.J. 19-20, 21
Bardach, E. 21
Bavaria 78
Belorgey, J.M. 51
'benchmarking' 308

benefit
  levels 299, 301-3
  reduction 31
Berlin 95-6, *95*
black grants, US 229
Blair, Tony 190
Bolderson, H. 304
Bourgeois, L. 45-6
Bremen 95-6, *95*
Bruhnes, B. 56

C

calculating unemployed 113-14
California 32, 223, 227, 240-2, 243, 250
  ideology *256, 282*
  negotiating placements 275, *275*
  placement types *270, 283*
  sanctioning *277, 284*
  strategy, 329
  target group *259*, 330
case management 263, 278, 289
case-work 29, 43, 307, 309, 311
  and financial assistance 309
cash-care provision 29, 72, 309-10, 312
Castels, R. 17
centralisation 297, 309, 310, 312, 321,
  328-30, 333
  and active labour market programmes
  323
centralised programmes 28, 265-7,
  278-80, 297, 307, 310
Centres for Work and Income
  (Netherlands) 124, 127
Children's Tax Credit (UK) 193
citizenship 67
  right to social assistance 299, 320
Clinton, Bill 226
Collective Utility Work (France) 59,
  60-1
Community Work Experience
  Program (CWEP) (US) 223, 224
compulsion xviii-xix, 7-8, 9-10, 288-
  9, 302, 317
  Denmark 161, 162
  and dependency 18, 21, 252
  and social exclusion 17-18
  UK 26, 181, 194, 201

US 26
conditionality *see* rights and
  responsibilities
conservative-corporatist welfare
  regimes viii, 27, 48, 320
contract-type job creation schemes
  59-60, 85-6, 96, 97
Contrat Emploi Solidarité (CES) (France)
  59-61
contributory principle, France 42
control 31
convergence xviii-xix, 2-3, 295, 303-
  12
  diffusion 304-8
  globalisation 304, 318
  nominal 305, 307, 311
  non-convergence 309
  programme effects 308-11
  qualified 304, 308-12
  see also divergence; new convergence
  theory
Cost-of-Living Assistance (Germany)
  76-8
Costello, A. 5
created public work placements *270*
cultural model of dependency 19-20,
  21
culture of poverty 20
curtailment 296, 298-303
  see also entitlement; workhouse test

D

Davis, P.L. 319, 322, 333
de Tocqueville, A. 18, 20
dead-weight problem 262
Dean, H. 22
decentralisation 310, 322, 329
decentralised programmes 265-7
decommodification 27
defensive workfare 29, 31
demand-side measures 5, 253, 255
democratisation 12
Denmark xvi-xvii, 159-61, 178-9
  Active Social Policy Act 32
  ALMPs *25*, 26, 323-4, 32-3
  compulsion 317
  re-designation 261

rights and responsibilities 10
social assistance 330
  convergence 310, 312
  expenditure 318
  typology 29, *30*, 320
social-democratic welfare regime xi,
  27, 317
structural context 23, *24-5*
unemployment 261, 318
workfare 26, 29, 31, 32, 300
  strategy 297, 30, 323, 329-30, 332
young people 260
see also activation
dependency 15, 16, 251, 305, 315-16,
  326-7, 330, 334
  long-term unemployment 260-1, 262
  Norway 137
  preventing 252, 255, *256*
  UK 186-7, 190
  US 221-3
  and worklessness 18-22
  young people 260
deservingness xiii, 314
differentiated poverty regime 28, 31
diffusion 304-8
  as dissemination of ideas 305-6
  geographical 304-5, 311
  hierarchical 308
  from US 305-8, 311
disability 261
  Netherlands 112
  UK 184, 187-8, 193, *198*
Disabled Person's Tax Credit (DPTC)
  (UK) 193
disincentives xii, 14-15
  Norway 136
  UK 191
displacement 236, 271-2
Ditch, J. 28
divergence 311-2
diversity xviii-xix, 3, 312-14
  and policy inheritance 319-24
  and politics 314-17
  and scale 317-19
  and target groups 324-8
  dual social assistance regimes 311, 320
Durkheim, E. 113

E

Eardley, T. 27, 299
Earned Income Tax Credit (EITC)
  (US) 193, 216, 219, 231
economy
  France 47-8, 56
  Netherlands 109-10
  and workfare 318
Ellwood, D. 19-20, 21
Emploi Jeunes (France) xv, 43-4, 61-2
  activities 63
  employers 62-3
  evaluation 65-6
  implementation 63-4
Emplois Familiaux (France) 58
Employment Solidarity Contract
  (France) 59-61
empowerment 31
Engbersen, G. 113
entitlement 3, 10, 290, 298, 328, 334-5
  UK 186-9
  US 230-1, 254
Esping-Andersen, G. xi-xii, 27, *30*, 320
European centralised programmes
  279-80, 281, 288, 297, 307, 310-11,
  320, 323, 327-8, 335
European Commission 308
European Union 14, 308
exclusion *see* social exclusion
exclusion score 29, *30*, 31
exclusion index 299
exclusion unemployment, France 47
expectancy model of dependency 19,
  20
expenditure 23, *24*, *25*, 250, 251-2
  France 54, *55*
  Germany 96
  Netherlands 112, 114
  Norway 133, 134-5, 152
  UK 185, 189

F

Family Support Act 1988 (FSA) (US)
  220, *221*, 225-6
Field, Frank 187
Finder, A. 236

flex jobs (Denmark) *164*
flexibility 31, 111
  Netherlands 115
  UK 182, 190
Flexibility and Security Act 1999
  (Netherlands) 115
Floyd Shoemaker, F. 305
food stamps (US) 76, 217, 218, 219, 231
form-based approaches 4, 5-6, 9-10
France xiv-xv, 32, 41-4, 66-7
  ALMPs 331
  conservative-corporatist welfare
    regime xi, 27, 320
  Contrat Emploi Solidarité 59-61
  economic context 47-8
  Emploi Jeunes xv, 43-4, 61-4, 65-6, 291
  expenditure 54, *55*, 252
  insertion policies and republican
    ideology 4, 44-6, 331
  institutional context 46-7
  labour market participation policies
    56-9
  rights and responsibilities 10, 11
  social assistance
    change 311
    typology 29, *30*, 315, 330-1
  social exclusion 16-17, 253, 314
  structural context 23, *24-5*
  TRACE 64-6
  Travaux d'Utilité Collective 59, 60-1
  unemployment 315, 330
  unemployment benefits 48-9, 331
  workfare strategies 297, 301, 311, 315
  young people 10
  see also Revenu Minimum d'Insertion
Fraser, N. 20
fraud 191
Fürsorgeprinzip 73, 74, 76-8

G

Gardiner, K. 189
General Assistance (US) 217, 334
Gerhardsen, Rune 148
Germany xv, 71-2
  compulsion 317
  conservative-corporatist welfare
    regime xi, 27, 317, 332

ideological shift 317, 331-2
rights and responsibilities 10
social assistance
  change   311
  recipiency   trends
    78-81
  typology 29, *30*, 320
  social exclusion 253
  structural context 23, *24-5*
  unemployment 317, 332
  welfare state 72-3, *74*, 75-8
  workfare 32, 301, 311
    strategies 297, 301, 311, 321
  see also Help Towards Work
ghettoes 20
'gift relationship' 325
Gilbert, B. 13
Gilbert, N. 13
globalisation 304, 306, 319
Goodin, R. 8, 21-2
Gordon, L. 20
Gough, I. 29, *30*, 31, 311, 320
Grimes, A. 8
Grover, C. 5

H

Hamburg 89, 95-6, *95*, 97
Handler, J. 19
handmaiden model of welfare
  provision 26
harshness 152
Hasenfeld, Y. 19
Heclo, H. 307
Help Towards Work (HTW) (*Hilfe zur
  Arbeit*) (Germany) xv, 32, 71-2, 249,
  278, 280, 331
  administration 266, *266*, 267, 331
  contract-type 85-6
  evaluation and outcomes 93-6,
    287-8
  expenditure 252
  future 97-8
  ideology *256*, *282*, 317
  implementation 301
  intra-national variation 88-93, 255,
    331
  negotiating placements 274, 275, *275*

non-contract 85
placement types 81-4, 269, *270*, 273, *283*
rights and responsibilities 254, 307
sanctioning 86-7, 276, *277*, 278, *284*
selectivity 264, 268
social assistance 299, 311
target group *258*, 327, 331
timing of intervention 263
workfare strategies 311, 323
young people 260
Hilfe Besonderen Lebenslagen (Germany) 76
Hilfe zum Lebensunterhalt (Germany) 76-8
housing programmes, France 49
Human Resource Development (HRD) 296-7, 301-3, 322-3, 335-6
convergence 310
and policy inheritance 320, 333
and politics 316
and scale 318
and target group 327-8, 332

I

ideology xiii, 15-22, *282*
comparative study 250-5, *256*
Denmark 177-8
European centralised programmes 279
France 44-6, 66
Netherlands 112-15
UK 190-1
in-work assistance, UK 186, 191
incentives xii, 14
Norway 136
UK 191
incomplete differentiated poverty regime 28, 31
Individual Action Plans (Denmark) 172
individualism 45
individuals 15, 52, 128, 286
US 251
see also dependency; rights and responsibilities
Ingram, H. 326
insertion 4, 17, 66-7

France 41, 42-3, 44-6, 50-1, 251, 252
see also Revenu Minimum d'Insertion
Netherlands 117
institutional context *see* administration
institutional-redistributive model of welfare provision 26-7, 28
institutionalised poverty regime 28, 31
instruments of curtailment 300
intra-national variation 10, 249-50, 310
administration 265, 267
Germany 88-93
Norway 133, 142, 150-1, 156
UK 201
workfare aims and ideology 255
see also state variation
irrational dependency 7

J

Jahoda, M. 113
Jessop, B. 5, 13, 15, 311
job creation 5
France 43, 56-7
Netherlands 116
Job Opportunities and Basic Skills (JOBS) (US) 225
Jobs for Youth Act 1997 (France) 32
Jobseekers' Act 1995 (UK) 32
Jobseeker's Allowance (JSA) (UK) 188-9, 190, 193, *196*, *197*
Jobseeker's Employment Act 1998 (JEA) (Netherlands) xvi, 32, 105-6, 117-19, 128, 249, 320
administration 265, *266*, 267
combating social exclusion 253
convergence 310, 312
as European centralised programme 279-80
funding and implementation 123-5
ideology *256*, *282*, 317
monitoring and research 125-7
negotiating placements 274, 275-6, *275*
placement types 119-22, *270*, 271, *283*
rights and responsibilities 254
sanctioning *277*, 278, *284*
social assistance contract 300-1

strategies 323
target group *258*
timing of intervention 263
universal programme 263, 264
as workfare 122-3
Jordan, B. 8, 9, 17
justifications 15-16

K

KAJA (Norway) 146
Knudsen, Grete 141

L

labour force attachment strategy, US
227, 241
labour force participation 23, *24*
Denmark 159
UK 181, 182, 183
labour market
distant from 324, 327, 332, 335
feminisation 27-8
tight 332, 334
Labour Market Attachment 296-7, 301-3, 307, 324-8, 334, 336
convergence 307
and ideology 319, 334
and policy inheritance 329
and scale 318-19
and target group 325-8, 334
labour market policies
expenditure *25*
France 42-3, 49, 56-9, 65-6
see also Emploi Jeunes; Trajet d'accès à l'emploi
Netherlands 114, 115-17
UK 181
Labour Party (Norway) 135, 148, 149-50
Labour Party (UK) 190-4
Larsson, A. 13
latin regimes 309
Lavangen hypothesis 152
Le Grand, J. 14
Leipzig 89, 90-1, 317
Leisering, L. 22
Lenoir, Renè 44

less eligibility 298, 302
see also curtailment
Levitas, R. 17
liberal welfare regimes xi, 27, 320
Lilley, Peter 187
Lister, R. 206
LMA *see* Labour Market Attachment
local authorities 265
Denmark 167, 168-9, 170, 176-7
Germany 78, 85
Netherlands 117, 124
Norway 136, 140, 141, 144, 146, 150, 153-4, 155
local variation *see* intra-national variation
Lødemel, I. 9, 26, 28, 29, *30*
lone parents 28, 316
Norway 140
UK 182, *198*
US 327, 334
long-term unemployment 23, *25*, 27-8, 262
France 47
Netherlands 105, 106, 110, 116
Norway 156
target group 260-1
UK 182-3, 184, 192
US 219
Lowell, Josephine Shaw 221
Luxembourg process 14

M

Mabbett, D. 304
macroeconomic policies 12
Netherlands 111-12
maintenance principle, Germany 73, 74, 75-6
making work pay
UK 191, 192-3
US 220, 241-2
Malthus, T. 18, 20, 335
Manpower Demonstration Research Corporation (MDRC) (US) 224
market workfare 5
Marshall, T.H. 8
Mead, L. 7-8, 9, 20, 21, 114
means testing, Norway 135

measuring rod 124-5, 127
Medicaid (US) 217-18, 231
Midré, G. 298
Minimum Income and Insertion Act 1989 (France) 32
minimum wage, UK 193
Modern Apprenticeships (MAs) (UK) 32, 187, *196*, 205
Moore, John 186-7
more–less equation 295-8, 302-3, 336
Morel, S. 4, 17
Murray, Charles 20, 113

N

Nathan, R.P. 4-5
National Childcare Strategy (UK) 193
National Traineeships (NTs) (UK) 32, 187, 194, *196*, 205
Netherlands xvi, 105-7, 127-8
  ALMPs 323-4
  compulsion 317
  economic developments and unemployment 109-11
  ideological shifts 112-15, 317
  labour market policy developments 115-17
  macroeconomic policy 111-12
  rights and responsibilities 10
  social assistance
    convergence 310, 312
    expenditure 318
    typology 29, *30*, 320
  social security provision 107-9
  structural context 23, *24-5*
  unemployment 261, 318
  welfare regime xi, 27, 320
  workfare strategy 297, 300, 323, 329-30, 332
  young people 260
  see also Jobseeker's Employment Act 1998
New ambitions for our country (UK Green Paper) 191
new convergence theory 304
New Deal for Disabled People (UK) 192, 194, *198*

New Deal for Lone Parents (UK) 192, 194, *198*, 316
New Deal for Over 25s (UK) 32, 192, *195*, 202, 206
New Deal for Over 50s (UK) *197*, 204, 208
New Deal for Partners of the Unemployed (UK) 192, 194, *198*
New Deal (UK) 191-2, 251, 300-1, 333
  criticism 206-7
New Deal for Young People (UK) xvii, 32, 192, *196*, 199, 201-3, 207-8, 249, 317
  administration 265, *266*, 267
  combating social exclusion 253
  compulsion 194
  convergence 310, 312
  as European centralised programme 278-80
  evaluation 287, 289-90
  ideology *256*, *282*, 317
  influences 311, 331
  negotiating placements 274, 275-6, *275*
  pathways *200*
  placement types *270*, 271, 272, 273, *283*
  rights and responsibilities 254
  sanctioning *277*, *284*
  social assistance 300-1
  strategies 312, 334
  target group *259*, 333
  timing of intervention 263
  universal programme 263, 264
New York City 32, 234-7, 243, 250, 302
  ideology *256*, *282*
  negotiating placements 275, *275*
  placement types *270*, 273, *283*
  sanctioning *277*, 278, *284*
  target group *259*
  timing of intervention 263
non-work placements *270*, 273-4
Norway xi, 133-4, 154-6
  ALMPs *25*, 26, 323, 331-2
  ideological shift 317
  policy context 143, 144-7, 316
  political process 143, 147-50
  public opinion 3

recent developments 153-4
rights and responsibilities 10, 11
social assistance 332
  convergence 310
  expenditure 318
  typology 29, *30*, 320
social-democratic welfare regime xi,
  27, 320
structural context 23, *24-5*
unemployment 316
welfare state 134-6
workfare
  development 303, 306
  implementation 302, 332
  strategy 298, 302-3, 318, 321-3, 332
see also Social Services Act 1991

O

obligation *see* rights and responsibilities
OECD 13, 308
offensive workfare 29, 31-2
Oldfield, N. 28
Omnibus Budget Reconciliation Act
  1981 (OBRA) (US) 220, *221*, 222,
  223-5, 242
ONE programme (UK) 192, 194, 207,
  261
opt-in programmes 250, 291
  see also Emploi Jeunes; Youth Training

P

passive policies 12-13, 252
paternalism 17, 21
path dependency 309, 319
  see also policy inheritance
Payne, J. 21
Personal Responsibility and Work
  Opportunity Reconciliation Act
  1996 (PRWORA) (US) 32, 221,
  221, 228-9, 243-4
block grants 229
end of entitlement 230-1
expansion of state latitude 229-30
participation requirements 231-3
rights and responsibilities 254
time limits 230

see also Temporary Assistance to
  Needy Families
placements 268-9, *270,* 278, 279, *283*
  created public work 273
  negotiating 274-6, *275*
  non-work 273-4
  subsidised work 272-3
  work-for-benefit 271-2
policy convergence *see* convergence
policy diversity *see* diversity
policy inheritance 319-24, 328, 330,
  332-4
  divergence from 322
policy transfer 311
political influence 303
politics
  and diversity 314-317
  and workfare 315, 332-4
Poor Laws 28, 306, 335
population 23, *24*
poverty 23, *24*, 306
  Netherlands 114-15
  and social exclusion 16, 17
  UK 190, 194
poverty regimes 28, *30*
programme effects 308-12, 321-2, 329,
  333
Project Work (UK) 188, 190, 192
protected work (Denmark) *164*
psycho-social model of dependency 19,
  20
Public Agenda 228
public opinion 3, 325-6
public welfare principle, Germany 73,
  74, 76-8
pull factors 28
push factors 28

R

rational dependency 7
rational model of dependency 19, 20
re-designation 261
Reagan, Ronald 223, 242
reciprocity 21
rehabilitation (Denmark) *163*
residual model of welfare provision 26,
  28

residual poverty regime 28, 31
responsibility *see* rights and responsibilities
Revenu Minimum d'Insertion (RMI) (France) xv, 42, 43, 49-50, 66-7, 249, 280-1, 298, 301, 330
   administration 266, *266*, 267
   and dependency 315
   effectiveness 287-8
   ideology 45, *256*, 279, *282*, 315
   implementation 301, 316
   intra-national variation 255
   negotiating placements 275, *275*, 276
   placement types *270*, *283*
   quasi-universal programme 263, 327-8
   rights and responsibilities 11, 50-2, 254
   sanctioning 276, *277*, *284*
   selectivity 268
   social assistance 300, 311, 330
   strategies 311, 316, 323, 330
   target group *258*, 328, 330
   timing of intervention 263
   young people 52-4
rights and responsibilities xii, 3, 10-11, 251, 253-4, 255, *256*, 306-7, 314-15
   Denmark 160, 166-9, 170
   France 45-6, 49-52
   Netherlands 108-9, 118
   Norway 133, 135, 137, 138
   UK 186-9, 207
   US 224, 225, 334
risk groups 324-6
   France 331
   Denmark 332
   Netherlands 332
risk society 12
Rogers, E.M. 305
Room, G. 17
Rose, R. 319, 322, 333

S

sanctioning 276, *277*, 278, 280, *284*
   Denmark 162
   France 52
   Germany 86-7, 92
   Norway 142
   UK 202
   US 224, 231, 235, 241, 243
scale 312, 316-17
Schmidtz, D. 8, 21-2
Schneider, A. 326-7
Schulte, B. 28, 29, *30*
Schumpeterian Workfare State 5, 312-13
Seeliger, R. 304
selectivity 263-4, 268, 288, 327-8
self-efficacy 20
self-employment, UK 202
self-reliance 21-2
Shragge, E. 9
Silver, H. 17
single parents *see* lone parents
skill development 31
social activation 278
   Denmark 161, 179
   Netherlands 116-17, 121-2
   UK 181
social assistance xii-xiv
   approaches 4
   continuity 321
   contract 10-12, 296-98, 300-2, 320, 335
   convergence 321
   curtailment 299-300, 222
   Denmark 167-8
   dependency 18
   divergence 211
   expenditure 23, *24*, 250, 251-2, 321
   France 49
   Germany 76, 78-81, 96, 99
   integration with workfare 323
   Netherlands 107, 108, 112
   Nordic model 311, 323, 330
   Norway 133, 134-5, 142, 144-5
   regimes 320-1
   rights-oriented 334
   target groups 257, 324-5
   traditions 323, 330
   typologies 27-9, *30*, 312, 320
   UK 185, 325
   US 215, 216-20
   see also workfare

Social Assistance Act 1961 (Germany) 32, 71

Social Assistance Act 1998 (Denmark) 261

Social Assistance Law 1965 (Netherlands) 108

Social Care Act 1964 (Norway) 136, 147-8

social cohesion 17, 44

social construction 326-7, 331-4

social contract 21

social control 299

social-democratic welfare regimes xi, 27, 320

social exclusion 15-18, 20, 251, 253, *256*, 315, 333, 335
France 41, 42, 43, 44, 66, 254
Netherlands 126-7
UK 190, 191

social inclusion 194

social insurance xiii, 324-5
Germany 73, 75
UK 185

social policies, France *see* insertion

social security, 336
Netherlands 107-9
UK 185-6

Social Security Act 1988 (UK) 187

social security expenditure 23, *24*
France 54, *55*
Netherlands 112, 114
UK 185

social security principle, Germany 73, *74*, 75

Social Services Act 1991 (Norway) 32, 133, 136-7, 249, 279, 280, 285
administration 265-6, *266*, 267
compliance 138-9
convergence 310, 322
dependency 252
divergence 311
duration 141-2
ideology *256*, *282*, 316, 318, 325
inter-agency cooperation 142-3
intra-national variation 255
negotiating placements 275, *275*
objectives 137-8, 150-2
placement types *270*, 271, *283*

political process 149-50
remuneration and financing 142
rights and responsibilities 254
sanctioning 142, *277*, *284*
scope 140
selectivity 268
social assistance 144
social assistance contract 298, 302
strategies 316, 318, 329
target group 139-40, *259*, 260
timing of intervention 263
training 141
work specifications 141

social work provision 28

societal-based justifications 15

solidarity 44-5, 66, 67, 325

Solidarity Job Contracts Act 1989 (France) 32

South Korea 304

Standing, G. 10, 15

state level contract 286

state responsibility 17, 286-7

state variation (US) 220, 228, 229-30, 243
Clinton waivers 220-1, *221*, 222, 226-7

Stewart, J. 5

stratification 27

subsidiarity 27
France 42, 49
Germany 72
Norway 137

subsidised work placements *270*, 272-3
France 43
Netherlands 116-17, 119-21, 122-3
UK 202, 203

Supplemental Security Income (SSI) (US) 76, 217, 219, 231

supply-side measures 5, 253, 255
UK 179, 206-7

Sweden 13, 307

T

target groups 257, *258-9*, 260-4, 285, 324-8, 330-1, 334
and diversity 313, 321-4

Norway 139-40
tax credits, UK 193
Taylor-Gooby, P. 22
temporalisation 12
Temporary Assistance to Needy
    Families (TANF) (US) 10, 216, *221*,
    228, 242, 250
    features 218, 219, 220
    participation requirements 232
    sanctioning 231
    target group 257, *259*
    time limits 230
    see also California; New York City;
        Personal Responsibility and Work
        Opportunity Reconciliation Act
        1996; Wisconsin
Therborn, G. 114
'third way' policies 317
time limits 261-3
    Norway 141-2
    US 18, 226, 230, 242, 252
Titmuss, R. 26-7, 28
top up social assistance 28
Torfing, J. 9, 26, 29, 31, 281, 319
trainfare 9
training 8-9, *270*, 273-4, 278, 326
    Denmark 161, *163*, 170, 172-4
    France 43, 59
    Germany 72, 83, 91-2, 99
    Netherlands 121-2
    Norway 141, 146-7
    UK 32, 187, 190, 202-3, 205-6
    US 226-7
Trajet d'accés à l'emploi (TRACE)
    (France) 44, 64-5
    evaluation 65-6
Travaux d'Utilité Collective (TUC)
    (France) 59, 60-1
Turok, I. 207

U

underclass 20, 190
unemployment 23, *25*, 27-8, 287, 317,
    327
    Denmark 178
    France 41-2, 47
    Germany 79, *80*

Netherlands 109-11
Norway 145, 154
UK 179, 182-3
young people 326-7
unemployment benefits
    France 48-9, 54, *55*
    Netherlands 107-9, 112
    Norway 145
    US 218-19
unemployment insurance 323-4, 333
unemployment traps, UK 192-3
uniformity provision, US 223-4
United Kingdom xvii, 181, 207-8
    ALMPs *25*, 26, 323-4, 330, 333
    challenges to compulsion 206-7, 317
    compulsory work measures 194,
        195-8, 199, *200*, 201-6
    conditionality 321
    curtailment 301, 333
    defensive workfare 29, 31
    and EU policy 308
    liberal welfare regime xi, 27
    Modern Apprenticeships 32
    National Traineeships 32
    New Labour's welfare reform 188-92,
        307, 333
    Poor Laws 18, 306, 335
    re-designation 259
    rights and responsibilities 10, 186-9
    social assistance 76, 321-2, 323
        convergence 310, 312
        expenditure 318
        typology 28-9, *30*, 319-20
        structural context 23, *24-5*
    unemployed people and social
        security 185-6
    unemployment 181-5, 261, 318
    unemployment insurance 323-4, 333
    workfare
        strategy 297-8, 301, 312, 322-3, 333
        target group 324, 333
    young people 10, 260
    Youth Training 291
    see also New Deal
United Nations, Copenhagen Summit
    13-14
United States xvii-xviii, 215, 243-4, 280
    1990s 2, 226-8

administration 266, *266*
ALMPs *25*, 26, 323-4, 334
curtailment 302-3
defensive workfare 29, 31
dependency 18, 19, 20, 22, 252, 315, 334
diffusion 305-8, 310
Earned Income Tax Credit 193
expenditure 252
Family Support Act 1988 225-6
incentive and disincentive measures 191
liberal welfare regime xi-xii, 27, 320
Omnibus Budget Reconciliation Act 1981 223-5
public opinion 3
quasi-universal programme 263
re-designation 261
recent experience 232-42
rights and responsibilities 10, 334-5
social assistance 76, 216-20
  contract 302
  convergence 310
  expenditure 318
  typology 29, *30*, 320
structural context 23, *24-5*
target group 257, 316, 334
unemployment 318
workfare xi, 4, 32, 220-2, 302
  development of 300, 323-4, 334-5
  strategy 298, 318, 302, 312, 315-16, 321-4, 329
  see also Aid to Families with Dependent Children; California; New York City; Personal Responsibility and Work Opportunity Reconciliation Act 1996; Temporary Assistance to Needy Families; Wisconsin
universal programmes 263-4, 279, 300, 327, 332-3
unmet needs, France 57-8

V

variation *see* diversity
Veierød, Tove 149
Versicherungsprinzip 73, *74*, 75
Versorgungsprinzip 73, *74*, 75-6
voluntary work
  Denmark 173
  UK 202

W

wage polarisation 27-8
waiver policy, US 220-1, *221*, 226
Walker, R. 22, 28
Webster, D. 207
welfare 1-2, 22, 187, 335
welfare dependency *see* dependency
welfare states 15
  France 48
  Germany 71, 72-3, *74*, 75-8
  Netherlands 121-2, 123
  Norway 134-6
  typology xi-xii, 26-7, *30*, 320
welfare-to-work 189, 190, 191-2, 194, 234
  influences 307
Wilensky, H. 303
Wisconsin 32, 226, 227, 237-40, 243, 250
  ideology *256*, *282*
  negotiating placements 275, *275*
  placement types *270*, 273, *283*
  sanctioning *277*, 278, *284*
  strategy 329
  target group *259*, 330
women 91
  UK 182
  US 222
work 8-9, 10, 113
  Denmark 161
  UK 207
  US 215
work ethic 19
  Norway 135-6, 148
work-for-benefit placements *270*, 271-2, 278

work-for-benefit policies
  divergence 268-9, *270*, 271-6, *277*, 278
  UK 207-8
Work Incentive Program (WIN) (US) 223
Work and Responsibility Act 1974 (US) 226
work tests
  Norway 144
  UK 186
  US 221
workfare
  case-work 29, 309, 322
  and centralisation 321, 330
  compulsion 7-8
  decommodification 27
  definitions xiv, 3-7, 249, 335
  and dependency 18, 20-1, 315
  development of 298-303, 307
  ideological contexts 15-22, 313-15, 317, 319, 330, 334
  impact on social assistance 308-11, 321, 330, 332
  implementation 309, 321, 323, 329
  integrated programmes 323-4, 327, 332-3, 335
  national context 313-14, 318
  as part of social assistance 7, 9-10, 309, 319-20, 328
  and politics 315, 332-4
  programme effects 304, 329
  as public investment 304
  racialised 334
  and scale of problem 332-4
  stratification 27
  strategies 328
   and target group 324-8, 330
   variations in 296, 302
  target group 314, 316, 324-8, 330-1, 333-5
  taxonomies 29, 31-2, 279-81
  trans-Atlantic differences 314, 327, 334-5
  and unemployment 317, 322
  US xi, 215
  work 7, 8-9
workfare states 15

workhouse test 298, 302-3
Working Age Agency (UK) 192
Working Families'Tax Credit (WFTC) (UK) 192-3
worklessness 250, 307
  causes 15, 306, 334
  cost 15
  and dependency 15, 16, 18-22
  passive to active policies 12-15
  and social exclusion 16-18
  supply-side deficiencies 253
  UK 184-5
worlds of welfare 27, *30*

Y

young people 10, 260, 264, 291
  Denmark 168, 169, 171, 177
  France 42, 43-4, 66
    Emploi Jeunes 61-4
    Revenu Minimum d'Insertion 52-4
    Trajet d'accés à l'emploi 64-5
    Travaux d'Utilité Collective 59
  Germany 91-2, 98
  Netherlands
    unemployment 109, 110, 308
    Youth Employment Scheme 105, 116, 120, 126-7
    see also Jobseeker's Employment Act
  Norway 139-40, 144-7
  UK 181-2, 187, 190-1, *195-6*, 205-6
    see also New Deal forYoung People
  US 219
Youth Allowance Act (Denmark) 177-8
Youth Allowance Scheme (Denmark) 160-1, 165-6, 169
Youth Employment Act (YEA) (Netherlands) 105, 120, 127
  funding 123-4
  monitoring and research 126
Youth Employment Programme (France) *see Emploi Jeunes*
Youth Training Scheme (UK) 187
Youth Training (UK) 187, 291